MIMESIS
INTERNATIONAL

POLITICS
n. 12

Ottavio Marzocca

BIOPOLITICS FOR BEGINNERS

Knowledge of life and government of people

MIMESIS
INTERNATIONAL

This book is published with the support of the University of Bari 'Aldo Moro'

© 2020 – MIMESIS INTERNATIONAL
(MILAN – UDINE)
www.mimesisinternational.com
e-mail: info@mimesisinternational.com

Isbn: 9788869771781
Book series: *Politics*, n. 12

© MIM Edizioni Srl
P.I. C.F. 02419370305

Translation from Italian by Sarah Donahue and Translation Agency sas - Ceresara
(MN) - Italy

TABLE OF CONTENTS

INTRODUCTION

The writing of this book began in one era and ended in another. Considering the month and year (June 2020) in which this text was completed, one can guess the reason. Of course, the many times in which it has recently been said that "nothing will be the same as before" seem to discredit in advance the claim to affirm also in this case that one era has ended, and another has started. After all, what started with the first serious pandemic of the third millennium could be "another era" only for the crossing of a threshold to which the event forced us, but still remain firmly tied to ways of being and acting rooted in the past. In fact, one wonders if the "passage" was traumatic enough to determine the radical change that one would expect or if it was too sudden to influence the ways of being in the world of those who experienced it. Certainly the pandemic had the power to lengthen the path that led to the conclusion of this book by requiring the addition of a chapter dedicated to it; at the same time it cleared up the doubts that initially curbed the intention to return to a theme such as biopolitics, which had become (apparently) out of date after years of the concept's use and abuse. The pandemic, in reality, has pronounced a definitive word in this regard, showing in a disruptive way both its conspicuously biopolitical character and its inexorable actuality.

In any case, the book – so to speak – easily foregoes being thankful for the spread of a lethal infection since it finds in its endeavour, deliberated in unsuspected times, the reason for dealing with issues that have gathered around the theme of biopolitics, starting from the most basic and trying to clarify those more complex. Hence the hope of offering the reader clear references to move on this terrain which – also because of what the pandemic has forced us to think – cannot be abandoned so easily, despite the inflation of biopolitics that took place between the two millennia recommend doing so. Hence also the title of the book, which leaves the reader the faculty to consider it modest or ambitious, ironic or serious.

The intent, however, is not to provide evidence of the hypothesis's validity that our history is structurally permeated by biopolitics. Rather, the book is inspired by the idea derived from Michel Foucault's research, according to which biopolitics is certainly a strategic form of modern politics, but does not constitute its paradigm; it is to be inscribed in a broader set of forms of government of society, which concern both ways of acting and life. The main arguments to support this thesis are proposed first and foremost – but not only – in the first chapter, dedicated precisely to Foucault.[1] In the same chapter, moreover, one can grasp the possibility that the accurate reading of certain Foucaultian texts offers to free the theme of biopolitics from generic declinations. In fact, it is clearly linked to the decisive role that modern medicine has assumed, at least since the 18th century, in defining precise forms of state biopower: it was a question of real medicalization processes of society, based primarily on the attention to the well-being of the population, that is, its demographic dynamics, public hygiene, the healthiness of spaces, infectious diseases, the health of the poor classes, the "defence" of society through its "purification" from "dangerous individuals", etc. Hence the need to recognize the essential link between biopolitics and modernity, a link that Foucault allows to focus on by contextualizing biopolitics itself within the framework of the hegemony that economic rationality exercises on the ways of governing modern societies. This connection – as will be seen – is decisive to avoid transforming biopolitics into a sort of metastorical concept.

It follows therefore the opportunity to investigate the hypothesis that the origin of the biopolitical vision of politics and state power can be found in antiquity. This is what the book attempts to do in the second chapter where Plato and Aristotle – as true or presumed precursors of our political culture – are considered as possible

---

1   All references to authors, proposed in this introduction, are resumed and clarified on the bibliographic level in the following chapters.

founders of a vision of this kind, examining its main political works. The hypothesis – recently supported by Mika Ojakangas – appears somewhat plausible especially with regard to Plato, but in reality it turns out to be rather weak if it occurs, among other things, in light of the contempt that the author reserves in the *Republic* to those who dedicate themselves to «this excessive care for the body», to those who «always fancy himself sick and never cease from anguishing about his body», and to the medicine that favours these excesses by conceiving «new-fangled and monstrous strange names of diseases». Ultimately, what prevents from attributing to Plato a biopolitical vision of state power is his denunciation and his rejection of what Foucault would call "medicalization" of the life of individuals and the *polis*, that is, the promotion of processes similar to those that in modernity have ended up placing the care and promotion of life among the fundamental tasks of governments.

It is true, on the other hand, that a eugenic tendency can be seen in the organization of the procreation and raising of rulers and helpers children, proposed by Plato in the *Republic*. However, the difficulty of contextualising it in a biopolitical vision of the state emerges if we consider essential aspects of the project that he illustrates in his fundamental work. The Greek philosopher does not intend to apply this organization to the entire collective body of the *polis*, but only to the political class that will have to govern and defend it. Much more important than this intention, on the other hand, is the idea that rulers and helpers – unlike other citizens – must live in a community of wives and children regime and in the absolute absence of private property. This indication does not tend to transform – as one might believe – the political class into a large family; on the contrary, it tends exactly to abolish the family and to dissolve the essentially private character of its logics. All this, according to Plato, will ensure that in the action of state rulers there is no room for the pursuit of one's own particular interest and the common good, – that is, justice, harmony and unity of the *polis* –, is decidedly privileged, finality anything but biopolitics of the state itself. For this reason too, neither those who govern nor the state in general will undertake the protection and strengthening – possibly in an aberrant way – of the individual and collective life as their fundamental political aim. Other surveys carried out in the same chapter through the *Laws* and *The Statesman* seem to confirm these outcomes of the analysis of the *Republic*.

For Aristotle things are different, especially in the sense that his vision of politics is an indirect, but fundamental, presupposition of the reflections that contemporary thought – from Hannah Arendt to Foucault – has dedicated to the intense attention that modern politics, differently from that of the ancients, devotes to life. Aristotle, from this point of view, is the one who clearly excludes that the power of the politician is comparable to that of the landlord, since the former is exercised on free men, while the latter is exercised on slaves so that their performances ensure the well-being, above all physical, of the family. For him, moreover, the specificity of political fellowship lies in the fact that it exists «for the sake of noble actions, not merely to living in common»: while originating «for the sake of life, it exists for the good life», that is to guarantee citizens a free existence based on the practice of virtue, «a full and independent life, which (...) constitutes a happy and noble life».

Undoubtedly, all this is connected to a hierarchical vision of human nature, a vision that legitimizes slavery and sometimes seems to imply "eugenic" temptations. For Aristotle, moreover, active political citizenship is a possibility reserved for male and free individuals as indigenous and in a position to practice leisure. On the other hand, precisely this attention – far from being secondary – to the need for leisure makes it possible to exclude that the political community advocated by Aristotle has as its essential aim the care and enhancement of life. Being in leisure is a sort of indispensable condition that the state must guarantee to the free citizen, since the good use of leisure is decisive for the cultivation of virtue; this, in turn, is the essential content of the happy and noble life that the political fellowship must set itself as the primary objective.

The centrality that – according to Aristotle – virtue must assume in public life is an essential element of his vision of politics, an element which – as is known – is found in very clear terms also in Plato. For both philosophers, the political quality of the state can be guaranteed above all through the exercise of virtue by citizens and rulers. From this point of view, it is important to consider that for neither of them economic activities represent favourable conditions for the acquisition and practice of virtue. Both condemn enrichment as an end in itself and theorize the need for moderation and balance in the acquisition of wealth; Plato considers the cultivation of private interests as a source of danger for the unity of the state; Aristotle not only exalts leisure as a condition of virtue, but also despises the activities of farmers, artisans and merchants, because «ignoble and inimical to virtue» and as an impediment to active citizenship. It is on foundations like these that – according to them – it is possible to pursue justice and the unity of the state (Plato) or to achieve a happy and noble life that finds its corroborative criterion in the same virtue as citizens (Aristotle). In visions like these, the biopolitical strengthening of the life of individuals or of the collective body does not find the conditions for becoming a strategic objective of the state. To prevent these conditions from being created is the clear prevalence of the moral aims of politics; but equally important is that in these visions productive and economic activities are not virtuous and qualifying activities for the state. This implies, on the one hand, that its economic strengthening cannot be a politically fundamental task and, on the other, that even the strengthening of the health of its collective body – as state wealth – cannot be.

***

Against the backdrop of the comparison between modern and ancient forms of politics lies the distinction between "life" and "political life" generally attributed to the Ancients; a distinction that Arendt – earlier and more clearly than Foucault – highlighted by recalling the importance that, according to her, it had for the Greeks. This distinction constitutes an essential reference of the debate on biopolitics, in which it is generally indicated by referring to the different meanings that the ancient Greek attributed to the terms *zoé* and *bios*: according to the prevailing translations, the first term corresponds to "natural life", while the second indicates life as "qualified" by a political or another form. In the third chapter, together with other questions, the main implications of the reflection on this issue are discussed taking into account the positions expressed by Giorgio Agamben, Antonio Negri and Roberto Esposito in their contributions to the debate on biopolitics. As will be seen, the three Italian philosophers agree in believing that the possibility of re-actualizing the distinction that the terms *zoé* and *bios* would indicate has been overcome. Agamben, in this sense, insists on the radical difficulty of separating "life" from the sphere of politics: the Greek distinction between *zoé* and *bios* – according to him – already implied that political life (*bios*) "captured" natural life (*zoé*) to qualify it politically, dominate it sovereignly and deny it substantially. Therefore, today it would be urgent to find ways in which between *zoé* and *bios* – life and form of life – there can be an interpenetration that excludes the imposition of an extrinsic form by a heteronomous biopower. Negri also argues that the distinction between *zoé* and *bios* today is completely unacceptable, since biopolitics is now the dimension in which life of bodies and political life, creativity of life and productivity of labor, coincide and create the conditions to release biopolitics itself from biopower: it is necessary, therefore, to ensure that the biopolitical productivity of the postmodern multitude unleashes its power to overcome the biopower of global capitalism. Finally, for Esposito himself, the difference between life and political life today has no validity. For him, life now places itself «at the centre of the global *polis*» positioning itself in a dimension that goes beyond the borders of the state and dissolves the very idea of a political body on which state biopower has historically been founded; therefore life today makes it possible and, at the same time, demands an affirmative biopolitics capable of overcoming the oscillations between politics of life and politics of death, which have tragically marked the history of modern politics leading to the Nazi catastrophe.

Moving beyond the reflections of these three authors, both in the third and in the sixth chapter, the exclusion of the possibility of referring to the distinction between *zoé* and *bios* is reconsidered in the light of the fact that Foucault in one of his last Courses had carefully examined this distinction. From his point of view, certainly the term *zoé* for the Greeks indicated the simple fact of living; the word *bios* instead indicated neither political life nor any other form of qualified life; rather it referred to the «life that can be qualified», the «course of existence» that the individual can try to live and qualify ethically. Therefore, if we share the result of Foucault's analysis, we can suppose that the reflection on biopolitics should not be limited to taking note of the decline of the separation between natural and political life; rather, it should rethink the distinction between *zoé* and *bios* by giving new importance to the idea of *existence*: it would be a matter of thinking of the latter as a span of time and dimension in which the singularity of a life takes place as irreducible both to the generality of the biological life and to biopolitical forms that it assumes when undergoing the powers of technology, economy or the state. In this sense it would be necessary to call into question – between *zoé* and *bios* – a third concept that emerges from the reflection of the last Foucault: that of *ethos* understood as a way of conducting oneself. It finds in the dimension of *bios* as existence, the sphere in which those who intend to be and remain free can try to form or transform it by critically interacting with power and taking care of their own self, that is by practicing what the French philosopher calls *ethopoiesis*, the formation of an *ethos*. The broad meaning that ancient Greek attributes to the term *ethos*, moreover, allows us to grasp the link that the idea of *way of conducting oneself* maintains with that of *way of dwelling*. Beyond what Foucault claims, it follows that the worldly and cosmic, terrestrial and ecosystem, local and global dimension of our dwelling is the area in which biopolitics and biopowers should be contextualized, problematized and exceeded ethically and politically, to reflect on and face the major threats to which life and existence appear exposed in our world, starting from the ecological one.

In any case, such a task cannot be properly focused upon if it is not referred to the main forms that biopolitics, on the one hand, and the government of our *ethos*, on the other, have taken on in the history of the last centuries. Therefore, in the fourth and fifth chapters, we first try to bring out the biopolitical character of some of the main government strategies of this history, considering in particular those that since the 19th century have established themselves with social security techniques, policies of the welfare state and, subsequently, with the imposition of neoliberal governmentality. From the path that is taken in this sense emerges the privileged relationship that the various forms of biopolitics have with the economic rationality that essentially permeates the ways of governing modern society; on the other hand, in the same way the fact emerges that *ethos* is one of the main stakes of the economic and biopolitical government of this society.

The authors who, in the fourth chapter, are considered to reconstruct the preconditions, circumstances and developments of the biopolitics of social security and welfare state go from Thomas R. Malthus to Karl Marx, from William Beveridge to Richard M. Titmuss, from Jacques Donzelot to Daniel Defert, from François Ewald to Robert Castel, from Pierre Rosanvallon to Foucault himself. With regard to biopolitics attributable to neoliberalism, however, in the following chapter the attention is mainly focused on – but not only – the analyses of Nikolas Rose and Melinda Cooper.

***

Already between the end of the 18th and the beginning of the 19th century many of the problems that will subsequently be addressed through social security systems and welfare state policies are announced with the attention that the state and the political economy address to the essentially biopolitical issue of the population. Malthus, in particular, identifies the imbalance between a tendentially unlimited demographic growth and the more uncertain development of the production of subsistence goods as the cause of the dangers of impoverishment and deterioration of the collective health, of which – according to him – they are victims and at the same time responsible especially the poor, because of their inclination to procreate too much. Marx, for his part, opposes this view by denouncing the conditions in which the industrial proletariat is placed by capitalism: this – on the one hand – attracts the labour force in the production processes, but – on the other – tends to increase the capital destined to the means of production at the expense of the labour; therefore, thus increasing the productivity of the labour force, it cyclically makes superfluous and expels large numbers of workers who end up falling into misery. Consequently, that recurrent imbalance between population growth and the availability of subsistence goods, which Malthus presents as a natural law, for Marx is the result of the continuous oscillation of capitalism between the increase of the labouring population and the production of a relative unemployed overpopulation.

Against the backdrop of scenarios and visions like these, the explosion of social conflict is one of the most frequent problems that the governments of emerging liberal societies will have to avoid in the 19th century; they will succeed in doing so – albeit partially – when they find a way to break down the massive issue of class exploitation and injustice into a plurality of mostly biopolitical problems: the most effective strategies in this sense will be those that will reduce the "social question" to a variety of limited problems such as accidents at work, invalidity, illness, unemployment, old age; they will be treated as risks or risk factors against which life must be insured beforehand and eventually indemnified in the event of "damage" (Donzelot, Ewald). In this way, the phenomenon of mutualism that workers' movements promote in order to supportively face the dangers and uncertainties of their condition, or to guarantee autonomy and resistance in their struggles, will be largely neutralized (Defert).

Insurance techniques will also become the paradigm of many of the policies that will be promoted by the welfare state in the 20th century. The idea that life should be protected from the unpredictability of events in an increasingly complex and economically active society is – in a sense – the inspiring principle of this form of government (Beveridge). The same catastrophic dimension that wars take on in this century, especially in Europe, becomes a decisive motivation for the creation of new systems for safeguarding life through the welfare state (Titmuss, Foucault, Rosanvallon). In reality, in various countries this form of government aspires to going beyond the simple protection of life and, in fact, also leans to some redistribution of income. However, the salaried worker guaranteed by a formal contract is the main reference figure of the welfare state (Castel); furthermore, his family is the social group to which the greatest attention is generally paid, especially with support for raising children (Titmuss). All this, on the other hand, implies that lesser protections are granted to marginal social figures with respect to productive activities or not conforming to the behaviour models corresponding to the work-family relationship (Foucault).

The most clearly biopolitical aspects of the welfare state strategies emerge through the functioning of the Health Care Systems created after the Second World War, which – at least in Europe – are generally supported by the state, albeit in different ways and measures. Even in the case of these systems it can be said that they tend to go beyond the limit of simply safeguarding life by trying to guarantee a wider "right to health" with performances corresponding to the advancements of medicine (Foucault). In this way, on the one hand, they satisfy and increase certain health needs, and on the other, they do not always manage to guarantee everyone an adequate and impartial access to their services. However, these systems help to make the medicalization of individual and collective life increasingly intense; at the same time, together with the welfare state in general, they become the target of neoliberal critics who denounce the anti-economic character of the expenses that the state incurs to respond to an indefinite demand for assistance and care for life. Especially since the end of the seventies, in the context of societies increasingly conditioned by a market economy in the process of globalization, trends of this type will eventually create the conditions for the crisis of the welfare state and a progressive privatization of medical services, encouraged by governments more and more sensitive to the argumentations of neoliberalism.

The processes that push towards privatization, in reality, find their important presupposition also in the individualization of the relationship with health, which – in a certain sense – the welfare state itself has promoted: it, in fact, has transformed citizens into simple users of services and personal services the costs of which are socialized, but whose management and use are extraneous to any form of empowerment, participation and solidarity sharing comparable, for example, to those of worker mutualism of the 19th century. From this point of view, it can be said that the welfare state ended up favouring a privatization of the citizen's *ethos*, which will indirectly contribute to the crisis of this form of government, depriving it of the social tension that can guarantee its legitimacy (Rosanvallon).

***

The crisis of the welfare state coincides with the emergence of medical practices increasingly dominated on a scientific and technological level by genetic research and molecular biology which, since the end of the seventies, have been the subject of constantly growing economic investments. This is a biomedicine that focuses its attention not only on full-blown diseases, but also or especially on those to which the individual and his relatives can be predisposed. In this sense, the individual and family genetic microcosm represents the privileged object of these medical practices which will find in neoliberal governmentality the conditions for the promotion of a private relationship with healthcare by both its various operators and by current and potential patients.

These and other aspects of the relationship between medicine and neoliberalism are examined in the fifth chapter discussing, in particular, the analyses of Rose and Cooper. The first author allows – among other things – to focus on the ways in which the genetic approach to health is combined with important political and ethical transformations which take place in what he defines as «advanced liberal societies». Rose expresses scepticism concerning the critical analyses of the role of genetics, particularly regarding two issues. First of all, he disagrees with the idea that the increasingly relevant role of genetics implies the reaffirmation of a deterministic vision of life, from which new forms of eugenics and political racism may derive. According to him, the combination of genetic research, biotechnology and new pharmacology today deeply reduces the importance of the concept of heredity: this combination, in fact, pushes doctors and patients to consider biological matter as substantially modifiable and malleable, that is in terms that are anything but deterministic. Furthermore, for Rose, the possibility of a political use of genetics in a eugenic and racist sense is substantially excluded due to the weakening of the unitary visions of the population, of society and of the nation, which – according to him – particularly characterizes advanced liberal societies: here the molecularization of medicine finds the best conditions to develop and to profoundly downsize the relationship between the individual body and the collective body of the population, on which eugenics and biopolitical racism of the past centuries have been based. According to Rose, the same unitary idea of body is deeply destabilized by contemporary medicine, since now tissues, cells, DNA fragments – as well as blood, organs, eggs, sperm, embryos – are normally extrapolated from the bodies and manipulated, reproduced, recombined, marketed and transferred from one body to another and from one place to another, regardless of the state borders and their political bodies. Therefore, for Rose, the growing influence of the new medicine prevents – especially in the advanced liberal societies – that nationalistic, state-centric or totalitarian forms of biopolitics find space in our era by leveraging the idea of a collective body. These theses are discussed in the book, among other things, in light of the fact that, in reality, new expressions of nationalism, souverainism, authoritarianism and racism have long characterized our era.

The second issue on which Rose disagrees with the critical views of the role of genetics is that of the centrality that the individual takes on in new medical practices: this, according to him, does not imply that the genetic approach isolates the individual from the social dimension; rather, genetics pushes him to establish responsible relationships with others, to the extent that the pathologies and genetic risks of which he may be a carrier, never concern him exclusively, but as a blood relative of other people. It is above all in this regard that Rose's analyses allow us to detect the ethical changes associated with the new medicine; changes to understand which the ideas of risk and genetic responsibility represent key concepts. The author is fully aware of the fact that, in this regard, genetics induces the individual to privilege the (private) relationship with his own family, current or future; but this, for him, is simply a test of the individual's openness not so much to society, as to sociality; a sociality that Rose defines as *biosociality* or *biological citizenship,* insisting on the idea that today the person urged by the new medicine to take responsibility for genetic risks actively interacts with genetic professionals and biomedical researchers, associations and movements animated by actual or potential patients and their relatives, medical institutions and biotechnological or pharmaceutical companies, etc.

In reality, the crux of the matter is not to understand whether the new medicine isolates the individual from social relations; rather, it is a question of considering that – as the "protagonist" of this medicine – the individual contributes to a general privatization of medical, biopolitical and economic attention to life, in which his genetic relationship with the private dimension of the family plays a decisive role. In fact, in this same dimension, that particular form of ethical responsibility which consists in the economic and private self-government of the human capital of the individual members of the family, as well as of marriages, procreation and careers, theorized by that authoritative exponent of neoliberal thought which is Gary S. Becker, featured prominently in our time.

Both Rose and Cooper offer many tools to place these trends within the context of the global capitalism of our era. Both authors in this sense speak of *biocapitalism* to indicate the new economy that develops around them; but while Rose assumes the affirmation of this economy as a datum without particular problems, Cooper puts it radically in discussion. According to her, biocapitalism finds the decisive conditions for its take-off in Reagan America: which in itself is proof of the link that it has had since its birth with neoliberalism, with the decline of the welfare state and with vast processes not only of privatization, but also financialisation and commercialization of the attention to life. One of the most important aspects of biocapitalism, from this point of view, is the connection that since its inception – especially in the USA – has been established between research and biotechnological production, on the one hand, and increasing financialisation of the economy, on the other. Financialisation, in a certain sense, impresses its mark on research and biotechnological production: it engages in them its essentially speculative logic which implies a constant projection of investments towards results and gains to be made in an indeterminate or continually deferred future. The activity that takes place in this bioeconomy – according to Cooper – is essentially "promissory" in the sense of both its constant projection towards the future and the intent to produce, regenerate or reproduce life in the most varied and variable forms. Its most advanced expression in this sense is regenerative medicine which

– as Cooper says – is based on a morphogenetic conception of life. By studying and manipulating stem cells, in particular, it tends to activate the most plastic and malleable form of living matter to «regenerate the geometries of the body otherwise»; ultimately it aspires to immortalize the potential of these cells to constantly make «the moment from which all possible forms of living matter can be regenerated» achievable.

For reasons like this, according to the author, *delirium* and *megalomania* must be seriously considered among the aspects of biocapitalism. This, however, does not authorize those who intend to draw inspiration from her analyses to take refuge in the idea that the material, biopolitical, economic and ethical effects of biocapitalism are essentially illusory or evanescent. Rather, Cooper's research urges us to explore the forms that biocapitalism can take with the progressive imposition of the new Asian powers (China and India, in particular) in the scenario of globalization: if American biocapitalism is linked to its speculative and promissory matrix, these powers propose themselves as subjects of an unprejudiced bioeconomy and of a global biopolitics capable of affecting more and more deeply in the materiality of life, its care, reproduction and regeneration of its forms. In fact, it is a question of reflecting and of opening up new areas of research on all this.

Among the most interesting issues of Cooper's studies is the case of introducing at least another, which became particularly relevant in the year in which this book was completed: the potentially pandemic epidemics of our time, which had their symbolically and concretely inaugural moment with the explosion of AIDS. This disease – as is known – had a vast and ruinous spread especially in sub-Saharan Africa where, according to Cooper, it revealed a series of implications of the political hegemony that neoliberalism was conquering worldwide. With the end of modern medicine's dream of defeating infectious diseases, through AIDS especially in the 1990s it became clear that the serious health problems that poor populations were facing were destined to be addressed as humanitarian emergencies rather than as public health problems to be entrusted to public health care systems. Through a famous legal action by the pharmaceutical companies against the possibility of using antiretroviral drugs at low cost, it was also clear that in the context of globalization, biocapitalism was ready to harshly counter attempts to remove the essential tools for the protection of life from the logic of the market.

***

Cooper does not fail to put into light, against the backdrop of the processes that she analyses, the ecological question, placing it in the context of global capitalism: in particular, according to her, the latter tends to tackle this question, on the one hand, trying to transform it into opportunities for new investments in biotechnological production, for example, with the use of modified microorganisms for the neutralization of polluting chemicals; on the other, treating it as a set of planetary-sized dangers and emergencies, for example, through pollution emissions trading or by planning geo-engineering interventions on gases present in the atmosphere to combat climate change.

However, if we want to fully grasp the biopolitical and governmental implications of the ecological question, it must be examined without linking it too closely to the urgencies of our time. As we try to show in the sixth chapter, this question arises at least since the life sciences have clearly assumed as a problem to investigate the relationships between living beings and the physical and organic conditions of their survival: going from the botanical geography of the early 19th century up to the ecosystem ecology of the 20th century, passing through Darwinian biology and population ecology, ecological scientific knowledge has clearly established itself for a long time. Well, since its origins, this knowledge has been clearly in tune with the biopolitical orientation of the dominant ways of governing society. It is sufficient to consider the crucial importance that, especially after the advent of Darwinian biology, in this knowledge has assumed the problem of living species as *populations* constantly exposed to the risks of growing too much, of shrinking or of extinction based on the influence of environmental conditions and their ability to adapt to them. It is certain, in any case, that an essentially Malthusian matrix characterizes much of the scientific ecology; in fact, it emerges quite clearly in the second half of the 20th century with the famous Report for the Club of Rome (1972), in which the relationship between the growth of the human population and the consumption of environmental resources emerges as a crucial problem.

The Malthusian matrix of this knowledge, on the other hand, makes reliable the hypothesis that scientific ecology maintains relationships and affinities important also with the economic rationality of the governmental policy dominant in recent centuries, a rationality of which Malthus has been an exemplary supporter. In any case, especially starting from the ecosystem ecology, ecological knowledge tends to present the functioning of the interactions between life and the environment as a form of economic rationality superior to that to which the prevailing governmentality and development models in our society adhere: from this point of view, ecosystems generally manage to maintain a lasting balance as life reproduces within them by efficiently using – i.e. without waste and without abuse – the energy and physical resources that the environment offers them.

Ultimately it can be said that in the 20th century the ecological discourse, while posing the problem of the excessive growth of the human population and that of the growing abuse of natural resources, aspires to establish a new biopolitics and a new economy based on a relationship of compatibility between population growth, production development and "functioning" of ecosystems. Indeed, it is precisely based on visions of this type that the various strategic proposals for sustainable development since the last decades of the last century have urged governments, societies, and economic players to reconcile production activities, consumption and demography with environmental balances. However, as we know, although the so-called green economy or ecologically correct behaviours sometimes give the impression of being able to assert themselves easily in our time, in general current societies still continue to prove incapable both of reducing the overall environmental unsustainability of their economic activities and to solve the biopolitical and ecological problem of world population growth. What this book hypothesises in this regard is that the very fact that the ecological discourse compares with modern governmentality on its economic and biopolitical terrain does not represent at all a favourable condition for the success of the strategies it proposes to "solve" the environmental crisis. On this ground, in fact, modern governmentality always has a multiplicity of possible options that ecological strategies do not have. Evidence, however indirect, of the reliability of this hypothesis is that, in recent decades, neoliberal governmentality has allowed global capitalism to both welcome "sustainable" production and consumption within its sphere, and to continue to welcome anti-ecological production and consumption. On the other hand, in the same governmental context – especially in richer societies – parental couples generally tend to have few children; these couples, therefore, contribute little to world population growth which, however, continues to assume enormous dimensions, just as the abuse of environmental resources continues to grow also with their contribution.

It should be added, in any case, that certain theoretical assumptions of ecological knowledge, from the second half of the 20th century, have been deeply destabilized by scientific visions that deal with problems similar to those of ecological knowledge in a different way: these are, in particular, the theory of dissipative structures and the so-called Gaia hypothesis, on which Cooper also insists. According to the first theory, there are open systems in nature that create complex structures that evolve creatively by consuming resources. Here the second principle of thermodynamics, according to which entropic processes constitute a universal and irreversible trend, in reality only applies to closed systems that inevitably have limited resources. But for systems open towards an undefined external environment, the idea that the dissipation of resources leads to their disintegration must be radically questioned. Our own planet is an open dissipative system that makes life possible by drawing energy from the sun and thus keeping away from the tendencies towards degradation. It is also important to note that for this theory the forms of biological life are the main dissipative structures; consequently the biological evolution itself occurs as a process of continuous creation and improvement of structures capable of freeing, precisely through dissipation, life from the limits that environmental conditions seem to impose upon it. In other words, from this point of view, life generally manages to assert itself because it is capable of transforming its dependence on environmental resources into possibilities for evolution and substantial independence.

On this basis, in a certain sense, it is possible to exclude that the ecological crisis is a problem that can be solved only by limiting the consumption of resources: if this crisis is such because it endangers life, it can also be said that life is capable of warding off this danger by continuing to consume energy and matter, and transforming this consumption into factor of evolution. Moving in a similar direction and insisting on the creative abilities of life, the theorists of the Gaia hypothesis, for their part, argue that pollution is an «inevitable consequence of life at work». In any case, for them, the production and accumulation of waste products can never block biological evolution as a whole; environmental crises occur periodically in the history of life, but the latter responds to them with «evolutionary innovations» that allow it to overcome them and continue to evolve.

Ultimately, the theory of dissipative structures and the Gaia hypothesis represent paradigms of a sort of "post-ecological knowledge" that escapes the "pessimism" of ecology since its main reference is neither "nature" nor "environment", but "life" as a productive and reproductive power capable of creating complexity and overcoming the problems of degradation that may arise from time to time. In fact, this knowledge radically downsizes the ecological question since it outlines a "bio-centric" rather than "eco-centric" vision of the environment; the world as an unmeasurable multiplicity of material and immaterial elements and relationships is placed decidedly in the background of an undisputed supremacy of biological life. From this point of view, therefore, the same unstoppable productive dynamism of contemporary societies can be considered a fundamental expression of the overall dynamism of life and its ability to impose itself on the conditioning of the world. In short, on these bases, the political problem of ecology can be transformed into a biopolitical and economic problem that finds its own solutions in itself. In this way, however, we end up considering irrelevant the fact that if life asserts itself, it can do so to the advantage of some of its forms and to the detriment of others. It is no coincidence, in fact, that an ecological crisis can occur precisely when the decline of certain forms of life tends to turn into extinction and a reduction in the biodiversity of the environment.

***

What ecological and post-ecological theories have in common today is a vision of the relationship between living beings and the environment focused on the consumption of primarily energy resources. From this point of view, the ecological question presents itself as an essentially bio-energy problem, no matter if it is considered to be fraught with serious or in any case solvable dangers. However, in reality, there is at least one other way of determining this question, which can subtract it from the predominance of the bio-energy paradigm and put it in a different perspective from that of biopolitical and economic governmentality. This is the *ecology of mind* theorized by Gregory Bateson: although it gives importance to the problem of resource consumption, it goes beyond the "physicalism" that induces ecological and post-ecological knowledge to place such consumption at the centre of the relationship between life and environment. The ecology of mind, on the other hand, overcomes the substantial dualism that conditions the prevailing visions of this relationship; in fact, it takes as its main reference exactly the *relationships* between living beings and between them and the environment, rather than the environment and life in their dialectical confrontation. In the Batesonian vision of ecology the concepts of the mind and the mental system play a fundamental role on the basis of these premises.

In short, according to Bateson, living beings are first of all minds and the aggregate they form among themselves and with their environments constitute mental systems in which the relationships between the parts are more important than the flows of energy and material resources. These relationships can be defined "mental" in the sense that they produce learning processes, that is, orientation or transformation of behaviours, not necessarily adequate for the maintenance or creative evolution of the mental systems in which relationships take place; these processes, in fact, can also trigger tendencies towards the disintegration and degradation of these systems. Man in particular tends to produce ecological crises with increasingly serious consequences since what he learns in his relations with the environment is generally conditioned by the essential purposefulness of his conscience; his «purposive consciousness» continually leads him to change his environmental contexts in an instrumental way to achieve the goals he pursues from time to time. Furthermore, his availability of increasingly powerful technologies only progressively aggravates the ecological consequences of the purposefulness of his behaviours.

The hypothesis that the ecology of mind can help us free the ecological question not only from the bio-energetic paradigm, but also from the governmental biopolitics-economy binomial appears reliable if the Batesonian ecology is made to interact with the Foucaultian vision of the experiences of *ethopoiesis*. In this sense, the sixth chapter shows the possibility that Foucault offers us to understand ethopoiesis as a form of learning that requires attention to our relations with the world, that is, to our *ethos* as a way of dwelling. Ethopoiesis can thus become an opening of our self towards the immense complexity of ecosystemic and mental relationships that connect us to the world and which should lead us to significantly reduce our claim to "govern" it to make life, the environment and its resources "productive".

***

The COVID-19 pandemic has revealed the extreme limit that the crisis has reached in the relations of our societies with the world, bringing to light this crisis primarily on an elementary level, that is, as an alteration of man's ecosystemic relations with animals, in particularly with wild ones: this alteration, in fact, is one of the decisive factors in the ever more frequent emergence in our time of potentially pandemic zoonotic infectious diseases. A multiplicity of processes of heavy and growing anthropization of the planet and its ecosystems contributes to this alteration in various ways: deforestation, urbanization, expansion of industrial farms, global mobility of humans, animals, goods, etc. In these and other ways, our societies tend to ignore not only the complexity of relationships that man inevitably has with other species, but also the fact that these relationships require anything but generic respect for their various ecosystems. Without this respect, in fact, unpredictable spillovers of pathogens from non-human animals can occur, such as – for example – those of viruses with far superior capacity than humans to adapt to environmental changes. They, in particular, easily learn how to behave in those new ecosystems which human bodies can suddenly become for them. The COVID-19 pandemic is basically the result of such a zoonotic process.

This was an opportunity for the deployment of various forms of biopolitics whose scenario was characterized by the role – primary and problematic at the same time – of the World Health Organization: the great contagion, even before it occurred, had to be the great test of the prevention and containment policies of the so-called *emerging infectious diseases* around which most of the strategies of this organization have been elaborated in the last decades. Among these strategies, the one based on global and technologically equipped surveillance systems on the dangers of epidemics stands out, in which the constant collection and processing of information and signals coming from every part of the planet on possible outbreaks play a central role. Clearly, these systems have not proven particularly effective. Nonetheless, they present themselves as a pillar of global biopolitics also for our tomorrow threatened by other pandemic dangers.

Their substantial ineffectiveness, in any case, made it necessary for other forms of anti-pandemic biopolitics to unfold, alternate and confront each other through the more or less strong intervention of the nation states. In general it can be said that these biopolitics – after an initial moment in which the emergency declination and uncertainty prevailed – began to oscillate between a "disciplinary" approach (lockdown and quarantine) and strategies for the "regulation" and "normalization" of the contagion, however promoted in the absence of a vaccine. Furthermore, a mixed and variable strategy between these two approaches was to individualize technological surveillance by adopting the so-called contact-tracing model, rather than the meta-geographic and global model of the WHO. Last but not least, it was the choice of certain governments to consider the intervention of political institutions on the contagion simply inappropriate, so that it could freely run its lethal course, putting some countries in front of a form of "normalization" similar to denying the problem. In one way or another, however, the extreme vulnerability of our globalized society has manifested itself in a sensational way.

Precisely for this reason the pandemic has been and remains a condition for attempting to change the dominant forms of our *ethos*, of our relationship with the world, with existence and with life. It has shown us, among other things, that the human animal does not connect to life only through its biological material, but also and above all through ecosystemic and interspecific relationships: being irreducible to a microcosm observable in the laboratory, these relationships can be underestimated and altered, thus becoming causes of unexpected and even catastrophic events. The great contagion, on the other hand, has shown us that transcending the sphere of individual life is not only the dimension of the family, society or population-species, but also what we can recognize by naming it from time to time "nature", "environment", "ecosystem" or in other ways. In any case, after entering profoundly in this dimension, we can no longer think that we have not authorized it to enter within us.

June 2020

ACKNOWLEDGMENTS

The elaboration of this book is the result of a path to which various people, to whom it is opportune to express gratitude, have contributed. Among these there is one that deserves to be thanked first: Yoshie Yanagihara, a scholar of the Tokyo Denki University, who – a few years ago – had the goodness of recognising me as one of her interlocutors for her research on biopolitics in Europe. From our meeting in Italy and from the subsequent exchanges of ideas at a distance the project of this volume arose, which she constantly encouraged me to achieve by showing me a trust that will be difficult to repay. Particularly comforting in my effort were the competence and sensitivity with which this attentive fellow companion followed my work.

On the other hand, since her merits exceed those of anyone else, I risk underestimating the gratitude that I owe also to other people who have often unwittingly created the conditions for the conception of this book over time. I am referring first of all to the group of researchers who in 2006, at University of Bari, carried out the project of the *Lessico di biopolitica* (*Biopolitics Lexicon*) – published in Italian and French – of which I was given the opportunity to coordinate the edition. Among them I must certainly thank in a special way Pierangelo Di Vittorio who – among other things – helped me to convincingly overcome my uncertainties about the idea that "psychiatric power" historically fall fully within the forms of biopower.

One scholar to whom I feel I have an important debt, of which he is perhaps unaware, is Thomas Lemke of the Goethe Universität in Frankfurt am Main; on various occasions and, above all, with his studies he offered me authentic enlightenment on the forms that biopolitics has assumed in the context of neoliberal governmentality. I also owe gratitude to Luigi Pellizzoni, of the University of Pisa, who in the many moments in which I was able to meet and listen to him allowed me to grasp precisely the enormous political implications of current life sciences and technologies.

I am also grateful to Laura Bazzicalupo, of the University of Salerno, and Salvo Vaccaro, of the University of Palermo, with whom I have had numerous opportunities to discuss political and philosophical topics almost always connected with the theme of the government of life.

For the attention to my research that finds expression in this book I cannot fail to be grateful also to: Vanessa Lemm and Miguel Vatter of the Flinders University; Emanuele Leonardi of the Universidade de Coimbra; Andrea Russo, Patricia Chiantera-Stutte, Renata Brandimarte, Ruggiero Gorgoglione, Massimiliano Di Modugno, Enrico Mastropierro and Letizia Konderak, companions of various adventures at the University of Bari. Thanks also to Paolo Castoro – a brilliant student at the same University in recent years – who has contributed with rigor and competence to place in order my bibliographical references.

Finally, in a way that is anything but ritual, I must express gratitude to my wife Liliana, for the patience with which she endured the "incursions" of the writing of this book in everyday life. Needless to say, the responsibility for what has been written here is mine alone.

CHAPTER ONE
BIOPOLITICS AND GOVERNMENT
OF PEOPLE
Starting again from Foucault

1. *Life as what is at stake*

Let's start with an observation. Especially since the nineties of the last century the topic of biopolitics has been at the center of a rich and lively debate based on the idea that in our society *life* is one of the privileged objects of the exercise of power. At that time, a very important reason for the great interest in this topic was the rediscovery of some lines of research followed by Foucault in the seventies. This rediscovery was motivated, in the short-term, by the re-publication of several little-known Foucaultian texts and, above all, the edition – released in 1997 in France – of his course entitled *"Society Must Be Defended"*, held at the Collège de France in the first months of 1976:[1] in it Foucault gives a particularly effective explanation of what, according to him, biopolitics is. In reading the text we were reminded that the French philosopher's attention to this theme had already been clearly demonstrated in the last

---

1   Michel Foucault, *"Society Must Be Defended": Lectures at the Collège de France – 1975-1976*, ed. by Mauro Bertani and Alessandro Fontana, trans. by David Macey (New York: Picador, 2003). A first edition of this course, not authorized by Foucault's heirs, had already been published in Italian in 1990. Other important texts on the subject of biopolitics became easily available when the great collection of essays, articles and interviews was published for the first time in France: Michel Foucault, *Dits et Écrits*, ed. by Daniel Defert and François Ewald (Paris: Gallimard, 1994), 4 vols. Moreover, later materials which are particularly useful for the deepening and framing of this topic within Foucault's thought were made available with the progressive publication of other courses held by the French philosopher at the Collège de France. These texts and materials will be cited on the following pages if necessary.

chapter of a well-known work, the first volume of the *History of Sexuality*, published in the same year in which he had taught the aforementioned Course.

According to what Foucault affirms in his lectures and in his 1976 book, since the 18th century, the state has constantly paid attention to the *life* of the population and of individuals, since it is a fundamental resource for the favorable conservation and growth of its own power. Therefore, it is actively involved in collective health and wellbeing and, to this end, it implements a set of knowledge, techniques and strategies that give rise to a *biopolitics*, i.e. to the exercise of a power over life, a *bio-power*.[2]

One of the most important results of the research carried out by Foucault in this area is certainly the identification of the exercise of biopower as the condition in which contemporary «state racism» is fostered and affirmed. In overseeing collective life and wellbeing, the state can consider dangerous to health and to general prosperity the existence of groups of individuals seen as «deviants», «degenerates», «abnormal» or as members of «inferior races»; in these extreme, but not exceptional, cases biopower, as power of life, can be turned into power of death and state racism can be the way in which this inversion is carried out.[3] In certain historical moments and in certain political contexts, killing or letting die people who belong to a «subrace» or an «inferior race» can be considered politically appropriate to guarantee full development, prosperity and the affirmation of the power of a «super-race» or a «superior race», since it is believed that the latter is the only form of life capable of living fully, of fully realizing the potential of a country, a state, a people, a nation.[4] This – according to Foucault – is the cause of the most tragic outcomes of the historical combination between biopower and sovereign power, which has been created in the contemporary state especially starting from the second half of the 19th century: sovereign power reactivates its traditional "life

---

2   Foucault, *"Society Must Be Defended"*, pp. 239-63; Michel Foucault, *The History of Sexuality. Volume 1: An Introduction* (New York: Pantheon Books, 1978), pp. 135-45.

3   Foucault, *"Society Must Be Defended"*, pp. 81, 83, 88, 89, 105, 107, 239, 254, 255.

4   *"Society Must Be Defended"*, pp. 61, 260.

and death power" leading the biopolitical declension of racism to extreme consequences.[5]

Obviously – according to the French philosopher – Nazism was the political regime that led these implications of biopower to extreme consequences in the most direct and systematic way. But it was certainly not the only example of its inversion into a power of death. Even in other contexts, and in more discrete ways, biopower can heavily influence or compromise *life* and, consequently, also the *freedom* of men. However, with regard to Nazism it is useful to underline that many of the concepts and metaphors that it used to "justify" the extermination of Jews and persons "unworthy to live" were of a *medical* and *biological* nature. These concepts referred mostly to the danger of "infection" of the "health" of the race and nation. The Jews in particular were seen, at different times, as bacteria, viruses, parasites, microbes, etc.[6] If we think in general about the ease and frequency with which we use, for example, the definition of parasite to scorn certain people, we can clearly understand that similar concepts and terms can be easily used by other political regimes to exclude, discriminate, possibly send to death or to let individuals or entire social groups die. In short, it is entirely plausible that the exercise of a biopower and its effects of death can be found in many other cases such as that – indicated by Foucault – of «the way socialist states (of the Soviet Union type) deal with the mentally ill, criminals, political adversaries, and so on».[7]

Regarding these aspects of biopower, it is interesting to note that, due to a very significant coincidence, the Foucaultian Course held in 1976 was published at a time (1997) in which the fierce inter-ethnic wars of the former Yugoslavia were exploding. These wars were one of the most catastrophic effects

---

5   See *"Society Must Be Defended"*, pp. 239-41; see also Foucault, *The History of Sexuality. Volume 1*, pp. 135-9.

6   See Roberto Esposito, *Bios: Biopolitics and Philosophy*, trans. by Timothy Campbell (Minneapolis: University of Minnesota Press, 2008), pp. 116-7.

7   *"Society Must Be Defended"*, p. 262; see also p. 83. On this topic see Sergei Prozorov, *The Biopolitics of Stalinism: Ideology and Life in Soviet Socialism* (Edinburgh: Edinburgh University Press, 2016).

of the collapse and disintegration of the socialist regimes of Eastern Europe, not only forms of military and political confrontation, civil war and secession, out of which new state realities emerged (Croatia, Serbia, Bosnia-Herzegovina, etc.); the various armies and fighting groups set out to set up new states on ethnic and racial grounds; therefore, they put into practice or indulged in the practices of ethnic cleansings, i.e. the preemptive racial purification of the collective political bodies that they intended to constitute. In a sense, they promoted a bio-politics that immediately translated into thanato-politics (death politics) and into clashes between state racisms, even before the independent states actually existed. Hence, even these events pushed the most attentive and critical political culture to focus on the biopolitical vocation of the modern state, and its catastrophic implications became tangibly evident at the very moment in which the new states were claimed as necessary foundations for the affirmation of the autonomy and identity of certain nations.

What is certain in any case is that, since the 1990s, the rediscovery of Foucault's research on biopolitics has intersected with a growing attention to life and its relations with death as a privileged terrain for conflicts, strategies, processes, public discussions, political choices, events (inter-ethnic wars, humanitarian wars, genocide, large migrations, biotechnology developments, and decisions on abortion, assisted procreation, euthanasia, etc.). For these reasons, among others, the reflection on biopolitics has progressively grown since then and today is far from being exhausted, after the publication of other courses held by Foucault, which – as we shall see later – refer to the same topic in various measure.

2. *Biopolitics and sovereignty*

Both the analysis presented in "*Society Must Be Defended*" and the one presented in the first volume of the *History of Sexuality* highlight two fundamental aspects of biopolitics. The first consists in the heterogeneity of biopower with respect to sovereign power, so that it seems a sort of juxtaposition has been created in the modern state between two essentially different forms of power: the first (biopower) based, above all, on biological and medical knowledge; the second (sovereign power) based on predominantly juridical knowledge. The other important aspect of biopolitics, according to Foucault, is instead that of the duplicity of levels on which biopower is exercised: the individual level and the collective level. From this point of view, biopolitics is historically said to have established itself – on the first level – above all through the *disciplines* that concern the *organic processes* and *behaviors* of the individual's *body* and – on the second – through the policies of *regulation* of the *biological processes* concerning the *population* as *species*.[8]

To adequately focus on these aspects of biopolitics from the Foucaultian point of view, it is opportune to frame them in the overall vision that emerges from the main research that Foucault did on power. The first fact to keep in mind is that the French philosopher deeply questions the importance that is generally attributed to the idea of *sovereignty*. According to him, power is not simply exercised through relationships in which someone is sovereign over someone else, that is, according to the schema with which the functioning of a state is usually described. Foucault, of course, does not deny that the institutions of power are fundamental instruments of the exercise of power, but – according to him – sovereignty is only the most evident part of the general economy of this exercise; most power relationships take place in other ways. And it is precisely in trying to highlight and analyze these other modes of power that Foucault, in the seventies, came to define a set of techniques, tools, and forms of knowledge that act on two levels: an individual level, which is mainly treated through disciplinary techniques and institutions, and a general level that is mostly the terrain of strategies for governing the collective body.

In summarizing these two levels of the functioning of power, it should first be remembered that Foucault deals with the first

---

8   Foucault, *The History of Sexuality. Volume 1*, pp. 139-40; *"Society Must Be Defended"*, 249-50. On the relationships between discipline and biopolitics see Salvo Vaccaro, *Biopolitica e discipline. Michel Foucault e l'esperienza del GIP* (Milan: Mimesis, 2005).

especially in *Discipline and Punish*, a book on the birth of the modern prison, which, however, also analyzes the overall affirmation of the disciplinary society in the West. According to the French philosopher, the main areas in which the *disciplines* were imposed, more or less between the 18th and the 19th centuries, are those of the *school*, of the *army*, of the *hospital*, of the *factory*, besides that of the *carceral system*. It is above all in these spheres that the techniques aimed at the *control of the individual's body* have been elaborated and used by means of education, training, healing, correction, requirement to work, punishment, re-education, etc., using, among others, forms of discrete and continuous *surveillance*.[9]

Regarding the collective level of the exercise of biopower – as has been mentioned – in his research Foucault speaks of strategies for regulating the phenomena concerning the population. It is above all at this level that the political centrality of biological life emerges clearly. Here, in fact, the focus is mainly on four crucial issues: 1) *birth and mortality rate*; 2) *morbidity*; 3) *disabilities*; 4) *effects of the milieu*.

These are issues for which biopower is, primarily: control over fertility, longevity, mortality and demographic phenomena in general; the statistical and administrative management of these issues; and policies aimed at increasing or moderating demographic growth. Secondly, biopower is health care for endemic diseases, as well as epidemic ones; therefore diseases are treated not only as the possible uncontrollable spread of death in collective and individual life, but especially as factors that decrease energy, reduce performance, and increase the social and economic costs of treatment, and which require permanent systems for the medical management of the forces of society. Thirdly, biopower is the control of events and phenomena that more or less seriously compromise the abilities and activities of individuals considered as a whole: accidents, infirmities, anomalies, old age. In this case, biopolitics is mostly carried out through forms of insurance that constitute the various types of social security. Finally, biopower is

---

9   Michel Foucault, *Discipline and Punish: The Birth of the Prison*, trans. by Alan Sheridan (New York: Vintage Books, 1995).

an intervention on the relationship between people and their milieu interpreted as both a natural environment (i.e. as a geographical, climatic, hydrographic context) and as an artificial environment resulting primarily from urbanization processes: exerting an unmistakable influence on collective life, the milieu requires the control of the effects of this influence.[10]

3. *Medicalization*

A rather surprising fact is that Foucault explicitly uses the terms biopolitics and biopower in only a few of his many texts published in the most disparate forms.[11] Nonetheless – as we can see in the following pages – it is certainly possible to clarify and precisely examine the terms of his thinking on this topics, relying above all on the results of his research in the seventies.

Among the texts that certainly cannot be ignored in this regard, we must first consider those of a few conferences held in October 1974 in Brazil on the theme of social medicine; considered as a whole, they are of great importance with regard to the theme of biopolitics. In one of these conferences, in particular, Foucault indicates the *medicalization* of society as the main factor in the emergence of biopolitics in the 18th century.[12] This indication is only apparently obvious. With it, in fact, the author seems

---

10   Above all, on these essential aspects of biopower, see: *"Society Must Be Defended"*, pp. 243-5.

11   See Valerio Marchetti, 'La naissance de la biopolitique', in Dominique Franche and others (ed. by), *Au risque de Foucault,* (Paris: Èditions du Centre Pompidou, 1977), pp. 239-48.

12   Michel Foucault, 'The Birth of Social Medicine', in *The essential works of Michel Foucault*, III, *Power*, ed. by James D. Faubion, trans. by Robert Hurley (New York: New Press, 2000), pp. 134-56. The other Brazilian conferences to which we will refer here are: Michel Foucault, 'The Crisis of Medicine or the Crisis of Antimedicine?', trans. by Edgar C. Knowlton Jr. and Clare O'Farrell, *Foucault Studies*, 1 (2004), 5-19; Michel Foucault, 'The Incorporation of the hospital into modern technology', trans. by Edgar Knowlton Jr., William J. King, Stuart Elden, in Jeremy W. Crampton and Stuart Elden (ed. by), *Space, knowledge and power: Foucault and geography* (Aldershot, UK: Ashgate Press,

to invite us never to lose sight of the fact that the advent of biopolitics is closely linked to the role historically played by medical knowledge and practices. In fact, if we ignore this basic fact, we will always run the risk of spreading the meaning of the concept of biopolitics excessively, as often happens in the debate around it. In short, according to Foucault, the decisive condition of the emergence of biopolitics was the assumption of the individual and collective *body* as an object of political control through medical intervention.[13]

Certainly this emergence is closely linked to that of capitalism; however, this does not mean that medicine took immediate action to include healthcare in an individualistic and privatized dimension, namely in the «market relation joining the doctor to the patient», and that it has remained «impervious to the global, collective dimension of society». In the historical context of the 18th and even of the 19th century, the fact that medicine was called to play a political role necessarily implied that it took place primarily as «social medicine»; modern medicine – according to Foucault – is above all «a social practice, and only one of its aspects is individualistic and valorizes the relations between the doctor and the patient».[14] It socialized the attention to the body, and through this socialization it transformed into a «biopolitical strategy», since «for capitalist society, it was biopolitics, the biological, the

2007), pp. 141-51. Other texts in which Foucault proposes the theme of biopolitics are: 'The Mesh of Power', trans. by Gerald Moore, in *Space, knowledge and power: Foucault and geography*, pp. 153-62; 'The Political Technology of Individuals', in Luther H. Martin, Huck Gutman, Patrick H. Hutton (ed. by), *Technologies of the Self: A Seminar with Michel Foucault*, (London: Tavistock, 1988), pp. 145-62; 'Bio-history and bio-politics', *Foucault Studies*, 18 (2014), 128-30. Also extremely important is 'La politique de la santé au XVIII siècle', in Foucault, *Dits et Écrits*, III, pp. 725-42.

13   Foucault, 'The Birth of Social Medicine', pp. 136-7.
14   'The Birth of Social Medicine', p. 136. Against the background of these theses by Foucault, his analysis of the birth of «a medicine of the social space» proposed in *The Birth of the Clinic: An Archeology of Medical Perception*, trans. by Alan Sheridan, (London: Routledge, 2003), pp. 16-44.

somatic, the corporal, that mattered more than anything else».[15] Ultimately, according to Foucault, the emergence of biopolitics was based on

> the fact that starting in the eighteenth century human existence, human behavior, and the human body were brought into an increasingly dense and important network of medicalization that allowed fewer and fewer things to escape.[16]

Certainly of note among the reasons for the growing attention to the body, which developed in this framework, was the need to transform it into «a factor of productive force, of labor power». But, actually, this need was not imposed immediately, since initially the body – both individually and collectively – was assumed to be a resource of the power of the state, rather than a merely productive factor; medical and biopolitical attention to «the proletarian's body, the human body, as an instrument of labor» was imposed only in the «second half of the nineteenth century».[17] To illustrate the ways and moments through which this was achieved, the French philosopher describes three different exemplary forms that medicine – according to him – has assumed during the course of its biopolitical socialization: German state medicine, French urban medicine and the English labor force medicine.

1. The first of these three forms, according to him, emerged in Germany at about the beginning of the 18th century in close relationship with the needs of the state, especially because that country – quite unlike France and England – was influenced by its fragmentation in a multiplicity of small and weak states that were joined in a united state only in the 19th century. In such a situation, the need to assume the state itself, its collective body, its resources, its apparatus and its institutions as objects of study, transformation and strengthening was already imposed in the 17th century and pushed Prussia in particular to promote a «science of the state» and a «state medicine». Obviously – as we already

---

15   'The Birth of Social Medicine', p. 137.
16   'The Birth of Social Medicine', p. 135.
17   'The Birth of Social Medicine', p. 137.

know –, according to Foucault, the population was destined to become a fundamental object of attention; but in Germany this attention translated into «a medical practice (...) actually devoted to the improvement of public health» well ahead of France and England.[18] In Germany, the assumption of the population and its health as essential bases of state power rapidly led to the creation of a large system of observation of sickness and of recording of the different epidemic and endemic phenomena, which, in turn, led, first of all, to a radical standardization of the medical profession; secondly, to the subordination of doctors to a general administration; and finally, to their incorporation into a state-controlled medical organization.[19] It was an overall process of the nationalization of medicine of which there were no examples of equal intensity in other countries and that, indeed, tended to assume the body of all people and each person not so much as «labor power», but as the «strength of the state in those conflict that set it against its neighbors – economic conflicts, no doubt, but also political ones».[20]

2. The most important aspect of what happened in France, however, lies in medicine's insistent reference to the problems created by the expansion of urban structures especially from the second half of the 18th century on.[21] In that period the impetuous growth of the cities as places of commerce, industrial production and concentration of a poor, laboring population, made urgent the need for a unitary system of government to overcome the plurality of powers that were exercised in the urban space by the seignorial authorities, by the Church, by the guilds, by the police, by the representatives of the crown, etc.[22] The growing city quickly became a place of fear caused by social turbulence, unrest, increasingly frequent revolts, as well as epidemics, dangerous throngs of people and things, the multiplication of factors of infection, etc.[23] French

18   'The Birth of Social Medicine', pp. 139-40.
19   'The Birth of Social Medicine', pp. 140-1.
20   'The Birth of Social Medicine', pp. 141-2.
21   'The Birth of Social Medicine', p. 142.
22   'The Birth of Social Medicine', p. 143.
23   'The Birth of Social Medicine', pp. 143-4.

urban medicine emerged in a context like this, first and foremost as a system of investigation and intervention on places where people and structures were concentrated, which could turn into sources of health hazards: the removal of the cemeteries and slaughterhouses to the city peripheries was one of the exemplary effects of this approach.[24] Similarly, medicine tackled the health problems that were thought to stem from the poor circulation of air and water or the risky coexistence in the urban space of structures for water and sewage distribution and disposal facilities, such as fountains, sewers, pumps, river washhouses, etc. The result was various interventions for the widening of roads and the demolition of buildings that were considered to hinder ventilation or the flow of water.[25]

Guaranteeing public hygiene was the main goal of this type of medical policy. In addressing these problems, medicine collaborated with other areas of scientific knowledge, first of all chemistry, in order to analyze air, water and other material conditions of collective life. In this way, it defined itself as a medicine of things rather than organisms, a medicine that turned its attention to the *environment* – even before this concept was established – and posed the question of the *salubrity* of spaces as a condition for the *health* of people.[26] Therefore, it can be said that this medicine passed «not from analysis of the organism to analysis of the environment», but «from analysis of the environment to that of the effects of the environment on the organism and, finally, to analysis of the organism itself».[27]

3. In England the process of the biopolitical socialization of medicine took place primarily through a path of "completion" on the medical level of the "Poor Law" of 1834 which aimed at ensuring a minimum of assistance to the neediest members of the population. In the first half of the 19th century the need for essential forms of medical care and control of the population in general was urgently felt because by then England was experiencing

---

24   'The Birth of Social Medicine', pp. 146-7.
25   'The Birth of Social Medicine', pp. 147-9.
26   'The Birth of Social Medicine', pp. 149-51.
27   'The Birth of Social Medicine', p. 150.

the problematic effects of the industrial revolution much more intensely than other European countries. A real proletariat had formed and the poor classes were perceived as bearers of various dangers, in particular health and political issues. According to Foucault, through the protection and medical control of the poor

> the wealthy classes, or their government representatives, would guarantee the health of the needy classes and, consequently, protect the privileged population. (...) Thus the wealthy freed themselves of the risk of being victims of epidemic phenomena issuing from the disadvantaged classes.[28]

This type of policy – according to the French philosopher – also continued to develop later through systems designed to control compliance with the obligation of vaccinations, and intervention on unhealthy places, and «record of epidemics and diseases capable of turning into an epidemic».[29] The general meaning of these strategies was to guarantee «a control of the health and the bodies of the needy classes, to make them more fit for labor and less dangerous to the wealthy classes».[30] Additionally, these policies allowed for the articulation of an overall system in which «a welfare medicine designed for the poorest people; an administrative medicine responsible for general problems such as vaccination, epidemics, and so on; and a private medicine benefiting those who could afford it» coexisted.[31] This articulation would then be perpetuated in different forms and ways also in the medical systems and in the biopolitics of «today's richest and most industrialized countries».[32]

4. *Hygienism*

According to Foucault's reconstruction, the socialization processes of medicine have largely been characterized by concern

---

28   'The Birth of Social Medicine', p. 153.
29   'The Birth of Social Medicine', p. 154.
30   'The Birth of Social Medicine', p. 155.
31   'The Birth of Social Medicine', pp. 155-6.
32   'The Birth of Social Medicine', p. 156.

for public hygiene. In France, this concern was the basis of a real scientific, cultural and political movement that took the name of hygienism (*hygiénisme*) and profoundly influenced medical, urban and political practices, not only in that country. Hygienism, among other things, largely inspired the urban changes that made Georges-Eugène Haussmann famous: he was the prefect of Paris who under the authoritarian regime of Napoleon III (1852-1870) deeply transformed the structure of the French capital. He greatly expanded and rectified many city streets and radically reorganized the urban distribution of circulation, residence, commerce and production spaces, making them more accessible and easier to cross. Therefore, he not only made a greater control of the health and sanitary risks possible, but he also created a structure of the city that appeared to be more functional to the maintenance of public order: expropriating and demolishing entire medieval neighborhoods considered narrow and unhealthy, he expelled the greater part of the poorer classes, who were considered dangerous, from the city center. Moreover, creating avenues of enormous width and length, he aimed to facilitate the repression of the revolts that had continued to mark Parisian history since the days of the French Revolution.[33]

If this kind of change concerned open spaces, the changes concerning the underground structures and the enclosed spaces of the city were equally important and radical. In this sense, the creation and hygienic rationalization of large systems for the circulation of water and sewage water were of great importance. Furthermore, the approach inspired by hygienism profoundly influenced the reorganization and management of the areas for accommodating people in need of special attention. It, therefore, contributed – both in France and elsewhere – to the design and creation of the contemporary hospital: in the 19th century the hospital stopped being «an institution of aid to the poor awaiting death» and progressively became «a site of collective medicalization».[34] Since then it has increasingly

---

33 See David Harvey, *Rebel Cities: From the Right to the Cities to the Urban Revolution* (London-New York: Verso, 2013), pp. 7-8, 16-7, 117.
34 Foucault, 'The Crisis of Medicine or the Crisis of Antimedicine?', p. 13.

tended to guarantee hygienic and healthy conditions within its premises as basic assumptions both for the health of bodies and for the effective exercise of medical intervention.[35] Moreover, as we have already seen, according to Foucault the medicalization processes did not only have the purpose of healing the diseases of the individual organism; above all they tended to prevent the possibility of illnesses and the dangers that they entail when they take on a social dimension. Therefore, even the hospital, perfecting itself as a medical institution, assumed its biopolitical role in both an individual and a collective sense: it has become an area of exercise of the power-knowledge of medicine for a growing number of problems in the lives of people and society. From this point of view, the disciplinary organization of its spaces has assumed very precise functions.

> With the application of the discipline of medical space, and by the fact that it is possible to isolate each individual, install him in a bed, prescribe for him a regimen, etc., one is led toward an individualizing medicine. In effect it is the individual who will be observed, surveyed, known and cured. The individual thus appears as an object of medical knowledge and practice.
>
> At the same time, through the same system of disciplined hospital space, one can observe a great number of individuals. The records obtained daily, when compared among hospitals and in diverse regions, permit the study of pathological phenomena common to the whole population.
>
> Thanks to hospital technology, the individual and the population present themselves at the same time as objects of knowledge and medical intervention. The redistribution of those two medicines will be a phenomenon of the nineteenth century. The medicine that is formed in the course of the eighteenth century is simultaneously a medicine of the individual and the population.[36]

The hospital of the 19th century, in short, placed itself at the intersection of the processes of individualization and the processes of totalization of the medical intervention in society. But while it is important to note, also in this regard, that the essential references of

35   In this regard, see above all Foucault, 'The Incorporation of the Hospital into Modern Technology', pp. 142-3.
36   'The Incorporation of the Hospital into Modern Technology', p. 151.

biopolitical strategies are both the individual and the population, it is equally important to consider another aspect of these trends: the hospital has also become a meeting place for two complementary declinations of hygienic attention to the collective space; it is an attention that finds its main justification in the transformations that medicine has undergone since the end of the 18th century, or when it started to become a social medicine. We have already seen that, in this way, it has also been transformed into «a medicine of the environment», which – explains Foucault – is directed «precisely to the intersection of the disease and the organism, as it is in the surrounding environment: air, water, temperature, the regimen, the food, etc.».[37] So, this transformation took place referring both to the urban environment and to the space inside the hospital and its relationship with the external space.

> In the first place it is a matter of knowing where to situate a hospital so that it does not continue to be a dark, obscure and confused place in the heart of the city where a person would arrive at the hour of death and spread dangerous miasma, contaminated air, dirty water, etc. (...)
> In the second place, one also had to calculate the internal distribution of the space of the hospital as a function of certain criteria: if it was certain that an action practiced in the environment would cure diseases, it would be necessary to create about each patient a small individualized space environment, specific to them and modifiable according to the patient, the disease, and its evolution.[38]

Ultimately, it can be said that the creation of the contemporary hospital is a fundamental part of the set of processes that Foucault sees as originating from the emergence of state medicine in Germany, urban medicine in France and labor force medicine in England. That is to say: the «appearance of a medical authority» as «a social authority that can make decisions concerning a town, a district, an institution, or a regulation»; the outlining of «a medical field of intervention distinct from diseases: air, water, construction, terrains, sewerage, etc.»; the organization of «mechanisms of medical administration» through which data are

---

37   'The Incorporation of the Hospital into Modern Technology', p. 148.
38   'The Incorporation of the Hospital into Modern Technology', p. 149.

recorded, statistics are compiled and compared, and so on. It is within the framework of these trends that the hospital is structured as a system of individual and social medicalization that goes beyond the limits of pure assistance. And it is on the basis of these same tendencies that – for Foucault – we can say that «in recent decades, medicine, in acting beyond its traditional boundaries of ill people and diseases, is taking over other areas».[39]

5. *Bio-politics and bio-history*

For all these reasons – according to the French philosopher – in our age it is not possible to consider ourselves free from the power that medicine has taken on in our society, imagining that we can easily find spheres of individual and collective life still free from this same power. «What is diabolical about the present situation is that whenever we want to refer to a realm outside medicine we find that it has been already been medicalized». So, Foucault argues that we must now go beyond the criticism of modern medicine developed, for example, by the representatives of so-called "antimedicine" such as Ivan Illich. According to the French author – they limit themselves to reporting errors, deficiencies and the harmful effects of medicine (iatrogenic diseases, lack of effectiveness, useless treatments, doctor-inflicted injuries);[40] and they also believe they can oppose the dominant forms of medicine with «a demedicalized art of health made up of hygiene, diet, lifestyle, work and housing conditions etc.». In short, they do not realize that in these aspects "antimedicine" is also substantially linked to «a series of rules set in place and codified by biological and medical knowledge».[41]

Beyond these evaluations of antimedicine, which can be more or less agreed upon,[42] what is worth highlighting here is another

---

39   'The Crisis of Medicine or the Crisis of Antimedicine?', pp. 13-4.
40   See 'The Crisis of Medicine or the Crisis of Antimedicine?', pp. 5-9, and Ivan Illich, *Medical Nemesis: The Expropriation of Health* (New York: Pantheon Books, 1976), especially pp. 13-36.
41   'The Crisis of Medicine or the Crisis of Antimedicine?', p. 14.
42   For a different evaluation of Illich's thought, see Michel Foucault, 'La philosophie analytique de la politique', in Foucault, *Dits et écrits*, III,

question: Foucault is especially interested in showing that the harmful effects of contemporary medicine are not so much the result of its failures or of its overall inadequacy, as much as the uncontrollable result of the undeniable advancements of its knowledge and of its technical intervention skills. In this sense he claims that, while previously «the harmfulness of medicine was judged in proportion to its non-scientificity», by the beginning of the 20th century «medicine could be dangerous, not through its ignorance and falseness, but through its knowledge, precisely because it was a science»;[43] in addition, he notes that today

> the instruments that doctors and medicine in general have at their disposal cause certain effects, precisely because of their efficacy. Some of these effects are purely harmful and others are unable to be controlled, which leads the human species into a perilous area of history, into a field of probabilities and risks, the magnitude of which cannot be precisely measured.[44]

It can be said, for example, that the same hygienistic approach, reaching a high level of effectiveness with the progress of anti-infectious medicine,

> led to a general decrease of the threshold of the organism's sensitivity to hostile agents. This means that to the extent that the organism can defend itself better, it protects itself, naturally, but on the other hand, it is more fragile and more exposed if one restricts contact with the stimuli which provoke defenses.[45]

Foucault's speech goes well beyond the indication of this kind of consequence, even envisaging the profound alterations of the biological mechanisms that may derive from the interference of the historical developments of modern medicine with the temporality of the phenomena of life; in this sense, in his opinion, it can be said that with these developments humanity has entered into the

---

pp. 545-6.
43   'The Crisis of Medicine or the Crisis of Antimedicine?', p. 9.
44   'The Crisis of Medicine or the Crisis of Antimedicine?', p. 10.
45   'The Crisis of Medicine or the Crisis of Antimedicine?', p. 10.

dimension of «bio-history».[46] It is a time dimension in which what is increasingly relevant is

> the effect of medical intervention at the biological level, the imprint left on human history, one may assume, by the strong medical intervention that began in the eighteenth century.[47]

Only by grasping the unprecedented intensity of the relationship that has since established itself between the history of medical strategies and the evolution of life phenomena can one succeed in properly framing the positive and negative effects of medical developments. Only in this way, moreover, are we in a position to focus on the enormous implications of the ever closer relationships that have been created in our era between medicine, biology and genetic research.

> Nobody knows – says Foucault – where the genetic manipulation of the genetic potential of living cells in bacteria or in viruses will lead. It has become technically possible to develop agents that attack the human body against which there are no means of defence. One could forge an absolute biological weapon against man and the human species without the means of defence against this absolute weapon being developed at the same time. (...)
> We thus enter a new dimension of what we might call medical risk. (...)
> Nowadays, with the techniques at the disposal of medicine, the possibility for modifying the genetic cell structure not only affects the individual or his descendant but the entire human race. Every aspects of life now becomes the subject of medical intervention. (...)
> A new dimension of medical possibilities arises that I shall call bio-history. The doctor and the biologist are no longer working at the level of the individual and his descendents, but are beginning to work at the level of life itself and its fundamental events. This is a very important element in bio-history.[48]

It is also for these reasons that, for Foucault, it is necessary to retrace precisely the conditions that historically allowed medicine

---

46   'The Crisis of Medicine or the Crisis of Antimedicine?', pp. 11-2.
47   'The Birth of Social Medicine', p. 134.
48   'The Crisis of Medicine or the Crisis of Antimedicine?', pp. 10-1.

to become a pillar of biopower, considering that «humanity did not remain immune to medicalization».[49] In fact, according to him, it is quite probable that medicalization began to influence the history of our species profoundly from an early date because of the broad and intensely social, environmental and political character it assumed from the beginning, that is even before an organic, microbiological, chemical and genetic medicine actually developed. In this sense, medicalization could have produced even more positive effects than those it aimed to achieve, without its promoters having a clear awareness of it: the decrease or disappearance of various infectious diseases from the West «even before the introduction of the twentieth century's great chemical therapy»; the disappearance of the plague during the 18th and 19th centuries «without our really knowing either the reasons for, nor the mechanisms of, that phenomenon»; the progressive reduction of patients who died of tuberculosis before Koch discovered «the bacillus that was to make him famous». They are all examples of the possibility that, long ago, mechanisms yet to be studied intervened «at the level of bio-history» with the decisive contribution of collective medicalization strategies. In any case, certainly a series of physical, social and political processes played an important role in this sense, among which we must consider: on the one hand, «the change of socio-economic conditions, the organism's phenomena of adaptation and resistance», the weakening of the infectious microorganisms; on the other, «the measures of hygiene and isolation», and, more generally, the interventions of medicine and different therapeutic techniques on the individual and collective level.[50]

However, while, on one hand, medicalization may have even contributed to the achievement of unexpectedly positive results, on the other, it may also have provoked, and still be provoking, perverse, uncontrollable effects. This is precisely the case of the alteration of the mechanisms of «bacterial and viral protection», which occurs «as a result of the therapeutic intervention» on infectious diseases. This intervention certainly produces immediate benefits, but, at the same time, it can cause a reduction

---

49   'The Birth of Social Medicine', p. 134.
50   'The Birth of Social Medicine', pp. 134-5.

in defense capabilities from «attacks against which the organism had previously been protected»; so

> through the very effects of medications – positive and therapeutic effects – there occurs a disturbance, even destruction, of the ecosystem, not only at the individual level, but also at the level of the human species itself.[51]

Precisely while considering this *ecosystemic dimension* in which Foucault projects the uncontrollable effects he discusses, one could also pose other problems than those that he himself indicates. In general, one might ask what ecosystemic effects are caused by a medicalization that, although it tends to contextualize life in its environmental conditions, actually assumes the environment as an external world with respect to life itself, as a set of circumstances that tend mostly to undermine it. But we will come back to this later.

For now, in light of what we have just seen, it is enough to repeat that – according to the French philosopher – not only the positive effects but also the negative effects of medicalization should be considered as results of the effectiveness, rather than the limits, of the success of medicine in society, of the hospital as its fundamental instrument, of hygienism as its historically essential strategy.

6. *A medicine of the soul*

Obviously, we must always bear in mind that all this – according to Foucault – results from the promotion of specific political strategies and the establishment of precise power relations. From this point of view, there is one aspect of the creation of the contemporary hospital that certainly should not be overlooked, namely the fact that it gave rise to a two-sided hospital system, the "organic" and the "psychological". In short, it is a matter of considering that the medicalization of individual and collective life

---

51   'The Crisis of Medicine or the Crisis of Antimedicine?', p. 10.

has evolved by directing growing attention not only to the body, but – so to speak – also to the soul, that is to the behavior of men starting from those who are generally considered madmen. Thus, since the 19th century, hospitals have primarily had two functions:

> (1) to confine those who were unable to work for physical reasons; (2) to confine those who could not work for nonphysical reasons. In this way, mental disorders had become the object of medicine and a social category called "psychiatry" was born. (...)
> [I]f this medicalization occurred, it was (...) essentially for economic and social reasons: that was how the madman was made identical to the mentally ill individual and an entity called "mental illness" was discovered and developed. Psychiatric hospitals were created as something symmetrical to hospitals for physical illnesses.[52]

The text in which Foucault expresses himself in these terms was published at a time that could be defined as transitional in the context of his fundamental studies of madness; those studies, after having achieved their first great result in the early sixties with *History of Madness*,[53] were later "updated" in two Courses held at the Collège de France respectively in the years 1973-1974 and 1974-1975.[54] Among the changes that occur in these Courses in comparison with the initial moment, the most important seems to consist precisely in the adoption of a clearer awareness, on the part of Foucault, of the role that power relations – starting from the 19th century – have played in the progressive medicalization of

---

52 Michel Foucault, 'Madness and Society', in *The essential works of Michel Foucault*, II, *Aesthetics, Method and Epistemology*, ed. by James D. Faubion, trans. by Robert Hurley (New York: New Press, 1998), p. 342.

53 Michel Foucault, *History of Madness*, ed. by Jean Khalfa, trans. by Jonathan Murphy and Jean Khalfa (London: Routledge, 2006). This edition is a translation of *Histoire de la Folie à l'âge classique* (Paris: Gallimard, 1972), first published in French as *Folie et Déraison: Histoire de la folie à l'âge classique* (Paris: Plon, 1961).

54 Michel Foucault, *Psychiatric Power: Lectures at the Collège de France – 1973-1974*, ed. by Jacques Lagrange, transl. by Graham Burchell (New York: Palgrave McMillan, 2006); Michel Foucault, *Abnormal: Lectures at the Collège de France – 1974-1975*, ed. by Valerio Marchetti and Antonella Salomoni, transl. by Graham Burchell (London: Verso, 2003).

madness, i.e. in the establishment of psychiatry as specific field of medical knowledge and of the asylum as the psychiatric hospital.

> Power relations – says Foucault – were the *a priori* of psychiatric practice: they conditioned how the asylum institution functioned, they determined the distribution of relationships between individuals within it, and they governed the forms of medical intervention. (...)
> Now, what these power relations involved first and foremost was the absolute right of nonmadness over madness. A right translated into terms of expertise being brought to bear on ignorance, of good sense (access to reality) correcting errors (illusions, hallucinations, fantasies), and of normality being imposed on disorder and deviation. This triple power constituted madness as a possible object of knowledge for a medical science, constituted it as illness, at the very moment that the "subject" affected by this illness was disqualified as mad – that is to say, stripped of all power and knowledge with regard to his illness.[55]

As in the case of the skepticism expressed in general toward "antimedicine", in one of his Brazilian conferences Foucault also expresses his perplexities on so-called "antipsychiatry" (including psychoanalysis in this definition) and its attempts to question the medicalization of madness implemented by psychiatry: in that conference antipsychiatry seems to him to be «a type of activity and discourse based on a medical perspective and knowledge»; so even in this case it seems to him that «one cannot get away

---

55   Foucault, *Psychiatric Power*, p. 345. As was observed by Jacques Lagrange – editor of this course –, Foucault does not adhere to a rigid vision of these power relationships. The disciplinary and relational character that medical power assumes in the psychiatric hospital does not exclude the reversibility, albeit paradoxical, of such relationships. An exemplary case would be that of women classified as hysterics by the great neuropsychiatrist Jean-Martin Charcot in the 19th century. They – so to speak – adhered faithfully to the diagnosis of "hysteria", manifesting a disproportionate amount of symptoms and giving vent to countless crises the content of which often consisted in talking about and simulating an irrepressible sexuality, which ended up representing a sort of "victory" on the part of the hysterics themselves against medical power. On this issue see *Psychiatric Power*, pp. 308-23; in this same volume, see also Jacques Lagrange, 'Course Context', pp. 354-5, 361-2.

from medicalization, and every effort toward this end ends up referring to medical knowledge».[56] Instead, in his Course entitled *Psychiatric Power* he seems to examine the matter more carefully and – excluding psychoanalysis from the field of antipsychiatry – he expresses himself in very different terms; in fact, he clearly indicates the reasons why antipsychiatric experiences – while remaining within the limits of medical practices – somehow managed to delineate a perspective of the «demedicalization of madness».[57] The validity of these experiences – in his opinion – is above all in the fact that they took place in the heart of that medical institution, exemplary and special at the same time, that is the psychiatric hospital: it is there that antipsychiatry succeeded in highlighting and, at the same time, destabilizing the power relations which were the historical basis on which the process of medicalization had classified madness as mental illness. Foucault says antipsychiatry was able to do all of this in the following way:

> giving the individual the task and right of taking his madness to the limit, of taking it right to the end, in an experience to which others may contribute, but never in the name of a power conferred on them by their reason or normality; detaching behavior, suffering, and desire from the medical status given to them, freeing them from a diagnosis and symptomatology that had the value not just of classification, but of decision and decree; invalidating, finally, the great retranscription of madness as mental illness that was begun in the seventeenth and completed in the nineteenth century.[58]

What emerges in general from the work that Foucault carried out in his Courses of the years 1973-1974 and 1974-1975 is that, in the 19th century, psychiatry certainly found in the asylum the

---

56   'The Crisis of Medicine or the Crisis of Antimedicine?', pp. 14-5.
57   *Psychiatric Power*, p. 346. The main references of Foucault in this regard are: David Cooper, *Psychiatry and Antipsychiatry* (London: Tavistock, 1967); Franco Basaglia (ed. by), *L'istituzione negata. Rapporto da un ospedale psichiatrico* (Turin: Einaudi, 1968). On the differences between the Foucaultian vision of psychiatric power and that of the exponents of the antipsychiatry, see Lagrange, 'Course Context', pp. 357-60.
58   *Psychiatric Power*, p. 345.

main place for the affirmation of its power-knowledge, but it also discovered the risk of being locked up with the madmen who it transforms into sick people and aspires to cure.

Moreover, the special character it attributes to its own knowledge and to the illness it deals with, often places it in a condition of lesser scientific authority than that which clinical and organic medicine conquers more easily with the help of biological, microbiological, chemistry and pharmacology research.[59] Be that as it may, the ambition of psychiatry to extend its sphere of influence to the whole of society is not inferior to that of other branches of medicine; it is very sensitive to the strategies of hygienism and to the aims of the protection of the social body that inspire most of the medicalization processes. In fact, it is precisely by interpreting these strategies and these purposes in its own way that it manages to go beyond the walls of the psychiatric hospital. Foucault insists on this theme both in his 1974-1975 Course and in a 1978 text:

> if psychiatry became so important in the nineteenth century, it was not simply because it applied a new medical rationality to mental or behavioral disorders, it was also because it functioned as a sort of public hygiene.[60]

As we have seen, medicine as a whole had begun to orient itself in this direction since the 18th century by addressing

> the question of human "populations", with their conditions of existence, of habitation, of nutrition, with their birth and mortality rate, with their pathological phenomena (epidemics, endemic diseases, infant mortality).

In the 19th century, psychiatry conformed to this orientation and, in this way, managed to attain its autonomy and its prestige «because it had been able to develop within the framework of

---

59   See Pierangelo Di Vittorio, 'Psichiatria', in Renata Brandimarte and others (ed. by), *Lessico di biopolitica*, coord. by Ottavio Marzocca (Rome: Manifestolibri, 2006), pp. 244-51.

60   Michel Foucault, 'About the Concept of the "Dangerous Individual" in 19th-Century Legal Psychiatry', *International Journal of Law and Psychiatry*, 1, 1978, 1-18 (p. 6); see also *Abnormal*, pp. 118-22 and 315-7.

a medical discipline conceived of as a reaction to the dangers inherent in the social body». In fact, psychiatrists did not take long to consider mental illness as

> a social "danger", either because insanity seemed to them to be linked to living conditions (overpopulation, overcrowding, urban life, alcoholism, debauchery), or because it was perceived as a source of danger for oneself, for others, for one's contemporaries, and also for one's descendants through heredity.[61]

7. *Social defence*

In this way, psychiatry made a decisive contribution to the functioning of a set of security mechanisms in a society that was increasingly worried about the increase of risks, dangers, accidents and fears. It would contribute to a sort of qualitative leap in these mechanisms, which – between the end of the 19th and the beginning of the 20th century – would find a general justification in the theory of *social defence*.[62]

According to Foucault, in truth, psychiatric medicine had already assumed an important role in this sense at the beginning of the 19th century, when it began to urge criminal justice to consider mental pathologies as a source of danger, even as a possible cause of involuntary crimes, "objective", more than subjective, for which the traditional concepts of guilt and responsibility were inadequate. A historical situation that was decisive for asserting these arguments was the case of some brutal murders that clamorously filled the news chronicles between 1800 and 1835; these were murders for

---

61 'About the Concept of the "Dangerous Individual" in 19th-Century Legal Psychiatry', pp. 6-7.

62 The main work in this regard is that of the jurist Adolphe Prins, *La Défense sociale et les Transformations du Droit pénal* (Bruxelles: Misch et Thron, 1919). On this subject see the texts presented during the seminar conducted by Foucault at the Catholic University of Louvain (Belgium) in 1981 and published in Françoise Tulkens (ed. by), *Généalogie de la défense sociale en Belgique*, (Bruxelles: Story-Scientia, 1988); additionally, see Maximo Sozzo, 'Difesa sociale', in *Lessico di biopolitica*, pp. 107-11.

which there were no reliable explanations, that were presented as crimes committed «without reason, [..] without profit, without passion, without motive».[63] The great psychiatrists of the era studied them and presented them as «monstrous crimes», as «crimes against nature»; in short, by insistently calling attention to these crimes, psychiatric medicine came to define the sphere of «criminal insanity or pathological crime».[64] For a while, the notion that psychiatry proposed to the judiciary to explain these cases and deal with them on a criminal level was that of «homicidal monomania».[65] This was a decidedly problematic notion that, in the long run, was abandoned; however, just by insisting on it psychiatry succeeded in imposing the idea that unsuspected mental illnesses can cause unpredictable crimes. In the 19th century – according to Foucault – crime became an important issue for psychiatry

> not because, after having gone through every other possible domain of madness, it came across this superfluous and excessive madness that consists in killing. In fact, it was interested straightaway in madness that kills because its problem was to constitute itself and advance its claims as a power and knowledge of protection within society.[66]

63   'About the Concept of the "Dangerous Individual" in 19th-Century Legal Psychiatry', p. 5; on these murders, see pp. 3-4. The most famous case studied by Foucault among these crimes, as is well-known, is that presented in *I, Pierre Rivière, having slaughtered my mother, my sister, and my brother....*, ed. by Michel Foucault, trans. by Frank Jellinek (New York: Pantheon Books, 1975).

64   'About the Concept of the "Dangerous Individual" in 19th-Century Legal Psychiatry', p. 5. The main Foucault references in this regard are: Jean-Étienne D. Esquirol, *Des maladies mentales considérées sous les rapports médical, hygiénique et médico-légal*, (Paris: Ballière, 1838), 2 vols; Etienne-Jean Georget, *Examen des procès criminels des nommés Léger, Feldtmann, Lecouffe, Jean-Pierre et Papavoine, suivi de quelques considérations médico-légales sur la liberté morale* (Paris: Migneret, 1825); William C. Ellis, *A Treatise on the Nature, Symptoms, Causes and Treatment of Insanity, with Practical Observations on Lunatic Asylums* (London: Holdsworth, 1838); Andrew Combe, *Observations on Mental Dérangement* (Edinburgh: Anderson, 1831).

65   'About the Concept of the "Dangerous Individual" in 19th-Century Legal Psychiatry', p. 6.

66   *Abnormal*, p.121; see also: 'About the Concept of the "Dangerous Individual" in 19th-Century Legal Psychiatry', p. 6.

Of course, a notion like that of homicidal monomania left open the possibility, however, that the authors of crimes "without motive" would go unpunished since they were "not responsible", insofar as it was believed that the unleashing of their pathology had overwhelmed them; but that notion also led to question of whether there were "dangerous individuals" whose behaviors had to be studied in order to control them and treat them, according to their degree of dangerousness.

According to Foucault's reconstruction, in the second half of the 19th century, the great influence of positivism and biological evolutionism made possible the affirmation of the *degeneration theory* that, however, psychiatry had developed even before Darwin published his most important work.[67] Through this theory psychiatry aimed to explain behaviors that were deviant from those considered normal, referring to a kind of regression of the biological structure of certain individuals, able both to be transmitted to their descendants and to produce dangerous mental diseases. In this way, psychiatry no longer limited itself to trying to recognize diseases so as to try to cure them; first of all, it aimed at identifying the possibility of these diseases in advance and safeguarding society and the species from the risks to which they were exposed since it claimed this degeneration could be transmitted by inheritance. So «it became possible for psychiatry to link any deviance, difference, and backwardness whatsoever to a condition of degeneration»; psychiatry «thereby gained a possibility of indefinite intervention in human behavior».[68]

Among the most radical attempts to use psychiatric medicine for the protection of society, Foucault indicates the one made by criminal anthropology near the end of the 19th century. In particular, Cesare Lombroso, its most famous exponent, in the different editions of his most important work, stubbornly aimed to classify various types of dangerous individuals starting

---

67   See *Psychiatric Power*, p. 223. The founding work of degeneration theory is universally recognized in Bénédict-Augustin Morel, *Traité des dégénérescences physiques, intellectuelles et morales de l'espèce humaine, et des causes qui produisent ces variétés maladives* (Paris: Baillière, 1857).

68   *Abnormal*, p. 315.

from the hypothesis of their natural disposition to crime, recognizable, above all, through anatomical, physiological and psychic anomalies.[69]

Critically interacting with the jurists of the time, criminal anthropology expanded and took to extreme consequences the idea that the danger of certain individuals could be not only demonstrated, but also used as a condition of treatment not simply when crimes had been committed, but – above all – when there was a risk that they be committed. For the management of the penal system criminal anthropology even proposed «putting aside the legality» and to substantially replace the law with criminological medicine: the latter would have been the solution to the problem of crime, since it made it possible to recognize its potential perpetrators and thus strike or neutralize them before any crime was actually committed.

> The Criminal Anthropologists – claims Foucault – emphasized that what is called "penalty" does not have to be a punishment, but rather a mechanism for the defence of society, and therefore noted that the relevant difference is not between legally responsible subjects to be found guilty, and legally irresponsible subjects to be released, but between absolutely and definitively dangerous subjects and those who can cease to be dangerous provided they receive certain treatment. They concluded there should be three main types of social reaction to crime or rather to the danger represented by the criminal: definitive elimination (by dead or by incarceration in an institution), temporary elimination (with treatment), and more or less relative and partial elimination (sterilization and castration).[70]

Of course, today we cannot help but recognize that both degeneration theory and criminal anthropology have been largely surpassed by the neurology and psychiatry of the 20th century. However, according to Foucault, this fact should not cause us to underestimate their exemplary meaning and the influence, albeit

---

69   Cesare Lombroso, *L'uomo delinquente studiato in rapporto all'antropologia, alla giurisprudenza, alle discipline carcerarie ed alla psichiatria* (Turin: Bocca, 1896-1897).

70   'About the Concept of the "Dangerous Individual" in 19th-Century Legal Psychiatry', p. 13.

indirect, that they may have exercised on the theories and practices that contemporary societies have adopted and continue to adopt in pursuing their own protection;[71] we must consider, in particular, that in the 19th century, through the theory of degeneration and criminal anthropology, psychiatry contributed to the birth of a particular kind of racism from which we have probably not yet freed ourselves.

> With this notion of degeneration and these analyses of heredity, you can see how psychiatry could plug into, or rather give rise to, a racism that was very different in this period from what could be called traditional, historical racism, from "ethnic racism".
> The racism that psychiatry gave birth to in this period is racism against the abnormal, against individuals who, as carriers of a condition, a stigmata, or any defect whatsoever, may more or less randomly transmit to their heirs the unpredictable consequences of the evil, or rather of the non-normal, that they carry within them.[72]

Faced with these theses it can also be thought that Foucault tends to attribute excessive historical responsibility to psychiatric medicine. But, in truth, he does not fail to recognize that «although it gave rise to this eugenics, psychiatry is far for being reducible to this form of racism, which covered or took over only a relatively limited part of it».[73]

Foucault's purpose is not to throw pure and simple discredit on this branch of contemporary medicine; rather he intends to problematize it so as to place its genesis within the framework of precise historical conditions and specific political motivations. In short, the main goal of the French philosopher is to question the idea of «protection of the social body», i.e. the perspective, still generally accepted in an uncritical way, according to which «society must be defended» – as the title in quotation marks of his 1975-1976 Course provocatively states. It is the same idea and the same perspective with which not only psychiatric practices, but also general strategies of medicalization, have impressed a

---

71 'About the Concept of the "Dangerous Individual" in 19th-Century Legal Psychiatry', p. 14.
72 *Abnormal*, pp. 316-7.
73 *Abnormal*, p. 317.

clear biopolitical orientation that is constantly exposed to the possibility of sliding into more or less evident forms of racism and thanatopolitics.

Ultimately, among Foucault's intentions, one must appreciate that of inviting us to reflect on the fact that the relationships between knowledge and power can create this kind of possibility insofar as they are established in a field in which health and suffering, freedom and dependence, life and death are constantly at stake.

On the other hand, the French philosopher, at the very moment in which he highlights these implications of the medicalization of society, also indicates the need to frame them in a "productive" and "positive" vision of the exercise of power. According to him, despite everything, the main purposes of the exercise of power in modern society are not the exclusion or radical discrimination of certain forms of life, but the normalization of the ways of being, of existing and of behaving that life itself conveys. In this sense, the essential perspective of the power strategies which include biopolitics is not that of the repressive imposition of a *law*, but rather that of the identification and the affirmation – albeit temporary – of a *norm*, of the definition and of the production of a *normality*. It is a perspective that – according to the French philosopher – was definitively imposed in the 20th century.

> If the jurists of the seventeenth and eighteenth centuries are considered to have invented a social system that had to be governed by a system of codified laws, it might be argued that in the twentieth century doctors are in the process of inventing a society, not of law, but of the norm. What governs society are not legal codes but the perpetual distinction between normal and abnormal, a perpetual enterprise of restoring the system of normality.[74]
>
> [T]he norm brings with it a principle of both qualification and correction. The norm's function is not to exclude and reject. Rather, it is always linked to a positive technique of intervention and transformation, to a sort of normative project.[75]

---

74   'The Crisis of Medicine or the Crisis of Antimedicine?', p. 13.
75   *Abnormal*, p. 50.

Evidently, the pursuit of this type of positive purpose in the name of the "protection" of society can also lead to aberrant or catastrophic consequences.

8. *Biopolitics or governmentality?*

The theme of biopolitics – at least in appearance – remained the subject of Foucault's attention until the early 1980s. Proof of this can be seen in the aims that he set for himself in the three courses held at the Collège de France between 1977 and 1980, naming them respectively: *Security, Territory, Population* (1977-1978); *The Birth of Biopolitics* (1978-1979); *On the Government of the Living* (1979-1980). Of the three titles, only the first does not explicitly refer to the relationship between power, or politics, and life. However, it is enough to focus on the terms *security* and *population* to understand that the biopolitical link between strategies to protect society and attention to the fate of the population as a living species is at the center of Foucault's interest. On the other hand, neither the title of the second nor that of the third Course need particular explanations; the intent to propose an analysis of the power exercised over life appears clear in them. But, beyond what the topics indicated in the titles say, the typical mobility of Foucault's thought and the experimental way in which he presents his research in the courses produce deviations, changes in perspective, and adjustments that, in fact, would progressively determine the consideration of biopolitics no longer as a central theme of his work, but as one of the main aspects of a broader framework of transformations of the exercise of power.

From the first two courses just mentioned (held by Foucault after a sabbatical year), an essential link emerges between the theme of biopolitics and that of the general forms of government, i.e. the complex of theories and political practices that the author indicates with the term *governmentality*. Precisely in this regard, it should be noted immediately that Foucault examines this last topic, articulating its examination so as to open fields of investigation wider than that of biopolitics.[76] The notion of governmentality indicates an interweaving of relationships between a general political rationality and a set of techniques and knowledge, which implies – as in the case of biopower – a necessary distinction between the idea of *government* and that of *sovereignty*.

The government does not constitute an immediate application of sovereign power, but, especially in modernity, it is rather an essential condition of its functioning, as it compensates for the limits of predominantly juridical, military and fiscal

---

76   The broad analytical potentialities of the notion of governmentality will cause it to become the subject of various research paths after the publication (in Italian and in English) of the text of a single lesson of the Course carried out by Foucault in 1977-1978 (which remained unpublished until 2004): Michel Foucault, 'La governamentalità', trans. by Pasquale Pasquino, *Aut aut*, 167-168 (1978), 12-29; Michel Foucault, 'Governmentality', trans. by Rosi Braidotti, *Ideology & Consciusness*, 6 (1979), pp. 5-21. On its importance and on the later editions of this text, see Sylvain Meyet, 'Les trajectoires d'un texte: "La gouvernementalité" de Michel Foucault', in Sylvain Meyet, Marie-Cécile Naves, Thomas Ribemont (ed. by), *Travailler avec Foucault. Retour sur le politique*, (Paris: L'Harmattan, 2005), pp. 13-36. After the publication of the lesson in English, the consistent phenomenon of *Governmentality Studies* emerged in the English-speaking countries and later similar research was carried out elsewhere. For the most relevant results of these studies, see: Graham Burchell, Colin Gordon, Peter Miller (ed. by), *The Foucault Effect: Studies in Governmentality*, (Chicago: The University of Chicago Press, 1991); Andrew Barry, Thomas Osborne, Nikolas Rose (ed by), *Foucault and Political Reason Liberalism: Neoliberalism and Rationalities of Government*, (London: UCL Press, 1996); Thomas Lemke, *Eine Kritik der politischen Vernunft: Foucault Analyse der modernen Gouvernementalität* (Hamburg, Berlin: Argument, 1997); Mitchell Dean, *Governmentality: Power and Rule in Modern Society* (Thousand Oaks, London, New Delhi: Sage, 1999); Ulrich Bröckling, Susanne Krasmann, Thomas Lemke (ed. by), *Gouvernementalität der Gegenwart*, (Frankfurt am Main: Suhrkamp, 2000). On the importance of the concept of *governmentality* in Foucault, see: Michel Senellart, 'Michel Foucault: "gouvernamentalité" et raison d'État', *La pensée politique*, 1 (1993), 276-303; Michel Senellart, 'La critique de la raison gouvernementale', in Guillaume Le Blanc, Jean Terrel (ed. by), *Foucault au Collège de France: un itinéraire*, (Bordeaux, Fr: Presses Universitaires de Bordeaux, 2003), pp. 101-29.

instrumentation of sovereignty, by tending to *direct* men, and their existential behaviors.

In this regard, Foucault states that the «arts of government» of modernity come from areas which are not strictly political, indicated with expressions such as: government of the family, government of children, government of the community, government of souls, etc. From this point of view, the most appropriate definition of governmentality is that of the «way in which one conducts the conduct of men».[77] But adopting a more general angle, according to Foucault, we can say that *pastoral power* constitutes a sort of model of the government which is found in Jewish tradition and which will be actively exercised by the Christian pastorate through the spiritual direction and the government of souls and conducts. For Foucault, the model of pastoral power and the shepherd metaphor are decisive tools for deciphering the political rationality which is affirmed by the «governmentalization» of the modern state: the shepherd's power is exercised on a multiplicity rather than on a territory; it tends toward the salvation of the whole of the flock and, at the same time, of every single sheep. Similarly, but on a different terrain, the modern *political government* does not have as its primary and immediate goal the possession or conquest of a land and the taking of its wealth, but the good management of the strength of the state and of the resources of the social body.[78]

In this context – as in the more specific one of biopower – it is the *population* that appears as the fundamental resource of the force of the state, with regard to which precise forms of knowledge and appropriate administration techniques will be developed.[79] On

---

77 Michel Foucault, *The Birth of Biopolitics: Lectures at The Collège de France – 1978-1979*, ed. by Michel Senellart, trans. by Graham Burchell (New York: Palgrave MacMillan, 2008), p. 186.

78 Michel Foucault, *Security, Territory, Population: Lectures at The Collège de France, 1977-1978,* ed. by Michel Senellart, trans. by Graham Burchell (New York: Palgrave MacMillan, 2007), pp. 123-30. See also: Michel Foucault, '*Omnes et Singulatim:* Towards a Criticism of "Political Reason"', in Sterling Mc Murrin (ed. by), *The Tanner Lectures on Human Values* (Salt Lake City, Utha: University of Utah Press, 1981), II, pp. 223-54.

79 See Foucault, *Security, Territory, Population*, especially pp. 29-86.

the other hand, an essential subject of knowledge and the power of government will necessarily be the individual himself, to the extent that he can contribute to the preservation and increase of the strength of the whole. Hence, the affirmation of life, health, the material and moral well-being of each and every person as the core points of reference of government practices. Hence also the importance that Foucault attributes to the duality of the ways of exercising this power, i.e., to the processes of *individualization* and *totalization* of this same exercise.[80]

These developments in Foucault's research allow us to say that biopolitics, as a government of life, constitutes an essential expression of modern governmentality, also because – as we have seen – already in the course entitled *"Society Must Be Defended"* and in the first volume of *History of Sexuality* it can be seen that biopower itself is exercised through a dual modality, that is by combining the individualizing approach, typical of disciplinary techniques, with the all-encompassing one of the regulation of the biological phenomena of the population.

In the Foucaultian analysis of modern governmentality a distinction is also made between two great historical phases. The first goes from about the end of the 16th to the mid-18th century and is characterized by the leading role played by absolutist monarchies and forms of power-knowledge such as the *doctrine of raison d'État* and the *theory of police*.[81] Instead, the second phase is that of liberal

---

80   Regarding this, see: Foucault, '*Omnes et Singulatim:* Towards a Criticism of "Political Reason"', p. 254; Michel Foucault, 'The Subject and Power', in Hubert L. Dreyfus and Paul Rabinow, *Michel Foucault: Beyond Structuralism and Hermeneutics*, (Chicago: The University of Chicago Press, 1983), 2nd edn, p. 216; Foucault, 'The Political Technology of Individuals', pp. 161-2.

81   *Security, Territory, Population*, pp. 236-341. Among Foucault's main references here above all we should point out, for the doctrine of *raison d'État*: Giovanni Botero, *Della ragion di Stato libri dieci* (Venice: Giolitti, 1589); Giovanni Antonio Palazzo, *Discorso del governo e della ragion vera di Stato* (Naples: G. B. Sottile, 1604); Bogislaw Philipp von Chemnitz, *Dissertatio de ratione status in imperio nostro romano-germanico* (Freistadii, 1647 – published with the pseudonym Hippolitus a Lapide); for the theory of police: Johann Heinrich Gottlob von Justi, *Grundsätze der Policey-Wissenschaft* (Göttingen: Van den Hoecks,

governmentality, in which the political economy imposes itself as the main knowledge of government. This phase differs from the former, above all because the problem of limiting the exercise of power by public authorities to avert the excesses and abuses characteristic of the previous phase is continuously set here.[82]

In both cases both the wealth of the state and the collective well-being are pursued as general, interconnected goals; nevertheless, with liberal governmentality the economy acquires its own definitive autonomy understood in two very precise ways: firstly, as scientific autonomy of the political economy from the orientation of the government; secondly, as independence of the economic initiative of individuals from the government: the freedom of the economic subjects, in fact, is conceived as a decisive tool for the pursuit of general prosperity. Liberalism, moreover, emphasizes the need for security, but in addition to it referring to the safeguarding of the physical well-being of the community and individuals, it also translates it into the securitarian protection of the various forms of freedom. In this way, the practice of liberal government often ends up protecting and promoting some freedoms to the detriment of others, or limiting some to the advantage of others, according to variable criteria of danger and cost-effectiveness.[83] However, for reasons that can be intuited, but which – in any case – may become clear in the following pages, it can be said that the combination of the pursuit of well-being and the promotion of freedoms on the basis of security criteria creates the conditions for liberalism to give rise to a biopolitics.

On the basis of these contents of Foucault's research, it can be assumed that, over the period between 1977 and 1980, the subject of government took the upper hand over that of biopolitics. But,

---

1756); Louis Turquet de Mayerne, *La monarchie aristodémocratique, ou le gouvernement composé et meslé des trois formes de légitimes Républiques* (Paris: Jean Berjon and Jean le Bouc, 1611); Nicolas Delamare, *Traité de la police*, 3 vols, (Paris: Jeanet Pierre Cot, 1705-1710); Peter Carl Wilhelm von Hohenthal, *Liber de politia, adspersis observationibus de causarum politiae et justitiae differentiis* (Leipzig: Christ. Gottlob Hilscherum, 1776).

82   *The Birth of Biopolitics*, pp. 4-47.
83   *The Birth of Biopolitics*, pp. 62-70.

in light of the first two of the courses of this same period, it can also be said that this change derives from the same general issue that underlies Foucault's attention to biopolitics. This is an issue that can be summarized in this simple question: *how has it come about that in our societies life has become a privileged object of the exercise of power?*[84] It is in an attempt to answer a question like this that, from a certain point in time onward, the dimension of government appears to Foucault to be the general framework that needs to be investigated to understand the reasons for the birth and the emergence of biopolitics. Along the way, however, the notion of *government* will assume such an importance and a breadth of significance as to push the French philosopher to analyze it in depth from various other points of view. In particular, he will feel the need to explore the possible specifications of the idea of government not only on the political, but also on the ethical and religious levels. This is clear in the third Course, despite its title (*On the Government of the Living*) seems strictly biopolitical. Here it will suffice to recall – in the words of Foucault himself – that within the «very general framework» of «the notion of 'government'» in this course «we studied the problem of the examination of conscience and of confession».[85]

9. *Government and security*

In general, it can be said that his attention to the theme of the government will influence Foucault's philosophical and ethical-political commitment throughout the period from 1978 until the year of his death. But the "turning point" towards this theme took form during the first lessons of the 1977-1978 Course, in which the French philosopher tried to verify the hypothesis that the birth of biopolitics can be explained by the prevailing in the 18th century of *security mechanisms* (or *apparatuses*) over the *legal*

---

84   *Security, Territory, Population*, p. 1.
85   Michel Foucault, *On The Government of the Living: Lectures at the Collège de France – 1979-1980*, ed. by Michel Senellart, trans by Graham Burchell (London: Palgrave Macmillan, 2014), p. 321.

system and over *disciplinary mechanisms* of power.[86] Therefore, in these same lessons, he tried to trace «a sort of history of technologies of security» examining the specific ways in which these technologies, from around the middle of the 18th century, had an effect on the issues of *space*, the *aleatory*, *normalization* and the *population*:[87] Foucault maintained that the mechanisms of security dominated the framework of the political strategies concerning these four issues through the processes and approaches that can be summarized in the following terms.

1. Definition of a more complex and dynamic political spatiality than those corresponding to the *centralized territory*, on which *sovereignty* is exercised, and to the rigidly structured *architectural space* of the *disciplines*: it is the spatiality that corresponds to the idea of *environment*, or more precisely of *milieu*, which towards the middle of the 18th century – according to Foucault – became relevant above all in the securitization of the urban space.[88]

2. Restructuring of the political approach to risky events, with exemplary importance given to the *scarcity* of food goods. This will no longer be taken as an eventuality that it is absolutely necessary to prevent or avoid, for example, with direct measures on exports and prices, but will be treated as an effect of an *oscillation* of the availability of agricultural goods, which must be corrected, slowed down or canceled, first of all by promoting freedom in the *circulation* of cereals and in price trends.[89]

3. Treatment of problems such as epidemics, not only by the care and isolation of the ill, but also with a *probabilistic and preventive approach* (inoculation and vaccination), which will "regulate" the general morbidity and mortality, bringing them to levels considered *normal,* and trying to make the health conditions of the individual parts of the collective body useful to these levels.[90]

4. In each of these cases, attribution of an unavoidable centrality to the *population* that will no longer be conceived of «as a collection of subjects of right, as a collection of subjects wills

---

86   See *Security, Territory, Population*, pp. 4-11.
87   *Security, Territory, Population*, p. 11.
88   *Security, Territory, Population*, p. 11-23.
89   *Security, Territory, Population*, pp. 29-49.
90   *Security, Territory, Population*, pp. 56-66.

who must obey the sovereign's will through the intermediary of regulations, laws, edicts, and so on». Rather «it will be considered as a set of processes to be managed at the level and on the basis of what is natural in this processes».[91]

In these changes, the *mechanisms of security* impose themselves or overlap with the mechanisms of sovereign power and disciplinary power, according to Foucault. This clearly emerges if we consider the main problems around which these changes revolve: the *town*, *circulation*, *naturalness* and the *population* itself. In fact, all these changes concern, above all, «the phenomenon of the town»,

> for in the end the problem of scarcity and grain is the problem of the market town, and problem of contagion and epidemic diseases is the problem of the town as the home of disease. The town as market is also the town as the place of revolt; the town as a center of diseases is the town as the site of miasmas and death. (...) And if it is true that the outline of the very complex technology of securities appeared around the middle of the eighteenth century, (...) it is to the extent that the town posed new and specific economic and political problems of government technique.[92]

Another crucial problem is that of *circulation*, since

> the town, scarcity, and epidemics (...) share the fact that they all more or less turn on the problem of circulation (...) in the very broad sense of movement, exchange, and contact, as form of dispersion, and also as form of distribution.[93]

In other words, according to Foucault, in these transformations

> we see the emergence of a completely different problem that is no longer that of fixing and demarcating the territory, but of allowing circulations to take place, of controlling them, sifting the good and the bad, ensuring that things are always in movement, constantly moving around, continually going from one point to another, but in such a way that the inherent dangers of this circulation are canceled out.[94]

---

91   *Security, Territory, Population*, p. 70. On all of these topics, see ibid., pp. 11-79.
92   *Security, Territory, Population*, pp. 63-4.
93   *Security, Territory, Population*, p. 64.
94   *Security, Territory, Population*, p. 65.

Moreover, the importance of the *naturalness* of the phenomena in which the technologies of security intervene must be understood in the sense that they «are connected to what the physiocrats called physical processes, which could be called natural processes, and which we could also call elements of reality». These are phenomena that the mechanisms of security do not tend to cancel «in the form of the prohibition (...), but in the form of a progressive self-cancellation of phenomena by the phenomena themselves» or by trying to contain them «within acceptable limits».[95]

As for the *population*, it has already been said that it represents for Foucault the central reference point of the changes he describes. What should be noted here more precisely is that the mechanisms of security referring to it are defined as

> the set of mechanisms that, for the government and those who govern, attach pertinence to quite specific phenomena that are not exactly individual phenomena, even if individuals do appear in a way, and there are specific processes of individualization.

This means that «the population with its specific phenomena and processes» imposes the *government* of all men and women as an adequate form of the power exercised according to the logic of security: while sovereignty and the disciplines refer to the multiplicity of persons considered individually; while the union of these forms of power implies «an exhaustive surveillance of individuals so that they are all constantly under the eyes of the sovereign in everything they do», in the government based on mechanisms of security «the relation between the individual and the collective (...) is made to function in a completely different way»[96]; in this case the dimension of the population assumes its own essential autonomy as the totality of social body, characterized by its specific variability due to a multiplicity of factors: the material surroundings, the circulation of wealth, the

---

95 *Security, Territory, Population*, pp. 65-6.
96 *Security, Territory, Population*, p. 66.

laws, people customs, the moral or religious values, the condition of means of subsistence.[97]

The biopolitical aspects of this change are quite evident: when Foucault says that through political attention to the population «the relation between the individual and the collective (...) is made to function in a completely different way», he alludes, among other things, to the maturation of an approach that will find a paradigmatic reference in the fundamental biological relationship between the species and the individual organism. However, it is equally evident that the biopolitical implications of this transformation do not limit its significance and scope. Therefore, in the course of 1977-1978, Foucault no longer bothers to point out these implications; he focuses instead on the urgency of giving space to the issue of government as «a set of mechanisms (...) that attach pertinence to quite specific phenomena».[98]

In this sense, there is an important fact that we need to address about the security mechanisms: from examining them it is clear that *liberalism* is the political regime that, more than others, favors their affirmation and development. Foucault clearly states that liberal freedom, which is «both ideology and technique of government», can only be understood if it is meant as «the correlative of the deployment of apparatuses of security». In fact – he adds –, «[a]n apparatus of security (...) cannot operate well except on condition that it is given freedom» in its liberal meaning, that is, first of all as «freedom in the broad sense of the term», as «possibility of movement, change of place, and processes of circulation of both people and things».[99]

Evidently, it is precisely for this link between the promotion of freedom and the security mechanisms that liberalism also represents «the framework of political rationality» within which the biopolitical problems became increasingly important for

---

97   *Security, Territory, Population*, pp. 70-1.
98   *Security, Territory, Population*, p. 66.
99   *Security, Territory, Population*, pp. 48-9.

the government of men.[100] But, for Foucault, this implication of his research does not at all represent a point of arrival or a conclusion. On the contrary, it can be said that starting from it, for the French philosopher, other indispensable problems arise. More precisely, the general analysis of the security mechanisms leaves two questions unanswered which can be expressed in the following terms: 1) what is the origin of the idea that men should be governed by paying constant attention to the relationship between collectivity and individuals, or – in biopolitical terms – the relationship between population-species and individual-organism? 2) How is it possible that the problems of the government become so important and assume a clearly biopolitical character precisely with liberalism, although the latter is characterized by its essential vocation to favor the autonomy of individuals over the fate of the community?[101]

In fact, in the last ten lessons of the 1977-1978 course, and then during the entire course of the 1978-1979 course, Foucault attempts to reply first to one and then to the other question. This implies that in this period the need to address the problem of government becomes the most important issue in his research. This need matured precisely when – in the first of these courses – he addressed the theme of the population more in depth. In the 1975-1976 Course, as we know, the French philosopher had clearly identified the population as the biopolitical object par excellence, that is «as political problem, as a problem that is at once scientific and political, as a biological problem and as power's problem»;[102] but now – as he himself says –, «looking more closely» at «the specific problems of population», we cannot but arrive «at the problem of government»: it is a question not only of power exercised over life, but also of the calculated management of resources, of the orientation of the behavior of individuals and of the society itself.[103]

---

100 *The Birth of Biopolitics*, p. 317.
101 See *The Birth of Biopolitics*, p. 317.
102 *"Society Must Be Defended"*, p. 245.
103 *Security, Territory, Population*, p. 88; see also pp. 103-6.

Considering the population as a privileged object of the government of men and women, and moving forward in his research, Foucault cannot but recognize the *political economy*, even more than medical and biological knowledge, as the most functional kind of knowledge in the forms of governmentality in modern societies. To explain his thought, he said, in fact, that the word «governmentality» must be understood first as

> the ensemble formed by institutions, procedures, analyses and reflections, calculations, and tactics that allow the exercise of this very specific, albeit very complex, power that has the population as its target, political economy as its major form of knowledge, and apparatuses of security as its essential technical instrument.[104]

From this definition we can deduce not only that – according to him – the nucleus of modern governmentality is essentially economic, but also that biopolitics is, in a sense, functional and complementary to the economic rationality of this governmentality; furthermore, on this basis it can be understood that for Foucault the most adequate regime for this rationality of government is *liberalism* insofar as it historically binds itself closely to the governmental use of political economy as a privileged form of knowledge. This will be particularly clear especially in the 1978-1979 course.

Obviously, all this does not exclude the possibility that, by reconstructing with Foucault the historical conditions in which the relationship between modern governmentality and population has matured, its specific biopolitical aspects may also emerge. This is what can be said, above all, about the vast system of government that – according to the French philosopher – the modern state defined and began to operate before the advent of liberalism, between the 17th and the 18th centuries, i.e. the *police*.

10. *Police*

In this regard, Foucault points out, above all, the fact that in the first centuries of modernity «the word "police" had a completely

---

104 *Security, Territory, Population*, p. 108.

different meaning from the one it has today».[105] As von Justi, «the greatest theorist of police», says:[106]

> under the name police we include the laws and regulations that concern the interior of a state, which endeavor to strengthen and increase its power, to make a good use of its forces, to procure the happiness of its subjects, (...) in view of the fact that the happiness of the state depends on the wisdom with which all these things are administered.[107]

From the most "advanced" literature on this theme, written above all in the 18th century, Foucault derives the main areas of intervention that were generally assigned to the police. These dealt with at least five major areas of the life of the state: 1) «the number of men» in «its relationship whit the set of forces: the size of the territory, natural resources, wealth, commercial activity, and so on»; 2) «the necessities of life», i.e., the quantity and the quality of the «provision of food, the so called basic needs»; 3 «health» which «is not just a problem for police in cases of epidemics», but also «a permanent object of police concern and intervention» above all to safeguard the salubrity of the urban space; 4) «the activity» of population, which means: «preventing idleness», ensure that those who are able to work do so, dividing aid among the «disabled poor», ensuring that «the regulations of professions» were respected and applied, etc.; 5) «circulation», i.e. not only

> the material network that allows the circulation of goods and possibly of men, but also (...) the set of regulations, constraints, and limits, or the facilities and encouragements that will allow the circulation of men and things.[108]

From all this, it emerges clearly that it was with the emergence of the police that the first fundamental conditions of biopolitics were created. This is also evident because the police

---

105 *Security, Territory, Population*, p. 312.
106 *Security, Territory, Population*, p. 314.
107 von Justi, *Grundsätze der Policey-Wissenschaft*, p. 4.
108 *Security, Territory, Population*, pp. 323-5; see also Foucault, 'La politique de la santé au XVIII siècle', in Foucault, *Dits et Écrits*, III, p. 730.

had a strong health vocation: in fact, it developed largely as
«medical police».[109] But also of importance is the broad scope
of policies inaugurated by the police, on which Foucault insists
particularly by observing that

> its fundamental object is all the forms of, let's say, men's coexistence
> with each other. It is the fact that they live together, reproduce, and
> that each of them needs a certain amount of food and air to live, to
> subsist; it is that they work alongside each other at different or similar
> professions, and also that they exist in a space of circulation.[110]

Moreover, it is evident here that through the police biopolitics
already demonstrates itself as something not reducible either
to a policy of the "capture" of biological life or to a perennial
exposition of life itself to the risk of death or to its treatment in
terms of mere "purification". Already with the police, in fact, it
goes far beyond these possibilities.

> With police – says Foucault – there is a circle that starts from the
> state as a power of rational and calculated intervention on individuals
> and comes back to the state as a growing set forces, or forces to be
> developed, passing through the life of individuals, which will now be
> precious to the state simply as life.

Therefore,

> [t]his circle will pass through the life of individuals, but it will also
> pass through their more than just living, that is to say, through what at
> the time was called men's convenience, their amenity, or even felicity.

«Men's happiness» is clearly indicated by all the most
authoritative 18th century police science theorists (Delamare,
Hohenthal, von Justi) as a fundamental purpose, «as the

---

109 See *Security, Territory, Population*, pp. 58-9. A fundamental
      reference in this regard is Johann Peter Franck, *System einer
      vollständigen medicinischen Polizey* (Mannheim: C.F. Schwan,
      1779-1790), 4 vols. Further bibliographical indications in this
      regard are provided by Foucault himself in 'La politique de la santé
      au XVIII siècle', pp. 740-2.
110 *Security, Territory, Population*, p. 326.

individual's better than just living» which «must in some way be drawn on and constituted into state utility».[111] According to the terminology of Delamare, in particular, *goodness*, the *preservation*, *convenience*, the *pleasures of life* are the goals that the police must pursue by turning their attention to both health and subsistence, as much as religion and morals, public peace, commerce, manufacture and mechanical arts, theater and games, the care and discipline of the poor, etc.[112]

In short, we can say that biopolitics, finding its first conditions of possibility in a context like this, immediately reveals that the governmental dimension in which it is grafted goes far beyond the limits of the mere exercise of a "life and death power". Obviously, the possibility of exercising such a power remains at the disposal of state sovereignty and will re-emerge especially when the latter claim to carry it out by means of state racism. Already with the police state, after all, biopolitics clearly reveals the danger of discrimination to which the different ways in which life itself is lived are exposed, if they do not correspond to the guidelines of government of society; the nascent biopolitics, moreover, immediately allows us to understand that there is no spontaneous correspondence between the increase in the potential of life that it promotes, and the increase in the liberties that individuals can enjoy: in the specific case of the pre-liberal state, this mismatch was due to the almost unlimited extension of control over society that the police demanded to exercise; but this non-correspondence was able to continue to reproduce itself in liberal society through the governmental link between the growth of the potential of life and the privileging of certain models of freedom and behavior to the detriment of others.

11. *Naturalness and freedom*

With regard to the issues mentioned above, through Foucault it must be stressed that at least until the end of the 18th century the

---

111 *Security, Territory, Population*, p. 327.
112 *Security, Territory, Population*, p. 334.

«police force extended its field well beyond the surveillance and maintenance of order»;[113] precisely for this reason it differs from what we mean by police today. This fact does not really deserve to be repeated if it did not indirectly serve to highlight that a large part of the transition from the governmentality of the police state to the liberal state took place precisely through the radical downsizing of the broad government functions initially assigned to the police itself and through their progressive reduction to substantially repressive tasks.[114]

Liberal governmentality, in fact, asserted itself starting from the criticism of the police state, even if it did not give rise to the surpassing, but rather to the "restructuring" of the police. The Foucaultian description of this change could be summarized by saying that it consists in a transition from a logic of authoritarian, artificial and meticulous regulation of the processes and activities to be governed, to their smooth and flexible regulation, inspired by the respect for their evolution which is considered "natural".

Artificial, meticulous, basically unlimited regulation is a general mode of police action during the era of absolutism: «[w]e are – says Foucault – in a world of indefinite regulation, of permanent, continually renewed, and increasingly detailed regulation» which makes use of tools like ordinances, interdictions, instructions, etc..[115] It is interesting to note that, in this way, the police force relates directly to the royal power, circumventing – so to speak – the power of the court. But this does not mean that it is placed in an area of arbitrary and "illegal" management of its power; rather, by elaborating and applying its

---

113 Foucault, 'La politique de la santé au XVIII siècle', p. 730.This text – which we have already mentioned earlier – is the modified and updated version, almost certainly on the basis of the research carried out by Foucault for the 1978-1979 Course, of an essay already published in 1976, of which there is an English version: Michel Foucault, 'The politics of health in the eighteenth century', trans. by Colin Gordon, in Michel Foucault, *Power/Knowledge: Selected Interviews and Other Writings, 1972-1977*, ed. by Colin Gordon (New York: Pantheon Books, 1980), pp. 166-82.

114 *Security, Territory, Population*, pp. 353-4.

115 *Security, Territory, Population*, p. 340.

own rules, it implements an extra-judicial extension of the law, which also allows it to achieve

> the permanent *coup d'État* that is exercised and functions in the name of and in terms of the principles of its own rationality, without having to mold or model itself on the otherwise given rules of justice.[116]

From the end of the 18th century, the police's pre-liberal aspiration to directly and without limits determine the course of things was gradually overtaken by the need to let the «naturalness» of the processes to be governed play out. Therefore, rather than systematically regulating them, it was a matter of encouraging their spontaneous self-regulation and «ensuring that the necessary and natural regulations work, or even to create regulations that enable natural regulations to work».[117]

The over-regulatory approach of the police state was perceived more and more as a forced intervention, destined in the long term to provoke results that are the opposite of those that it pursues. One cannot think, for example, of avoiding scarcity or of guaranteeing the growth of the export of cereals, while continuing to keep prices low. It is necessary to allow them to rise spontaneously so that farmers are encouraged to increase production so that a certain lowering of the prices may follow, corresponding to the game of supply and demand. This game is the real guarantee of the availability of food, of flourishing commerce and of the overall growth of wealth.[118] It is, therefore, a question of replacing, as much as possible, the artificiality of police regulations with the naturalness of the processes and their management. This, evidently, is valid, above all, for the economic processes which thus assume an autonomy with respect to the action of government; economic knowledge will refer precisely to this autonomy on which it bases, on the one hand, its scientific claims and, on the other hand, the requests addressed to the rulers to respect the naturalness of the functioning of the market in order to be able to govern well.[119]

---

116 *Security, Territory, Population*, p. 339.
117 *Security, Territory, Population*, p. 353.
118 *Security, Territory, Population*, pp. 341-4.
119 *Security, Territory, Population*, pp. 350-1.

In truth, according to Foucault, naturalness imposes itself as an essential feature of almost all the objects of political action starting from the processes that concern the whole of all men and women that the government takes care of. Hence the decisive evolution that undergoes the biopolitical, as well as the economic, problem of the population. It will no longer be conceived of as a good in and of itself, whose consistency must be increased indefinitely. According to the new perspective,

> there will be a spontaneous regulation of the population that ensures (...) [that] you will always have the number of people that is naturally determined by the situation in a given place. (...) Population is not therefore an indefinitely modifiable datum.[120]

This naturalness of the phenomena to be governed, on the other hand, it is not «the naturalness of processes of nature itself, as the nature of the world». Rather, it is a naturalness which corresponds «to what happens spontaneously» when the men «cohabit, come together, exchange, work, and produce». According to Foucault, it is «a naturalness that basically did not exist until then and which (...) begins to be thought of and analyzed as the naturalness of society».[121]

Insisting on these changes at the end of his 1977-1978 Course, Foucault evidently developed the indications proposed in the first lessons on the birth of the mechanisms of security. But now it is quite clear that with liberalism these mechanisms tend to guarantee the "natural" regulation of phenomena which should preferably be left free «in such a way that they do not veer off course, or in such a way that clumsy, arbitrary, and blind intervention does not make the veer off course». Hence the importance of the link between security and freedom and

> the insertion of freedom within governmentality, not only as the right of individuals legitimately opposed to the power, usurpations, and

---

120 *Security, Territory, Population*, p. 345.
121 *Security, Territory, Population*, p. 349.

abuses of the sovereign or the government, but as an element that has become indispensable to governmentality itself.[122]

It is through these changes that the «exhaustive and unitary project of police» is disarticulated and most of its functions are delegated to other systems that will leave the police with a merely repressive task. Therefore – Foucault says –

> [o]n the one hand will be a whole series of mechanisms that fall within the province of the economy and the management of the population with the function of increasing the forces of the state. Then, on the other hand, there will be an apparatus or instruments for ensuring the prevention or repression of disorder, irregularity, illegality, and delinquency.[123]

However, despite the depth of all these changes, the framework of the political rationality inaugurated by the theories of *raison d'État* and practiced by the police state is not exceeded. In the new governmentality «the objective will still be to increase the state's forces».[124]

Once again, therefore, we can say that Foucault, on the one hand, offers us the possibility of clearly grasping the biopolitical elements of the changes he analyzes, on the other, he places these elements within the framework of an evolution of governmentality to which he attaches greater importance than its biopolitical aspects. This fact will also be confirmed by the work he will do during the 1978-1979 Course. In it, the need to prioritize – with respect to biopolitics – research on governmentality, deepening its liberal articulation, will be expressed quite clearly in the following terms.

> I thought I could do a course on biopolitics this year. I will try to show how the central core of all the problems that I am presently trying to identify is what is called population. Consequently, this is the basis on which something like biopolitics could be formed. But it seems to me that the analysis of biopolitics can only get under way

---

122 *Security, Territory, Population*, p. 353.
123 *Security, Territory, Population*, p. 353.
124 *Security, Territory, Population*, p. 348.

when we have understood the general regime of this governmental reason I have talked about, this general regime that we can call the question of truth, of economic truth in the first place, within governmental reason. Consequently, it seems to me that it is only when we understand what is at stake in this regime of liberalism opposed to *raison d'État* – or rather, fundamentally modifying [it] without, perhaps, questioning its bases – only when we know what this governmental regime called liberalism was, will we be able to grasp what biopolitics is.[125]

The growing interest that Foucault will manifest first for liberal governmentality and then – in the last years of his life – for the various ethical and philosophical aspects of the «government of self and others» will ultimately push biopolitics into the background.

---

125 *The Birth of Biopolitics*, pp. 21-2. On the relationships between the courses held in 1977-1978 and 1978-1979 see Sandro Chignola (ed. by), *Governare la vita. Un seminario sui Corsi di Michel Foucault al Collège de France (1977-1979)* (Verona: Ombre corte, 2006).

CHAPTER TWO
THE ANCIENTS AND THE POWER
OVER LIFE
Plato and Aristotle
between Arendt and Foucault

1. *Political power and the domestic administration of life*

According to Foucault, biological life has become a fully political issue only with modernity; the substantial extraneousness of the problems of life to the sphere of politics has characterized our history until, with modern society, «the life of the species is wagered on its own political strategies». In this regard – as is known – one of the most quoted expressions of the French philosopher is the following:

> For millennia, man remained what he was for Aristotle: a living animal with the additional capacity for a political existence; modern man is an animal whose politics places his existence as a living being in question.[1]

In fact, to the extent that Aristotle represents one of the most authoritative exponents of classical political thought, his point of view can help us to understand various aspects of this question. As is known, in *Politics* he makes a clear distinction between the public sphere of politics and the private sphere of reproduction and preservation of life; taking pains above all to distinguish the way the statesman exercises his power as compared to the ways in which it is exercised by the royal ruler, the estate ruler and the master of the family,[2] he distinguishes – additionally – the

---

1   Foucault, *The History of Sexuality. Volume 1*, p. 143.
2   Aristotle, *Politics*, trans. by Horace Rackham (London: William Heinemann/Cambridge, Mass.: Harvard University Press, 1959), 1252a, 8-14, p. 3.

reasons why men unite in a family from those for which they join together in a state: especially in the case of the family they come together because they «are unable to exist without one another»; this happens in particular in the «union of female and male for the continuance of the species», a union which – in ancient Greece – was often connected to that of masters and slaves «for the sake of security», that is to guarantee the preservation of life.[3] Differently the state, as it «comes into existence for the sake of life, it exists for the good life».[4]

With this, evidently, Aristotle means to say that the good life is something different from survival in good health, from physical well-being and from material security, which represent the main purposes of family organization. The good life is rather a happy and free way of life that politics and the state itself must be concerned with, taking care of, first of all, «civic virtue». In fact, what makes it possible to say that a state as a political fellowship truly exists is that within it there is concern about the «proper moral character» of the citizens, as an essential condition of the good life itself.[5] From this point of view, the state is not simply the organization that allows men to live in the same place or an alliance that allows them to defend themselves from aggression or to facilitate exchanges between them; but rather:

> a state is the partnership of clans and villages in a full and independent life, which in our view constitutes a happy and noble life; the political fellowship must therefore be deemed to exist for the sake of noble actions, not merely to living in common.[6]

Since – as we have said – the point of view of Aristotle, obviously, can be considered particularly representative of the political culture to which he belongs, we can legitimately suppose, on the one hand, that in classical antiquity attention to the natural necessities of life was generally excluded from political activities or, in any case, was given little political

---

3   *Politics*, 1252a, 26-35, p. 5.
4   *Politics*, 1252b, 30-31, p. 9.
5   See *Politics*, 1280a, 31-1280b, 9, pp. 213-5.
6   *Politics*, 1280b, 30-1281a, 5, pp. 217-9.

attention; while, on the other hand, that which we today call biopolitics is a different thing, at least from the main classical forms of politics and the exercise of public power. In this sense we must consider the fact that Aristotle clearly distinguishes the power of the statesman from that of other figures: as a political power, it must guarantee the conditions of civic coexistence based on the virtuous and independent practice of citizenship, and, therefore, differs in particular from the power of the master of the family. In fact, the task of the latter is to ensure the well-being of family members by exercising his power for this purpose not in the public space, but in the private sphere of the *oikos* and the *oikonomia* (household management).[7] To clearly grasp the sense of this distinction between political power and family mastership it will suffice here to recall the following passage of *Politics*.

> Republican government controls men who are by nature free, the master's authority men who are by tasks, and nature slaves; and the government of a household is monarchy (since every house is governed by a single ruler), whereas statesmanship is the government of men free and equal.[8]

Hannah Arendt, referring to Aristotle herself, insists on the clear-cut nature of the difference between these two forms of power, and authorizes us to hypothesize that the historical transformations that may have led to overcoming it and to focusing attention on the needs of life in the political sphere, must have been truly profound. Not surprisingly, in fact, the author – although she never used the terms "biopolitics" or "biopower" – became one of the main points of reference in the debate on the topic that these terms indicate.[9]

> The distinctive trait of the household sphere – she writes – was that in it men lived together because they were driven by their wants and needs. The driving force was life itself (...) which, for its

---

7   On these topics see *Politics*, 1252a, 7-14, p. 3; 1253b, 1-12, pp. 13-5; 1255 b, 16-21, p. 29.
8   *Politics*, 1255 b, 19-21. p. 29.
9   On this, see Catherine Mills, *Biopolitics* (Abingdon, Oxon; New York: Routledge, 2018), especially pp. 58-80.

individual maintenance and its survival as the life of the species needs the company of others. (...) Natural community in the household therefore was born of necessity, and necessity ruled over all activities performed in it.

The realm of the *polis*, on the contrary, was the sphere of freedom, and if there was a relationship between these two spheres, it was a matter of course that the mastering of the necessities of life in the household was the condition for the freedom of the *polis*.[10]

In that regard, Arendt clearly states that in ancient times the power exercised in the domestic dimension for the preservation of life was not a political power, but rather a *prepolitical* power.[11] The author also reflects on the unmistakable derivation of the modern term economy from the word *oikonomia* with which the exercise of this power was defined in large part in ancient Greece. According to her, this derivation easily induces us to think of a substantial affinity between the activities that the two terms indicate; household management, in fact, is carried out through a good "economic" management of goods and wealth for the wellbeing of people. Despite this affinity, however, what we need to consider, according to Arendt, is that only in modernity has the economy assumed such political importance that it could also be defined as a *political economy*. Otherwise,

according to the ancient thought (...), the very term "political economy" would have been a contradiction in terms: whatever was "economic," related to the life of the individual and the survival of the species, was a non-political, household affair by definition.[12]

If, instead, in the modern age the idea of a political economy is completely acceptable and obvious, this depends on the fact that

the decisive division between the public and the private realms, between the sphere of the *polis* and the sphere of household and family, and, finally, between activities related to a common world and

---

10   Hannah Arendt, *The Human Condition* (Chicago: The University of Chicago Press, 1998, 2nd edn), pp. 30-1.

11   *The Human Condition*, p. 31

12   *The Human Condition*, p. 29.

those related to the maintenance of life (...) is entirely blurred, because
we see the body of peoples and political communities in the image of
a family whose everyday affairs have to be taken care of by a gigantic,
nation-wide administration of housekeeping.[13]

What can be found here is a substantial convergence of Arendt's
theses with those of Foucault regarding the decisive role that the
prevalence of economic rationality may have assumed on the forms
of public power in the historical transformations that allowed for
life to become one of the main concerns of politics. But from this
point of view, if we give credit to what Foucault says in his 1977-
1978 course, the differences between antiquity and modernity
regarding the role of the economy can be further clarified by going
even farther than the suggestions proposed by Arendt.

As we have seen, according to the French philosopher, from at
least the 18th century on the political economy becomes, in a very
precise sense, the «major form of knowledge» among those that
inform the governmentality of modern society. From his point of
view, however, the economy, assuming its own specific modern
meaning, does not simply impose itself in the form of «a gigantic
administration of housekeeping»; it also, and above all, asserts
itself as power-knowledge and as the rationality of government that
considers the state, society and individuals as essentially economic
subjects whose economic growth needs to be constantly promoted as
a fundamental condition of well-being, health and general prosperity.
Now, if we return to Aristotle, comparing this way of conceiving
the economy with the ancient *oikonomia*, the differences between
modernity and antiquity appear even clearer and more meaningful.

According to the great Greek philosopher, *oikonomia* necessarily
implies an activity of acquisition of goods and wealth, which
he generally defines with the term *chrematistics*;[14] this does not
mean, however, that household management has to tend toward
enriching the family and its members without limits. Rather, it
must procure «those goods (...) which are necessary for life», the
amount of which cannot be unlimited. Likewise, even the amount
of wealth that the state should dispose of cannot and must not be

---

13   *The Human Condition*, p. 28.
14   in Greek: *chrematistikè techne*.

unlimited. In short, in general the acquisition of wealth should not be conceived of as a primary purpose of human communities, but simply as «a collection of tools for the householder and the statesman».[15] On the other hand, Aristotle recognizes that there is «another kind of acquisition that is specially called wealth-getting (...) and to this kind it is due that there is thought to be no limit to riches and property».[16] This type of acquisition does not tend toward the use of the goods it procures as simple tools, as happens – or should happen – in the context of *oikonomia* or a virtuous politics; it tends toward the unlimited commercial exchange of such goods, an exchange that focuses on the indefinite growth of properties and money. Therefore, this form of acquisition must be considered «not natural» or «unnecessary» chrematistics:[17]

> these riches, that are derived from this art of wealth-getting, are truly unlimited; (...). But the household branch of wealth-getting has a limit, inasmuch as the acquisition of money is not the function of household management. (...) [S]ome people suppose that it is the function of household management to increase property, and they are continually under the idea that it is their duty to be either safeguarding their substance in money or increasing it to an unlimited amount. The cause of this state of mind is that their interests are set upon life but not upon the good life.[18]

Undoubtedly, it must be borne in mind that both this distinction (between the acquisition of goods that is part of *oikonomia* and that which is not part of it) and the distinction between political power and family mastership or household management, are part of a sort of paradigmatic vision of the *polis*; more precisely, they are part of a kind of model of social coexistence that Aristotle seems to want to regenerate or restore. We must also consider that these distinctions are generally inspired by the intent to define concepts, forms of power and aggregation, roles, activities, etc. on the basis of the recognition of what is "natural" with respect to what is not.[19]

---

15   Aristotle, *Politics*, 1256b, 29-38, p. 39.
16   *Politics*, 1256b, 40-1257a,1, p. 39.
17   Aristotle, *Politics*, 1257a, 5, p. 39; 1258a, 15-1258b, 8, pp. 49-51.
18   *Politics*, 1257b, 24-1258a, 1, pp. 45-7.
19   All of the first book of *Politics* exemplifies this kind of recognition.

This – as is well-known – leads the Greek philosopher on the one hand, to indicate the predisposition to politics as an essential part of man's nature and, on the other, even to consider slavery to be "natural", in the same sense in which it is generally accepted and practiced in the ancient city.[20] Well, precisely the fact that Aristotle's reflection takes this approach allows us to consider that his main concern was to revitalize a model of coexistence that his contemporaries would recognize as "natural" and would widely share. Therefore, it seems plausible that the same distinctions cited thus far are part of a vision which would generally shared.

Now, if this reasoning has any validity, it cannot but confirm the idea that radical historical transformations were necessary so that certain distinctions would no longer be considered "natural" and would lapse, i.e., that the political power would make economic administration of collective wealth its primary task, so that this administration would take on the indefinite enrichment of society – that is, Aristotle's not natural chrematistics – as its essential logic and make the management and the biopolitical strengthening of the force of the state its own fundamental strategic articulation.

Evidently, it is on the basis of hypotheses like these that it is possible to consider reliable Foucault's idea, according to which only with modernity is «the life of the species [...] wagered on its own political strategies».[21]

2. *Eugenics for guardians*

In fact, in more or less recent years some authors have sustained, from different points of view and with different intensities, that the political thought of ancient Greece – and, therefore, also that of Aristotle – actually tends to promote the exercise of a biopower by the state or, in any case, creates the premises of biopolitics.[22] It

---

20 *Politics*, 1253a, 3-4; 1254a, 14-1255a, 3; pp. 9, 19-25.
21 Foucault, *The History of Sexuality. Volume 1*, p. 143.
22 Among the authors who have expressed themselves in this way, we must first of all mention Giorgio Agamben who supports similar arguments in his *Homo Sacer: Sovereign Power and Bare Life*, transl. by Daniel Heller-Roazen (Stanford: Stanford University Press, 1998). Among the texts of

is a hypothesis that it is best not only to explain clearly, but also to check carefully starting from the main political work of he who is considered the most important exponent of classical political thought: Plato.

In *The Republic*, which is also considered the most radical of his political works, the theme around which his biopolitical inclinations seem to express themselves clearly is the well-known one of the «community of wives and children». According to him, this is one of the three fundamental conditions of the creation of the ideal state, to which should be added that of the exercise of the same functions by men and women[23] and that, most important of all, in which «either philosophers become kings in our states or those whom we now call our kings and rulers take to the pursuit of philosophy seriously and adequately».[24]

According to Plato, the community of wives and children, together with the absence of any private property, must form the basis of the organization of the life of the «guardians», composed of «rulers» and «helpers», who will respectively be responsible for guiding and defending the state. What becomes necessary for this purpose is a law like the following.

> That these women shall all be common to all these men, and that none shall cohabit with any privately; and that the children shall be common, and that no parent shall know its own offspring nor any child its parent.[25]

---

other authors who express themselves in similar terms, we must point out in particular: Peter Sloterdijk, 'Rules for the Human Zoo: a response to the *Letter on Humanism*', in *Not Saved: Essays after Heidegger*, trans. by Ian Alexander Moore and Christopher Turner (Cambridge, UK: Polity Press, 2017), pp. 193-216; Jacques Derrida, *The Beast and the Sovereign*, transl. by Geoffrey Bennington (Chicago: Chicago University Press, 2009, vol. I); Mika Ojakangas, *On the Greek Origins of Biopolitics: A Reinterpretation of the History of Biopolitics* (London and New York: Routledge, 2016). In this chapter we will refer, above all, to the very clear theses of the latter author.

23   Plato, *The Republic*, trans. by Paul Shorey (London: William Heinemann/ Cambridge, Mass.: Harvard University Press, 1937), 451c-457b, vol. I, pp. 433-53.

24   *The Republic*, 473c, vol. I, p. 509; see also 473c-480a, vol. I, pp. 509-35.

25   *The Republic*, 457c-d, vol. I, pp. 453-5.

To achieve these goals, the lawgiver must choose both the men and the women destined to live together.

> And they, having houses and meals in common, and no private possessions of that kind, will dwell together, and being commingled in gymnastics and in all their life and education, will be conducted by innate necessity to sexual union.[26]

However, this does not mean that they will be allowed «disorder and promiscuity in these unions». The rulers in office, in fact, will have to «arrange marriages, sacramental so far as may be. And the most sacred marriages would be those that were most beneficial». To obtain these beneficial marriages the rulers can use «falsehood and deception» or «certain ingenious lots» so that «the best men (...) cohabit with the best women in as many cases as possible and the worst with the worst in the fewest». Plato does not hesitate to compare this strategy to the approach that is used in organizing the unions and procreations of «hunting-dogs», «pedigree cocks», «horses and other animals», to the point that – according to him – after having favored the union of the «best» with the «best» and, if it cannot be avoided, that of the «worst» with the «worst», «the offspring of the one must be reared and that of the other not, if the flock is to be as perfect as possible». A whole series of prescriptions and attentions must be followed to ensure, among other things, that a stable number of individuals is generated so that, «so far as possible, our city may not grow too great or too small».[27] Moreover, the «officials appointed for this» will take care of the nurturing of the children who will be born in the framework of this organization.

> The offspring of the good (...) they will take to the pen or creche, to certain nurses who live apart in a quarter of the city, but the offspring of the inferior, and any of those of the other sort who are born defective, they will properly dispose of in secret, so that no one will know what has become of them. (...) They will also supervise the

---

26   *The Republic*, 458c-d, vol. I, p. 457.
27   *The Republic*, 458d-460a, vol. I, pp. 459-463.

nursing of the children, conducting the mothers to the pen when their breasts are full, but employing every device to prevent anyone from recognizing her own infant. And they will provide others who have milk if the mothers are insufficient.[28]

Particular injunctions, prohibitions and controls will then have to be imposed to make sure that «the offspring (...) come from parents in their prime» and to ensure, definitively, «that ever better offspring may spring from good sires and from fathers helpful to the state sons more helpful still».[29] Children born under these conditions will be raised and treated as the children of all; no parent will be able to recognize their own, no son and no daughter will be able to distinguish their brothers and sisters,

except that a man will call all male offspring born in the tenth and in the seventh month after he became a bridegroom his sons, and all female, daughters, and they will call him father. And, similarly, he will call their offspring his grandchildren and they will call his group grandfathers and grandmothers. And all children born in the period in which their fathers and mothers were procreating will regard one another as brothers and sisters.[30]

The perspective outlined by Plato effectively makes it possible to attribute to him the intent to promote a biopolitical strategy characterized by an attention to the quality and quantity of individuals, considerably similar to eugenics. A thesis of this kind, in fact, is sustained and argued in a particularly clear way by Mika Ojakangas. This author does not limit himself to looking for evidence of his thesis in *The Republic*, but he strives to demonstrate its validity by also referring to the two other great political works by Plato – *Statesman* and *Laws* –, in particular the latter. Ojakangas, furthermore, extends his analysis beyond the limits of Platonic thought, trying to go back to what he defines «the Greek origins of biopolitics»; moreover, he sustains along these lines that Aristotle himself can be considered a theorist of biopower, especially in light of some non-negligible aspects of

---

28   *The Republic*, 460b-460d, vol. I, pp. 463-465.
29   *The Republic*, 460d-461a, vol. I, p. 465.
30   *The Republic*, 461d-e, vol. I, p. 467.

Politics. The Finnish author radicalizes this interpretation of the thought of the two Greek philosophers to the point of affirming that «Plato's and Aristotle's understanding of politics was profoundly biopolitical».[31] According to him, the political culture of the two philosophers – although they were very attentive to the need for the state to be equipped with laws – was largely extraneous to the idea of *natural, universal and immutable justice* that was formed through the experience of ancient Rome and the Christian vision of man, and finally translated into the modern «juridico-insitutitonal model of politics, revolving around laws, legal subjects, contracts, liberties, obligations, rights, and duties».[32] Ultimately, according to Ojakangas, although they certainly also represent fundamental references for modern political culture, Plato and Aristotle were largely insensitive to the characteristic preoccupation of this culture for the certainty of the law and for the freedom of individuals as subjects of law. Which could be explained precisely with the marked biopolitical orientation of platonic-aristotelian philosophy, i.e. with the fact that

> both Plato and Aristotle thought that the ultimate aim of all politics, namely the security (*asphaleia*) and well-being (*eudamonia*) of the city-state, depends primarily on the quantity and quality of its population.[33]

The hierarchical vision of human nature that characterizes the thinking of both Greek philosophers and the intent to assert this vision in the political organization of the *polis* – according to Ojakangas – allows us to say that their conception of the government of the state foreruns modern biopolitics; perhaps, it is even «more biopolitical than the modern one, for Plato and Aristotle had no need to 'compromise' their biopolitical vision of politics with concepts alien to it»[34], such as the universalist, modern and egalitarian concepts of human nature, justice and law. Therefore, he believes even their conception of justice is closely linked to a

---

31   Ojakangas, *On the Greek Origins of Biopolitics*, p. 9.
32   *On the Greek Origins of Biopolitics*, p. 6; see also pp. 100-15.
33   *On the Greek Origins of Biopolitics*, p. 7.
34   *On the Greek Origins of Biopolitics*, p. 137.

hierarchical vision of human nature: «[f]or Plato and Aristotle (...) natural justice entails hierarchy, not equality, subordination, not autonomy». But what matters most in this regard – according to Ojakangas – is that

> Platonic-Aristotelian natural justice resembles more that justice inherent in the naturalism of modern human sciences, particularly in eugenics and thereby in Nazism, than the justice of natural moral law.[35]

According to the Finnish scholar, one can even say that Plato anticipated the biopolitical theories and strategies of Nazism, but, at the same time, that he was not «a precursor of Nazism alone»; more generally, in fact, it can also be argued that

> [h]e was a precursor of modern biopolitics, particularly the biopolitics of state racism based on the idea that selective breeding and killing the 'unfit' can better the race – and that this betterment alone is able to bring about a well-ordered, just, and happy society.[36]

Regarding Plato's *The Republic*, naturally, one cannot ignore what even Ojakangas does not overlook: that is, the policies for managing procreation and raising children are proposed only for the ruling *elite* of the guardians and not for the entire political body of the state. Nevertheless, this does not change the fact that these policies can legitimately be considered biopolitical. However, it may also be opportune to try to highlight at least some aspects of these same policies that can prevent their meaning from being over-simplified.

3. *A metallic nature*

First of all, it is important to note that Plato's clear propensity to conceive in eugenic terms the strategies he proposes does not seem to imply a deterministic view of the nature of the individuals who would be generated and bred according to these strategies. There

---

35   *On the Greek Origins of Biopolitics*, p. 113.
36   *On the Greek Origins of Biopolitics*, p. 96; see also pp. 12-4.

is no doubt that he has a hierarchical conception of human nature, according to which men are not all the same, but have different natures and, therefore, it would be useful for the state if they were to carry out different tasks and have roles at different levels within the *polis*. However, this conception does not imply a particular rigidity in the destinies of those born from parents with one nature or another. We cannot be certain, in particular, that the children born from the union of the "best men" with the "best women" will always be able to perform for the good of the state the same governmental or defensive tasks that are the responsibility of their classes of origin. Therefore, if necessary, the children who are more suitable for carrying out tasks other than those carried out by their parents can move from the lower to the upper classes and vice versa. To this end, the rulers in charge, referring to the myth of the birth of men from the earth, will tell the citizens that the divinity that shaped them has mixed gold in those who are destined to govern, silver in those who will courageously defend the state, iron and bronze in those who will have to dedicate themselves to the activities of farmer and artisan.[37] This story, however, must be completed as follows:

> as you are all akin, though for the most part you will breed after your kinds, it may sometimes happen that a golden father would beget a silver son and that a golden offspring would come from a silver sire and that the rest would in like manner be born of one another. So that the first and chief injunction that the god lays upon the rulers is that of nothing else are they to be such careful guardians and so intently observant as of the intermixture of these metals in the souls of their offspring, and if sons are born to them with an infusion of brass or iron they shall by no means give way to pity in their treatment of them, but shall assign to each the status due to his nature and thrust them out among the artizans or the farmers. And again, if from these there is born a son with unexpected gold or silver in his composition they shall honour such and bid them go up higher, some to the office of guardian, some to the assistanceship, alleging that there is an oracle that the state shall then be overthrown when the man of iron or brass is its guardian.[38]

---

37   *The Republic*, 414d-415a, vol. I, pp. 303-5.
38   *The Republic*, 415a-c, vol. I, pp. 305-7.

As has been observed by Maria Moneti Codignola, it is true that according to the Platonic vision «the beautiful and the good are naturally favored» and it is «entirely legitimate to program their birth»; however, «there is not a superior race in the city that is self-reproducing, but instead every new born must be assigned to a class on the basis of the observation of its natural characteristics».[39] In any case, it is important not to neglect the character that is not only mythological, but also definitely "false", of the story that Plato recommends be proposed to convince the citizens, firstly, that they are in some way destined by nature to the tasks that they must perform for the good of the state and, secondly, that no one can be sure that the nature of their class of origin represents the basis of a sort of predestination for each of them. This story is a true political-ideological stratagem or, more precisely, one of those «opportune falsehoods» that – according to Plato – the rulers are allowed to say to «enemies and citizens for the benefit of the state».[40]

Some important clarifications can be made on all this: the uncertainty of the results of procreation, brought to light in the story, makes the idea that the Platonic view of human nature is of a deterministic kind not credible; on the other hand, the "falsity" and the instrumentality of the story itself also render problematic the idea that Plato's greatest concern is to naturalize – or even to biologize – in an indisputable manner the differences and destinies of men, even in a non-deterministic context.[41] Finally, it should be considered that the need for this false narrative in *The Republic* is indicated by Socrates – with much embarrassment – at the end of a long reasoning on the primary importance that a moral education must have, first of all, in the ideal state. This must concern, above all, the citizens who can be part of the elite group of guardians and who, moreover, will have to pass rigorous tests before being accepted in it. In short, for the author of *The*

---

39   Maria Moneti Codignola, *Il paese che non c'è e i suoi abitanti* (Florence: La Nuova Italia, 1992), p. 57.
40   *The Republic*, 414b and 389b, vol. I, pp. 301 and 213.
41   On this, see Mario Vegetti, 'La "razza pura"', in *Platone, La Repubblica*, ed. by Mario Vegetti, vol. IV, book V, (Naples: Bibliopolis, 2000), pp. 295-300.

Republic, while we should look for the different vocations of men in their different natures, their moral education will, nevertheless, be the fundamental and essential premise for the good government of the ideal state.[42]

Reasons such as these show that the purpose of Plato's eugenic strategies was not to create or strengthen a superior race from a biological or ethnic point of view, but to constitute an aristocracy capable of politically practicing virtue based not only on one's innate gifts, but also, and above all, on one's acquired moral qualities.[43] In any case, the importance that Plato assigned to education was an absolutely central element of his ideal state project: with the objective of making the citizens virtuous and responsible for the common good, the education would contribute decisively to ensuring cohesion and unity of the state, which for him, together with justice, represented the main purposes of politics. It is in the light of these goals, in fact, that the community of wives and children can be adequately assessed, since they are the essential motivation of this same community.[44] In any case, it can be said that precisely by grasping this aspect of the Platonic project, further verification can be made of the actual possibility of interpreting this project in biopolitical terms.

4. *The family as a danger*

As we have seen, in *The Republic* Plato openly theorizes the need to place an elite group of guardians in command of the state, composed of rulers and helpers: the former must have an essential philosophical predisposition and the latter a military type of dedication towards the state. They must be imposed with a regime

---

42 *The Republic*, 376e-414b, vol. I, pp. 175-301.
43 On this, see Esposito, *Bios: Biopolitics and Philosophy*, p. 54; see also the critical considerations on what Esposito claims in this regard in Ojakangas, *On the Greek Origins of Biopolitics*, pp. 18-9. Furthermore, see Simona Forti, 'The Biopolitics of Souls: Racism, Nazism, and Plato', *Political Theory*, 34, 1 (2006), 9-32.
44 *The Republic*, 461e-467d, pp. 469-83.

of a community of wives and children, which will be accompanied by the prohibition not only of having a family, but also of having property and a private sphere.

So, precisely because it must be conceived and practiced in these terms, for Plato, the community of wives and children can represent a fundamental guarantee of the maximum good of the state, that is to say, precisely of its unity and its cohesion. This can be explained briefly in this way: a family, the generation and rearing of one's own children, the possession of personal property, having private affairs, all compromise the possibility that the rulers and defenders of the state will preserve the morality necessary to pursue the common good, that is to guide the state in the best way and to guarantee its union and harmony.[45]

Precisely in this regard, in his second book of *Politics* Aristotle addresses very clear criticism to Plato arguing that the «community of children, women and possessions» involves a kind of excessive compaction of the state, which, in reality, creates the danger that it will disintegrate instead of remaining unified. According to Aristotle, it is not possible to unify the areas of personal, family and political life without altering the nature of the city-state and ending up by destroying it.

> Yet it is clear that if the process of unification advances beyond a certain point, the city will not be a city at all; for a state essentially consists of a multitude of persons, and if its unification is carried beyond a certain point, city will be reduced to family and family to individual, for we should pronounce the family to be a more complete unity than the city, and the single person than the family; so that even if any lawgiver were able to unify the state, he must not do so, for he will destroy it in the process.[46]

In reality the risk that the state designed by Plato be reduced to a family is real only to the extent that it is the class of guardians who would have to share a whole set of relationships normally included in the private sphere of the *oikos*: the state management of these relationships would entail, in particular, that the children born be

---

45   *The Republic*, 416 d-417 b, 457 d-466 d, vol. I, pp. 311-3; 453-83.
46   Aristotle, *Politics*, 1261a, 17-24, p. 71.

considered and raised as children of the state itself. However, with his objection, Aristotle seems to make a criticism of Plato analogous to that which Hannah Arendt made of modern society, arguing – as we have seen – that it «blurred the decisive division between the public and the private realms, between the sphere of the *polis* and the sphere of household and family» tending to see the political community «in the image of a family whose everyday affairs have to be taken care of by a gigantic, nation-wide administration of housekeeping».[47] Now, if such a criticism were unquestionably valid also with regard to Plato, the hypothesis that the ideal state proposed in *The Republic* is a decidedly biopolitical state would be substantially well-founded. Even in this regard, however, the situation must be considered with caution.

It is not simply a question of reiterating that the elimination of the boundary between private and public in *The Republic* only concerns the guardians; it is also and above all a question of focusing on the reason why Plato exposes the class of guardians to the possibility, or the risk, of becoming a large family. The reason lies in his desire not so much to break down the boundary between private and public, as to abolish the private sphere and the family altogether. In short, the hypothesis in which Plato seems to want to transform the elite of his ideal state into a large family should be completed by pointing out that for him this is necessary precisely to free the guardians from the family in its normal and private sense. In fact, what Plato identifies as the greatest danger for the state is that its rulers and defenders be conditioned by their private interests, which find their most favorable condition precisely in the family founded on the traditional marital relationship, on the generation and raising of one's own children and the ownership of personal property. By prescribing, instead, that the guardians consider neither conjugal partners, nor children, nor material goods, as their own, they would be placed in the conditions of maximum disinterest and they would thus be able to guarantee the maximum cohesion of the state, since cohesion would reign among them, above all:

---

47   *The Human Condition*, p. 28.

these (...) prescriptions tend to make them still more truly guardians and prevent them from distracting the city by referring 'mine' not to the same but to different things, one man dragging off to his own house anything he is able to acquire apart from the rest, and another doing the same to his own separate house, and having women and children apart, thus introducing into the state the pleasures and pains of individuals. They should all rather (...) share one conviction about their own, tend to one goal, and so far as practicable have one experience of pleasure and pain. (...) [L]aw-suits and accusations against one another [will] vanish, one may say, from among them, because they have nothing in private possession but their bodies, but all else in common (...). So that we can count on their being free from the dissensions that arise among men from the possession of property, children, and kin.[48]

Paradoxically, therefore, by proposing to annul the family and the private dimension, Plato wants to respond in a radical and definitive way to the same need that would be dear to his most famous pupil, Aristotle: the need to separate and distinguish the private sphere of particular interests from the public sphere of the common good. However, Plato does not believe that the simple practical, conceptual and moral distinction between the private *oikonomia* and the public sphere of political citizenship represents an effective remedy for the inclination of men to make the interests that mature in the former prevail to the detriment of the ends pursued in the second. The virtuous execution of the duties of those destined to guide and defend the state can be realized best only if the family and private sphere are dissolved, neutralized or diluted within a dimension of the general sharing of material goods and physical, affective and procreative relationships. Therefore, while manifesting disturbing eugenics inclinations, Plato has as his main aspiration not the constitution of a healthy and strong social organism in terms of physical power and biological integrity, but the formation of a political community in which the conditions of virtue and attention to what is common are actually created and endure. Hence, also and above all, the fundamental importance of the moral education which the state itself must be concerned with, as – indeed – the citizens themselves.

---

48   Plato, *The Republic*, 464 c-e, vol. I, p. 477.

5. *A medicine without biopolitics*

As part of the discourse on education, Plato proposes – among other topics – his vision of the «art of medicine» by relating it to that of the «art of justice». This is a vision that Ojakangas interprets as a decisive proof of the biopolitical propensity of the Greek philosopher.[49] In any case, this is certainly a crucial aspect for understanding if and to what extent *The Republic* of Plato tends to transform politics into biopolitics.

In a passage from the third book of the work, on which Ojakangas bases most of his interpretation, the Greek philosopher – after praising the medical practice that in the past was inspired by Asclepius (god of medicine) – claims that the medical art should take a drastic position towards those who are incurable and that the administration of justice should assume a similar one towards those who are criminally incorrigible:

> these arts will care for the bodies and souls of such of (..) citizens as are truly well born, but of those who are not, such as are defective in body they will suffer to die and those who are evil-natured and incurable in soul they will themselves put to death.[50]

Ojakangas does not hesitate to state that here Plato assigns to medicine the same «prophylactic function» towards society that, according to Foucault, it would only assume in the 19th century when its biopolitical role would be fully defined. The Finnish author argues, rather, that «medicine has embraced that prophylactic function from the very beginning – at least if we are to believe Plato's testimony of Asclepius».[51] However, if we carefully consider both the overall discourse in which Plato's statements are placed and Foucault's point of view, we can arrive at very different, and even opposite, conclusions from those of Ojakangas. In extreme synthesis, the fact that Plato tends to assign thanato-political tasks to medicine does not mean that these tasks necessarily fall within a biopolitical perspective, for a very simple

---

49 *On the Greek Origins of Biopolitics*, pp. 66-7.
50 *The Republic*, 409e-410a, vol. I, p. 287.
51 *On the Greek Origins of Biopolitics*, p. 67.

reason: he declares himself clearly opposed to assigning medicine a central role in the life of individuals and the community. In Foucaultian terms we could say that he wants to avoid, in any way, the individual and collective medicalization that would allow medical power-knowledge to become the pillar of a politics that would thus become biopolitical. His reference to the ancient medical practice inspired by Asclepius has exactly this meaning. In fact, Plato would like to end the increasingly frequent recourse to medicine made by his contemporaries ever since the teachings of Asclepius had been forgotten.[52]

According to Plato, medicine is increasingly important in people's lives, especially because individuals and the state are less and less concerned about cultivating education based on the simplest forms of music and gymnastics. Instead, he insistently proposes the promotion of musical education, including in this not only music in the strict sense, but also culture in general (especially poetry and narration); he equally strongly insists on the need to promote gymnastics, referring to the forms of physical exercise and diet that can give rise to a healthy and sober lifestyle.[53]

However, one should not believe that the importance attributed to gymnastics by Plato implies an exaltation of the body and its muscular power. Gymnastics certainly has the purpose of maintaining the health and vigor of the body, but its primary purpose is to contribute, in harmonious combination with musical education, to creating a good soul. In fact, with regard to gymnastics, Plato says through Socrates: «I, for my part, do not believe that a sound body by its excellence makes the soul good, but on the contrary that a good soul by its virtue renders the body the best that is possible».[54] Therefore, gymnastics is important in so far as it can contribute to education in virtue: it can do so if it does not become an end in itself, if it is practiced in relation to musical education which, in turn, must always be connected to gymnastics. These two disciplines, remaining in a balanced combination, can generate sobriety (music) and bravery (gymnastics) and avoid

---

52   *The Republic*, 405c-408b, vol. I, pp. 271-81.
53   *The Republic*, 375e-405a and 410a-412a, pp. 169-269 and 287-93.
54   *The Republic*, 403d, vol. I, p. 265.

the risks that each of them entails, if practiced exclusively, of producing softness and savagery, respectively.[55] For reasons like these – according to Plato – we can say that «those who established an education in music and gymnastics had not the purpose in view that some attribute to them in so instituting, namely to treat the body by one and the soul by the other»; rather it must be recognized «that they ordained both chiefly for the soul's sake».[56]

Plato's insistence on the educational and moral role that gymnastics and music should play could be enough to demonstrate what is well-known, namely that the ideal state project he proposes in *The Republic* – no matter how aberrant, questionable or utopian – it is no more than a project of radical ethical re-establishment of the *polis*; and it is, above all, for this reason that it cannot be reduced to an essentially biopolitical perspective. Moreover, beyond this general consideration, of great importance are the precise reasons why Plato places the role of medicine alongside that of the art of justice when he maintains – as we have seen – that the former should let those who are «defective in body» die, and the latter should condemn to death those who are «evil-natured and incurable in soul».

There is no doubt that thinking in these terms the Greek philosopher offers an excellent argument to those who accuse him of racism; but it cannot be ignored, on the other hand, that he openly affirms that the city-states in which medicine and the art of justice progressively extend their influence are realities in which the moral education that tends to harmonize sobriety in souls and health in bodies no longer finds space or no longer has the effectiveness it should have; for this reason «licentiousness and disease multiply» and «many courts of law and dispensaries [are] opened».[57] In fact, according to him, the most evident proof of «an evil and shameful state of education in a city» is precisely «the necessity of first-rate physicians and judges»; it is particularly «disgraceful», in this sense, «to require medicine (...) not merely for wounds or the incidence of some seasonal maladies, but,

---

55   *The Republic*, 410a-412a, vol. I, pp. 287-93.
56   *The Republic*, 410b-c, vol. I, p. 289.
57   *The Republic*, 405a, vol. I, p. 269.

because of sloth and such a regimen as we described», that is, excesses in physical activity, in eating, etc. This is what had been happening for a long time, according to Plato, and the growing use of medicine had led doctors to devise «new-fangled and monstrous strange names of diseases», names that did not exist «in the days of Asclepius»:[58]

> this excessive care for the body that goes beyond simple gymnastics (...) is troublesome in household affairs and military service and sedentary offices in the city. And, chief of all, it puts difficulties in the way of any kind of instruction, thinking, or private meditation, forever imagining headaches and dizziness and attributing their origin to philosophy. So that wherever this kind of virtue is practised and tested it is in every way a hindrance. For it makes the man always fancy himself sick and never cease from anguishing about his body.[59]

Thus, even if Plato were willing to attribute a political and thanato-political role to the medicine of Asclepius, this role would still have to agree with the fact that – for the Greek philosopher – Asclepius was clearly opposed to medicalizing the life of each and every person; therefore, he would *never* have contributed to promoting a biopolitics truly worthy of the name. In short, it is impossible to consider secondary the fact that – according to Plato's Asclepius – the influence of medicine had to be limited as much as possible in people's lives. It is in this perspective, then, that the harshness of the hypothetical role that medicine would assume in the Platonic state must be evaluated, without assuming that it would be a biopolitical role. In fact, for the Greek philosopher, Asclepius believed that «excessive care for the body that goes beyond simple gymnastics» could only hinder the activities of men and their efforts to practice virtue.

> Then – Plato says through Socrates – shall we not say that it was because Asclepius knew this – that for those who were by nature and course of life sound of body but had some localized disease, (...) for such (...) and for this habit he revealed the art of medicine, and, driving out their disease by drugs and surgery, prescribed for them

---

58   *The Republic*, 405a-d, vol. I, pp. 271-273.
59   *The Republic*, 407b-c, vol. I, pp. 277-279.

their customary regimen in order not to interfere with their civic duties, but that, when bodies were diseased inwardly and throughout, he did not attempt by diet and by gradual evacuations and infusions to prolong a wretched existence for the man and have him beget in all likelihood similar wretched offspring? But if a man was incapable of living in the established round and order of life, he did not think it worthwhile to treat him, since such a fellow is of no use either to himself or to the state.[60]

Ultimately, only a certain simplification of the discourse on the physical health of citizens proposed in *The Republic* makes it possible to argue that it is essentially biopolitical, as believed by Ojakangas, who moreover – as already mentioned – also judges the two other main political works by Plato and *Politics* by Aristotle in similar terms.

6. *The skeptical legislator*

In effect, even for these works it is worthwhile to take the time not so much to discuss Ojakangas' evaluations, but to do some further general verification of the possibility of attributing to the two Greek philosophers an unequivocal biopolitical vocation.

Let us first consider Plato's *Laws*. First of all, it is important to note that in this work he – albeit reluctantly – in fact renounces the possibility of achieving what he considers a fundamental base of the perfect state, namely

this condition in which there is community of wives, children, and all chattels, and all that is called "private" is everywhere and by every means rooted out of our life, and so far as possible it is contrived that even things naturally "private" have become in a way "communized".[61]

Here it is interesting to observe that the Greek philosopher, on the one hand, radicalizes the idea of the abolition of every private

---

60   *The Republic*, 407d-e, vol. I, p. 279.
61   Plato, *Laws*, trans. by R. G. Bury (Cambridge, Mass.: Harvard University Press/London: William Heinemann, 1961), 739c, vol. I, p. 363.

sphere far beyond what he proposed in *The Republic* limiting this abolition to the circle of guardians; on the other hand, he argues that, if one keeps faith with the ideal reasons for which this abolition would be appropriate, one can also accept the possibility of granting property and a domestic sphere to citizens. The perfect state must continue to represent the ideal model of constitution, but in everyday reality it can be pragmatically accepted that «the land and houses» be divided among the citizens, provided «the apportionment» is done

> with this intention – that the man who receives the portion should still regard it as common property of the whole state, and should tend the land, which is his fatherland, more diligently than a mother tends her children.[62]

Here, therefore, Plato, at least in appearance, accepts a certain distinction between "private" and "public", but – at the same time – emphasizes that both individual property and the domestic sphere («the land and houses») belong to the common dimension of the state. It is in the context of a moral dedication to this dimension that he places a specific discourse on marriage and procreation in *Laws*.

In particular, when considering the moment when it is appropriate for a young man «of noble sires» to marry, he proposes as the main rule for a good choice of the bride to «neither to shun connexion with a poor family, nor to pursue ardently connexion with a rich one, but, other things being equal, to prefer always an alliance with a family of moderate means».[63] Through this indication, Plato assigns primary importance to the moral criteria that citizens must follow in their decisions so that they benefit the state. This is not simply a question of guaranteeing a balanced distribution of wealth among families, but also of morally condemning «inordinate wealth».[64] The search for equilibrium, on the other hand, is a politically beneficial rule as a general principle of morality to be applied not only through

---

62   *Laws*, 739e-740a, vol. I, p. 365.
63   *Laws*, 773a, vol. I, p. 461.
64   *Laws*, 773e, vol. I, p. 465.

the moderation of wealth, but also through the combination of the different inclinations of citizens, which can be achieved with weddings. No biopolitical intent seems to prevail over this moral framework of the question of marriage unions and their political implications.

> Such a course will benefit both the state and the united families, since in respect of excellence what is evenly balanced and symmetrical is infinitely superior to what is untempered. The man who knows he is unduly hasty and violent in all his actions should win a bride sprung from steady parents; while the man that is of a contrary nature should proceed to mate himself with one of the opposite kind.[65]

In *The Republic* the need for a balanced combination between the different natural and moral predispositions of the citizens represented a general orientation to be applied to the whole of the state to ensure that everyone carried out his or her tasks without interfering in the tasks of others;[66] in the framework of that work, however, on the procreative level the combination of "equal" rather than "different" types remained necessary, in particular between the "best" men and women, for the formation of the elite of the guardians. In *Laws* this perspective is overcome or, better, it is transformed through a vision of marriage relationships that tends to favor a mixture rather than the homogenization of conditions and characters; therefore, certain heavy-handed eugenic strategies, proposed in the *Republic* with the community of wives and children, seem destined to be scaled down.

In any case, there is no doubt that Plato in the *Laws* proposes to pay maximum attention to marriages and their procreative aspects. He argues that men and women should feel the duty to marry and do so at the right age. He recommends – among other things – that spouses always use «their mind» in procreation, so that it always has the best results for the benefit of the political community.

---

65 *Laws*, 773a-b, vol. I, p. 463.
66 *The Republic*, 433a-434c, vol. I, pp. 367-373; 443b-444a, vol. I, pp. 413-7.

> The bride and bridegroom must set their minds to produce for the state children of the greatest possible goodness and beauty. (...) The bridegroom, therefore, shall apply his mind both to the bride and to the work of procreation, and the bride shall do likewise, especially during the period when they have no children yet born.[67]

It does not seem, however, that the concern for the quality of the children that are generated must be understood first of all in physical or biological terms, just as the criteria of beauty, physical prowess or material wealth, for Plato, cannot prevail over that of virtue in recognizing the value of citizens.

> Nor indeed is it right that pre-eminent honours in a state should be conferred on a man because he is specially wealthy, any more than it is right to confer them because he is swift or comely or strong without any virtue, or with a virtue devoid of temperance.[68]

In any case, Plato believes that the state should organize a specific surveillance of marital behavior as far as procreation is concerned;[69] the latter, however, corresponds to a duty that can only be described as universal: «a duty to lay hold on the ever living reality by providing servants for God in our own stead».[70] According to Plato, this duty – like that of marrying – corresponds to the necessity that the reproduction of humanity as a whole continues to take place, rather than the strengthening of an ethnic group or a special race.

> A man shall marry when he is thirty years old and under thirty-five, bearing in mind that this is the way by which the human race, by nature's ordinance, shares in immortality, a thing for which nature has implanted in everyone a keen desire. The desire to win glory, instead of lying in a nameless grave, aims at a like object. Thus mankind is by nature coeval with the whole of time, in that it accompanies it continually both now and in the future; and the means by which it is immortal is this: by leaving behind it children's children and continuing ever one and the same, it thus by reproduction shares in immortality.[71]

---

67   *Laws*, 783d-784a, vol. I, p. 497.
68   *Laws*, 696b, vol. I, pp. 231-3.
69   *Laws*, 784a-e, vol. I, pp. 497-501.
70   *Laws*, 773e-774a, vol. I, p. 465.
71   *Laws*, 721b-c, vol. I, pp. 311-3.

However, Plato believes that in the political regulation of marital relations and procreation, the instrument of persuasion should be preferred, avoiding too much legislation or intervention in an authoritarian way in this area, except in cases of obvious deviation from the tasks that – according to him – every marriage implies, or deviation from the duty to marry.[72] In a certain sense, he only indicates the "conjugal duties" in the most canonical sense of the expression as functional tasks useful to the state.

It is also for this reason that Plato is concerned with distinguishing from his point of view healthy sexual relations from dangerous ones; but also in this regard his aim is markedly moral and far from being biopolitical: to avoid abandoning oneself to erotic passions (homosexuality, auto-eroticism, concubinage, pedophilia) which weaken or destroy the possibility of acquiring the virtues which the citizens of a just state should have. And, while recognizing that it is very difficult to legislate in this area, he thinks that lawmakers should, nevertheless, turn their attention to these issues.[73]

In general, therefore, it can be said that the discourse on sexual and procreative relationships that Plato proposes in *Laws* does not create the actual conditions of a biopolitics since it falls within an ethical-political vision in which both individual and collective life and its security never take on a value higher than

---

72 *Laws*, 720e-721e; 773c-e; 784e-785a, vol. I, pp. 309-13; 463-5; 499-501. Foucault, in *The Use of Peasure: Volume 2 of The History of Sexuality*, trans by Robert Hurley (New York: Vintage Books, 1990), pp. 167-70, referring to *Laws* indicates Plato's general orientation to consider marriage and procreation as duties of citizens to be related to the needs of the state. According to Foucault, Plato outlines in this way «a system of authoritarian regulation of behaviors in the context of an ideal city» (p. 166). Therefore, the prescriptions that the Greek philosopher seems to want to impose on matrimonial relations «take the form, not of a voluntary ethics, but of a coercive regimentation», although he realizes the «difficulty of legislating in this area» (p. 167). In this sense Foucault observes that «Plato puts only a limited amount of trust in the law when it is a question of regulating sexual conduct. He does not believe it will achieve adequate results if one does not use measures other than its prescriptions and threats for controlling such violent desires. More effective means of persuasion are needed for this». (p. 168).

73 *Laws*, 835d-842a, vol. II, pp. 149-69.

that of virtue. Not surprisingly, in fact, speaking of the victories that the Greeks achieved in their heroic wars against the Persians, Plato maintains that the battles that really saved them were those in which they avoided every form of cowardice, becoming better on a moral level:

> so that we differ from most people in not regarding mere safety and existence as the most precious thing men can possess, but rather the gaining of all possible goodness and the keeping of it throughout life.

Therefore, for him, it is fundamental to establish whether, in defining a just political constitution, «we are travelling by the same road which we took then, as being the best for states in the matter of settlements and modes of legislation».[74]

7. *Rulers, shepherds and guard dogs*

A theme that seems to testify in favor of the biopolitical character of the Platonic vision of power is that of the comparison between the ruler and the shepherd. As Ojakangas observes, this theme appears in various works by Plato, among which the more political ones stand out: *The Republic*, *Statesman* and *Laws*.[75] We have already seen that Foucault himself insists on the political meaning of this theme in his 1977-1978 Course and, according to Ojakangas, this means that from a Foucaultian point of view pastoral power can be considered a sort of paradigm of biopolitical power, since the shepherd is a breeder of living beings. Therefore, the Finnish author does not give great importance to the fact that the French philosopher, in reality, assumes pastoral power as a model not so much of biopower, as of that broader and more complex form of power that is the government, in which the exercise of a biopower can be also included.[76]

In any case, according to Foucault, the use of the metaphor of the shepherd is not particularly relevant in the political culture

---

74   *Laws*, 707d, vol. I, p. 265.
75   *On the Greek Origins of Biopolitics*, pp. 3-4, 79-83, 134.
76   *On the Greek Origins of Biopolitics*, pp. 33-4.

of classical antiquity; the case of Plato, for him, represents a sort of exception that does not, however, imply a clear assumption of this metaphor as a model of political power. The theme of the shepherd, for Foucault, is much more important in middle-eastern cultures and, in particular, in the Jewish culture from which Christianity borrowed it and then transformed the pastorate into a real system of power.[77] In supporting these theses, the French philosopher considers the Christian pastorate exactly as «model and matrix of procedures for the government of men», since it is a power exercised not simply on the lives, but above all on the souls, on the *ethos* of individuals.[78] Foucault dedicated three important lessons of his 1977-1978 course to the theme of pastoral power and did so for one reason only: to try to make clear the specificity of the government with respect to other forms of power such as those exercised through segregation, the disciplines or biopolitics, forms to which the government cannot be reduced. Ultimately, his analysis of the pastorate is part of a larger attempt to

> talk of something like a "governmentality" that would be to the state what techniques of segregation were to psychiatry, what techniques of discipline were to the penal system, and what biopolitics was to medical institutions.[79]

Thus the attribution to pastoral power of an exemplary meaning as a «model and matrix» of the government, for him, implies a consideration of the pastorate primarily as a «spiritual direction» and, more generally, as «*oikonomia psuchōn*, that is to say, the economy of souls», rather than as a simple breeding of living beings.[80] In short, it is a question of assuming the idea of the pastor as a good administrator of the ways of behaving more than of the physical health of individuals.

---

77 See *Security, Territory, Population*, pp. 122-85. For a different point of view on the use of the theme of the shepherd by Plato, see the already mentioned Sloterdijk, 'Rules for the Human Zoo: a response to the *Letter on Humanism*'.

78 *Security, Territory, Population*, p. 147; see also pp. 148-51.

79 *Security, Territory, Population*, p. 120.

80 *Security, Territory, Population*, pp. 123, 192.

For his part, Ojakangas, in addition to interpreting the Foucaultian analysis of the pastorate in immediately biopolitical terms, maintains that Foucault underestimates the importance of the use that Plato makes of the metaphor of the shepherd in his works. Which, according to him, represents significant proof of Foucault's oversight of the Greek origins of biopolitics.[81]

In fact, the idea that the French philosopher underestimates the importance of the Platonic theme of the shepherd does not seem completely unfounded.[82] Nevertheless, supposing that there is this underestimation on his part, it can still not be seen as a lack of attention to the alleged Greek origins of biopolitics. Foucault – as has already been said – looks to cases where the pastoral power has been assimilated to the political one, for the roots of something broader and more complex than biopolitics, that is, the management of the behavior of men, which can *even* be practiced through a power exercised over their lives.[83]

Once this fact has been highlighted, it is certainly also appropriate to consider the terms in which Plato makes use of the metaphor of the pastor on the political level, in an attempt to verify if and to what extent this use represents a proof of the biopolitical orientation of his thought.

One of the places in *The Republic* where he compares the shepherd to the ruler is one in which he excludes the possibility of being able to accept the idea that «the real rulers (...) think of anything else night and day than the sources of their own profit».[84] This idea is as unacceptable to him as that according to which the true shepherd takes care of his flock simply to gain material advantages and money:[85]

---

81   *On the Greek Origins of Biopolitics*, pp. 77-83.
82   See *Security, Territory, Population*, pp. 138-47.
83   From this point of view, it does not make much sense to oppose Foucault by trying to prove that the «Christian pastoral power» does not represent a prelude to modern biopolitics and that, instead, the deployment of the latter «goes hand in hand with the *decline* of Christian pastoral ideals» (*On the Greek Origins of Biopolitics*, p. 2). In fact, Foucault does not consider the Christian pastorate as an immediate paradigm of biopower, but, above all, as an emblematic form of governing the ways in which men act.
84   *The Republic*, 343b-c, vol. I, p. 65.
85   *The Republic*, 345c-d, vol. I, p. 65.

the art of the shepherd surely is concerned with nothing else than how to provide what is best for that over which it is set, since its own affairs, its own best estate, are surely sufficiently provided for so long as it in nowise fails of being the shepherd's art. And in like manner (...) every form of rule in so far as it is rule considers what is best for nothing else than that which is governed and cared for by it, alike in political and private rule.[86]

Here, in reality, the comparison of the art of the ruler with the art of the shepherd is not proposed in order to assimilate the first to the second considering both as arts of breeding, but rather because the pastoral art can be considered an art of government in the same way that other arts can also be considered as such. In any case, here Plato through an articulated argument wants to highlight that «each of the arts is different from others because its power or function is different» and, additionally, that «each art also yield us benefit that is peculiar to itself and not general, as for example medicine health, the pilot's art safety at sea, and the other arts similarly».[87] Precisely because each of the arts considered differs from the others on the basis of its own power, its function and the various benefits it provides, it is not possible to lump them together by tracing them back to the supposed common purpose of procuring advantages for those who exercise them; each in fact «provides and enjoins what is beneficial to its subject, considering the advantage of that, the weaker, and not the advantage of the stronger».[88] Therefore, in a sense, the art of the ruler can be compared not only to the art of the shepherd, but also to other arts to the extent that each of them pursues in its own way what is beneficial to its subjects. Consequently, from this point of view, there is no special similarity between the art of the ruler and that of the shepherd. Rather it can be said that the other arts, including that of the shepherd, are similar to that of the ruler since each of them represents a way of governing different objects and spheres of activity. Ultimately, according to Plato, there is no art that can be considered truly paradigmatic with respect to political power;

---

86   *The Republic*, 345d-e, vol. I, p. 75.
87   *The Republic*, 346a, vol. I, pp. 75-77.
88   *The Republic*, 346e, vol. I, p. 79.

rather the opposite is true, because each of «the arts do hold rule» and «no art considers or enjoins the advantage of the stronger but every art that of the weaker which is ruled by it».[89] Therefore, it is probably precisely this possibility of comparing different arts to the political government, to the extent that each of them expresses a form of rule, that pushes Plato to compare the figure of the ruler (also) to that of the pastor: in fact, the second, in its own way, governs like the first does; but it cannot be said that the former necessarily governs as a pastor in his role as a breeder. Which – as we will see later – will emerge clearly in the *Statesman*.

In any case, this comparison of the two figures appears in two other short passages of *The Republic*, in which in truth there is no mention of the relationship between the shepherd and the flock, but of that between guard dogs and shepherds.[90] «The helpers» who have the task of defending the state and protecting citizens are compared to the dogs, «as it were dogs subject to the rulers who are as it were the shepherds of the city».[91] If here the rulers are compared to the shepherds it is, above all, because they are destined to have the role of guide because they are inclined and educated to wisdom, that is, to the use of reason. This, among the various vocations of the souls of citizens (the rational, the appetitive and the high spirited), is that which allows rulers to pursue justice rather than (biopolitical) aims such as safety and health. It is a task that the rulers will be able to carry out by ensuring that each person performs the task that is right for him according to his vocation, governing the state with the support of the helpers and the courage to which they must be educated by strengthening their inclination in this direction.[92] Therefore, Plato says,

> [i]t is surely the most monstrous and shameful thing in the world for shepherds to breed the dogs who are to help them with their flocks in such wise and of such a nature that from indiscipline or hunger or some other evil condition the dogs themselves shall attack the sheep and injure them and be likened to wolves instead of dogs.[93]

---

89   *The Republic*, 342c-d, vol. I, p. 63.
90   *The Republic*, 416a-b and 440d, vol. I, pp. 309 and 403.
91   *The Republic*, 440d, vol. I, p. 403.
92   See *The Republic*, 427d-444e, vol. I, pp. 345-419.
93   *The Republic*, 416a, vol. I, p. 309.

This comparison of the rulers to the shepherds (or herdsmen) and of the helpers to watch-dogs is also proposed in the *Laws*, where Plato intends to exclude that the gods can be compared to these figures or to the rulers of any kind of activity.[94]

Also in this case, Plato's discourse is oriented in a clearly moral sense. In fact, he intends to oppose «those wicked men» who think «they had gained the right to act as they chose – those men who wickedly hold all those false notions about the gods».[95] These men are the same ones who think they can get material advantages at the expense of others and bribe those who exercise power to avoid the consequences of their behavior.[96] Therefore, if the comparison between the gods and the herdsmen or the watch-dogs were possible, it would have to be admitted that the deities are corruptible,

> that the gods are always merciful to unjust men and those who act unjustly, provided that one gives them a share of one's unjust gains; it is just as if wolves were to give small bits of their prey to watch-dogs, and they being mollified by the gifts were to allow them to go ravening among the flocks.[97]

In reality, the part of the *Laws* in which the metaphor of the pastor seems to be used in biopolitical terms is another. Nevertheless, even in this case we can go beyond this first impression. It is a passage in which the Greek philosopher considers the possibility that the creation of a just state requires a preemptive «appropriate purge», similar to the type «the shepherd or cowherd, or the keeper

---

94   *Laws*, 905d-907b, vol. II, pp. 371-7.
95   *Laws*, 907b-c, vol. II, p. 377.
96   *Laws*, 906a-c, vol. II, pp. 373-5: «there are certain souls that dwell on earth and have acquired unjust gain which, being plainly bestial, beseech the souls of the guardians – whether they be watch-dogs or herdsmen or the most exalted of masters – trying to convince them by fawning words and prayerful incantations that (as the tales of evil men relate) they can profiteer among men on earth without any severe penalty: but we assert that the sin now mentioned, of profiteering or "over-gaining," is what is called in the case of fleshly bodies "disease," in that of seasons and years "pestilence," and in that of states and polities, by a verbal change, this same sin is called "injustice"».
97   *Laws*, 906d, vol. II, p. 375.

of horses or any such animals» would implement «[i]n dealing with a flock of any kind», separating «the sound from the unsound, and the well-bred from the ill-bred», and sending «the latter to other herds, while keeping the former under his own care».[98] Here Plato proposes arguments similar to those he uses in *The Republic*, in particular when he compares the tasks of medicine, practiced according to the teachings of Asclepius, with those of the institutions of justice. Indeed, specifying that «[o]f the many possible modes of purging, some are milder, some more severe», without excluding either one, he adds:

> those that are severest and best a lawgiver who was also a despot might be able to effect, but a lawgiver without despotic power might be well content if, in establishing a new polity and laws, he could effect even the mildest of purgations. The best purge is painful, like all medicines of a drastic nature, – the purge which hales to punishments by means of justice linked with vengeance, crowning the vengeance with exile or death: it, as a rule, clears out the greatest criminals when they are incurable and cause serious damage to the state.[99]

Here the main concern of Plato is to free the state from the presences that constitute a danger for the maintenance of harmony; but it is not so much a matter of eugenically purifying the body of the political community, as guaranteeing what we would call public order. Certainly, according to him, the most effective ways of pursuing this goal are very painful, as are «all medicines of a drastic nature»; in this case, however, it is not so much the medical approach that can exercise a function, but a radically punitive use of justice. Moreover, the need to purify the state to safeguard harmony remains even in the case in which a «milder form of purge» can be adopted; in any case, it is a question of avoiding not so much a risk of physical and biological degeneration of the collective body as the danger of disorder like that which – according to Plato – presents itself when the people suffering from a lack of food are guided by seditious leaders to attack the property of the rich. It is in a case like this that «a milder form of purge» can suffice.

---

98   *Laws*, 735b, vol. I, p. 349.
99   *Laws*, 735d-e, vol. I, p. 351.

> A milder form of purge is one of the following kind: – when, owing to scarcity of food, people are in want, and display a readiness to follow their leaders in an attack on the property of the wealthy, – then the lawgiver, regarding all such as a plague inherent in the body politic, ships them abroad as gently as possible, giving the euphemistic title of "emigration" to their evacuation. By some means or other this must be done by every legislator at the beginning.[100]

More generally, even in cases where order and collective harmony are not in danger, it is still necessary to keep out morally unreliable people who might threaten the country:

> we shall test thoroughly by every kind of test and by length of time the vicious among those who attempt to enter our present state as citizens, and so prevent their arrival, whereas we shall welcome the virtuous with all possible graciousness and goodwill.

Also in this case, therefore, it is important to understand in a moral rather than a biopolitical sense the "purifications" and "selections" that Plato purports to propose when outlining his strategies for re-founding the state – not that this makes them more acceptable or even appreciable, naturally. In this sense, however, it cannot be ignored that the main dangers that he believes should be avoided are those deriving from the imbalances in the distribution of wealth, or «fierce and dangerous strife concerning the distribution of land and money and the cancelling of debts».[101] That these are – according to him – the main sources of danger is shown by the conviction with which he claims that men should make «a kind of rule of moderation» and believe

> that poverty consists, not in decreasing one's substance, but in increasing one's greed. For this is the main foundation of the security of a state, and on this as on a firm keel it is possible to build whatever kind of civic organisation.

---

100 *Laws*, 735e-736a, vol. I, p. 351.
101 *Laws*, 736c, vol. I, p. 353.

The security of the state and the possibility that it constitutes a true civic organization find their main basis not in the physical power of its collective body, but in a general morality that consists first of all in moderating appetites and, in particular «in renouncing avarice by the aid of justice».[102]

8. *The difficulty of being breeders*

As is known, it is in the *Statesman* – intermediate work from a chronological point of view between *The Republic* and the *Laws* – that Plato carries out a particularly wide reflection on the possibility of comparing he who exercises power over the state to the figure of the pastor as a breeder. In reality although this comparison – after a long series of in-depth analyses – seems to be feasible, it subsequently proves to be substantially erroneous. In fact, according to Plato, it must be noted, first of all, that there are many figures that could claim, together with the statesman, to be breeders of men.

> For instance, merchant, husbandmen, and all who prepare grain for use, and also gymnastic trainers and physicians would certainly all dispute with the herdsmen of humanity, whom we have called statesmen, and would assert that they themselves take care of the tending of humanity, and not the tending of the common herd only, but even that of the rulers themselves.[103]

Secondly, the comparison between the shepherd and he who exercises power over the community appears more adequate if it refers to the divinity that, in the mythical time of Cronus, presided over the life of humanity whose needs, moreover, were easily satisfied at that time by the abundance of resources naturally guaranteed by the earth; not surprisingly in that situation «there were no states», so politics were not necessary.[104] That divine

---

102 *Laws*, 736e, vol. I, p. 355.
103 Plato, *The Statesman*, in Plato, *The Statesman*, *Philebus*, trans. by Harold N. Fowler, *Ion*, trans. by W. R. Lamb (Cambridge Mass.: Harvard University / London: William Heinemann, 1952), 267e-268a, p. 45.
104 *The Statesman*, 272a, p. 59.

shepherd – according to Plato – is he «who alone ought to have the care of human beings as shepherds and neat herds care for their flocks and herds, and therefore alone deserves to be honoured with that appellation».[105]

In any case, the main reason for considering the statesman's comparison to the shepherd or herdsman inadequate is that the definition of breeder of men is more appropriate for other figures. Plato insists on this by proposing, among others, an argument similar to the one he already proposed in *The Republic* where – as we have seen – he believes it is possible to compare the art of the ruler with other arts, including that of the shepherd, only to the extent in which they «do hold rule», each pursuing in its own way «what is beneficial to its subject».[106] Here, in fact, is how he expresses himself in the *Statesman* when it seems clear to him that it is necessary to go beyond the hypothesis of comparing one who governs the state to a shepherd or herdsman:

> All the other herdsmen have this in common that they feed their respective herds; but the statesman does not, yet we gave him the name of herdsman, when we ought to have given him one which is common to them all. (...) Is not caring for herds common to them all, with no especial mention of feeding or another activity? If we called it an art of tending herds or caring for them or managing them, as all herdsmen do, we could wrap up the statesman with the rest, since the argument showed that we ought to do so.[107]

Therefore, the idea of caring or managing, and not that of breeding or feeding, allows us to characterize in general the activity of the statesman without having to compare it to that of a particular figure of which it must be considered a sort of political derivative. Indeed, according to Plato, «no other art would advance a stronger claim than that of kingship to be the art of caring for the whole human community and ruling all mankind».[108] Once the political art as an art of caring has been distinguished from the art of breeding, it will

---

105 *The Statesman*, 275b, p. 69.
106 *The Republic*, 342c-d and 346e, vol. I, pp. 63 and 79.
107 *The Statesman*, 275d-e, p. 71.
108 *The Statesman*, 276b-c, p. 73.

be possible to understand that what makes it political in a full sense is the way of exercising the power that corresponds to it.

> And if we call the art of those who use compulsion tyrannical or something of the sort and the voluntary care of voluntary bipeds political, may we not declare that he who possesses this latter art of caretaking is really the true king and statesman?[109]

It is not possible, therefore, to believe that the Platonic statesman is a breeder of men for the simple reason that, despite everything, he is not comparable to a shepherd or a herdsman. As is known, Plato goes so far as to argue that the politician must be compared to the weaver as he is capable of intertwining and harmonizing the different and better natures of men in the political community, in particular those of «the decorous» with those of «the courageous» people.[110] It cannot, therefore, be argued that the weaver, after all, is nothing but «a manager of shepherds, an owner of the ranch who takes care of the whole community by ruling over the shepherds who in turn look after its individual members».[111] Plato, first of all, believes that the specificity of the activity of the statesman can be defined and maintained only if it is distinguished and kept at a distance from the various activities that are subordinate to it in the city-state.[112] Moreover, if it is true that the statesman cannot, however, do without having direct collaborators, in reality not even these will be comparable to shepherds. There are three main sciences which these collaborators will use: rhetoric which has «the power of persuading a multitude or a mob by telling edifying stories»;[113] military science which has «[t]he power of determining how war shall be waged against those upon whom we have declared war»;[114] the science of the righteous judge who «is guardian of laws and a servant of the kingly power».[115]

---

109 *The Statesman*, 276e, p. 75.
110 *The Statesman*, 308b-311c, pp. 185-95.
111 *On the Greek Origins of Biopolitics*, p. 82.
112 *The Statesman*, 287b-291b, pp. 111-23.
113 *The Statesman*, 304c-d, p. 171.
114 *The Statesman*, 304e, p. 171.
115 *The Statesman*, 305b-c, p. 173.

In any case, even the *Statesman* confronts us with Plato's insistent concern to construct a political community based on harmony, and capable of averting its breakdown in any way. Therefore, even in this work, for him the education of citizens in the virtues necessary for this purpose cannot fail to play a fundamental role; as in his other political works, on the other hand, he does not believe that education always gives appreciable results.[116] In fact, he does not rule out using «the punishment of death and exile and deprivation of the most important civic rights» against those «who have no capacity for courage and self-restraint» or to put «under the yoke of slavery» those «who wallow in ignorance and craven humility».[117] Therefore, finally, he considers it appropriate to encourage marriages that allow for the balanced combination of the best natures, or, once again, the «decorous» people with the «courageous» ones so that the right mix of these characteristics can be found in their children.[118] On the other hand, it is precisely in this regard that politics, as an art of weaving, rather than as a pastoral art, can fully fulfill its essential educational function, striving to create conditions in which «both classes have one and the same opinion about the honourable and the good».

> For indeed the whole business of the kingly weaving is comprised in this and this alone, – in never allowing the self-restrained characters to be separated from the courageous, but in weaving them together by common beliefs and honours and dishonours and opinions and interchanges of pledges, thus making of them a smooth and, as we say, well-woven fabric, and then entrusting to them in common for ever the offices of the state.[119]

Despite the perplexities or concerns that this ethical-political perspective can raise, it is, nevertheless, difficult to maintain that it is oriented and motivated by an essentially biopolitical intent.

---

116 *The Statesman*, 308d-e, pp. 185-7.
117 *The Statesman*, 308e-309a, p. 187.
118 *The Statesman*, 310c-d, p. 193.
119 *The Statesman*, 310e-311a, pp. 193-5.

9. *Number of citizens and the need for leisure*

Finally, it is necessary to consider the hypothesis that Aristotle himself was not immune to a certain biopolitical inclination or that, indeed, for him «the central topics of biopolitics are the very keystone of politics and the art of government».[120] Ojakangas maintains that the proof of the marked biopolitical orientation of Aristotle's thought is the fact that, for him,

> the ultimate aim of the art of government is to promote the happiness of the city-state and felicity of its inhabitant, the main means for achieving this being the regulation of the quality and quantity of population according to the immanent norms of life known through the scientific inquiry of human nature.[121]

In fact, in *Politics*, in the authoritative English translation we consider here, Aristotle seems to want to address in biopolitical terms the question that is indicated with the expression «supply of population».[122] However, in the original text Aristotle does not use terms corresponding to our idea of population. Indeed, the expression translated with «supply of population» is «*plethos ton anthropon*», literally: "number" or "multitude of men". Moreover, in other parts of the same chapter, Aristotle uses expressions such as «*plethos ton enoikounton*» ("number" or "multitude of inhabitants") or simply «*plethos*» ("number" or "multitude").[123] In short, we can say that there is no real reference to the population as a demographic, biological or ethnic community; therefore, Aristotle cannot be attributed too easily with the primary intent of promoting the happiness of the city-state in a biopolitical sense, namely to preserve and increase above all the well-being and physical health of the community. It will suffice here to consider that, even before examining the question of the "number of men", he clearly

---

120 *On the Greek Origins of Biopolitics*, p. 6.
121 *On the Greek Origins of Biopolitics*, p. 39.
122 Aristotle, *Politics*, 1326a, 7-9, p. 553. This translation of Aristotle's work corresponds to the 1959 reprint of the same 1944 edition referred to by Ojakangas.
123 *Politics*, 1325b, 33-1326b, 25, pp. 552-9.

states that his real purpose is to understand what could be the best «number of citizens» («*plethos politón*»).[124] This inescapable preliminary clarification implies that it is not so much a matter of establishing the right amount of inhabitants in a generic sense, as of understanding how to ensure that the inhabitants include an adequate quantity of citizens with full rights, that is, free men able to participate in public life and to actively practice citizenship. It does not seem that there is another way of understanding what Aristotle explains in these terms:

> even if it be right to judge the state by the test of its multitude, this ought not to be done with regard to the multitude of any and every class (for states are doubtless bound to contain a large number of slaves and resident aliens and foreigners), but the test should be the number of those who are a portion of the state – the special parts of which a state consists.[125]

Aristotle's reference to «slaves, and resident aliens and foreigners», that necessarily live in a state, means that, since they are not citizens as per material and juridical conditions, they cannot actively participate in political life and cannot even be considered decisive parties as far as the state carrying out its task of guaranteeing happiness. Therefore, it is precisely the presence of an adequate «number of those who are in a portion of the state», i.e. of men in a position to actively practice citizenship, which must be considered absolutely necessary for this purpose.

On the other hand, the fact that – as we have already seen – for Aristotle the happiness that the state must promote does not consist simply in health and material well-being is reaffirmed here through the clear indication of this purpose in the possibility of practicing virtue to the benefit of the political community itself. In fact, it is in relation to happiness understood in this way that – according to him – we can distinguish the forms of political constitution and arrive at identifying the best composition of the state that can also guarantee the indispensable material, military, economic, religious and juridical conditions of the same happiness:

---

124 *Politics*, 1325b, 40-41, p. 553, Greek text, p. 552.
125 *Politics*, 1326a, 18-22, p. 555.

the state is one form of partnership of similar people, and its object is the best life that is possible. And since the greatest good is happiness, and this is some perfect activity or employment of virtue, and since it has so come about that it is possible for some men to participate in it, but for others only to a small extent or not at all, it is clear that this is the cause for there arising different kinds and varieties of state and several forms of constitution; for as each set of people pursues participation in happiness in a different manner and by different means they make for themselves different modes of life and different constitutions. And we must also further consider how many there are of these things referred to that are indispensable for the existence of a state; for among them will be the things which we pronounce to be parts of a state, owing to which their presence is essential.[126]

The conclusion of this reasoning is that self-sufficiency (*autàrkeia*) is the basic general assumption of the existence of the state and that the classes indispensable for this purpose are: «a number of farmers who will provide the food, and craftsmen, and the military class, and the wealthy, and priests and judges to decide questions of necessity and of interests».[127] In other words, with the presence and the activities of these classes the set of pre-political conditions of the fully political life of the city-state can be guaranteed.

Of course, the question of the total quantity of inhabitants is far from irrelevant in this sense, but it too, like many other issues, must be addressed using the criteria of measurement and equilibrium. In this respect too, indeed, it is necessary that its main purpose be not the indefinite strengthening of the state, but its self-sufficiency which is the indispensable condition of its independence, of its own political freedom and, therefore, also of the practicability of «the best life» and «the happiness» as «perfect activity or employment of virtue»:

for certainly beauty is usually found in number and magnitude, but there is a due measure of magnitude for a city-state as there also is for all other things – animals, plants, tools. (...) Similarly a state consisting

---

126 *Politics*, 1328a, 35-1328b4, p. 571.
127 *Politics*, 1328b, 20-23, p. 573.

of too few people will not be self-sufficing (which is an essential quality of a state), and one consisting of too many, though self-sufficing in the mere necessaries, will be so in the way in which a nation (*ethnos*) is, and not as a state, since it will not be easy for it to possess constitutional government – for who will command its over-swollen multitude in war? or who will serve as its herald, unless he have the lungs of a Stentor? It follows that the lowest limit for the existence of a state is when it consists of a population (*plethous*) that reaches the minimum number (*plethos*) that is self-sufficient for the purpose of living the good life after the manner of a political community.[128]

Here it is evident that the total number of inhabitants must not be excessive since increasing it indefinitely would perhaps make it possible to form or reinforce an *ethnos*, a collectivity as an ethnic entity, but not to establish and provide for the existence of a fully political community. This number must be contained within a certain limit, not because this guarantees the selection of the healthiest men and, therefore, the most capable of increasing the power of the community; the limit and the balance that must be maintained in the quantity of inhabitants, besides being necessary conditions for reaching and maintaining the state's self-sufficiency, are, above all, indispensable bases of the feasibility of political life in its various forms.

> The activities of the state are those of the rulers and those of the persons ruled, and the work of a ruler is to direct the administration and to judge law-suits; but in order to decide questions of justice and in order to distribute the offices according to merit it is necessary for the citizens to know each other's personal characters, since where this does not happen to be the case the business of electing officials and trying law-suits is bound to go badly; haphazard decision is unjust in both matters, and this must obviously prevail in an excessively numerous community.

Certainly Aristotle's discourse implies a discriminatory orientation towards certain social figures, an orientation that is expressed, above all, in his conception of the right to citizenship

---

128 *Politics*, 1326a, 34-1326b, 10, p. 557.

and the active practice of the latter. He himself makes this orientation clear when he indicates not only the slaves, but also the resident aliens and foreigners as those who – in one way or another – cannot enjoy the rights of the citizen.[129] This was a consolidated vision and generally shared by the inhabitants of the Greek *poleis* and even by Aristotle, a «resident alien» himself in Athens. He had no intention of questioning this vision; what he purported to do, rather, was to take it as a reference point to define the conditions in which political participation and active and virtuous citizenship would really be possible for those who were entitled to it. And here, undoubtedly, his specific conception of human nature plays a fundamental role. In particular, with regard to slaves, as we have already seen, this conception includes the idea that there are both slaves and free men by nature; the exclusion of slaves from citizenship, for him, can only derive from this as a necessary consequence. Furthermore, Aristotle accepts as an obvious fact the total or partial exclusion of foreigners and metics (resident aliens) from citizenship rights; which, of course, is explained by the fundamental importance that is generally attributed to autochthony in the Greek cities. But if we hasten to deduce that Aristotle's willingness to exclude a large number of inhabitants from citizenship is proof of his biopolitical inclination, we risk missing out on what is almost certainly the fundamental motivation for this attitude. It is the contempt that Aristotle, and the Greek culture of his time, reserved as much for the work of slaves as for overly strenuous activities – such as agriculture – and those activities that limit individuals to their private interests, such as the crafts and commerce which resident aliens were normally engaged in.[130]

---

129 *Politics*, 1326b, 21-24, p. 559: «it is easy for foreigners and resident aliens to usurp the rights of citizenship, for the excessive number of the population makes it not difficult to escape detection».

130 See Arendt, *The Human Condition*, pp. 81-3, including footnote n. 7. On the contempt that the Athenian citizens reserved for commercial activity at the time of Aristotle, see also Karl Polanyi, 'Market Elements and Economic Planning in Antiquity', in *For a New West: Essays, 1919-1958*, ed. by Giorgio Resta and Mariavittoria Catanzariti (Cambridge, UK: Polity Press, 2014), especially pp. 155-62.

These activities – according to Aristotle – can only hinder the virtuous practice of free citizenship and the political pursuit of the common good. This is how one can interpret what the Greek philosopher says when he denied the possibility for craftsmen, merchants and farmers to be truly citizens, even if they carried out activities that were, for the most part, indispensable for the state, and they were often free men.

> But at present we are studying the best constitution, and this is the constitution under which the state would be most happy, and it has been stated before that happiness cannot be forthcoming without virtue; it is therefore clear from these considerations that in the most nobly constituted state, and the one that possesses men that are absolutely just, not merely just relatively to the principle that is the basis of the constitution, the citizens must not live a mechanic or a mercantile life (for such a life is ignoble and inimical to virtue), nor yet must those who are to be citizens in the best state be tillers of the soil (for leisure is needed both for the development of virtue and for active participation in politics).[131]

In short, from this point of view, we can say that the real object of Aristotle's discriminations are certain activities rather than specific social figures; precisely this would imply the exclusion of, or, at least, the need to consider with great caution, the idea that it is a biopolitical intent that guides his effort to identify the best number and quality of the inhabitants of a city-state. Moreover, even the fundamental importance that, according to him, should be attributed to leisure (the condition that the Greeks indicated with the term *scholé*) in order to be able to practice citizenship makes it very difficult to include his vision of politics in a biopolitical perspective. In this vision, leisure and the virtuous use of it are so important that they constitute the decisive conditions of a good life and the happiness that politics and the state must promote. Leisure is one of the main objectives that both men and states must pursue in their existence, thus avoiding dedicating themselves to the pure increase of wealth, power and domination:

---

131 *Politics*, 1328b, 34-1329a, 2, p. 575.

life as a whole is divided into business and leisure, and war and peace, and our actions are aimed some of them at things necessary and useful, others at things noble. (...) [W]ar must be for the sake of peace, business for the sake of leisure, things necessary and useful for the purpose of things noble. The statesman therefore must legislate with all these considerations in view (...) and aiming more particularly at the greater goods and the ends. And the same principle applies in regard to modes of life and choices of conduct: a man should be capable of engaging in business and war, but still more capable of living in peace and leisure; and he should do what is necessary and useful, but still more should he do what is noble.[132]

Therefore, «to be able to employ leisure» is both an objective and an essential condition of an education to virtue that must be practiced both by the state as a whole and by individuals.[133] If citizens are able to employ leisure in a virtuous manner, they will be able to practice citizenship in a virtuous manner. Therefore, education must not limit itself to teaching «reading and writing and drawing», as «useful for the purposes of life», and «gymnastics as contributing to manly courage»; in fact, «nature itself seeks to be able not only to engage rightly in business but also to occupy leisure nobly; for (...) this is the first principle of all things».[134] For these reasons, among the disciplines that young people should be taught, music must certainly be included, because it «is useful as a pastime in leisure, which is evidently the purpose for which people actually introduce it, for they rank it as a form of pastime that they think proper for free men».[135] Moreover, the state will certainly have to deal with military education, but this will have to have precise goals that cannot be limited to the increase of its power and its domination over others.[136] Even war training, therefore, must be practiced in view of leisure and peace.[137]

---

132 *Politics*, 1333a, 31-1333b, 2, pp. 607-9.
133 *Politics*, 1334a, 14-17, p. 613.
134 *Politics*, 1337b, 31-34, p. 639.
135 *Politics*, 1338a, 21-24, p. 643.
136 *Politics*, 1333b, 29-32, p. 611; see also 1333b, 40-1334a, 3, p. 611.
137 *Politics*, 1334a, 3-11, p. 611-3.

Of course, it is far from easy to acquire, together with the others, the virtues necessary to be able to employ leisure. Therefore, according to Aristotle, it is necessary to pay specific attention to the «nature and habit and reason» of men, making sure to educate them through good habits and reason. This means that the state must implement its educational tasks in a precise order:

> in the first place it is necessary for the training of the body to precede that of the mind, and secondly for the training of the appetite to precede that of the intelligence; but the training of the appetite must be for the sake of the intellect, and that of the body for the sake of the soul.[138]

Now, since in these concatenations the training of the body represents a preliminary step to others, the state cannot help but to make this training be preceded by a specific attention to procreation, to encourage the birth of children endowed with the nature best adapted to guarantee the best results of virtue education. Therefore, in this regard, the lawgiver «must first pay attention to the union of the sexes, and settle when and in what condition a couple should practise matrimonial intercourse»;[139] in this sense Aristotle is concerned with establishing

> for how long a time it is suitable for them to serve the state in the matter of producing children. For the offspring of too elderly parents, as those of too young ones, are born imperfect both in body and mind, and the children of those that have arrived at old age are weaklings.[140]

Above all, there are prescriptions regarding age, season and climatic conditions in which it is appropriate to practice the marital relationships that Aristotle believes it is necessary to propose;[141] equally important for him is to establish rules concerning «the particular kind of bodily constitution in the parents that will be most beneficial for the offspring». These rules, however, will not simply aim to identify the best physical structures of the parents;

---

138 *Politics*, 1334b, 7-28, pp. 615-7.
139 *Politics*, 1334b, 30-33, p. 617.
140 *Politics*, 1335b, 29-32, p. 625.
141 *Politics*, 1334b, 29- 1335b, 3, pp. 617-23.

rather they will tend to favor the «bodily habits» that «have been trained by exercise, but not by exercises that are violent, and not for one form of labour only, as is the athlete's habit of body, but for the pursuits of free men».[142] Finally, it is in a framework like this that it seems appropriate to Aristotle that

> there be a law that no deformed child shall be reared; but on the ground of number of children, if the regular customs hinder any of those born being exposed, there must be a limit fixed to the procreation of offspring, and if any people have a child as a result of intercourse in contravention of these regulations, abortion must be practised on it before it has developed sensation and life; for the line between lawful and unlawful abortion will be marked by the fact of having sensation and being alive.[143]

It may be considered that these aspects of Aristotle's discourse have a biopolitical flavor; but it is, however, difficult to maintain that they constitute the characterizing element of his political philosophy.

10. *Between despotism and virtue*

When considering from a general point of view the possibility of interpreting Aristotelian thought in biopolitical terms, it may be important to clarify precisely if and in what sense – according to the Greek philosopher – there must be usefulness of family life for the state or the political sphere.

Returning to Hannah Arendt, in this regard it is appropriate to recall her thesis according to which in antiquity «the mastering of the necessities of life in the household was the condition for the freedom of the *polis*».[144] In this sense, the author highlights the "despotic" and even violent nature of the power that the head of the family could exercise in the *oikos* sphere so that the incessant necessities of life could be faced and satisfied. In her opinion, in the private household organization in antiquity

---

142 *Politics*, 1335b, 9-12, p. 623.
143 *Politics*, 1335b, 21-27, pp. 623-5.
144 Arendt, *The Human Condition*, pp. 30-1.

> force and violence are justified (...) because they are the only means to master necessity – for instance, by ruling over slaves – and to become free. Because all human beings are subject to necessity, they are entitled to violence toward others; violence is the prepolitical act of liberating oneself from the necessity of life for the freedom of world.[145]

This thesis by Arendt tends to mark the difference that – according to her – existed in ancient Greece between the domestic sphere, in which the harsh necessities of life were dealt with, and the public space of the *polis*, in which the conditions were created for the free practice of citizenship and political participation. With this thesis, however, the author also risks leading us to believe that the aim of the ancient *oikonomia* was purely and simply to guarantee the conditions of physical health and material well-being so that the free citizens who made up the family could intervene in public life without difficulties. Furthermore, by insisting on the idea that «the household head ruled with uncontested, despotic power» over family life,[146] in actual fact, Arendt underestimates the complexity and importance of the moral problems that those who had the power as the head of the family had to face and resolve.

In this sense it must be emphasized that in *Politics* Aristotle insists on the differences between the various power relations that the head of the household must establish with the various members of the family, such as relationships between «master and slave, husband and wife, father and children». According to him, only the relationship with the slaves, unlike the others, could have a despotic nature, i.e. that of master (in Greek: *despotes*), since «the free rules the slave, the male the female, and the man the child in a different way».[147] He thus shows that the head of the family had to know how to vary the use of his power in a far more flexible way than would seem necessary in the exercise of an authority without limits: if over the slave he must exercise the authority of the «master», «over the wife» he had «to exercise republican

---

145 *The Human Condition*, p. 31.
146 *The Human Condition*, p. 27.
147 Aristotle, *Politics*, 1253b 5-10; 1260a, 10-11, pp. 13-5, 63.

government and over the children monarchical».[148] Moreover, even the power exercised over slaves by no means implies that with them he should «use command only; for admonition is more properly employed with slaves than with children».[149] In short, according to Aristotle, the power of the head of the family cannot be adequately exercised without being properly adapted and regulated, without being oriented by a strong moral concern for the different forms of excellence, i.e. of virtue (*aretè*), of the various members of the family, a concern that must permeate the *oikonomia* itself. According to him, in fact,

> household management takes more interest in the human members of the household than in its inanimate property, and in excellence of these than in that of its property, which we style riches, and more in that of its free members than in that of slaves.[150]

It is, above all if guided by this moral concern of the head of the household, that, for the author of *Politics*, the *oikonomia* can be beneficial for the destiny of the *polis*, since it is expressed in the solicitation of the virtue of the various members of the family and, in particular, in the education of the children and the wife.

> For since every household is part of a state, and these relationships are part of the household, and the excellence of the part must have regard to that of the whole, it is necessary that the education both of the children and of the women should be carried on with a regard to the form of the constitution, if it makes any difference as regards the goodness of the state for the children and the women to be good. And it must necessarily make a difference; for the women are a half of the free population, and the children grow up to be the partners in the government of the state.[151]

Here, in short, it appears evident that – according to Aristotle – a truly positive relationship between the private and public

---

148 *Politics*, 1259a 38-1259b, 4, pp. 58-9.
149 *Politics*, 1260b, 7-8, p. 67.
150 *Politics*, 1259b, 18-19, p. 59.
151 *Politics*, 1260b, 14-21, p. 67. On the relations between the political constitution and the formation of the virtue of citizens see also *ibid.*, 1332a, 34-1332b, 11, pp. 599-601.

dimensions cannot be based simply on the material contribution that the *oikonomia* can give to the well-being and to the overall health of the *polis*; it must be based, above all, on the ethical commitment of the head of the family and on the moral education of its members. Therefore, this fundamental aspect of household management seems to confirm the idea that in the Aristotelian *polis* no immediate and systematic relationships are established between the attention of the *oikonomia* to biological life and the attention of politics to the exercise of public power and citizenship; indeed, we can say more precisely that, if these relations are given, they are subordinated to the pre-eminence of the ethical tasks to which the *oikonomia* is called to respond. From this point of view, the ethical qualification of the *oikonomia* seems to take on a sort of "civic" function that goes beyond the material and biological purposes of household management. It is also evident that the essential presupposition of this ethical qualification cannot but be the willingness of the one who exercises power over the *oikos* to govern, first of all, his *ethos* in order to be able to govern and also to form the *ethos* of the members of his family.[152]

This is what Foucault highlights on a more general level in his research on the practice of the *care of the self*, through which – according to him – the free man of antiquity, especially in Greece, tried to acquire and maintain an ethical mastery of his own behavior, which he would not have achieved if he had let himself indulge in the abuse of his power, of his position, of his role.[153] According to the French philosopher, this practice found in the relationship between spouses an important terrain for verifying its effectiveness precisely because in terms of power this relationship was clearly

---

152 On this topic see Aristotle, *Politics*, 1259b, 18-1260b, 20, pp. 59-67; on the general relationship between *ethos* and virtue see: Aristotle, *Nicomachean Ethics,* trans. by Horace Rackham (London: William Heinemann/Cambridge, Mass.: Harvard University Press, 1968), 1103a, 17-110b, 7, pp. 71-3; Aristotle, *Politics*, 1332a, 39-1332b, 11, p. 601.

153 Foucault, *The Use of Pleasure*, p. 23; see also Michel Foucault, 'The Ethics of the Concern for Self as a Practice of Freedom', in *The essential works of Michel Foucault*, I, *Ethics: Subjectivity and Truth*, ed. by Paul Rabinow, trans. by Robert Hurley and others (New York: The New Press, 1997), p. 288.

unbalanced to the benefit of the male, on the legal level as well.[154] Generally, the wife had to adhere almost unquestionably to a relationship of submission and loyalty to her husband; vice versa, the latter, although he had obligations of protection towards his wife, was not obliged to have an exclusive sexual relationship with her. Nevertheless – Foucault argues – from the reflections that various thinkers (Isocrates, Xenophon, Plato, Aristotle) devoted to the marriage relationship, clear indications emerge in favor of austerity and the limitation of men's extramarital relations.[155] Xenophon and Aristotle in particular suggested the groom pay attention to the sensitivity of the bride, since such attention would allow him to become fully worthy of his power as head of the family and landlord. Respect for his wife had to be part of an effort to match his behavior to the need to govern the *oikos* well.[156] In this sense, he had to worry not only about his personal relationship with his wife, but also about the domestic *ménage* over which he could feel morally entitled to exercise an authority if he had gained temperance and a mastery of himself (*enkràteia*) that would allow him a balanced use of his power. Moreover, the husband's self-accountability towards his wife and towards the home could produce important effects on his public reputation and his ability to act politically: by virtuously carrying out his private role, he would show that he could also perform his political role virtuously.[157]

Ultimately, Foucault's analysis of these issues also suggests that in the context of the *oikos* in its relationship with the *polis*, the formation of virtuous behaviors was generally more relevant than the attention to health and well-being – as indeed even our previous direct reading of Aristotle's *Politics* seems to demonstrate.

---

154 *The Use of Pleasure*, Part Three: 'Economics'.
155 In *The Use of Pleasure* Michel Foucault refers above all to the work of: Isocrates, *To Nicocles*; Xenophon, *Economics*; Plato, *Laws;* Aristotle, *Politics* and *Economics*.
156 *The Use of Pleasure*, p. 165.
157 *The Use of Pleasure*, p. 151. On the issue of *care of the self* see, in addition to this work: Michel Foucault, *The Care of the Self*, trans. by Robert Hurley (New York: Pantheon Books, 1986); Michel Foucault, *The Hermeneutics of the Subject. Lectures at the Collège de France, 1981-1982*, ed. by Fréderic Gros, trans. by Graham Burchell (New York: Palgrave McMillan, 2005).

11. *An unproductive biopolitics?*

Therefore, if we want to draw some conclusions about the hypothesis of attributing to Plato and Aristotle the role of "theorists" or even the "founders" of biopolitics, we can say, at least, that those elements in their thought that seem to testify in favor of this hypothesis, in reality do not make it possible to effectively characterize this thought itself as biopolitical. Their insistence on the indispensable supremacy that virtue must assume in the ambits of both public and private existence and the marked moral qualification of their political perspectives represent almost insurmountable impediments to this possibility. In other words, since for both philosophers the political quality of the state can be guaranteed, first of all, through the exercise of virtue and the care of the *ethos* of rulers and citizens, it is not possible for the preservation and enhancement of life to overlap with this fundamental requirement and take on the value of primary political aims. From this point of view, there is an element common to their visions that must be considered essential: the fact that they do not allow the economic activities and productive capacities of individuals and the community to be considered as determining and qualifying factors of the destiny of the state. Here it will suffice to recall the importance and implications that these visions have: the general need for moderation and balance or the condemnation of enrichment as an end in itself, which both philosophers express; the consideration by Plato of the sphere of private interests as a source of danger for the cohesion and unity of the state; contempt for work and commercial activity or the exaltation of leisure as an essential purpose of the existence of the citizen and the state, by Aristotle, etc.

Noting non-negligible aspects such as these indirectly serves to highlight that only by assuming the productive and economic development of the community as a strategic task, could the political perspectives of Plato and Aristotle effectively create the conditions for translating the administration and strengthening of life into a primary political purpose. With this we mean that to speak of biopolitics in the strict sense we cannot ignore the precise meanings that the exercise of biopower has assumed in modernity and the factors that have allowed its systematic and increasing development. In this sense, it is not possible to believe that a biopolitics would ever really have emerged without the specific forms of naturalization of collective existence that have led to the transformation of modern society into a set of forces and productive resources to be promoted, governed and developed. This naturalization found its first conditions in the assumption of the economy as an essential element of the nature and life of the state at the time of mercantilist policies and police state. It then became established and developed through the identification of the very nature of the economy with the spontaneous functioning of the free market, that is, after the rise of liberal governmentality. Finally, it was founded on the scientific thematization of life as a natural phenomenon endowed with regularity and capable of self-regulation which, on the one hand, results from the dynamic interaction between a collective level (population-species) and an individual level (body-organism) of its own explication; on the other hand, it is always susceptible to adaptation, regulation or normalization aimed mainly at the real or presumed improvement of its potential. Especially political economy, biological sciences, social medicine, demography played a fundamental role exactly to the extent that they are essentially modern powers-knowledge.[158]

The hierarchical and discriminatory conceptions of human nature that form the backdrop to the political visions of Plato and Aristotle may also imply a "selection", possibly a thanatopolitics, of individuals based on their "natural" vocations and ethical inclinations. However, they are not suitable for transforming society into an aggregation of living beings that tend to increase their physical, biological and productive power as a condition of

---

158 On all this we refer once again here to Foucault's research referred to in the previous chapter and, in particular, to *Security, Territory, Population*, pp. 29-79, 333-58. On the importance and the political implications of the new economic-biological naturalism that emerges in the 18th century, also see Andrea Cavazzini, 'Vie, conduite, économie. Essai épistémologico-politique', *La Rose de Personne*, 6 (2012), 95-124.

enrichment, prosperity and the growth of individual and collective capacities to dominate the world or others.

From this point of view, if there is a role that the Christian pastoral power, or Christianity in general, may have exercised on the genesis of biopolitics as an essentially modern phenomenon, it must not be sought in improbable pastoral strategies of systematic management and manipulation of the fate and potential of natural life; rather, this role can be found in the influence that the Christian sacralization of life and the projection of its salvation in a dimension of an afterlife may have exercised on the genesis of the *ethos* of modern man. As Hannah Arendt argues, the importance that modernity attaches to the phenomena of life is the other side of the «world alienation» of modern man, to which Christianity indirectly contributed through its «fundamental belief in the sacredness of life» and the transfer of the goal of human aspirations to a otherworldly sphere.

> The reason why life asserted itself as the ultimate point of reference in the modern age and has remained the highest good of modern society is that the modern reversal operated within the fabric of a Christian society whose fundamental belief in the sacredness of life has survived, and has even remained completely unshaken by, secularization and the general decline of the Christian faith. In other words, the modern reversal followed and left unchallenged the most important reversal with which Christianity had broken into the ancient world, a reversal that was politically even more far-reaching and, historically at any rate, more enduring than any specific dogmatic content or belief. For the Christian "glad tidings" of the immortality of the individual human life had reversed the ancient relationship between man and world and promoted the most mortal thing, human life, to the position of immortality, which up to then the cosmos had held.[159]

The secularization processes of modern society – according to Arendt – have not brought man back into the world; «modern man at any rate did not gain this world when he lost the other

---

159 *The Human Condition*, p. 313-4.

world».[160] Modernity, since its beginnings, has been marked by a progressive distancing of man from the materiality of the earth and the common world exemplarily represented by the *polis* in antiquity. The cause of this departure can be found in different ways in: «the invention of telescope and the development of a new science that considers the nature of the earth from the viewpoint of the universe»;[161] the «shrinkage of the globe» initiated by the great geographical discoveries and completed by the speed of contemporary means of communication;[162] the affirmation of the «innerworldly asceticism» promoted by the Protestant Reformation, which Max Weber identified as «the innermost spring of the new capitalist mentality»;[163] «the expropriation of the peasantry», in which an indefinite sequence of expropriations and appropriations of land, functional to economic accumulation, was initiated in Europe;[164] and finally, the affirmation of subjectivism in modern philosophical thought starting from Descartes.[165]

It is, in fact, in the context of an overall world alienation caused by processes like these that – according to Arendt – life has established itself as an object to which modern man pays increasing attention. He did not respond to the decline of his faith in an otherworldly immortality by reconnecting to "immortality" or to the simple permanence of an earthly and tangible world.[166] Rather, he has turned in on himself, on his vital needs, desires, processes and impulses that pass through him, making him feel a material reality which immediately belongs to him, but, at the same time, escapes him because it constantly exposes him to death.

---

160 *The Human Condition*, p. 320.
161 *The Human Condition*, p. 248.
162 *The Human Condition*, pp. 250-1.
163 *The Human Condition*, p. 251. According to Arendt, Max Weber demonstrated in a particularly effective way that for modern man the accumulation of wealth is possible by limiting himself to caring only about himself and his salvation, or that «an enormous, strictly mundane activity is possible without any care for or enjoyment of the world whatever». (p. 254).
164 *The Human Condition*, pp. 251-2.
165 *The Human Condition*, pp. 273-89.
166 *The Human Condition*, pp. 320-1.

What was left was a "natural force", the force of the life process itself, to which all men and all human activities were equally submitted (...) and whose only aim, if it had an aim at all, was survival of the animal species man. (...); individual life became part of the life process, and to labor, to assure the continuity of one's own life and life of his family, was all that was needed.[167]

Rather than adhering unconditionally to theses such as these, it seems appropriate instead not to underestimate their meaning, scope and implications.

---

167 *The Human Condition*, p. 321.

CHAPTER THREE
FROM THE *POLIS* TO GLOBALIZATION
Biopolitics and Philosophy
in Agamben, Negri, Esposito

0. *Preamble*

Among the scholars who have attributed crucial importance to the hypothesis that the roots of biopolitics can be traced back to the culture of ancient Greece certainly one cannot neglect Giorgio Agamben. Moreover, the Italian philosopher has carried out a reflection on biopolitics that goes far beyond the limits of the verification of this hypothesis and has become one of the main references of the intense debate that has developed on this subject since the nineties of the last century. The great influence that this author now exerts on the general reception of the concept of biopolitics makes his theses essential, considering also that they relate to Foucault's analysis in a rather critical, as well as particularly original, way. Therefore, it is opportune to examine his positions here, not only because they allow us to deepen further the possibility of tracing the origins of biopolitics back to antiquity, but also for the considerable implications that the author derives from this hypothesis, showing how it interacts with other important elements of his reflection on biopolitics.

It is worth noting, on the other hand, that the importance and density of Agamben's research indirectly testify to a particular vivacity that Italian philosophical research on biopolitics has expressed in recent decades, attracting notable international attention. In this chapter, therefore, the theses of two other Italian philosophers, Antonio Negri and Roberto Esposito, who have offered a significant contribution to the debate on biopolitics certainly comparable to that of Agamben, will also be examined, as they have also received great attention worldwide.

Among these authors, Esposito attributed special significance and importance to the common Italian origin of their intense reflection on biopolitics. He argued that this reflection is only a recent expression of a cultural tradition that, at least since Machiavelli, has always been characterized by a special vocation to combine the activity of thought with political commitment and life itself.[1] The deepening of a thesis like this certainly does not fall within the scope of this book; however, here we can at least say that Agamben, Negri and Esposito acquired a great part of the international attention they have been subjected to precisely since they began to treat biopolitics as one of the main themes of their research: the remarkable quality of their reflection has contributed to increasing sensitivity to this issue, which, in turn, was a decisive reason for the vast appreciation they received. Therefore, at least for these reasons, it can be assumed that these exponents of Italian philosophy have a marked ability to link philosophical research with the problems of life itself.[2]

---

1   See Roberto Esposito, *Living Thought: The Origins and Actuality of Italian Philosophy*, trans. by Zakiya Hanafi (Stanford: Stanford University Press, 2012). On the importance that in the last decades a certain political thought of Italian origin has acquired on the world level and on the importance that reflection on biopolitics has assumed in it, see: Lorenzo Chiesa and Alberto Toscano (ed. by), *The Italian Difference: Between Nihilism and Biopolitics* (Melbourne: re.press, 2009); Dario Gentili, *Italian Theory. Dall'operaismo alla biopolitica* (Bologna: il Mulino, 2012); Dario Gentili and Elettra Stimilli (ed. by), *Differenze italiane. Politica e filosofia: mappe e sconfinamenti*, (Rome: DeriveApprodi, 2015); Ruggiero Gorgoglione, *Paradoxien der Biopolitik. Politische Philosophie und Gesellschaftstheorie in Italien* (Bielefeld: transcript, 2016). Also see: Enrica Lisciani-Petrini and Giusi Strummiello (ed. by), *Effetto Italian Thought*, (Macerata: Quodlibet, 2017); Pier Paolo Portinaro, *Le mani su Machiavelli. Una critica dell'"Italian Theory"* (Rome: Donzelli, 2018).

2   There is no doubt, on the other hand, that, among these scholars, Negri is the clearest example of conjugation between an intense activity of *thought* and a *life* (or an existence) clearly marked by *political commitment*. On this, see Antonio Negri, *Galera ed esilio. Storia di un comunista*, ed. by Girolamo De Michele (Florence: Ponte alle Grazie, 2015).

1. *Agamben: the biopolitical structure of sovereignty*

1.1 *Exception and bare life*

Giorgio Agamben recognizes that Foucault was certainly the first to clearly focus on the fact that in modernity «the species and the individual as a simple living body become what is at stake in a society's political strategies».[3] If it is true that biopolitics and biopower are issues on which philosophical investigation must be developed in a radically critical way, the work already carried out by Foucault cannot but constitute its essential starting point. But a first necessity that arises in this regard, according to Agamben, is to make Foucault interact with Hannah Arendt. In fact, the Italian author highlights the fact that the latter, two decades earlier than the French philosopher, «had already analyzed the process that brings *homo laborans* – and with it, biological life as such – gradually to occupy the very center of the political scene of modernity». In agreement with what Foucault later claimed, Arendt – Agamben says – had already linked the profound alteration that, according to her, politics underwent in modern times, precisely to this centrality that biological life has assumed in the public space. However, the fact remains that «Foucault was able to begin his studies of biopolitics with no reference to Arendt's work (which remains, even today, practically without continuation)».[4]

The intersection between the Foucaultian and Arendtian perspectives – according to the Italian philosopher – appears to be necessary, above all because it makes it possible to take research on biopolitics beyond the «difficulties» and «resistances» of both authors so as to be able to grasp some very important implications

---

3   Giorgio Agamben, *Homo Sacer: Sovereign Power and Bare Life*, p. 3. As is known, this is the first of nine books that form the research path that the author has called "Homo Sacer". Recently, they have been collected and rearranged in a single volume: *The Omnibus Homo Sacer* (Stanford: Stanford University Press, 2017). The books of this series that are referred to in this chapter are cited in the editions that preceded the publication of the collection.

4   *Homo Sacer*, p. 6.

of their own reflections on the entry of natural life into the sphere of politics. Foucault, for his part, did not interpret the *concentration camp*, conceived of as an emblematic expression of totalitarianism, as the most representative and consequential form of biopower, since it was inscribed from the beginning in a power that systematically and directly intervenes on the fate of life. Arendt, on the other hand, was not able to connect the reflection proposed in *The Human Condition* on the «very primacy of natural life on political action», with the «penetrating analysis» of totalitarianism, which she had previously done.[5] According to Agamben, in fact, «only because in our age politics had been entirely transformed into biopolitics was it possible for politics to be constituted as totalitarian politics to a degree hitherto unknown».[6]

The importance that Agamben attributes to the *camp* leads him to consider it not only as a paradigmatic form of biopolitics, but also as «the hidden paradigm of the political space of modernity»,[7] to the extent that biopolitics, for him, represents the essential form of the modern exercise of power. Therefore, it is particularly interesting to understand why – according to the Italian author – Foucault was not able to recognize the paradigmatic value of the camp:[8] for Agamben, the main reason for this lack of recognition should lie in the fact that Foucault excludes, from the beginning of his biopower genealogy, the idea that its main focus lies in sovereign power. As is known, the French philosopher presents biopower as heterogeneous with respect to sovereignty, although he is fully aware of the fact that the two forms of power are integrated and interact in the modern state. Vice versa, Agamben believes that the link between biopower and sovereignty is, so to speak, structural: «the inclusion of bare life in the political realm constitutes the original – if concealed – nucleus of sovereign

---

5   *Homo Sacer*, p. 4.
6   *Homo Sacer*, p. 120.
7   *Homo Sacer*, p. 123; see also pp. 119-88. The author has further developed his reflection on the *camp* in Giorgio Agamben, *Remnants of Auschwitz: The Witness and the Archive*, trans. by Daniel Heller-Roazen (New York: Zone Books, 1999).
8   *Homo Sacer*, p. 123.

power. *It can even be said that the production of a biopolitical body is the original activity of sovereign power».*[9]

The author proposes this thesis in such radical terms as to claim that, ultimately, since its inception Western politics has concealed an intimate biopolitical vocation within itself. And this, in his opinion, can be shown by focusing on the separation – which would have been typical of ancient Greece and on which the Aristotelian conception of the *polis* is based – between *zoé* and *bios* or, more precisely, between *the sphere of natural life* and *sphere of political life*. This separation – according to Agamben – does not at all constitute an obstacle to the transformation of politics into biopolitics, since it involves «at the same time an implication (...) of bare life in politically qualified life». If it is true, in fact, that the conceptual distinction between *zoé* and *bios*, or between life and a good life, refers to the concrete distinction of the private space of biological reproduction (*oikos*) from the public space of political action (*polis*), it is equally true that it also implicates

an inclusive exclusion (an *exceptio*) of *zoé* in the *polis*, almost as if politics were the place in which life had to transform itself into good life and in which what had to be politicized were always already bare life.

Therefore, according to Agamben, the ousting of the "bare life" from the public sphere is not simply a necessary effect of

---

9   *Homo Sacer*, p. 6. As is known, Agamben takes up the expression and concept of "bare life" from Walter Benjamin. In particular by this author, see: 'Critique of Violence', and 'Goethe's Elective Affinities', in *Selected Writings, vol. I: 1913-1926*, ed. by Marcus Bullock and Michael W. Jennings (Cambridge, Mass.: Harvard University Press,1996), pp. 236-56 and 297-360. For a discussion of the topic in relation to Agamben's reflection, also see: Laurent Dubreuil, 'Leaving Politics: Bios, Zoe, Life', *Diacritics*, 2 (2006), 83-98; Ernesto Laclau, 'Bare Life or Social Indeterminacy?', in Matthew Calarco and Steven De Caroli (ed. by), *Sovereignty & Life* (Stanford: Stanford University Press, 2007), pp. 11-22; Ewa Plonowska Ziarek, 'Bare Life on Strike: Notes on the Biopolitics of Race and Gender', *The South Atlantic Quarterly,* 1 (2008), 89-105; Miguel Vatter, *The Republic of the Living. Biopolitics and the Critique of Civil Society* (New York: Fordham University Press, 2014), pp. 99-128.

delimiting the political space of the *polis*; it is, above all, the
condition that authorizes politics to make life itself the material
to be politically qualified and transformed, that is to say to be
bio-politicized.[10]

Agamben means to push philosophical research to develop the
genealogy of biopolitics in a direction that Foucault may have
hastily rejected. However, the fact remains that his discourse
involves theoretical problems that should not be underestimated.
In particular, it risks nullifying the importance that Agamben
himself attributes to the common assumption that makes
interaction between Foucault's and Arendt's research possible and
opportune. As the Italian philosopher observes, this assumption
in Foucault is expressed in the well-known thesis that the birth
of biopolitics coincides with the decline of the Aristotelian
definition of man as «a living animal with the additional capacity
for a political existence» and with its transformation into «an
animal whose politics places his existence as a living being
in question».[11] In Arendt, instead, this common assumption
manifests itself in the attribution of the decadence of politics to
the disappearance of the Greek distinction between the sphere of
political life and the sphere of natural life.[12] Therefore, we can say
that this distinction and its historical overcoming make it possible
respectively: for Foucault to focus on the advent of biopolitics
in modernity, for Arendt to denounce the biological alteration
that politics undergoes in modern times, and for Agamben to
connect their positions. But by claiming that the origin of the
"complicity" between Western politics and biopolitics dates
back to the Greek *polis*, Agamben risks destabilizing precisely
this essential basis of his discourse, as he ends up considering
the distinction between *zoé* and *bios* (*oikos* and *polis*) in two
very different and substantially contrasting ways: for him, on the
one hand, this distinction is a valid instrument for recognizing
the biopolitical mutation of politics, which was realized through
its obsolescence in modernity; on the other, it is a fictitious

10   *Homo Sacer*, p. 7.
11   Foucault, *The History of Sexuality. Volume 1,* p. 143.
12   *Homo Sacer*, pp. 3-4. See *The Human Condition*, pp. 28-31.

distinction which, in reality, hides the original capture by which the *zoé* has always been included in the *bios*, also masking the essential biopolitical vocation of Western politics.

Furthermore, by dating the original conditions of biopolitics back to ancient Greece, the Italian author risks making appear irrelevant the historical-cultural discontinuity between the forms of political action as practice of citizenship expressed in the *polis*, and the tendencies that transform political action into the mere exercise of sovereign power over the territory and over "subjects". From this point of view, Agamben's theses seem to imply not only the nullification of the heterogeneity hypothesized by Foucault between sovereignty and biopower, but also the substantial dispersion of every specificity of politics as a practice of freedom and civic virtue with respect to the simple exercise of a sovereign power, as well as with respect to biopower.

1.2 *Biopower as a suspension of life*

However, the real pivot of Agamben's discourse on biopolitics is the thesis according to which biopower is structurally inscribed in sovereign power: it is the recognition of this inscription which allows us to fully grasp the paradigmatic form of biopolitics in the *camp*. To this end – according to the Italian author – it is decisive to focus on the element of sovereignty, the absolute centrality of which is generally underestimated: it is *the state of exception*, that is, the essential condition of the full exercise of sovereign power. In this regard, Agamben considers it essential to refer to Carl Schmitt, according to him, the only one to have thought to the fullest about the necessary link between *sovereign power, exception* and *unconditional decision*. With his definition of "sovereign" as «he who decides on the exception», the German philosopher helps us to understand that sovereignty is «at the same time, outside and inside of the juridical order», and that «the sovereign is truly the one to whom the juridical order grants the power of proclaiming a state of exception and, therefore, of suspending the orders own validity».[13] It is in sovereignty understood in this sense that – according to Agamben – one can recognize the biopolitical crux in which it grips life. In the decision on the exception it becomes evident that sovereignty consists in having at ones disposal life itself, in the possibility of "suspending it" together with the law, exposing it to the indefinite oscillation between pure survival and the possibility of its suppression. Therefore, it can be said that through the power of the decision on the exception «[t]he sovereign decides not the licit and illicit but the originary inclusion of the living in the sphere of law».[14]

This direct implication of life in the exercise of sovereignty – the author maintains – can be grasped in a primitive and paradigmatic form through the notion of *homo sacer* used by archaic Roman law to indicate a person who was banned, i.e. excluded from both the civil and religious community. The *homo sacer* could not be put to death neither with legal punishment nor with a sacrificial rite, but those who killed him were not convicted of murder; therefore, a *homo sacer* was one who could be killed but not sacrificed. Well, – according to Agamben – the original biopolitical nucleus of sovereignty is exemplarily shown in this figure because «[t]he sovereign sphere is the sphere in which it is permitted to kill without committing homicide and without celebrating a sacrifice, and sacred life – that is, life that may be killed but not sacrificed – is the life that has been captured in this sphere».[15]

---

13 *Homo Sacer*, pp. 11-2, 15. See Carl Schmitt, *Political Theology: Four Chapters on the Concept of Sovereignty*, trans. by George Schwab (Chicago: University of Chicago Press, 2005), pp. 5-7. Agamben returned to discuss these topics in his *State of Exception,* trans. by Kevin Attell (Chicago: The University of Chicago Press, 2005).

14 *Homo Sacer*, p. 26.

15 *Homo Sacer*, p. 83. It certainly cannot be said that, by giving importance to the Latin figure of the *homo sacer*, Agamben intends to mark a certain discontinuity or difference between the Greek and Roman traditions. On the contrary, in his discourse the *homo sacer* seems to constitute a sort of hinge between the two traditions because, finding his place beyond the criminal law and sacrificial rituality, he «presents the originary figure of life taken into the sovereign ban and preserves the memory of the originary exclusion through which the political dimension was first

Therefore, it can be said not only that, for Agamben, biopower and sovereign power are structurally connected, but also that bio-politics is necessarily destined to shift into thanato-politics. This also explains the fundamental thesis of the author, according to which the camp is the biopolitical paradigm of modernity.

Obviously, when speaking of *camp* Agamben is referring above all to the Nazi *Lager*. But it should not be thought that, according to him, the paradigmatic meaning of the *camp* from a biopolitical point of view was manifested only through the eugenic extermination of the lives of the inmates which Nazism practiced there. For the author, the "purification of the race" constituted the prevailing strategy, but not the only way in which Nazism put into practice its bio-thanato-political suspension of life strategies. It would be enough to consider that Hitler also systematically and atrociously promoted medical experimentation on the so-called *Versuchspersonen* (human guinea pigs) and the extermination of defenseless individuals through the "Euthanasia Program for the Incurably Ill". In both cases – says Agamben – eugenic aims were not pursued. Therefore, in general, it can be said that Nazism aimed not only at the "improvement of the race", but also, and above all, at having complete control over life that lies in the hands of the sovereign power. If we understand that the true biopolitical nucleus of Nazi power was the *sovereign decision* «on the value or the nonvalue of life as such»,[16] we can also understand that the camp simply took to its extreme consequences a biopower that even the other forms of the sovereignty of our time are ready to exercise. According to the Italian author, this is demonstrated, for example, by the fact that in the 20th century lethal or very high-risk medical experiments were carried out on prisoners and those sentenced to death on a large scale in the United States.[17]

---

constituted» (ibid.). In any case, a particularly thorough examination of the Roman juridical tradition is carried out by Agamben in his *State of Exception*, trans. by Kevin Attell (Chicago: Chicago University Press, 2005), pp. 41-51, 74-88.

16   *Homo Sacer*, p. 142.
17   *Homo Sacer*, pp. 156-9.

1.3 *The sovereign and the physician*

Clearly, Agamben does not neglect the fundamental role that medical knowledge plays in the area of biopower and, in this regard, does not refer only to the cases of the Nazi "Euthanasia Program" or the "questionable" medical experiments practiced in the United States; among other things, he also considers exemplary contemporary medicine's identification of "brain death" as a condition sufficient to proceed with the removal of organs for transplantation.[18] This, like other examples, indicates – in his opinion – that at this point «the sovereign decision on bare life comes to be displaced from strictly political motivations and areas to a more ambiguous terrain in which the physician and the sovereign seem to exchange roles».[19]

In reality, this important hypothesis in which the figures of the sovereign and the doctor now tend to exchange roles is proposed by Agamben in terms that are less radical than they may seem. In fact, this hypothesis is a seeming possibility because what remains steady in the author's thought is that the fundamental condition of the exercise of biopower is the essential relationship that sovereignty has – even if only potentially – with «the state of exception as the original structure in which law encompasses living beings by means of its own suspension».[20]

This seems to make it impossible for a medical power to actually become biopolitical without first taking on the features of sovereign power; the latter, on the other hand, is, however, intrinsically biopolitical because of its essential relationship with the exception, even if it is not connected with a medical type of power. In fact, for Agamben, ours is the epoch of the triumph

---

18   *Homo Sacer*, pp. 160-5.
19   *Homo Sacer*, p. 143; see also pp. 136-42 and 154-9.
20   Agamben, *State of Exception*, p. 3. In *Homo Sacer*, p. 28, the author gives a definition similar to this one of sovereignty: «If the exception is the structure of sovereignty, then sovereignty is not an exclusively political concept, an exclusively juridical category, a power external to law (Schmitt), or the supreme rule of the juridical order (Hans Kelsen): it is the originary structure in which law refers to life and includes it in itself by suspending it».

of biopolitics mainly because «the state of exception tends increasingly to appear as the dominant paradigm of government in contemporary politics».[21]

Setting his reflection in these terms, the Italian philosopher effectively leaves unexplored a crucial question that can be summarized by asking questions such as the following: has sovereign power always been biopolitical as it is capable of exercising itself unconditionally on life? Or does it become truly biopolitical if it uses knowledge and techniques specific to the treatment of life? Was the Nazi power fully biopolitical as an absolute power that could have at any time renounced the support of bio-medical knowledge? Or did it have to rely on this knowledge since without it, it would not have been fully biopolitical?[22]

These questions arise for a reason as simple as they themselves are: if the exercise of a sovereignly unconditional power were sufficient to fully express the biopolitical vocation of sovereignty, perhaps the absolute power of the *Ancien Régime* monarchies could already have immediately realized this vocation. But, if some importance is attributed to the political genealogy of Foucault, one cannot consider secondary the fact that – according to him – it was exactly the inadequacy of the absolutist sovereignty of the modern state with respect to the systematic administration of life that pushed the state to equip itself progressively with specifically biopolitical knowledge and government tools.

Ultimately, although Agamben obviously recognizes the biopolitical importance of medicine, he does not effectively address the fundamental Foucaultian question of power-knowledge; more precisely, he does not discuss the general idea that the sovereign power of the state really promoted biopolitical strategies when it became governmentalized in order to make the specific régimes of truth of a set of scientific discourses function to its advantage. According to Foucault, in fact, this has happened since the state power managed to translate the effects of knowledge of such discourses into effects of power and, vice versa, to make these

21   Agamben, *State of Exception*, p. 2.
22   In this regard, see Simon Enoch, 'The Contagion of Difference: Identity, Bio-politics and National Socialism', *Foucault Studies*, 1 (2004), 53-70.

power effects work in factors of further production of politically effective truths. In this regard, it will suffice to recall the decisive function which – according to him – the police sciences, the political economy and the life sciences have had in determining what he defines «a shift of emphasis» from a territorial state to a population state.[23] The idea of this "shift" indicates that the modern state actually began to practice a biopolitics when it no longer limited itself to using the *law* to maintain or restore an *order* (possibly also through the "exceptional" suspension of the law itself), but has tended, above all, to affirm a *norm* and to produce a *normality*: for this purpose it has had to make use of knowledge and techniques of the government of the collective body, more than of control of its own territorial jurisdiction.[24] Consequently, from this point of view, the main reference for the exercise of power was no longer the territory, but the whole of individuals considered as a population and placed in relation to the processes it undergoes and that connect it to the environmental contexts in which it lives.[25]

In general, therefore, it can be assumed that the biopolitical government of modern society implies, on the one hand, the pursuit of the *normalization* of individual behavior and collective phenomena, on the other, a certain tendency to the *deterritorialization* of the exercise of power. Thus, if – as Schmitt himself maintains – the territorial foundation of the sovereignty of the modern state constitutes an essential condition of its exercise, the reshaping that this foundation could have already undergone through the shift of political attention from the territory to the population cannot fail to have also led to an erosion of the same political principle of sovereignty.[26] After all, in these

---

23 *Security, Territory, Population*, p. 363. On the question of *régimes of truth* see Michel Foucault, 'Truth and Power', in Michel Foucault, *Power/Knowledge: Selected Interviews and Other Writings, 1972-1977*, ed. by Colin Gordon, trans. by Colin Gordon and others (New York: Pantheon Books, 1980), pp. 109-33.
24 *Security, Territory, Population*, pp. 55-66.
25 *Security, Territory, Population*, pp. 20-3.
26 See Carl Schmitt, *The* Nomos *of the Earth in the International Law of the* Jus Publicum Europaeum, trans. by G. L. Ulmen (New York: Telos

terms we could also interpret that «process of dissolution» into which – according to Agamben himself – today «the great state structures have entered».[27] As is known, in fact, the current crisis of the nation state can generally be linked to the processes of deterritorialization, i.e. to the progressive reduction of the importance of the terrestrial space as the main reference point for political relations, caused by the globalization of the market economy and media communication.[28] All this certainly does not lead to the decline of the political paradigm of sovereignty, but nor does it imply its unshakable capacity always and in any case to prevail over any other mode of exercising power.

1.4 *Between globalization and normalization*

Taking into account the analyses developed by Foucault in the Courses held between 1977 and 1979, it can be said that the

---

Press, 2006).

27 See *Homo Sacer*, p. 12.

28 Here the term "deterritorialization" is used recalling in a very broad sense the general meaning that Gilles Deleuze and Felix Guattari attribute to it in *A Thousand Plateaus: Capitalism and Schizophrenia*, trans. by Brian Massumi (Minneapolis: University of Minnesota Press, 1987). It should be pointed out, however, that the two French philosophers do not theorize an unequivocally territorial character of the state. The latter – according to them – is defined as "territorial" because «it makes the earth an object of its higher unity, a forced aggregate of coexistence, instead of the free play of territories among themselves and with the lineages». It can be said that – according to the two authors – the state refers to the land to dissolve the territorializing relationship that traditional local societies have with it. «Capitalism, on the other hand, is not at all territorial, even in its beginnings: its power of deterritorialization consists in taking as its object, not the earth, but "materialized labour," the commodity» (pp. 453-4). From this point of view, in short, the relationship between the state and the «power of deterritorialization» of capitalism consists in being able to «moderate the superior deterritorialization of capital and to provide the latter with compensatory reterritorializations» (p. 455). Also very useful on these topics is Claude Raffestin, 'Territorializzazione, deterritorializzazione, riterritorializzazione e informazione', trans. by Paola Morelli, in Angelo Turco (ed. by), *Regione e regionalizzazione*, (Milan: Franco Angeli, 1984), pp. 69-82.

control of the population implemented by the police state, and the "frugal government" strategies pursued by liberalism, historically give rise to very different versions of the intertwining of normalization policies and deterritorialization processes.[29] In any case, assuming his point of view, it can be said that it is liberalism that clearly advances this intertwining and its effects of reducing the importance of sovereignty in the exercise of power: on the one hand, the assimilation of the "natural" functioning of the market economy to the naturalness of the biological processes of the population contributes to creating the conditions for the pursuit of *normality* by limiting the intervention of the state and leaving private subjects an ever larger space for autonomy and freedom of initiative;[30] on the other hand, the projection of this tendency into the dimension of the global market causes that process that Schmitt himself describes as the upper hand of the «international law of free trade and free economy» on the «political sovereignty of the individual territorial systems closed in itself».[31]

Therefore, on the basis of such a framework, along the historical sequence from the police state to the era of globalization, passing through liberalism and neoliberalism, the recurrent outbreaks of nationalism, totalitarianism, protectionism or sovereignism represent more or less successful attempts to reconstitute the centrality of sovereign power by reconnecting the biopolitical government of the community with policies of exaltation and–or expansion of the political territory. Nazism, in this sense, presents itself as the "perfect" and extreme conjugation of the territorializing exercise of sovereignty with the normalizing one of biopower. What seems certain, in any case, is that that regime would not have been able to deploy all its bio-thanato-political weight if it had limited

---

29   Foucault uses the expression "frugal government" to define liberal governmentality in *The Birth of Biopolitics*, pp. 28-37.

30   See *Security, Territory, Population*, pp. 33-49, 341-54; *The Birth of Biopolitics*, pp. 53-62.

31   Carl Schmitt, 'Übersicht über nicht staatsbezogene Möglichkeiten und Elemente des Völkerrechts', in *Der Begriff des Politischen. Text von 1932 mit einem Vorwort und drei Corollarien* (Berlin: Duncker & Humblot, 1963), p. 115.

itself to the sovereign appropriation of *Boden* (soil) and had not also pursued the full technical mastery of the *Blut* (blood).

On the other hand, if it is true that today biopolitics is an increasingly important dimension of the exercise of power, this may *not* be – as Agamben claims – the consequence of the fact that at this point, in the context of globalization, «the "juridical empty" space of the state of exception (...) has transgressed its spatiotemporal boundaries and now, overflowing outside them, is starting to coincide with the normal order, in which everything again become possible».[32] Rather, the current spread of the most varied forms – state and extra-state – of biopower could be the final result of the recurrent processes of the re-dimensioning of sovereign power, caused primarily by the biopolitical governmentalization of the modern state, secondly by the prevalence of a liberal governmentality and, finally, by economic globalization: in the framework of the latter the branches of biopower multiply beyond the limits of the sphere of the state due to the combination of the vertiginous developments of biomedical technoscience with the processes of deterritorialization of the market economy, and with the hegemony of neoliberalism. The freedom of initiative that private subjects can enjoy in this scenario the more they stand out in global competition, places them in a position to act more and more freely in the medical, pharmacological, biotechnological, etc. fields, both as economic subjects and as biopolitical subjects.[33]

Instead, according to Agamben's point of view, as an alternative to this type of hypothesis, we can only think that the state of exception represents a sort of metahistorical paradigm, immune from any setback coming from the upheavals that the sovereign power undergoes.

It must be considered, however, that – in one of the most interesting developments of his research – the Italian author seems to recognize the irreducible specificity of biopower with respect to sovereignty; at this point he speaks openly of «two paradigms» the first of which corresponds to «the transcendence of sovereign power» and the second to the «idea of an *oikonomia*, conceived as an

---

32 *Homo Sacer*, p. 38.
33 For a framework of this perspective see the fifth chapter of this book.

immanent ordering». So, it can be said that «[p]olitical philosophy and the modern theory of sovereignty derive from the first paradigm; modern biopolitics up to the current triumph of economy and government over every other aspect of social life derive from the second paradigm».[34] Ultimately, at this point Agamben recognizes, in the «economic» and «administrative» nature of government power, the specificities that clearly distinguish it from sovereignty, as well as the requirements that indirectly explain how biopolitics belongs to the governmental sphere.[35]

In spite of everything, however, his refined investigation into this duality of paradigms leads to an outcome that is entirely consistent with the premises of the path begun with his most important book on biopolitics (*Homo Sacer*): the relationship between sovereign power and state of exception in fact still constitutes the unitary center from which, in our societies, power is said to be exercised through the articulation of sovereignty and biopower; but this centrality now reaffirms itself through the mediation of the concept of «glory». In the "exceptional" relationship that is traditionally established between the sovereign and his subjects through the «glorification» and the «acclamation» of the former by the latter, Agamben not only identifies the origin of the fundamental function that the media exaltation of leaders plays today in the creation of political consensus, but also «the central mystery of power» which allows the principle of sovereignty to continue to exercise its hegemony, even if it is not always so evident.[36]

---

34   Giorgio Agamben, *The Kingdom and the Glory: For a Theological Genealogy of Economy and Government*, trans. by Lorenzo Chiesa with Matteo Mandarini (Stanford: Stanford University Press, 2011), p. 1.

35   *The Kingdom and the Glory*, p. 17; see also pp. XI-XIII, 1-52, 67-98. On this evolution of the thought of the Italian philosopher see Sophie Fuggle, 'Excavating Government: Giorgio Agamben's Archaeological Dig', *Foucault Studies*, 7 (2009), 89-95.

36   *The Kingdom and the Glory*, p. XII; see also pp. 167–260. For a deeper look at the possibility of using Agamben's theses in the analysis of neoliberalism and globalization, see the two contrasting points of view of: Alberto Toscano, 'Divine Management: Critical Remarks on Giorgio Agamben's *The Kingdom and the Glory*', *Angelaki: Journal of the Theoretical Humanities*, 16 (2011), 125-36, and German Eduardo Primera, 'Economic Theology, Governance and

1.5 *The use of life*

Finally, some considerations must be made about certain recent results of the reflection initiated by Agamben with *Homo Sacer*. In the final phase of this train of thought, he is increasingly concerned about identifying the conditions in which life can escape the danger inherent in constantly remaining subject to the power of a biopolitical sovereignty or government. These conditions, according to him, must be sought or created by ensuring that the separation between life and its form – between *zoé* and *bios* – no longer has reason to exist and one can coincide with the other.

Among the experiences that allude to this possibility, the Italian author considers in particular those of Christian monasticism. A peculiar aspect of these experiences – according to him – is the commitment to place *life* and the *rule* in a relationship that transforms the second into the immediate *form* of the first. In this sense, these experiences go beyond the effort to adhere to a system of precepts and commandments imposed from the outside on life itself; they are, therefore, not reducible to the pure submission of human actions to a transcendent authority: the Christian monk, grafting the *rule* into *life* itself through his incessant practice, renders one indiscernible from the other and, thus, creates a *habitus* which is his *habitatio*, a way of being, a form of life that is his life itself.[37] In this regard, Agamben highlights the meaning of the term *cenoby* which indicates the place where the monastic community lives: cenoby derives etymologically from the Greek expression *koinos bios* (*common life*). Therefore, it «does not name only a place, but first of all a form of life» which implies the constant sharing of life itself and the rule that constitutes its form.[38]

It is important to note that – according to Agamben's analysis – in Christian monasticism the main way to connect the rule

---

Neoliberalism: Lessons of «The Kingdom and the Glory»'. *Praktyka Teoretyczna*, 17 (2015), 106–22.

37 Giorgio Agamben, *The Highest Poverty: Monastic Rules and Form-of-Life*, trans. by Adam Kotsko (Stanford: Stanford University Press, 2013), p. 13.

38 *The Highest Poverty*, p. 11.

to life is to internalize it by rigorously marking the passing of time; this articulation of time translates not only in the precise chronological organization of material activities, but also, and above all, in the regular performance of the spiritual activity of prayer and meditation: thus «corresponding to the meticulous chronological regulation of every exterior act is a temporal scansion of the interior discourse that is just as punctilious».[39] Time, as a dimension of the internalization of the form of life through prayer and meditation, becomes the decisive factor of detachment from the world which this life must tend toward. In this sense, Agamben insists on what, from his point of view, cannot but be the true limit of Christian monasticism: the fact that living in common in the cenoby is based on a «flight from the world», on a voluntary exile due to the need to project life itself towards the transcendent dimension of divine power.[40]

With respect to these general aspects of Christian monasticism, Franciscanism has historically produced a kind of turning point: it radicalizes the need for interpenetration of *form* and *life* going beyond the assumption of «liturgy and incessant prayer» as the main answers to this need. In fact, Franciscanism identifies *poverty* as the fundamental way in which this interpenetration must take place;[41] from this point of view, it transforms the renunciation of the world into renunciation of ownership. In this regard, however, it is not able to avoid doctrinal confrontation with the hierarchies of the Church: on the one hand, it rejects *property* and, on the other, it has to justify the *use* of goods indispensable to life. In this sense, Franciscanism shows that use is a natural fact and necessary for the preservation of life; it can, therefore, be separated from ownership: use as a practice founded on itself – unlike property – does not require legal legitimacy; even though it may derive from a *right*, as a simple fact use does not necessarily depend on it; ultimately it depends neither on property nor on the law that legitimates it.[42]

---

39   *The Highest Poverty*, p. 25; see also pp. 18-27.
40   *The Highest Poverty*, pp. 48-51.
41   *The Highest Poverty*, p. 119.
42   See *The Highest Poverty*, pp. 109-16.

In this way, by opposing property and law, Franciscanism seems to make a frontal attack on two fundamental instruments of the power to which life is generally subjected. Nevertheless, according to Agamben, precisely by defining use in negative terms with respect to property and law, the Franciscans end up being imprisoned within the limits of legal argumentation. «On the one hand, they use its conceptuality and never call into question its validity or foundations, while on the other, they think they can secure with juridical arguments the possibility, through abdicating the law, of pursuing an existence outside the law».[43] Therefore, Franciscanism could not avoid the papacy's neutralization of its attempt; in fact it succeeded in obtaining it precisely by adopting and reversing the legal arguments proposed by the Franciscans: John XXII denied the possibility of separating ownership and use by insisting on the case of things «essential to the life» the use of which coincides with their consumption, hence «the separation of ownership from use is impossible».[44] In this way, in short, the Church was able to radically question the very possibility of basing the rule of poverty on the independence of use from property.

What Agamben is interested in highlighting in this regard is the fact that the Franciscans are unable to elaborate and practice «a definition of use in itself and not only in opposition to law».[45] Only by elaborating a definition of this kind and starting from it – according to him – could the conditions be identified for an effective liberation of life from powers, rules, laws or decisions that are foreign to it. This seems to be the conviction that also inspires the last passages of the train of thought begun by Agamben in *Homo Sacer*. In that regard, in *The Use of Bodies* the possibility of liberating life through the re-elaboration of the concept of use is based clearly on the reference to the bodies of individuals as living beings. In an apparently paradoxical way, Agamben outlines this possibility starting from a radical review of the condition of the slave described by Aristotle.[46]

---

43   *The Highest Poverty*, pp. 137-8.
44   *The Highest Poverty*, p. 129-30.
45   *The Highest Poverty*, p. 139.
46   Giorgio Agamben, *The Use of Bodies*, trans. by Adam Kotsko (Stanford: Stanford University Press, 2015).

As is well known, the latter defines the slave as a *living tool* which, as such, is the master of the house's object of use.[47] From Agamben's point of view, this description can be reinterpreted as a definition of a life whose form is immediately determined by its use.[48] According to the Italian philosopher, what counts here is, first of all, the fact that it is a living body that is immediately the object of use; it is important, furthermore, that the use defines the life of the slave as irreducible to that of the producer or the political actor: the use of the body of the slave does not produce objective results or acts distinct from its unfolding; its essential characteristic is that its effect coincides with its course. The use of body, from this point of view, gives shape to an inoperative life, to a life that does not produce "works".

In this regard, for Agamben, it is fundamental to resume and also rethink the Aristotelian relationship between potency and act, going beyond the idea that every potency is essentially subordinated to the act, or to the work, into which it is destined to be translated. According to him, in fact, use is a practice that defines a «form-of-life», a «habit» or a «habitual use» in which potency is never exhausted in the act, but persists as potency;[49] political action, production and working, instead, consume their own potency by actualizing themselves into an objective result.

All this does not mean that use as a habit consists in a total inertia or absence of works. Rather, it gives rise to a relationship with the works which is radically different from that which, according to the prevailing view, exists between potency and act; here «[t]he work is not the result or achievement of a potential, which is realized and consumed in it: the work is that in which potential and habit are still present, still in use».[50]

Framed in these terms, the concept of use can and must be rethought outside the conceptual schemes of economics and politics as forms of command and government of life. Unlike what happened in the Franciscan experience, moreover, use

---

47   See *Politics*, 1253b 25-1254a 19, pp. 15-9.
48   *The Use of Bodies*, pp. 3-23.
49   *The Use of Bodies*, pp. 58-62.
50   *The Use of Bodies*, p. 62.

must be freed from juridical conceptuality and redefined as an ontological modality, i.e. as a form of life that determines its being by coinciding with it. Agamben's discourse on use, in short, tends to elaborate a «modal ontology», overcoming the traditional ontological visions that find their cornerstone in the dualistic relationship between potency and the act:[51] the reflection on being must no longer consist in a questioning about *what*, but in one on the *as* of being.[52] A modal ontology, according to the Italian philosopher, becomes possible if being itself is thought of as life, as life itself's multiplicity of ways of being, as form generated by living.[53]

Returning to the centrality that bodies assume in this vision, it seems appropriate to make a concluding consideration on the paradigmatic character that Agamben attributes to the condition of the slave, taking into account what he claims about the relationship between the latter and his master. According to the author, in the rigid form that this relationship has assumed in our history as a relationship of unilateral and irreversible power

> the subjects whom we call master and slave are in such a "community of life" that the juridical definition of their relationship in terms of property is rendered necessary, almost as if otherwise they would slide into a confusion and *koinonia tes zoes* that the juridical order cannot admit except in the striking and despotic intimacy between master and slave.

The «scandalous» property rights of one person over another that is established here, according to Agamben, might be nothing more than «the originary form of property, the capture (the *ex-ceptio*) of the use of bodies in the juridical order».[54] In any case, evidently in this relationship the potency of the use of bodies is "imprisoned" by the unilateral nature of ownership and the exercise of power by

---

51 *The Use of Bodies*, pp. 146-75.On this topic see Gorgoglione, *Paradoxien der Biopolitik*, pp. 128-33, and by the same author: 'El uso de las mentes. Ontología para una política de la vida ecológica', *Soft Power*, 1 (2017), 187-99.
52 *The Use of Bodies*, p.172.
53 *The Use of Bodies*, pp. 220-3.
54 *The Use of Bodies*, p. 36.

the master. Therefore, taking up some suggestions from Foucault, Agamben maintains that the possibilities of "unlocking" this potency can be grasped in the form that the relationship between slave and master assumes in sadomasochistic practices.[55] Here, first of all, it is possible for the two roles to be interchangeable, to the extent that in these practices a power relationship is simulated in a ritual way; but what is most interesting – according to the Italian author – is that these practices create the conditions for a totally unique experience of subjectivation:

> the one whose body is (or seems to be) used is actually constituted to the same extent as subject of its being used, assumes it and experiences pleasure in it (...).Vice versa, the one who seems to use the body of the other can in some way be used by the other for his own pleasure.

In other words, according to Agamben, «*sadomasochism exhibits the truth of use, which does not know subject and object, agent and patient. And in being taken up in this indetermination, pleasure is also made non-despotic and common*».[56]

What perhaps may be objected about this perspective of overcoming the powers that condition and threaten life, is that perhaps any erotic (and loving, in general) relationship is, or should be, describable in these terms. Moreover, on the almost "paradigmatic" value that Agamben attributes to the figure of the slave, it can be observed that the author in fact underestimates the *servile* character of his activity, namely the fact that it generally consists of a *service* enjoyed and consummated while it takes place. In other words, if this activity can be defined as "inoperative" it is so, above all, to the extent that it produces services or performances, rather than works; therefore, it is not (only) the concept of use that allows it to be defined in this way. Although Hannah Arendt – as Agamben claims – may have anachronistically compared the slave's activity to modern labour, in any case, she has clearly

55   See 'Michel Foucault, an Interview: Sex, Power and the Politics of Identity', with B. Gallagher and A. Wilson, *The Advocate*, 400 (1984), 26-30 and 58.
56   *The Use of Bodies*, p. 35.

highlighted the essential characteristic of this activity as *servile labour*: for her it consists in the fact «that it leaves nothing behind, that the result of its effort is almost as quickly consumed as the effort is spent».[57] As a service or body performance, the activity of the slave leaves nothing behind; therefore, it is used and consumed simultaneously as it is carried out.

This observation is proposed here simply to advance a more radical hypothesis than that inherent in the assimilation of the activity of domestic slaves to modern productive labour: the hypothesis that the ancient importance of the slave's servile labour prefigures the centrality that is taken on, in our "post-industrial societies", by the activities that are used while they are carried out (transport, care, education, communication, information, entertainment, etc.), which are often given the general definition of services. It is almost superfluous to note that many of these activities are today based on the most effective forms of exercising power over the existence and very life of men and women; instead it is not superfluous to point out that today in many of these activities the practice of consumption takes precedence over that of the (lasting and repeated) use of life and the things of the world.

2. *Negri, Foucault and the ontology of biopolitical labour*

2.1. *The political economy of life*

Antonio Negri addresses the issue of biopolitics by framing it immediately in the context of globalization. But the enormous dimension that biopolitics can have in this scenario does not lead Negri simply to fear that a globalized biopower could become

---

57 *The Human Condition*, p. 87. As is known, Arendt here critically refers to Adam Smith and Karl Marx according to which workers who provide personal services and performances generally have to be considered economically unproductive. See Adam Smith, *An Inquiry into the Nature and Causes of the Wealth of Nations*, ed. by Edwin Cannan (London: Methuen & Co., 1904), vol. I, especially pp. 313-21. Karl Marx, *Theories of Surplus Value*, trans. by G. A. Bonner and Emile Burns (London: Lawrence & Wishart, 1951), pp. 148-75.

uncontrollable for society; according to him, we must imagine that biopolitics is not inevitably destined to strengthen a power external to life; therefore, it is necessary to distinguish clearly, on a conceptual level, biopower from biopolitics: with the first term we can indicate the «technologies» and the «mechanisms» of the power that is exercised over life itself; with the second, instead, the «experiences of subjectification and freedom», the «complex of resistances» and «the spaces in which relations, struggles and productions of power are developed».[58]

Negri's main intent is to reaffirm – consistent with his radical Marxism – «the importance of production within the biopolitical process of the social constitution» and to lead biopolitics back «to the ontology of production».[59] Foucault – according to the Italian author – was not able to fully appreciate the ontological importance of production, since his «interest in the economic factors of development and in the critique of political economy is much less deep than his interest in the study of all the other conditions and activities of development».[60] Therefore, Negri also claims that the French philosopher was too hesitant in thinking of biopolitics as «a political economy of life in general». At least in a first phase of his research on biopolitics, Foucault may have dawdled around the idea that it is intimately linked to the logic of strengthening the state and the need to maintain social order through "police science"; only later did he remove biopolitics from these limits, placing it in direct relation to the economic logic of our society.[61]

In reality – as we saw in the first chapter of this book – Foucault soon placed the subject of biopolitics in the more general framework of the economic rationality of the government of society through the courses held between 1977 and 1979. In this context, for him,

---

58   Antonio Negri, *Reflections on* Empire, trans. by Ed Emery (Cambridge, UK: Polity Press, 2008), pp. 73-4. See also Michael Hardt and Antonio Negri, *Commonwealth*, (Cambridge, Mass: Harvard University Press, 2009), pp. 56-63.

59   Michael Hardt and Antonio Negri, *Empire* (Cambridge, Mass: Harvard University Press, 2000), pp. 29 and 30.

60   Antonio Negri, *Empire and Beyond*, trans. by Ed Emery (Cambridge, UK: Polity Press, 2008), p. 231.

61   Negri, *Reflections on* Empire, p. 72.

economic knowledge immediately assumes a primary importance and is proposed, above all, as a fundamental instrument of governmentalization of the state through the centralistic and protectionist strategies of mercantilism; subsequently, this knowledge insists on the need to reduce the role of the state in the government of society with the free trade theories of political economy. Thus, Foucault's interest in economic processes can only appear unsatisfactory if compared with an overwhelming need, such as that felt by Negri, to lead biopolitics back «to the ontology of production».[62]

One of the concerns that push Negri to make his critical remarks on Foucault seems to be to avoid framing biopolitics as destined to decline with the crisis of the modern state and with the advent of economic globalization. Negri, however, does not seem to realize that *heterogeneity* itself, brought to light by the French philosopher, between the sphere of *governmentality* and *biopolitics*, on the one hand, and that of *state sovereignty*, on the other, is the presupposition for the relative independence from the state logic that biopolitics is gaining today by connecting with the economic needs of the strongest players on the global market.

2.2. *The production of subjectivity*

Negri's effort to lead biopolitics back to «the ontology of production» is combined with his insistence on the intellectual, communicative and linguistic characteristics of postmodern labour: according to him, these characters express the immediately social and relational quality of the labour of our era and they project it just as immediately in the perspective of the collective reconquest of its productive power controlled by capital.[63] However, according to Negri, when these "immaterial" connotations of post-modern labour are brought to light, it is easy to lose sight of its biopolitical quality, if one does not also grasp the connection that directly links these connotations to «the productivity of the corporeal, the somatic». Today language, communication, intellectuality and

---

62   *Empire*, p. 30.
63   *Empire*, pp. 28-9.

sociality are essential elements of labour since it is immediately embodied in «multitude of singular and determinate bodies that seek relation».[64] Consequently, contemporary labour must be considered in all respects as a «biopolitical labour».[65]

According to Negri, the social knowledge and the intellectual abilities that develop in contemporary capitalist society in relation to technological progress, are no longer alienated and rigidly incorporated into machines to be counterposed to labour. Today «mass intellectuality» no longer allows for this rigidity, since the main tool of production is now language, through which «the human brain reappropriates the instrument of labour» creating «the embodiment of general intellect».[66] It is also in this way that bodies and life itself come into play in productive cooperation, because at this point «labour is the productive activity of a general intellect and a general body outside measure».[67] Ultimately, in the multiform activities of contemporary labour it is no longer possible to distinguish material and immaterial production from the reproduction of life and its multiple relational, affective and bodily expressions. Therefore, according to Negri, it can be said that biopolitics is now the condition for the possibility of «a sort of counterpower, of a *potenza*, a production of subjectivity» that frees itself from biopower and is «expressed by life itself, not only

---

64   *Empire*, pp. 29-30.
65   Hardt and Negri, *Commonwealth*, p. 140.
66   *Reflections on* Empire, pp. 65 and 75. This view of the relationship between social knowledge and technological tools is based on a sort of reformulation of the Marxian concept of *general intellect*, that is, on the overcoming of the theoretical schema proposed in Karl Marx, *Grundrisse: Foundations of the Critique of Political Economy*, trans. by Martin Nicolaus (London: Penguin Books, 1993), pp. 614-26. The *general intellect* would no longer be incorporated – as Marx maintains – in the capitalist system of machines inasmuch as it is capable of objectifying the knowledge that develops in productive cooperation and of transforming it into an instrument of command, of intensive labour exploitation and devaluation of its role; today the definition of *general intellect* seems to directly concern labour due to its growing intellectual capacities, its aptitude to incorporate in itself and to socialize knowledge that is produced in the productive cooperation of the communication society.
67   *Empire*, p. 358.

in labour and in language, but also in bodies, in affects, desire and sexuality».[68] Biopolitics, in short, is not only a field of struggle and confrontation with biopower, but also, and above all, a process of subjectivation.

By applying this solution to his own reflections, Negri takes to the extreme his reaffirmation of the centrality of production and labour: since the productive power of labour is no longer simply economic, but is increasingly biopolitical, this implies the immediate productive involvement of life itself; which – according to the Italian philosopher – also constitutes an immediate possibility for labour to *produce* autonomous and free subjectivities, capable of resisting and avoiding the dominion of capital. In this sense, Negri also takes up the research carried out by Foucault on the ethical practices of antiquity, i.e. the arts of existence the main expression of which is the *care of the self*.[69] As subjectivation practices, for Negri these arts represent a prefiguration of the enormous «ability to construct the subject» that today the productive and biopolitical force of the multitude is able to reach by projecting itself in a perspective of overcoming capitalism.[70]

2.3 *Liberation and freedom*

Therefore, it can be said that Negri carried out two main operations around biopolitics. The first consists in defining in ontological terms the productive autonomy of «biopolitical labour» in comparison with biopower; the second consists in updating and framing in a biopolitical dimension the practices of ethical subjectivation highlighted by Foucault, identifying their source of energy in the labour of the multitude. Thus, the biopolitical interweaving of life and labour finds the definitive sanction of its productive power in the ethical-political construction of new subjectivities.

In reality, above all with the first operation – despite the importance he nonetheless attaches to Foucault's research – Negri

---

68   *Reflections on* Empire, p. 72.
69   See *Reflections on* Empire, pp. 127-9.
70   *Reflections on* Empire, p. 129.

risks losing fundamental results of the genealogical research of the French philosopher. Foucault, in fact, would be decidedly resistant to recognizing what the Italian philosopher calls «the ontological substance of social production»;[71] for him, especially in modernity, productive labour is, above all, a compulsory attitude produced historically by the political imposition of a certain social ethics.[72] To grasp the distance that separates Foucault from Negri and his Marxist vision of labour (or work), it will suffice here to consider what the former maintained in a 1978 conversation with American students:

> Marx thought, and he has written, that work constitutes the concrete essence of man. I think this is a typical Hegelian idea. Work is not the concrete essence of man. If man works, if the human body is a productive force, it is because man is obliged to work. He is obliged to work because he is invested by political forces, because he is inserted into power mechanisms and so forth.[73]

In the light of a position like this, it seems rather unlikely that Foucault would agree with Negri on the possibility of relating, not only work or labour, but also care of the self – as an ethical practice of subjectivation – to something like an «ontological substance» of production.

There is no doubt that for Foucault the care of the self and the practices of subjectivation in general do not constitute a sphere detached from economic and political relations: they represent ways of self-regulation that those who take care of themselves put in place

---

71   *Empire*, p. 28.
72   See Michel Foucault, *History of Madness*, trans. by Jonathan Murphy and Jean Khalfa, ed. by Jean Khalfa (London: Routledge, 2006),pp. 62-77; Foucault, *Discipline and Punish*, pp. 239-44. More generally, it should be added here that if a Foucaultian ontology is given, it can only be historical and certainly not "substantial". In this sense, see Michel Foucault, 'What Is Enlightenment?', trans. by Catherine Porter, in *The Foucault Reader*, ed. by Paul Rabinow (New York: Pantheon Books, 1984), pp. 44-50; see also Michel Foucault, *The Government of Self and Others. Lectures at the Collège de France 1982-1983*, ed. by Frédéric Gros, trans. by Graham Burchell (London: Palgrave MacMillan, 2010), pp. 20-1.
73   Michel Foucault, 'Dialogue on Power', in *Chez Foucault*, ed. by Simeon Wade (Los Angeles: Circabook, 1978), pp. 12-3.

to give an ethical form to their involvement in these relationships. According to Foucault, in Greek-Roman antiquity, the main aim of those who practices an art of existence like the care of the self is to maintain a certain detachment from these relationships so as not to be influenced by them. He who could do this is a free citizen in status and material condition, who – in one way or another – might find himself exercising power over others. Therefore, he does not simply aspire to release himself from a heteronomous power, but, above all, to demonstrate to himself and to others that he is worthy of the freedom he possesses by trying not to take advantage of it beyond measure. In the case of classical Greece, the «practices of the self» tend to achieve «an ethics of selfdelimiting domination»[74] in the context of both relationships in the private, reproductive and affective sphere, and those in the public and political sphere. In imperial Rome, on the other hand, such practices tend to guarantee an «ethics of self-mastering» aimed not only at moderating the exercise of one's power over others, but also, and above all, at becoming aware of the complexity of the world and the political relationships in which one is immersed: this creates the need for a self-critical sense of one's own limits, of an ethical distance from one's activities and power, even when exercizing it. In this regard Foucault attaches great importance to the connection between «knowledge of the truth» and «right action»: the man who takes care of himself, does it first of all by seeking and telling the truth about the problematic nature of the situation in which he lives, i.e. by criticizing any claim, his or others, to unilaterally "produce" or "command" events and political relations. It is on this basis, therefore, that the free man manages to shape his own actions at a critical distance from the exercise of power and from the activities in which he takes part.[75]

When Foucault transfers the need for practices like these into modernity, he presents as indispensable their collocation – so to speak – *on this side* of the exercise of power and *beyond* the dynamics of liberation. According to him, the practices

---

74 Foucault, *The Use of Pleasure*, p. 184.
75 See Foucault, *The Hermeneutics of the Subject*, pp. 371-81; Frédéric Gros, 'Course Context', ibid., pp. 539-45; Foucault, *The Care of the Self*, pp. 81-95.

of ethical subjectivation must actively problematize both the existing relationships and systems of power and the liberating outcomes of social evolution or political struggles. In this sense, the ancient arts of existence must be updated as *practices of freedom* and clearly distinct from the *processes of liberation*: going beyond the limits of these processes is no less important than escaping the exercise of power. According to Foucault, the «practice of liberation is not in itself sufficient to define the practices of freedom that will still be needed». In short, even «[l]iberation paves the way for new power relationships, which must be controlled by practices of freedom».[76] But this kind of problem arises even before a liberation movement or process is activated, because – according to the French philosopher – in our society we always enjoy a certain degree of freedom: «if there are relations of power in every social field, this is because there is freedom everywhere».[77] Therefore – says Foucault –, it is the relative freedom which, in any case, we have to constitute «the ontological condition of ethics» and it is this freedom that must be practiced ethically. In short, for him, ethics is «the conscious practice of freedom», the «form that freedom takes when it is informed by reflection».[78] Therefore, the Foucaultian practices of subjectivation neither in antiquity nor in the contemporary world seem to be able to find their main resource in an ontological substance or in a productive force; rather, they find this resource in an ontologically unstable and ethically problematic *condition* of relative freedom, which we must be able to recognize, examine, criticize, transform.

Of course, with his distinction between processes of liberation and practices of freedom, Foucault certainly does not intend to diminish the importance of liberation struggles and their conquests, but wants to focus precisely on their limits. Already in the first volume of the *History of Sexuality* he links the affirmation of a normalizing biopower with the

---

76 Foucault, 'The Ethics of the Concern for Self as a Practice of Freedom', pp. 282 and 284.

77 Foucault, 'The Ethics of the Concern for Self as a Practice of Freedom', p. 292.

78 'The Ethics of the Concern for Self as a Practice of Freedom', pp. 284-5.

manifestation of a series of specifically biopolitical struggles. He points out that in these struggles what is being claimed is «life, understood as the basic needs, man's concrete essence, the realization of his potential, a plenitude of the possible».[79] But this characterization of these struggles does not at all have the sense of an unconditional appreciation; it does not mean that in the biopolitical dimension of such struggles life is immediately considered «the place of emergence of a sort of counterpower, of a *potenza*, a production of subjectivity», nor that here is realized «the transition from the political to the ethical, or rather a perspective for constructing an ethics of the body, of the life of pleasures and of the life of labour».[80] For Foucault, an evaluation like this would imply the interpretation of the relationship between biopolitical struggles and biopower as a condition of the immediate solution to a problem that instead this relationship implicates: the biopolitical dimension of this relationship creates not so much the possibility of a passage «from the political to the ethical», as much as the need for an overcoming of biopolitics in the direction of ethics, conceived as a condition for a new politics.

According to Foucault, biopolitical struggles, despite their disruptive strength, represent a sort of conditioned reflex with respect to the imposition of biopower: in them, life, having become a political object, is assumed as such and used against the system. Thus, the protagonists of these struggles certainly achieve remarkable freedoms, but they also tend to underestimate the fact that biopower does not relate to life only by tending to repress it, but it generally takes a positive approach to life itself; therefore, they end up being inspired by a "mythological" and improperly ontological vision of life, conceiving of it as a place of «[t]he "right" to life, to one's body, to health, to happiness, to the satisfaction of needs, and beyond all the oppressions or "alienations," the "right" to rediscover what one is and all that one can be».[81] Ultimately, despite their historical novelty, these

---

79   *The History of Sexuality. Volume 1*, p. 145.
80   Negri, *Reflections on* Empire, p. 72.
81   Foucault, *The History of Sexuality. Volume 1*, p. 145.

struggles do not go beyond the relationship that biopower itself claims to establish with «the truth about desire, life, nature, body, and so on».[82] Consequently, they do not necessarily make a real ethical-political innovation possible.

In other words, in Foucault the transition to ethics requires a radical *problematization of our spontaneous thinking of ourselves as subjects of desire*, as holders of a productive, essential and decisive power for our own purposes to constitute ourselves as subjects. Indeed, it can be said that this problematization is the real dominant motif of the genealogy of the Western subject that the French philosopher has carried out through his "history of sexuality."[83] The constancy with which he insisted on this motif led him – as is well known – to a profound disagreement with Deleuze. It is significant, therefore, that Negri, underlining this divergence, has clearly expressed his greater affinity with Deleuze, precisely because, unlike the latter, Foucault never assigned an ethically or politically constitutive function to the force of desire.[84] The Foucaultian privileging of "pleasures", in fact, indicates precisely his attention not to emphasize desire neither as a fearsome force nor as an irrepressible power.

2.4 *The new man and the critical ontology*

The vision of ethics as a practice of freedom constitutes, for Foucault, an attempt to respond to a precise and crucial question: the question of the problematic relationship that is created in

---

82   Michel Foucault, 'On the Genealogy of Ethics: An Overview of Work in Progress', in *The Foucault Reader*, p. 350.

83   See Foucault, 'On the Genealogy of Ethics: An Overview of Work in Progress', pp. 351-9.

84   See *Empire*, pp. 28 and 422, n14; Gilles Deleuze, 'Desire and pleasure', in Arnold I. Davidson (ed. by), *Foucault and His Interlocutors*, (Chicago: University of Chicago Press, 1997), pp. 185-6; Michel Foucault, "Structuralism and post-structuralism", trans. by Jeremy Harding, in *The Essential Works of Michel Foucault, II, Aesthetics, Method and Epistemology*, p. 446. See also Foucault, 'The Ethics of the Concern for Self as a Practice of Freedom', pp. 283-4.

modern society between «the acquisition of capabilities and the struggle for freedom»:

> we can see that throughout the entire history of Western societies (...) the acquisition of capabilities and the struggle for freedom have constituted permanent elements. Now the relations between the growth of capabilities and the growth of autonomy are not as simple as the eighteenth century may have believed. And we have been able to see what forms of power relation were conveyed by various technologies (whether we are speaking of productions with economic aims, or institutions whose goal is social regulation, or of techniques of communication): disciplines, both collective and individual procedures of normalization exercised in the name of the power of the state, demands of society or of population zones, are examples. What is at stake, then, is this: How can the growth of capabilities be disconnected from the intensification of power relations?[85]

Hence the need to critically distance ethical subjectivation practices from the production processes, political strategies and communication techniques, not to abstract them, but to better relate them to the present and to make them respond adequately to the task of elaborating oneself. This – for the French philosopher – is what, in a certain sense, emerges from the experience of the modernity conceived of and practiced by Baudelaire. He – according to Foucault – urges us to actively seek to be modern while still remaining independent of modernity; to practice with detachment the relationship with our present through his «ironic heroization», to use it for the «transfiguring play of freedom with reality», to actively withdraw us from its continuous changes, without claiming to free our supposed alienated essence, but rather forming our own way of being free through an «ascetic elaboration of the self».

> Modern man, for Baudelaire, is not the man who goes off to discover himself, his secrets and his hidden truth; he is the man who tries to invent himself. This modernity does not "liberate man in his own being"; it compels him to face the task of producing himself.

---

85   Foucault, 'What Is Enlightenment?', pp. 47-8.

The arts of existence understood in these terms, for Foucault, cannot «have any place in society itself, or in the body politic. They can only be produced in another, a different place, which Baudelaire calls art».[86]

Returning to Negri's discourse, we could say that – according to Foucault – there is no guarantee that the increased biopolitical power of post-modern labour will not give rise to new and fearsome relationships of power. The productive liberation of this power, without the elaboration of adequate practices of freedom, does not necessarily translate into increased possibilities of political autonomy. Therefore, we must avoid indulging in «the empty dream of freedom» and dedicate ourselves rather to a «historical ontology», to a «critical ontology of ourselves». This ontology is itself an ethical practice that must «put itself to the test of reality, of contemporary reality, both to grasp the points where change is possible and desirable, and to determine the precise form this change should take». According to Foucault, this «historical ontology of ourselves must turn away from all projects that claim to be global or radical». Rather than projects of this type we should prefer

> the very specific transformations that have proved to be possible (...) in a certain number of areas that concern our ways of being and thinking, relations to authority, relations between the sexes, the way in which we perceive insanity or illness.

Ultimately, the critical ontology of ourselves consists in testing our ability to practice freedom, on the one hand, by problematizing the growth of the biopolitical power of life and, on the other hand, trying to escape the vagaries and dangers of «the programs for a new man».[87] This justifies hypothesizing a substantial extraneousness of such an ontology compared to what Negri defines as an «ontological line of passional constitution of the new human being who (...) can construct a new world».[88]

---

86   Foucault, 'What Is Enlightenment?', p. 42; see also pp. 39-41.
87   'What Is Enlightenment?', pp. 46-7.
88   Negri, *Empire and Beyond*, p. 177.

3. *Esposito: from politics that immunizes to philosophy of the impersonal*

3.1. *Power that preserves, power that destroys*

Among contemporary philosophers who have relocated the genesis of biopolitics in the sphere of influence of biomedical knowledge, Roberto Esposito certainly occupies a prominent place. This would suggest that he established a relationship of substantial consonance with Foucault's thought; but, in reality, things are not so simple.

The main problem that Esposito faces is that of coexistence in the context of the biopolitics of politics that preserve and politics that destroy life. Esposito acknowledges that Foucault has clearly highlighted the tendency of bio-politics to overflow into thanatopolitics, but he also maintains that the French philosopher has not convincingly identified the causes for this. He believes that the proof of this lacuna emerges, in particular, through the uncertainties that he feels characterize the Foucaultian attempt to define the relationship between biopower and sovereignty: sometimes Foucault insists on the differences and on the discontinuity between these two forms of power to underscore the positive attention to life that he believes characterizes only biopower; at other times he theorizes a relationship of complementarity between the two forms, arguing that bio-politics translates into thanato-politics when sovereignty puts its traditional power of life and death at the disposal of biopower.[89]

All this, according to Esposito, derives from the fact that Foucault thinks of biopolitics while maintaining the concepts of life and politics «in their absoluteness», «as originally distinct and only later joined in a manner that is still extraneous to them»;[90] therefore, in the context of his discourse it is not possible to focus

---

89   Roberto Esposito, *Bíos: Biopolitics and Philosophy*, trans. by Timothy Campbell (Minneapolis: University of Minnesota Press, 2008), pp. 24-44. The author refers above all to the theses that Foucault exposes in *"Society Must Be Defended"* and in *The History of Sexuality. Volume 1.*

90   *Bíos: Biopolitics and Philosophy*, pp. 43-4.

on the inextricable intertwining between life and politics that was created from the beginning in modern politics. In other words, Foucault's reflection lacks a theoretical paradigm suitable to clarify both the reasons for which this politics produces a biopolitics and those for which the latter is expressed through an almost inevitable oscillation between power that preserves life and power that destroys it. This paradigm, for Esposito, can be indicated by the term *immunitas* (immunity); it allows us to understand that the relationship between life and death that is established in the sphere of modern politics is not accidental, but essential, and that the factor that links the two elements consists in the intrinsically «immunitary» character of this politics.[91] For the Italian author, in short, it must be recognized that the history of this form of politics is deeply characterized by the tendency of society to immunize itself in order to protect itself from the dangers of disintegration. Of course, modern society protects itself like all other societies in history; however, it is not limited to counteracting the factors of disintegration, but is opposed to them by the immunitary inclusion of what it intends to hinder. Thus it subjects the political body «to a condition that simultaneously negates or reduces its power to expand». Ultimately, the approach of modern society to its own protection is comparable to the «medical practice of vaccinating the individual body», since «the immunization of the political body functions similarly, introducing within it a fragment of the same pathogen from which it wants to protect itself, by blocking and contradicting natural development».[92]

An exemplary proof of this essential immunitary character of our political practices, according to Esposito, can be seen in

---

91   *Bíos: Biopolitics and Philosophy*, p. 9.
92   *Bíos: Biopolitics and Philosophy*, p. 46. On the immunitary paradigm, see Roberto Esposito: *Immunitas: The Protection and Negation of Life*, trans. by Zakiya Hanafi (Cambridge, UK: Polity Press, 2011); 'Biopolitica, immunità, comunità', in Laura Bazzicalupo and Roberto Esposito (ed. by), *Politica della vita* (Rome-Bari: Laterza, 2003), pp. 123-33; *Terms of the Political: Community, Immunity, Biopolitics*, trans. by Rhiannon N. Welch (New York: Fordham University Press, 2013); also see Thimoty Campbell, 'Bíos, Immunity, Life', in Esposito, *Bíos: Biopolitics and Philosophy*, pp. VII-XLII.

the relationship between modern society and the individual. In this society the social bond is paradoxically reproduced through «the exemption» of individuals from the original intensity of the community relationship, or exactly through the immunization of the members of the society from the "risk" of deep involvement that the community relationship would entail. In this sense, modern society remains alive as a *communitas* through the *immunitas*, that is, by functionally contrasting the private sphere of the individual and the common sphere of society. Thus modernity immunizes «the same community in a form that both preserves and negates it» preventing it «from coinciding with itself». In this sense, the *immunitas* is the complementary and, at the same time, negative form of the *communitas*.[93]

In this way, according to Esposito, our society inevitably creates the conditions for life to become a privileged subject of politics and, at the same time, remain exposed to the possibility of its denial by power; in fact, if it is pursued beyond a certain limit, the political immunization of society triggers a mechanism similar to that of an autoimmune disease in which the protection of life «attacks the very body that it should protect».[94]

3.2. *A non-metaphorical biopower*

Nazism, for Esposito, represents the extreme manifestation of the immunitary vocation of modern politics: it systematically pursued the immunization of the political body and pushed intervention in the life and health of the community well beyond the limits to which other political regimes had led it.[95] This uniqueness of the Nazi regime, according to the Italian philosopher, is not adequately highlighted by Foucault because he claims that, «[a]fter all, Nazism was in fact the paroxysmal development of the new power mechanisms that had been established since the eighteenth century».[96] Therefore, Esposito has good reasons to believe that

---

93 *Bíos: Biopolitics and Philosophy*, 50-2.
94 Roberto Esposito, 'Nazism and Us', in *Terms of the Political*, p. 84.
95 See *Bíos: Biopolitics and Philosophy*, pp. 110-4.
96 Foucault, *"Society Must Be Defended"*, p. 259.

the French philosopher tends to see in the biopolitical character of Nazism above all an element of continuity with the previous regimes, losing sight precisely of its radical uniqueness.[97]

However, while this is plausible, the Italian author's thesis appears rather debatable, according to which Hitler's regime, by biologizing in an extreme way the exercise of its power, would have pushed its immunitary intent beyond any metaphorical meaning.[98] Certainly – as Esposito says –

[t]he deadly battle that was waged and disseminated by the regime's propaganda placed the originally healthy body and blood of the German nation in opposition to the invasive germs that had penetrated the nation with the intent of sapping its unity and its very life.[99]

From this point of view, it is indisputable that Nazism pursued an immunitary purpose; but – as Esposito himself shows – it first pursued it through «the regime's propaganda», that is, intensely using rhetorical and metaphorical language. Of course, this does not mean that Nazism did not take the biologization of politics to its extreme consequences. Precisely for this reason, however, the use of immunological terminology could only remain largely propagandistic and metaphorical, since it did not correspond to the now concretely and decidedly eugenic logic that characterized its radically racist biopolitics. Indeed, Esposito himself observes that the Reich ideologues used «the epidemiological» and «bacteriological» repertoire artificially to represent the Jews as «"bacilli", "bacteria", "parasites", "viruses" and "microbes"»;[100] he also points out that «this representation was in patent contrast with the Mendelian theory of the genetic, and therefore not contagious, character of racial determination».[101] But all this does not mean only that the Nazis instrumentally confused infectious diseases with hereditary diseases.[102] For Nazism, in fact, the

---

97   *Bíos: Biopolitics and Philosophy*, p. 111.
98   *Bíos: Biopolitics and Philosophy*, pp. 112-3.
99   Esposito, 'Nazism and Us', p. 85.
100 *Bíos: Biopolitics and Philosophy*, p. 116.
101 Esposito, 'Nazism and Us', p. 86.
102 *Bíos: Biopolitics and Philosophy*, p. 122.

problem of inheritance of diseases was more important than that of their contagious character; therefore, while it is true that the regime radically intensified the biologization of politics, this happened because it also promoted a strategy of active manipulation of life, which included, among other things, a systematic production of death aimed in an aberrant way at a "genetic empowerment" and not only at the "defence" of the race. Which ultimately means that Nazism, to fully and completely exercise its biopower, went far beyond the limits of the immunitary paradigm by projecting the protection of the race onto the broader horizon of its strengthening.

On the other hand, as far as it may seem plausible, it is difficult to object that even the Nazi purpose of genetic breeding was largely propagandistic and metaphorical; an objection such as this, in fact, would make the very idea that Nazism had pushed the biologization of politics beyond all limits problematic. The question, in any case, should be set in other terms: whatever the weight of the propagandistic and metaphorical aspects of Nazi biopolitics, its radicality and its uniqueness can be proven especially taking into account the fundamental importance that its eugenic intent had in it. Esposito himself allows us to focus on the importance of this by recalling the words of Otmar F.von Verschuer – Josef Mengele's teacher and protagonist in the regime's genetic research – who, not by chance, insisted on the centrality of demographic strategies:

> demographic politics is that of the protection of the ethnic body by maintaining and improving the healthy patrimony, the elimination of its sick elements, and the conservation of the racial character of the people.[103]

---

103 Otmar F. von Verschuer, *Leitfaden der Rassenhygiene* (Leeipzig: Georg Thieme Verlag, 1941), quoted in Esposito, *Bíos: Biopolitics and Philosophy*, p. 143.On the role of genetic research in support of the racist strategies of Nazism see: Peter Weingart and others, *Rasse, Blut und Gene* (Frankfurt am Main: Suhrkamp, 1992), pp. 367-561; Benno Müller-Hill, 'A Dark Side of Science in Difficult Times', in Giorgio Semenza and A. J. Turner (ed. by), *A History of Biochemistry. Selected Topics in the History of Biochemistry: Personal Recollections. VII* (Amsterdam: Elsevier Science, 2003), pp. 501-90. By Müller-Hill also see: *Murderous Science. Elimination by Scientific Selection of Jews, Gypsies, and Others in Germany 1933-1945*, trans. by G. R. Fraser (Oxford: Oxford University Press, 1988).

3.3. *Revitalize biopolitics?*

An important task which Esposito tries to respond to is to identify the ways in which it is possible to overturn the thanatopolitical "destiny" of modern biopolitics. In this sense he argues that we must, above all, try to disassemble and overturn the «bio-thanatological principles» of Nazism precisely because this was what fully realized this destiny.[104]

To this end – according to Esposito – we should, first of all, dissolve the centrality that our culture generally attributes to the concept of "political body" and that Nazism emphasized to an extreme extent. This concept should be contrasted with the idea, proposed by Maurice Merleau-Ponty, of «flesh of the world» understood as an «undifferential layer (and thus for this reason exposed to difference), in which the same notion of body, anything but enclosed, is now turned outside in an irreducible heterogeneity».[105] This idea would, above all, allow us to grasp the biopolitically positive potential of globalization which, compromising the boundaries and the cohesion of the political body of the state, could cause a sort of «extension of the somatic surface to the entire globe»; in which, «[i]f everything is the body, nothing will rigidly define it, which is to say no precise immunitary borders will mark and circumscribe it». In a similar scenario, according to Esposito, life can finally be placed «at the center of the global *polis*» and can attain an affirmative political force.[106]

Furthermore, according to the Italian philosopher, it would be necessary to free the idea of *birth* from the dispositif of suppressing it, that worked in Nazism in an apparently contradictory way through «the exhibition and the strengthening of the generative capacity of the German people» and, on the other hand, «the homicidal fury that is destined inevitably to

---

104 *Bíos: Biopolitics and Philosophy*, p. 157.
105 *Bíos: Biopolitics and Philosophy*, p. 159; see also pp. 157-62. Furthermore, see Maurice Merleau-Ponty, *The Visible and the Invisible*, ed. by Claude Lefort, trans. by Alphonso Lingis (Evanston, Ill.: Northwestern University Press, 1968).
106 *Bíos: Biopolitics and Philosophy*, p. 166.

inhibit it».[107] Esposito contrasts – so to speak – this dispositif with the theory of Gilbert Simondon according to whom life is a «perpetual birth» in which there is «an unending series of successive individuations» and

> the relation to both the world outside and to the collective is in fact a dimension of the individuation in which the individual participates due to its connection with the preindividual reality that undergoes gradual individuation.[108]

In this vision – says Esposito – «[e]very individual structure, at the moment of its greatest expansion, always preserves a remainder that cannot be integrated within its own dimension without reaching a successive phase of development».[109] So that here the «collective, (...) far from being its simple contrary or the neutralization of individuality, is itself a form of more elaborate individuation».[110] The essentially open nature of life processes, the substantial indistinction between birth and life, the reciprocal implication between individuality and collectivity would make this conception another essential presupposition of an affirmative biopolitics.

3.4. *Immunity and genetic calculations*

Insisting on the need to overturn the assumptions of Nazi biopolitics, Esposito also argues that it is important to dissolve the conditions of possibility of the «*absolute normativization of life*» realized by the law of the third Reich: this normativization

---

107 *Bíos: Biopolitics and Philosophy*, p. 169.
108 Gilbert Simondon, 'The Genesis of the Individual', trans. by Mark Cohen and Sanford Kwinter, in *Incorporations*, ed. by Jonathan Crary and Sanford Kwinter (New York: Zone Books, 1992), pp. 307 and 309. The text just quoted is a partial English translation of Gilbert Simondon, *L'individu et sa genèse physico-biologique* (Paris: Presses Universitaires de France, 1964); see also Gilbert Simondon, *L'individuation psychique et collective* (Paris: Éditions Aubier, 1989), and Esposito, *Bíos: Biopolitics and Philosophy*, pp. 180-1.
109 *Bíos: Biopolitics and Philosophy*, p. 180.
110 *Bíos: Biopolitics and Philosophy*, pp. 181-2.

was based on the assumption, on the one hand, of the «facticity of life» (the "natural" datum of race) as «privileged content» of the norm and, on the other hand, on the fixing of the discriminating «caesura» between lives «of different value» in the same legal norm.[111] However, it is not be a question of pursuing a dissolution of the relationship between life and norm, but of intensifying it in a completely different direction, accepting the idea that every form of life has its norm and that this is no more than «the singular and plural mode that nature every so often assumes in all the range of its expressions».[112]

On the subject of the relationship between life and norm, for Esposito, the perspectives of an «affirmative biopolitics» are clearly delineated. Here – according to him – Canguilhem's philosophy of biology is of decisive importance, or, more precisely, his idea of the norm as a «pure mode or state of being», that compromises any «transcendent role of command» and any «prescriptive function» of the norm itself; so that «not only health but also disease constitutes a norm that is not superimposed on life, but expresses a specific situation of life».[113]

In this regard it can be observed that, by attributing a fundamental importance to the thought of Canguilhem, Esposito indirectly contributes to highlighting the limits of his thesis according to which the essential and problematic core of the dominant biopolitics consists in its immunitary character. In fact, when Canguilhem insists on the idea that «a human organism's norm is its coincidence with the organism itself» he does so also with the intention of denouncing and averting the risk that the norm itself may «coincide with the calculations of a eugenic geneticist».[114] Precisely in this way he allows us to understand that, in our age, biopolitics is, above all, a field of confrontation and possibly conflict with a biopower that does not limit itself to perpetuating the domain of the immunological

---

111 *Bíos: Biopolitics and Philosophy*, pp. 182-4.
112 *Bíos: Biopolitics and Philosophy*, p. 186.
113 *Bíos: Biopolitics and Philosophy*, pp. 186 and 189.
114 Georges Canguilhem, *The Normal and the Pathological*, trans. by Carolyn R. Fawcett and Robert S. Cohen (New York: Zone Books, 1991), p. 259.

paradigm, but renews itself by leveraging the genetic paradigm. Therefore, if it is in the "genetic calculations" that many problems and dangers of contemporary biopower are lurking, it is not certain that it is sufficient to elaborate «a different philosophy of immunization» to deal with them.[115]

Far from claiming that the immunitary aims of modern biopolitics are destined to ebb,[116] we can hypothesize that the engineering and "recombinant" approach of contemporary genetics now tends to reabsorb – or interact with – the defensive and protective purpose of immunization in the ambition to produce genetically "better" organisms, both in their capacity for self-defense and in their "possibilities of life", understood as a biological, economic and political "power" in the broad sense. From this point of view – although it may be considered naive or "delirious" – the idea of overcoming the limits of the species, contained in the theories of *trans-humanism*, corresponds better than the notion of *immunity* to many of the biopolitical perspectives of postmodernity.[117] It is a biopolitics of performance, of competition and of the consequent economic, political and ethical hierarchies that is affirmed in this way. This is how we can reinterpret Foucault's hypothesis regarding the union that in our society seems to be realized between the applications of genetics and those of the neoliberal theory of human capital:

> good genetic make-ups – that is to say, [those] able to produce individuals with low risk or with a level of risk which will not be harmful for themselves, those around them, or society – will certainly become scarce, and insofar as they are scarce they may perfectly well

---

115 Esposito, 'Biopolitica, immunità, comunità', p. 130.
116 We will return to this issue in the last chapter.
117 Regarding this, see: Paola Borgna 'Postumano', in *Lessico di biopolitica*, pp. 225-9; Mark O'Connell, *To Be a Machine: Adventures Among Cyborgs, Utopians, Hackers, and the Futurists Solving the Modest Problem of Death* (London: Granta Book, 2017); James Barrat, *Our Final Invention: Artificial Intelligence and the End of the Human Era* (New York: Thomas Dunne Books, 2015); Ray Kurzweil, *The Singularity is Near: When Humans Transcend Biology* (London: Duckworth Overlook, 2005).

[enter], and this is entirely normal, into economic circuits or calculations.[118]

From this point of view, «the political problem of the use of genetics – as Foucault says – arises in terms of the formation, growth, accumulation, and improvement of human capital».[119] The task that contemporary biopolitics imposes on us, therefore, is not only that of overturning its thanatopolitical inclination, as Esposito believes, but also that of problematizing it because it produces, among other things, not negligible effects of power concerning behavior and ways of practicing the freedom of individuals and society. It is worthy of critical attention not only because it touches or endangers life, but also because it is a form of government of individuals that, by putting their lives at stake, influences their existence, orients their coexistence, and structures or determines their *ethos*.

After all, it is this type of reason that led Foucault to reabsorb the genealogy of biopower in that of governmentality. This is why, deepening his investigation, he first focused on the importance that, with liberalism and neoliberalism, freedom assumes as «both ideology and technique of government»;[120] subsequently he sought in the practices of ethical self-government an indispensable condition of attempts to reduce the grip of biopower on *life* and that of the heteronomous government of individuals over their own *existence*.

3.5. *Impersonal biopolitics*

The importance attributed to the concept of «flesh of the world» proposed by Merleau-Ponty, and the reference to Simondon's fluid vision of the relationship between «preindividual reality», individuality and collectivity, as well as the emphasis assigned to the liberating values of Canguilhem's philosophy of biology constitute a sort of

---

118 *Birth of Biopolitics*, p. 228.
119 Ibid.
120 *Security, Territory, Population,* p. 48.

announcement of the main outcome of Esposito's reflection on biopolitics. It is the radical questioning of the importance that – according to the Italian author – the philosophical, ethical and political tradition of the West generally attributes to the notion of *person*.[121] This notion – in his opinion – was strongly re-launched after the Second World War and today represents an essential point of reference on the juridical, as well as philosophical and ethical levels, both for secular and religious culture. The idea of person was assumed as a concept capable of finally guaranteeing respect for human rights, which Nazism had made impossible because it had linked the idea of man to whether or not a living being was a member of a superior race. The notion of person, moreover, is today seen as a condition of overcoming the unbridged gap between the concepts of man and citizen that with the French Revolution had been improperly considered as connected with each other and set side by side in the *Declaration* of 1789; it is on the concept of person, in fact, that the formulation of the *Universal Declaration of Human Rights* of 1948 was also based.[122]

In reality, the idea of person – according to Esposito – is completely inadequate to warding off the risk that modern politics, through biopolitics, could produce the radical discrimination of those who do not correspond to the definition that can be given from time to time to who is included under the umbrella of human rights. Today, in fact, when globalization seems to be the best condition for overcoming the limits of national citizenship as a prerequisite for the recognition of these rights, the latter – starting from the right to life – are guaranteed increasingly less: «the growing number of deaths from hunger, war and epidemics is an eloquent testimony to the ineffectiveness of what has come to be called "human rights"».[123]

---

121 See Roberto Esposito, *Third Person: Politics of Life and Philosophy of Impersonal*, trans. by Zakiya Hanafi (Cambridge, UK: Politiy Press, 2012) and Esposito, 'Toward a Philosophy of the Impersonal', in *Terms of the Political*, pp. 112-22.

122 Esposito, *Third Person*, pp. 1-4 and 67-73; Esposito, 'Toward a Philosophy of the Impersonal', pp. 112-3.

123 Esposito, *Third Person*, p. 4; see also Esposito, ' Toward a Philosophy

According to the Italian philosopher, the extreme inadequacy of the concept of person can be explained by going back to its original juridical conception which established itself at the time of ancient Rome; it is also necessary to consider that this concept is deeply rooted in our culture through the combination that has historically been created between the Roman and Christian traditions. In Roman law, in particular, being qualified as a person was an indispensable condition for the full enjoyment of the liberties of the citizen. This qualification, however, was not attributed to just any human being; it entailed a clear distinction between persons legally guaranteed in their freedom and those considered non-persons: not only slaves, but also women and young people constituted different expressions and gradations of the condition of non-person. In the emblematic case of the slave, his eventual liberation from the state of "thing" at his master's disposal and his transformation into person implied both his passage through various intermediate stages between slavery and freedom and the possibility of the reversal of the process of his liberation.

> Ultimately, freedom was nothing but a "remnant" or residue – a narrow, fragile projection – of the natural horizon of slavery. No human being was a person by nature – not as such. Certainly not the slave, but not the free man either: before he became *pater*, that is a legal subject, he still had to pass through the state of *filius in potestate*, which reflected the fact that, in the changeable dispositif of the person, since human beings arrived into life from the world of things, they could always be thrust back into it.[124]

According to Esposito, this discrepancy between the abstractly legal figure of the person and «the concrete existence and corporeal density of an individual human being»[125] reproduces itself in the Christian tradition through the schism between body and soul, human nature and divine nature; therefore, in actual fact, in this tradition

---

of the Impersonal', p. 114.
124 *Third Person*, p. 79.
125 *Third Person*, p. 76.

the separation between the person and the living body (...) grants entry into the afterlife. Both the idea of the double nature of Christ and that of the Trinity confirm this inner gap, this structural doubling of the personal dimension.[126]

Modernity, on the other hand, welcomes and reproduces in other ways the «dispositif that separates and excludes», which underlies the concept of person.[127] It is true that when the French revolution introduced the equality of all men, this separating dispositif seemed destined to disappear, since all men were declared to have rights. In truth – says Esposito – it still functioned by installing itself directly in the individual, since the juridical subjectivity that is recognized to him is identified with his «rational and volitional or moral part»; the human being, therefore, is split into two elements: «a biological body and a site of legal imputation, the first being subjected to the discretionary control of the second».[128] In short, according to Esposito, «this attribution of subjectivity refers to a noncorporeal, or more-than-corporeal element that inhabits the body, and which divides it in two parts: one rational, spiritual, or moral (which is the personal), and the other animal».[129]

The reproduction in different forms of a split between what makes and what does not make someone a person is what perpetuates the possibility for life to remain exposed to the dominion of a biopower ready to become a thanatopower; it is a split – says Esposito – that reaffirms itself in contemporary culture even, or above all, in the areas in which one would expected that it could be easily overcome. This, in particular, is the extremely significant case of liberal bioethics, about which Esposito's theses certainly appear to be convincing. The theories of the major exponents of liberal bioethics, in fact, are completely based on the centrality of the person and on the distinction of the human figures to whom the quality of person can be recognized or not.

---

126 Esposito, ' Toward a Philosophy of the Impersonal', p. 115.
127 Esposito, ' Toward a Philosophy of the Impersonal', p. 117.
128 *Third Person*, pp. 82 and 83; see also pp. 96-7.
129 Esposito, ' Toward a Philosophy of the Impersonal', pp. 116-7.

In any case, whether you start from the beginning or from the end of life, what really qualifies as 'person' only occupies the central section: that of adult, healthy individuals. Before and after this lies the no man's land of the non-person (the fetus), the quasi-person (the infant), the semi-person (the elderly, no longer mentally or physically able), the no-longer-person (the patient in a vegetative state), and, finally, the anti-person (the fool [...]).[130]

It is on this basis that – as Esposito observes – liberal bioethics, although based on «strict moral protocols», ends up assigning the person the function of «'deciding' machine» which «legally separates life from itself» turning it into a terrain of decision «about what must live and what may die, because it is a simple thing in the hands of those who, thanks to their superior ontological status, are exclusively qualified to dispose of it».[131]

Esposito does not fail to point out that not only the contemporary secular culture, but also the Christian one supports and legitimizes the functioning of the separating dispositif of the person. Which – according to him – clearly emerges, for example, from the theses of Jacques Maritain, principal exponent of christian personalism. This author – who participated actively in the writing of the *Declaration* of 1948 – claims that the human person possesses rights since he embodies the sovereignty over himself that has been assigned to man by divine sovereignty.[132] To the extent that this idea of person is based on the exercise of a sovereignty, it is entirely comparable to the secular and liberal vision which, already through John Locke and John S. Mill, finds the foundation of the freedom of the individual in the ownership of himself.[133] In both cases – according to Esposito – what is realized is a reification of the body, its reduction to an object, without which no sovereignty of man over himself and no

---

130   *Third Person*, p. 97; see also pp. 96-9. Esposito refers in particular to Hugo T. Engelhardt, *The Foundations of Bioethics* (New York: Oxford University Press, 1986) and Peter Singer, *Writings on an Ethical Life* (New York: Ecco Press, 2000).

131   *Third Person*, p. 99.

132   *Third Person*, pp. 72-3; see also pp. 12, 88-93, and Jacques Maritain, *The Rights of Man and Natural Law*, trans. by Doris C. Anson (New York: Gordian Press, 1971).

133   *Third Person*, pp. 91-2.

personalization of the human being can be possible; nor could any ownership of oneself by the individual, no bioethical supremacy of the person over the non-person nor the fate of his living organism be exercised.[134]

The perspective that Esposito outlines to attempt to free life from the discriminating mechanism of the person is that of a philosophy of the impersonal. In this sense, he relies on the thoughts of some thinkers among whom Simone Weil and Gilles Deleuze stand out.[135] In particular, Esposito takes from Weil the radical distinction between justice and rights and the clear preference for the former over to the latter. According to Weil, in fact, «the notion of rights, by its very mediocrity, leads naturally to that of the person, for rights are related to personal things».[136] What Weil denies, recognizing its connection with «the exclusionary dispositif of the person», is «the character of the "right" – particularistic per se, at once private and privative».[137] Therefore, the French author explicitly contrasts the impersonal dimension with the personal one: according to her, in fact, «[e]verithing which is impersonal in man is sacred, and nothing else».[138] If Weil distinguishes and gives priority to justice with respect to rights, it is because only the first «pertains to the impersonal, the anonymous – that which, not having a name, stands before or after the personal subject».[139] Ultimately, the French thinker aspires to dissolve the particularism that seems structurally connected with "rights" with respect to which she intends to re-establish the primacy of obligations. As Esposito observes, appreciating the theses of Weil, «the obligation of each, added to that of all others, corresponds in a global count to the rights of the entire human community».[140]

---

134 *Third Person*, pp. 92-3, 98-9, and 147.
135 Esposito searches for other elements of a philosophy of the impersonal in Émile Benveniste, Alexandre Kojève, Vladimir Jankélévitch, Emmanuel Lèvinas, Maurice Blanchot and in Michel Foucault; see *Third Person*, pp. 104-42.
136 Simone Weil, 'Human Personality', in *Simone Weil: An Anthology,* ed. by Sian Miles (New York: Grove Press, 1986), p. 62.
137 *Third Person*, p. 101.
138 Weil, 'Human Personality', p. 54.
139 *Third Person*, pp. 101-2.
140 *Third Person*, p. 103.

Esposito, nevertheless, while accepting the ideas of Weil, believes that the possibility of defusing the excluding mechanism of the person should not be entrusted solely to the community dimension, but should be sought in the person himself; according to him, it is a matter of recognizing and valuing «the relational impulse that makes the person something different from the isolated individual» and, at the same time, to extract and free «the singular element that is still implicit in the idea of a person» from the personal dimension.[141] The notion of *singular* – according to the Italian philosopher – is not the opposite of the impersonal; it rather allows one to think of human beings «for what they have that is most unique, but also for what they most have in common with each other».[142]

It is also for reasons like this that Esposito claims that «t]he most compelling encounter between contemporary philosophy and the power of the impersonal is certainly to be found in the work of Gilles Deleuze».[143] For the Italian author, Deleuze offers us the clearest possibility of thinking about an impersonal and affirmative biopolitics in his last essay devoted precisely to the theme of life. Life in its immanence, in its becoming and in being one with itself here presents itself as what unites all living beings without eliminating their singularity and multiplicity, and, at the same time, without involving the separation between a subject and an object, between a person and his body.[144] On the other hand, it is in the concept of "becoming-animal", developed by Deleuze together with Felix Guattari, that Esposito traces the most fruitful conceptual tool for the perspective of a philosophy of the impersonal.[145] Paradoxically, precisely because the animality of the body is what the exclusionary mechanism of the person

---

141 *Third Person*, p. 103.
142 *Third Person*, p. 102-3.
143 *Third Person*, p. 142.
144 *Third Person*, p. 147. See Gilles Deleuze, 'Immanence: A Life', in *Pure Immanence: Essays on a Life*, trans. by Anne Boyman (New York: Zone Books, 2001), pp. 25-33; see also *Bíos: Biopolitics and Philosophy*, pp. 191-4.
145 See Gilles Deleuze and Felix Guattari, *A Thousand Plateaus. Capitalism and Schizophrenia* (Minneapolis: University of Minnesota Press, 1987).

presumes to submit to its supremacy; precisely because, on the other hand, the reduction of man to the animality of his life has historically been the devastating condition of the thanatopolitical overthrow of biopolitics, the idea of "becoming-animal" can be a tool of radical contrast both of the dispositif of the person and of the thanatopolitical "destiny" of biopolitics. The "becoming-animal" must be understood, however, not only as an invitation to behave and remain in rapport with the animality of which we are a part; it must also be understood, above all, as adhesion to the becoming as such, to transformation and to the change which constantly affects life. It does not exclude reference to the person, but alters and declines it as a living person, «as an inseparable *synolon* of form and force, external and internal, *bios* and *zoé*».[146]

What is worth observing here is that the unconditional acceptance of our animality could still leave us exposed to the bio-thanato-political dangers that we hope to avoid; this could derive exactly from the fact that it seems to imply a definitive renunciation of seeking a political horizon different from that of biopolitics, a renunciation of the specificity of political action and perhaps even the illusion of being able to escape from the conflictual nature of relations of power.[147]

4. *Beyond the zoé and the bios*

We can say that Esposito offers his own declination of a perspective also substantially shared by Agamben and Negri: a perspective within which it is assumed to be almost impossible to escape the centrality that biopolitics attributes to life in its natural, generative, productive or reproductive immediacy. In general,

---

146 *Third Person*, p. 151; see also pp. 149-50. For a very interesting treatment of the theme of animality in biopolitical terms see Vanessa Lemm, *Nietzsche Animal's philosophy: Culture, Politics, and the Animality of the Human Being* (New York: Fordham University, 2009), especially pp. 152-6.

147 In this regard, see Laura Bazzicalupo, *Biopolitica. Una mappa concettuale* (Rome: Carocci, 2010), pp. 117-26.

however, the positions of the three authors are distinguished by the different importance they attribute to the possibility of practicing an affirmative biopolitics: Agamben does not seem to assign great credit to this possibility, while Negri explicitly maintains that it is immediately practicable, and Esposito assumes it as a hypothesis that the current situation requires us to actively explore.

Lying behind their different positions, the problem of the distinction between *zoé* and *bios* remains – in other words, between the sphere of "natural life" and that of "qualified life" of which, for the ancient Greeks, "political life" would have been the exemplary form.[148] Agamben – as we have seen – sets this distinction at the basis of his reflection, presenting it, moreover, as the common assumption that would make possible a fruitful interaction between the thought of Foucault and that of Arendt, since both explain many of the radical changes that Western politics has undergone in modernity precisely with the dissolution of this distinction.[149] At the same time, the author of *Homo Sacer* argues that in antiquity this distinction was nevertheless functional to the imperative of politically subjecting the «bare life» (*zoé*) to the «qualified life» (*bios*), which could not fail to lead to the biopolitical overcoming of the distinction itself and of its importance in our age.[150]

Through a more direct discourse, Negri also considers the distinction between *zoé* and *bios* to be useless today; therefore, he believes that at this time there is no longer any privileged link – as Hannah Arendt believed – between *zoé* and labour intended as an activity designed to respond simply to the biological needs of life. Today – says Negri – «the presence of labour at the center of the life world and the extension of social cooperation across society becomes total».[151] Therefore, «in the biopolitical world (...) social, economic, and political production and reproduction coincide, the

---

148 On this distinction and its importance in the debate on biopolitics, see Antonella Moscati, 'Zoé/bios', in *Lessico di biopolitica*, pp. 336-41.

149 See *Homo Sacer*, pp. 9-10 and 71.

150 See *Homo Sacer*, pp. 104-5.

151 Michael Hardt and Antonio Negri, *Labour of Dionysus: A Critique of the state-Form* (Minneapolis: University of Minnesota Press, 1994), pp. 10-1.

ontological perspective and the anthropological perspective tend to overlap»;[152] labour now also includes the qualities of *bios*, the potential of politics, and, therefore, represents a general capacity to free biopolitics from biopower.[153]

Also Esposito, for his part, refuses to renew the importance of the distinction between *zoé* and *bios*, claiming, moreover, that Hannah Arendt was able to rehabilitate it only by basing it «on the unverified premise according to which the only valid form of political activity is what is attributable to the experience of the Greek *polis*».[154] This distinction – according to him – no longer serves any purpose regarding the current problems and potentialities of biopolitics. Far more important in this regard is the fact that «*bios*» – interpreted as «flesh» and as a life without specifications – today «is reintroduced not on the margins or the thresholds, but at the center of the global *polis*».[155]

In the light of this common refusal by the three authors to attribute validity and relevance to the conceptual distinction between *zoé* and *bios*, it may be interesting to consider that Foucault, for his part, was not at all insensitive to this distinction, although he was aware of its uselessness in our age. In reality, one can perhaps say that, for him, it was not so much a question of denying the decline of the *zoé-bios* dualism, as of rethinking it to make room for a third element, namely *ethos*, the ethical detachment of singular and multiple existences from power over life and from the socialization of the productive force and the impersonal carnality of life itself.

In a Course held in 1980-1981, the French philosopher carefully examined the distinction between *zoé* and *bios*; he did not feel the need to examine it deeply in his previous years' research on biopolitics, but he felt it at that moment, as he began the journey that lead him to deal with the care of the self. He takes for granted that for the Greeks the term *zoé* corresponds to the simple and natural fact of living; vice versa, he does not link the word *bios* to "qualified life" or

152 *Empire*, p. 388.
153 See *Empire*, pp. 386-9; Hardt and Negri, *Commonwealth*, pp. 354-5.
154 *Bíos: Biopolitics and Philosophy*, p. 150; see also pp. 14-5.
155 *Bíos: Biopolitics and Philosophy*, p. 166.

"political life"; instead, he links it to the «life that can be qualified», to the «course of existence (...) inseparably linked to the possibility of managing it, transforming it, directing it in this or that direction». For him, this is the reason why – especially in the Hellenistic period – *bios* was the specific object of the ethical subjectivation practices of the care of the self, defined not by chance with expressions such as *tekhnai peri bion* or *technē peri bion*, i.e., «art of existence» and «technique that concerns the existence understood as life to be led».[156]

Therefore – according to his analysis – the *bios* is not a qualified life, but a life to be qualified; which does not mean that it has to do with mere biological life, with a bare life, with a vital power or with an impersonal physicality; rather it is existence understood as something necessarily singular. Foucault argues that in ancient times the *bios* refers in some way to the idea of subjectivity, even if the fact that the Greeks do not use this concept is obviously not negligible; in any case it is a "subjectivity" which is always "subjectivising" through practices of formation and transformation, that is, of self-government.[157]

When, in his last Course, Foucault analyzes philosophical *parrhēsia*, that is the courage of the truth which – in his opinion – philosophy dating back to Socrates has assumed as an ethical task and as a way of existence, he says clearly: «through the emergence and foundation of Socratic *parrhēsia*, existence (*bios*) was constituted in Greek thought as an aesthetic object, as an object of aesthetic elaboration and perception: *bios* as a beautiful work».[158]

It can probably be deduced that, from his point of view, it is, first of all, through an ethical art of existence that one escapes the biopower and the indefinite expansion of biopolitics, circumscribing the management of problems of *zoé* to the

---

156 Michel Foucault, *Subjectivity and Truth. Lectures at the Collège de France, 1980-1981,* ed. by Frédéric Gros, trans. by Graham Burchell (London: Palgrave MacMillan, 2017), pp. 33-5 and 251-4; see also Foucault, *The Hermeneutics of the Subject,*p. 447.

157 Foucault, *Subjectivity and Truth*, pp. 253-4.

158 Michel Foucault, *The Courage of the Truth The Government of Self and Others II. Lectures at the Collège de France, 1983–1984*, ed. by Frédéric Gros, trans. by Graham Burchell (London: Palgrave MacMillan, 2011), p. 162; see also pp. 126-7.

productive and reproductive sphere. Despite the apparent obviousness, it is significant the clarification that, in his 1980-1981 Course, Foucault felt the need to do by saying that the Greek expression *tekhnai peri bion* cannot be translated with the term "bio-tecniques", since today this word leads us to think of a completely different kind of practice.[159] In fact, in contemporary biotechniques (or biotechnology), there is constantly at stake the possibility that problems of life such as *zoé* can overtake those of the *bios* as an existence that must be ethically transformed, first and even more than politically, so that the problems of life itself will be handled with the appropriate attention.

As an ethical practice, *parrhēsia* – «a practice which finds its function of truth in the criticism of illusion, deception, trickery, and flattery» – necessarily implies a critical relationship with power and politics: those who want to practice freedom ethically must do so first by telling the truth about relations of power.[160] From this point of view, before wondering if and how biopolitics could free itself from biopower, we should have the courage to say and to tell ourselves an elementary truth: biopower is not simply an institution, a structure or a poorly made system, but often it is the unexpected effect of the most innocent practices.

159 Foucault, *Subjectivity and Truth*, p. 34.
160 Foucault, *The Government of Self and Others. Lectures at the Collège de France, 1982–1983*, pp. 353-4.

CHAPTER FOUR
BIOPOWER AND ECONOMIC RATIONALITY
Family Life, Social Security, Human Capital

1. *The modern family and the expansion of life*

1.1 *From model to instrument of government*

As we have already seen, according to Foucault, at the beginning of modernity European monarchies begin to become aware of not being able to effectively exercise their power by relying only on their sovereignty; therefore, they begin to elaborate and develop an art of government. Recalling authors – such as Guillame de La Perrière and François de La Mothe Le Vayer – who between the 16th and 17th centuries carried out particularly detailed thoughts on the subject, the French philosopher highlights the fact that, in this phase, the family *oikonomia* of antiquity is taken as a model in the elaboration of this art of government.[1]

> The art of government essentially appears in this literature as having to answer the question of how to introduce economy – that is to say, the proper way of managing individuals, goods, and wealth, like the management of a family by a father who knows how to direct his wife, his children, and his servants, who knows how to make his family's fortune prosper, and how to arrange suitable alliances for it – how to introduce this meticulous attention, this type of relationship between father and the family, into the management of the state?[2]

---

1   *Security, Territory, Population*, pp. 92-108.
2   *Security, Territory, Population*, pp. 94-5. The texts that Foucault refers to most in this regard are: Guillame de La Perrière, *Le miroire politique, œuvre non moins utile que nécessaire à tous monarches, roys, princes, seigneurs, magistrats, et autre surintendants et gouverneurs de Republicque* (Paris: V. Norment and J. Bruneau, 1567, 2nd edn.); François de La Mothe Le Vayer, *L'oeconomique du prince* (Paris: A. Courbé, 1653).

Foucault also shows that at the end of this period «the family disappears as the model of government»;[3] Rousseau, for example, clearly indicating the administration of the state with the expression *political economy*, insists on the impossibility of continuing to consider the *oikonomia*, or the household management, as a model of this administration, given the enormous difference in size and complexity of the respective areas. He also clearly distinguishes the political economy from the exercise of sovereignty, identifying the first with government; he defines the state as a «great family», but at the same time argues that «domestic government» and «civil government» cannot be exercised in the same way.[4]

Nevertheless, according to Foucault's reconstruction, the renunciation of considering the family *oikonomia* as a model of political government will not involve the exclusion of the family from the scenario of governmental strategies at all; rather it will take on a new and far from irrelevant role. And, also in this case, to give a decisive impulse in this sense will be the increasing attention that will be devoted to the biopolitical object par excellence, or to the population.

In other words, prior to the emergence of the problematic of population, the art of government could only be conceived on the basis of the model of the family, in terms of economy understood as management of the family. When, however, the population appears as absolutely irreducible to the family, the result is that the latter falls to a lower level than the population; it appears as an element within the population. It is therefore no longer a model; it is a segment whose privilege is simply that when one wants to obtain something from the population concerning sexual behavior, demography, the birth rate, or consumption, then one has to utilize the family. The family will change from being a model to being an instrument; it will become a privileged instrument for the government of the population rather than a chimerical model for good government. (...) And in actual fact, from the middle of the eighteenth century, the family really does

---

3   *Security, Territory, Population*, p. 104.
4   Jean-Jacques Rousseau, A *Discourse on Political Economy,* trans. by George Douglas Howard Cole (London: J. M. Dent, 1993), p. 128. See Foucault, *Security, Territory, Population*, pp. 106-7.

appear in this instrumental relation to the population, in the campaigns on mortality, campaigns concerning marriage, vaccinations, and inoculations, and so on.[5]

Evidently, according to this framing of the issue, the new role of the family is defined around problems that more clearly biopolitical could not be: «sexual behaviour, demography, the birth rate, or consumption, (...) the campaigns on mortality, campaigns concerning marriage, vaccinations, and inoculations». Moreover, from this framework it clearly emerges that a large part of the new role of the family will also be played in the ethical sphere, that is, in terms of the formation of adequate and functional behaviours to the not simply biopolitical, but also and above all economical governmentality that is being established. The family will become «a privileged instrument for the government of the population» transforming itself into a place where the strategic pursuit of biopolitical aims will be intertwined with the promotion of an individual and social *ethos* inspired by economic rationality.

1.2 *Familiarizing the economic* ethos

Accepting these indications deriving from the work of Foucault, it is important to consider the interweaving of biopolitical, economic and moral aims that begins to unfold when the government of a society is still entrusted to the police state, at the time of absolutism. In particular – as Jacques Donzelot observes – in the exemplary situation of *Ancien Régime* France, a convergence of interests is created between families and the police regarding the treatment of people whose behaviours are perceived as dangerous for the family reputation, on the one hand, and for the power of the state, on the other. For example, the internment of young prostitutes or wandering adolescents in segregation or correctional institutions is generally requested by their own families, while the abandonment of adulterous children in foundling hospitals is used by families as a possibility to save their conscience and their honour. The police, for their part, favour these practices endeavouring to create the

---

5   *Security, Territory, Population*, pp. 104–5.

conditions for transforming "useless" individuals into active forces to produce wealth and for the strengthening of the state. Therefore, this ensures that the «convents for the preservation and correction of young girls, supervised brothels for prostitutes, and foundling hospitals» have «the explicit purpose to reconcile the interest of families and the interest of the state, to bring harmony to families through the moralization of behaviour, and to consolidate the force of the state through the treatment of the inevitable casualties of this family regime».[6]

In the 19th century, liberal culture denounced the ineffectiveness and onerousness of these systems by showing, for example: that many families also abandon their legitimate children at the foundling hospitals so that the state would take responsibility for their maintenance; that their mothers with various deceptions often managed to have them returned as wet-nurses, receiving a salary for this task. Therefore, the system of anonymous abandonment of new-borns at the foundling hospitals was progressively discouraged and replaced by a set of offices that directly control and assist those mothers whose conditions would easily lead them to abandon or neglect their children: single mothers, widows, working women, mothers of large families. It is also important to note that this assistance is based on forms of inspection and surveillance on the hygienic, sanitary and educational conditions in which families live and children are raised.[7]

This kind of transformation is mostly supported by philanthropic associations which, being interested above all in the poorer classes of industrial cities, promote strategies of "familiarization" of their daily life to face the phenomena of "social deviance". These associations identify the family as both a place of moral responsibility and a means to alleviate the expenses of the state by promoting mutual help between people

---

6   Jacques Donzelot, *The Policing of Family*, trans. by Robert Hurley (New York: Pantheon Books, 1979), pp. 23 and 24. See also Arlette Farge and Michel Foucault, *Disorderly Families: Infamous Letters from the Bastille Archives,* ed. by Nancy Luxon, trans. by Thomas Scott-Railton (Minneapolis and London: University of Minnesota Press, 2016).

7   Donzelot, *The Policing of Family*, pp. 25-31.

and reducing the number of illegitimate children to be entrusted to assistance institutions. They therefore actively encourage marriages to limit the precariousness of relations between men and women, fight concubinage, engage in child protection, and tend to give women the role of guarantor of family stability. In this sense, without denying the right of women to work, these organizations denounce the poor conditions in which they work in factories and the degrading competition they give men in the labour market. Philanthropy also disputes the custom of sending poor girls to the workhouses of convents to enable them to obtain a dowry for their marriage, since this custom would not allow them to acquire the willpower and responsibility they will have as wives and mothers. To overcome these situations, philanthropic associations encourage and help the women from the working classes to take on the role of guardian of the hearth and to transform their homes into places where the temptations of the road for children and the tavern for men will have to weaken.[8]

Philanthropy, placing itself halfway between the state and the market, became a very important tool in the 19th century to counter the social problems arising from the growing presence in the large cities of the industrial grassroots and the multitudes of poor people; it carries out its endeavour, however, taking care to contain the involvement of the state: it is a question of tackling the problem of poverty without burdening the state with excessive social care functions; it is also a question of establishing a discipline for the working classes in a situation in which traditional corporate and community ties are declining and can no longer guarantee the reproduction of a social order now endangered by revolutionary movements. As Donzelot shows, the attentions that philanthropy addresses to the family have a decisive importance in the social diffusion of a morality compatible with the free market economy. In the philanthropic strategies, in fact, the promotion of the attitude of the family to saving has a central position «for reabsorbing individuals for whom it had been inclined to relinquish responsibility, calling upon the state instead as the agency politically responsible for their subsistence and well-

---

8   *The Policing of Family*, pp. 31-47.

being».[9] Indeed, in the 19th century *savings banks* experienced a significant growth and indirectly contributed to the transformation of poverty and social marginalization into a problem of lacking economic morality.[10]

1.3 *Vice and misery, moral restraint and savings*

Many philanthropy theorists are inspired at least in part by Thomas R. Malthus. In his most famous work, published and republished in various editions from 1798, it was he that insisted on the importance that encouragement towards workers to save should be given in a liberal society. This practice, according to him, has a great moralizing force, since it induces and accustoms people to the virtues of foresight and prudence.[11] What should be emphasized here is that these virtues – according to Malthus – are necessary primarily to face the main problem in which the working classes must be taught responsibility: the exquisitely biopolitical problem of population growth.

This growth – in his opinion – tends spontaneously to overcome the development of the production of subsistence means, causing the deterioration of living conditions for the population. The author, in his *Essay*, proposes a general theory of population growth,[12] which can be summarized in the following terms.

The consistency of the population, if it does not encounter obstacles, doubles every 25 years according to a «geometrical ratio», while the production of sustenance goods, at best, increases according to an «arithmetical ratio». The main reason for this difference – according to Malthus – is in the decreasing yield of the land as it is subjected to cultivation to satisfy the nutritional needs of the population itself: once all the fertile land has been occupied, the fertility of which is anyway different, one can only

---

9   *The Policing of Family*, p. 58.
10   See *The Policing of Family*, pp. 53-70; see also Foucault, *The Birth of Biopolitics*, p. 66.
11   Thomas R. Malthus, *An Essay on the Principle of Population* (London: John Murray, 1826, 6th edn), vol. II, pp. 407-11.
12   See Malthus, *An Essay on the Principle of Population*, vol. I, in particular pp. 1-24.

try to improve the productivity of the land already cultivated with various technical means. However, their overall productive capacity, also due to the increasing exploitation, will tend to decrease and therefore, evidently, it will never be able to increase proportionally to the population growth.[13] This can only give rise to negative consequences for the life of the population: hunger, poverty, disease, worsening of the collective health conditions, increased mortality, etc. According to Malthus, these effects constitute a first form of «obstacles» that can slow down or halt population growth; the author defines them as a whole: «misery». However, they fall within a broader set of obstacles to the increase of population, which Malthus distinguishes in «preventive», «positive» and «of mixed nature» and, furthermore, articulates in three general types: «moral restraint, vice and misery». This is how he summarizes his thoughts in this regard:

> On examining these obstacles to the increase of population which I have classed under the heads of preventive and positive checks, it will appear that they are all resolvable into moral restraint, vice, and misery.
> Of the preventive checks, the restraint from marriage which is not followed by irregular gratifications may properly be termed moral restraint.
> Promiscuous intercourse, unnatural passions, violations of the marriage bed, and improper arts to conceal the consequences of irregular connexions, are preventive checks that clearly come under the head of vice.
> Of the positive checks, those which appear to arise unavoidably from the laws of nature, may be called exclusively misery; and those which we obviously bring upon ourselves, such as wars, excesses, and many others which it would be in our power to avoid, are of a mixed nature. They are brought upon us by vice, and their consequences are misery.[14]

---

13 *An Essay on the Principle of Population*, vol. I, pp. 6-11. In this regard, an important convergence can be found between Malthus and David Ricardo, as noted by Michel Foucault in *The Order of Things: An archaeology of the human sciences*, trans. by Alan Sheridan (London and New York: Routledge, 2002), pp. 279-82. See David Ricardo, *On the Principles of Political Economy and Taxation* (London: Jhon Murray, 1817), pp. 49-76, 549-89.

14 *An Essay on the Principle of Population*, vol. I, pp. 15-6.

Malthus was not only an economist, but also an Anglican priest. It can therefore be hypothesized that his pastoral role could have led him to clearly highlight the moral transformations that the promotion of the free market economy requires. In this sense, of course, it is significant that he accredits fundamental importance to «the restraint from marriage which is not followed by irregular gratifications» and «may properly be termed moral restraint».[15] This is a remedy for the uncontrolled increase in population that – according to him – must be actively promoted since it is the only one that does not imply moral evils or material suffering, vice or misery, but rather improves individual and collective well-being on both an economic and moral levels. It must also be said, that if the pastoral role of Malthus may have had an influence in this sense, it never translated into the affirmation of abstractly religious principles. In fact, the author clearly places the «moral restraint» within the framework of a substantially economic utilitarian and individualistic ethic, an ethic which – according to him – must be able to impose itself as the most natural and the most rational, interacting with the «command of God» of chastity to be maintained before marriage.

> Judging merely from the light of nature – Malthus writes –, if we feel convinced of the misery arising from a redundant population on the one hand, and of the evils and unhappiness, particularly to the female sex, arising from promiscuous intercourse, on the other, I do not see how it is possible for any person who acknowledges the principle of utility, as the great criterion of moral rules, to escape the conclusion, that moral restraint, or the abstaining from marriage till we are in a condition to support a family, with a perfectly moral conduct during that period, is the strict line of duty. [...]

---

15   On the importance of the pastoral role not only of Malthus but of a large number of supporters of population-theories similar to his are of great interest the considerations that Marx plays in a long footnote of the first Volume of *Capital*, where he argues that «most of population-theory teachers are Protestant parsons». Here, too, he openly states that the work that made Malthus famous «in its first form is nothing more than a schoolboyish, superficial plagiary of De Foe, Sir James Steuart, Townsend, Franklin, Wallace, &c., and does not contain a single sentence thought out by himself». Karl Marx, *Capital Volume I*, in *Marx & Engels Collected Works* (London: Lawrence & Wishart – Electric Book, 2010), vol. 35, pp. 611-3.

The happiness of the whole is to be the result of the happiness of individuals, and to begin first with them. No cooperation is required. Every step tells. He who performs his duty faithfully will reap the full fruits of it, whatever may be the number of others who fail. This duty is intelligible to the humblest capacity. It is merely, that he is not to bring beings into the world, for whom he cannot find the means of support. [...]. If he cannot support his children, they must starve; and if he marry in the face of a fair probability that he shall not be able to support his children, he is guilty of all the evils, which he thus brings upon himself, his wife and his offspring. It is clearly his interest, and will tend greatly to promote his happiness, to defer marrying, till by industry and economy he is in a capacity to support the children that he may reasonably expect from his marriage; and as he cannot in the meantime gratify his passions without violating an express command of God, and running a great risk of injuring himself, or some of his fellow-creatures, considerations of his own interest and happiness will dictate to him the strong obligation to a moral conduct while he remains unmarried.[16]

It is therefore a matter of transforming the need to delay marriages and to practice chastity into a rule of individual and social conduct until one is able to maintain children. According to Malthus, it is impossible to hope that this rule «will be universally or even generally practised»,[17] nor can it be thought that it must necessarily give rise to legal retribution when it is violated. There is, however, a very effective way to obtain good results in this regard: progressively abolish the poor-laws that guarantee assistance to those who fall into poverty due to having generated children they cannot feed and bring up. If they are left to themselves, these thoughtless individuals will naturally receive the just punishment by having to live pitifully.[18] As one can imagine, on the other hand, Malthus considers it absolutely necessary for governments to promote «a system of national education» which provides for instructing «the people in the real nature of their situation», to teach them that

---

16 *An Essay on the Principle of Population*, vol. II, pp. 283 and 285.
17 *An Essay on the Principle of Population*, vol. II, p. 283.
18 *An Essay on the Principle of Population*, vol. II, pp 335-50.

without an increase of their own industry and prudence no change of government could essentially better their condition; that, though they might get rid of some particular grievance, yet in the great point of supporting their families they would be but little, or perhaps not at all benefited.[19]

It is within a framework of this type that the incitement to save becomes a fundamental tool for the formation of an economic *ethos* capable of functioning also as a resolving mechanism of biopolitical problems: saving is the best antidote to assistance that encourages the improvidence, and therefore it is the best means of economic moralization of people's lives, of their idea of marriage and their relationship with procreation.

[A] young man, who had been saving from fourteen or fifteen with a view to marriage at four or five and twenty, or perhaps much earlier, would probably be induced to wait two or three years longer if the times were unfavourable; if corn were high; if wages were low; or if the sum he had saved had been found by experience not to be sufficient to furnish a tolerable security against want. A habit of saving a portion of present earnings for future contingencies can scarcely be supposed to exist without general habits of prudence and foresight.[20]

1.4 *The overpopulation between Malthus and Marx*

As is known, on the problem of population, a position very different from that of Malthus is expressed by Marx in his analyses of the question of «surplus population» that can be created in capitalist society. Directly or indirectly, Malthus is Marx's main critical target in this regard. According to the author of the *Capital*, there is no doubt that in modern society we are periodically faced with a sort of surplus population, but the resulting problems cannot be considered as a question of disproportion between people and amount of means of support. More precisely, we can say that, on the one hand, Marx agrees with Malthus in summing up population growth not as a problem

---

19   *An Essay on the Principle of Population*, vol. II, p. 358.
20   *An Essay on the Principle of Population*, vol. II, p. 408.

in itself, but as a condition in which a part of the population may find itself living in poverty and suffering the devastating consequences; on the other hand, however, he is clearly opposed to the Malthusian reduction of population growth to a natural tendency that – depending on the circumstances – can be hindered by equally natural factors (such as hunger, disease, death caused by misery) or by certain behaviours deliberately adopted by individuals (such as vice and moral restraint). From his point of view we must say rather that, if the real problem is misery with its negative effects on life, it cannot be explained by the naturalization of the «geometrical ratio» of the population growth, on the one hand, and of the «arithmetical ratio» of the development of agricultural production, on the other. For Marx both the surplus population and the misery in which this ends up in order to live, are entirely artificial effects of the logic according to which it functions «the specifically capitalist mode of production.»[21]

To summarize Marx's reasoning in this regard, we can say that – according to him – this mode of production grows progressively intensifying the productive power of labour by increasing the amount of capital invested in means of production (constant capital) compared to that earmarked for wages (variable capital). From this derives, among other things, the strengthening of the technological component of the total capital, which causes increase in labour productivity without necessarily increasing the number of workers employed. In fact, the variable capital – even if it sometimes grows in absolute terms – tends to undergo a proportional decrease compared to the constant capital which grows anyway. This ultimately means that capitalism develops causing, on one hand, the increase in the labouring population and, on the other, «the constant transformation of a part of the labouring population into unemployed or half-employed hands». Therefore, according to Marx, it can be said that the development of the capitalist mode of production involves the progressive production of a relative surplus population.[22]

---

21 See Marx, *Capital Volume I*, especially pp. 623-34.
22 *Capital Volume I*, p. 623.

It is only in the context of such reasoning that the question of population can be correctly analyzed, according to him. If in modern society a surplus population is created that is found to live in poverty, this happens because it is a capitalist society in which

> [t]he labouring population (...) produces, along with the accumulation
> of capital produced by it, the means by which it itself is made
> relatively superfluous, is turned into a relative surplus population;
> and it does this to an always increasing extent.

We cannot therefore think of being able to elaborate a theory or a general law of population; rather, it must be recognized that

> a law of population peculiar to the capitalist mode of production
> exists; and in fact every special historic mode of production has its
> own special laws of population, historically valid within its limits
> alone. An abstract law of population exists for plants and animals
> only, and only in so far as man has not interfered with them.[23]

For Marx, in short, it makes little sense to speak abstractly of population growth and of surplus population as causes of misery and a consequent population decrease. Rather, we must speak of «a surplus labouring population» as «a necessary product of accumulation or of the development of wealth on a capitalist basis». According to him, moreover,

> this surplus population becomes, conversely, the lever of capitalistic
> accumulation, nay, a condition of existence of the capitalist mode of
> production. It forms a disposable industrial reserve army that belongs
> to capital quite as absolutely as if the latter had bred it at its own cost.

If Marx speaks of relative surplus population (or relative overpopulation) it is because it is not the simple result of population increase, which may also occur; rather, it corresponds to the variable part of the labouring population created by capitalist development, of which the capital can manage to do without due to its own development and the consequent growth of labour productivity. This relative surplus population, moreover, constitutes «a

---

23   *Capital Volume I*, pp. 625-6.

disposable industrial reserve army» since it can always be drawn again towards production that continues to develop, also or above all to compete with the employed population and to replace it by accepting lower wages and conditions worse than those in force.[24]

All this cannot be understood by considering the population growth as a natural process that can encounter natural or artificial obstacles in its way. For this reason, what is important for Marx is to emphasize that the surplus labouring population, «[i]ndependently of the limits of the actual increase of population, [...] creates, for the changing needs of the self-expansion of capital, a mass of human material always ready for exploitation».[25]

Foucault, comparing the points of view of Malthus and Marx, argues appropriately that

> [f]or Malthus, the problem of population basically has to be thought as a bio-economic problem, whereas Marx tried to circumvent the problem and to get rid of the very notion of population, but only to rediscover it in the non longer bio-economic form, but in the specifically historical-political form of class, of class confrontation and class struggle.[26]

To such an assessment, however, we can add that, if the bioeconomic and biopolitical character of Malthus's theses are evident, even the Marxian discourse often takes on a biopolitical flavour. But, in order to grasp it, we have to consider that for Marx the contrast between the capitalist production of wealth and the production of the surplus population as «a mass of human material always ready for exploitation» represents one of the major limits, one of the inevitable and most striking contradictions of the development of capitalism itself. This limit derives from the fact that in the capitalist mode of production «capital and its self-expansion appear as the starting and the closing point, the motive and the purpose of production». Well, the biopolitical meaning of the indication of this limit clearly emerges when Marx insists on the fact that here «production

---

24 See *Capital Volume I*, pp. 633-4.
25 *Capital Volume I*, pp. 625-6.
26 *Security, Territory, Population*, p. 77.

is only production for capital and not vice versa, the means of production are not mere means for a constant expansion of the living process of the society of producers».[27] This precise clarification has implications that go beyond the idea that Marx – as Foucault says – tends to frame the problem of population in the historical-political terms of class confrontation and class struggle; there is no doubt about this, but it must be added that here the author of the *Capital* actually considers, in terms of anything but metaphorically biopolitical, the development that production could have as «a constant expansion of the living process of the society of producers», if capitalism were overcome politically. It is an expansion of which capitalism creates the possibility without realizing it because of its contradictions and its limits which, on the other hand, are the result of the «social relations of production», namely the class relations on which it itself is based.[28] In a society in which these social relations of production were overcome by the class struggle against capital, production as «expansion of the living process of the society of producers» would have a free course and «the growth of the labouring population» would not produce «an artificial overpopulation».[29]

It can therefore be said on the comparison between Malthus and Marx that the biopolitical content of the theses of the former consists in its need for a government of demographic processes that adapt the latter to those which he considers structural limits of the production of subsistence goods, a production that must however, remain anchored to the logic of the free market and capitalism. The biopolitical sense of Marx's perspective, instead, lies in his conviction that, once freed from capitalism, the productive force of the labouring population, as a pillar of «the living process of the society of producers», can fully realize the expansive vocation of modern production, which manifests itself partially and distortedly in the capitalist development.

---

27   Karl Marx, *Capital Volume III*, in *Marx & Engels Collected Works* (London: Lawrence & Wishart – Electric Book, 2010),vol. 37, pp. 248-9.
28   *Capital Volume III*, p. 249.
29   *Capital Volume III*, p. 248.

Certainly, this does not mean that Marx's perspective, once translated into a concrete political strategy, would necessarily give rise to a sort of biopolitical regime. Here, rather, it is a question of bringing out the significant biopolitical implications of the Marxian discourse using and, at the same time, going beyond the analytical framework of which Foucault offers us the essential elements. It is no coincidence, in fact, that – as we saw in the third chapter – Marxist thinkers like Negri and Hardt come to theorize the perspective of overcoming capitalism in terms of an affirmative biopolitics based on the liberation of the "living" and productive power of labour. We can now understand – if nothing – that the elements that allow a theorization like this of overcoming capitalism are very evident in Marx. All this, in any case, leaves intact and, in a certain sense, reinforces the perplexities that we have already expressed about this theorization in that chapter, perplexities based largely on the reflections of Foucault himself.

However, Marx's theses certainly must be considered in all their complexity. In particular, we cannot overlook the fact that, having to deal with a widely accepted theory of population like that of Malthus, he tries to show its unreliability by bringing out the entirely political depth of the relationship between overpopulation and capitalist production and thus contesting the tendency of this theory to naturalize not only the population growth, but also its relations with the economy, with poverty and misery.[30] It is also true, on the other hand, that with regard to overpopulation, in a passage from Volume III of *Capital*, Marx manifests a clear ambivalence of his attitude towards the Malthusian theory, getting very close to it, while implicitly expressing the impossibility of sharing it. Indeed, speaking of the possibility of «a momentary excess of surplus capital over the working population it has commandeered», he argues that

> [it] would have a two-fold effect. It would, on the one hand, by raising wages, mitigate the adverse conditions which decimate the offspring

---

30 This rejection of the Malthus theory is not expressed only in the pages of the *Capital* that we have referred to, but, in a very clear manner, even in *Grundrisse: Foundations of the Critique of Political Economy*, pp. 526-33.

of the labourers and would make marriages easier among them, so as gradually to increase the population. On the other hand, by applying methods which yield relative surplus value (introduction and improvement of machinery) it would produce a far more rapid, artificial, relative overpopulation, which in its turn, would be a breeding ground for a really swift propagation of the population, since under capitalist production misery produces population.[31]

Here, in fact, Marx believes not only that there is a relationship between population growth and the development of production, but also that the increase in wages makes marriages easier and increases the population, in some way accepting the idea that labourers find, in the growth of their income, the conditions for more or less responsible procreation advocated by Malthus; on the other hand, as we have seen, Marx argues that the «misery» in which the relative overpopulation created by capital finds itself, «would produce to make more rapid, artificial, relative overpopulation, which in its turn, would be a breeding ground for a really swift propagation of the population». This corresponds to a description not very distant from that of Malthus, according to which the impoverishment of the poor leads them to increase their offspring even or precisely when they fall into misery.

2. Biopolitics and social security: for a genealogy of the welfare state

2.1 From the protector state to the provident state

The alarm raised by Malthus on the dangers that he believes derive from overpopulation has historically been taken seriously by most philanthropic organizations; these, however, have endeavoured to avert these dangers through a less rigid approach than his towards marriage. In the 19th century, they acted in this sense by assuming marriage and family as vehicles for the behaviours and habits necessary to face both these dangers and the risks caused by the development of the industrial society. They did so by actively promoting attitudes of foresight not

---

31   *Capital Volume III*, pp. 216-7.

only encouraging savings, but also the inclusion of the family in circuits of scholastic education, hygiene education, preventive health care, etc.[32]

However, beyond the experiences of philanthropy, saving has maintained a paradigmatic value as a way of approaching social issues and their biopolitical aspects. The first forms of insurance against accidents, illnesses and the problems of old age in the 19th century, as well as the social security systems of the 20th century welfare state, were based in large on the socialization of the ethics of economic foresight that both Malthus and philanthropy sought to instil in families through saving. It is a conception of the future as essentially conditioned by the danger that makes the promotion of such an ethical attitude credible and effective; moreover, it is an idea of danger as a calculable and compensable risk that gives this ethic its specific character of economic morality the application of which clearly implies the exercise of a government or a self-government of life.

These references to the logic of foresight bring us back to the centrality that the pursuit of security has assumed in the biopolitical government of individuals, according to Foucault. In fact, security as a general purpose of government practices and the idea of risk as a pivotal concept and instrument of these practices have played and still play an essential function in our society.[33] Considering the analyses by some authors, we can say that the modern state did not wait for real biopolitical strategies to be developed to reveal its attention to security, at the centre of which – in one way or another – life could only be placed. According to what Robert Castel reminds us, the modern state has proposed itself since its founding as a guarantor of security; the sovereignty of the state, theorized by Hobbes at the dawn of modernity, is based above all on the protection of life which it guarantees to individuals who decide to

---

32 See Donzelot, *The Policing of Family*, pp. 70-95.
33 See François Ewald, *L'État providence* (Paris: Grasset, 1986); by the same author, see: *Histoire de l'État providence. Les origines de la solidarité* (Paris: Grasset & Fasquelle, 1996); 'Insurance and risk', in *The Foucault Effect: Studies in Governmentality*, pp. 197-210. See also Daniel Defert, '"Popular life" and insurance technology', in *The Foucault Effect: Studies in Governmentality*, pp. 211-33.

submit to this sovereignty precisely for this reason: being exposed to the danger of the war of all against all, men realize sooner or later the need to stipulate a pact with which they undertake to refrain from the violence of one against the other and accept, therefore, the establishment of a sovereign power that enforces the pact by protecting them. They voluntarily surrender, to an institution or a person, the power to carry out the necessary actions to guarantee the peace, the safety and the survival of all.[34] This originally protective character – which not only Robert Castel, but also other authors attribute to the modern state – implies that the latter's privileged interlocutor is the *individual* as an isolated being, as the bearer of rights, above all *personal* and *private*, which must be guaranteed and defended. It is not by chance that the primary rights that the modern state undertakes to protect are individual rights to life and property. In this sense – according to Castel and Pierre Rosanvallon – the substantial convergence between an authoritarian thinker like Hobbes and a liberal philosopher like Locke is very significant.[35] Both link the protection of the individual's right to life with the protection of his property. In particular, Locke connects with absolute clarity the need to protect the life of individuals to that to safeguard property and freedom. Castel in this regard appropriately insists on the fundamental value that the protection of property assumes in this view. According to Locke, in fact, both life and freedom fall within the realm of property, since they, together with the material goods of the individual, are different expressions of their property. Men feel the need to aggregate and organize themselves politically because, if they remain in the state of nature, despite being free, they will still be in a condition of «full of fears and continual dangers»; therefore – says Locke – sooner or later they «unite for the mutual Preservation of their Lives, Liberties and Estates, which I call by the general Name, Property».[36]

---

34   Robert Castel, *L'insécurité sociale: qu'est-ce qu'être protégé?* (Paris: Éditions du Seuil, 2003), pp. 12-5. See Thomas Hobbes, *Leviathan*, ed. by Richard Tuck (Cambridge, UK: Cambridge University Press, 1996).
35   Castel, *L'insécurité sociale*, pp. 15-7; Pierre Rosanvallon, *La crise de l'État-providence* (Paris: Éditions du Seuil, 1981), pp. 21-2.
36   John Locke, *The Second Treatise of Government*, in *Two Treatises of Government*, ed. by Peter Laslett (Cambridge, UK: Cambridge

Consistent with this concept, according to Castel, in the nineteenth century the liberal state tended to guarantee the life and freedom of the individual through the protection of their property. In this way, not only will it perpetuate the protective vocation of the modern state, but – the French author maintains – will project itself into the same perspective in which the welfare state will later openly be placed. Undoubtedly, the liberal state generally presents itself as a State of law which, as such, wants above all to guarantee *civil security*, namely the safeguarding of public order and the prevention of crime, trying not to become a despotic and police state. However, by actively protecting the property, it in fact aspires in its own way to guarantee *social security*. «It must be understood in this way – says Castel – that private property guarantees, in the full sense of the term, against the contingencies of social existence (in the case of illness, accident, discontinuance of labour, etc.)».[37] From this point of view, however, the problem to which liberalism remains profoundly insensitive is that of the *non-owner individual*. In fact, the protection of owners by the state neither guarantees the creation of new owners nor the protection of non-owners. Therefore, social insecurity, as the widespread absence of safeguards from life's setbacks due to lack of property, is a politically explosive problem that soon arises in the history of liberal society, precisely because this is limited to assuming private property as a tool of social protection.[38]

To overcome a situation like this, social security systems promoted by the state will gradually be affirmed, which especially in Europe will find their full expansion in the thirty years following the Second World War. However, according to Castel, what will generally be called the welfare state will play, in a renewed manner, the protective role that seems to characterize the modern state since its inception, with the difference that it will play this role above all as a *risk reducer* by adopting insurance techniques as the main approach.[39] In this sense – as Rosanvallon says – the

---

University Press, 2014), p. 350. See Castel, *L'insécurité sociale*, pp. 15-7.
37 Castel, *L'insécurité sociale*, p. 20.
38 Castel, *L'insécurité sociale*, pp. 26-30.
39 Castel, *L'insécurité sociale*, pp. pp. 30-2. See also Rosanvallon, *La*

birth of the welfare state can be described as the transformation of the «protective state (of security)» into a «welfare state (of insurance)».[40]

2.2 *From security to insurance*

Both Castel and Rosanvallon rightly indicate in the predominantly insurance character the main aspect that the intervention of the contemporary state will assume with its growing attention to the problems of health, illness, old age, accidents at work, etc.; in this way, these authors highlight an essential evolution of the relationship of contemporary society with life, its security and the dangers it runs.

In this evolution it is precisely the concept of risk that assumes a crucial importance. This can be fully understood if one considers that the insurance techniques used in the welfare state are not simply a result of the struggles of which workers' movements have been protagonists since the 19th century. Undoubtedly, it cannot be denied that these struggles have played a fundamental role in this regard. However, what needs to be pointed out is that the assumption of the insurance approach to the problems raised by these movements was not the necessary or inevitable outcome of their struggles. As Daniel Defert says, «the workers movement only gradually came to give its endorsement to this solution, eventually embracing a piece of legislation originally passed without its support».[41] In fact, the social security systems that were formed through the privileging of the insurance techniques have their roots in the major approaches in which liberal society, since its origins, has been related to the uncertainties of life.

Conceiving itself first and foremost as a society that promotes the freedom of individuals more than others, liberal society asks them to be ready to face the dangers that this freedom entails. From this point of view, the very notion of risk is the conceptual, technical and political tool that allows one to think and face the

---

crise de l'État-providence, pp. 24-7.
40   Rosanvallon, *La crise de l'État-providence*, p. 26.
41   Defert, '"Popular life" and insurance technology', p. 211.

insecurity in which life takes place not only as something to be feared, but also as inevitable and even acceptable and appreciable. In the history of liberal society, in fact, the production of techniques of governing the uncertainty of existence – such as those proposed by Malthus or philanthropy – has combined in different ways with the promotion of an individual and social ethic of the readiness to accept and live with the risk.

It is almost superfluous to recall that in this perspective we can first of all understand the cult of the risk of free economic initiative, which liberalism promotes from the moment it is imposed on a political, cultural and ethical level. In particular, the modern entrepreneur, as an individual master of his own destiny, must show his moral aptitude for autonomy by being willing to face the unpredictability of the outcomes of his choices and decisions. He cannot consider himself an entrepreneur, if he is not willing to run the risk of investing and possibly losing his money or of asking for a loan from a bank without being able to repay the debt, to be able to make profits.[42]

In reality, risk soon plays a fundamental role also in the formation of the modern worker's *ethos*. As Rosanvallon argues, it is no coincidence that after the French Revolution the poor – along with domestic workers, young people and women in general – remained excluded from voting for a long period, as they were deemed unfit to take the risks of freedom gained with the Revolution itself. Their attitude to freedom, on the other hand, could only really manifest itself if they were willing to work in the conditions created by revolutionary emancipation, that is to offer their workforce on the free market by accepting all the consequences, positive or negative, that this entailed.[43] In this sense it is significant what two important French authors – who dealt intensively with the question of public assistance – wrote in the first decades of the 19th century. We are

---

42 On the fundamental importance of «willingness to take risks» for the modern entrepreneur, economy and culture, see Peter Sloterdijk, *In the World Interior of Capital: For a Philosophical Theory of Globalization*, trans. by Wieland Hoban (Cambridge: Polity Press, 2013), especially pp. 47-52.

43 See Pierre Rosanvallon, *The New Social Question* (Princeton: Princeton University Press, 2000), pp. 89-91.

referring to Tanneguy Duchatel (several times minister between 1834 and 1848, committed supporter of the ideas of Malthus on the improvidence of the poor) and Joseph-Marie de Gerando (multifaceted intellectual, particularly sensitive to the demands of philanthropy). This is how the first expressed himself by referring to the relationship between worker and master:

> With the free contract, in its present form, on the one hand there is no subjection, on the other there is no duty of protection: the worker offers his work, the master pays the agreed salary; these are their mutual obligations. When the business of the master goes badly and his industry is in decline, he mercilessly sends the worker away, and not wanting any more work, he stops paying the salary. He cares little that the worker has no job or can find another job, that his misery is extreme or that some savings protect him from poverty. From the moment he no longer needs his manpower, he fires him; it is up to the worker to get by as he can. This is what our laws want. And that they are not accused of injustice: they merely express all the consequences that exactingly derive from the independence of the worker. This, therefore, is the inevitable result of the freedom of work: it makes the condition of the workers more precarious.[44]

Gerando, on his part, referring to the new condition in which the worker found himself after the emancipation that the Revolution had secured for him, maintained the following.

> From the moment in which man has emancipated himself, the use of his freedom exposes him to a multitude of unexpected events. He becomes free only on the condition of behaving wisely, of redoubling his efforts and facing obstacles. He injures himself while working; while navigating he exposes himself to failure; acting he enters the battle with a multitude of obstacles; (...). The man who, with the development of civilization, comes into possession of a new existence, encounters new dangers: sometimes he suffers setbacks as a deserved punishment; sometimes the fear of suffering them excites his activity.[45]

---

44   Tanneguy Duchâtel, *De la Charité, dans ses rapports avec l'état moral et le bien-être des classes inférieures de la société* (Paris: Alexandre Mesnier, 1829), pp. 342-3.
45   Joseph-Marie de Gérando, *De la bienfaisance publique* (Bruxelles: Société Belge de Librairie, 1839), vol. I, p. 82.

It is against the backdrop of such a conception of the existence of the free man that will end up affirming not only the concept of risk, but also the insurance approach to the biopolitical management of its possible translation into damage. It is in this same context that the constant exposure of individual life to danger, emphasized as an inescapable fact, will take on a foundational value for the creation of a system of insurance as «a paradigm of social solutions to all cases of non-labour: first that of industrial accidents, then sickness and old age, and finally unemployment».[46] Here, in any case, we are talking about a trend that will only begin to be fully realized in the second half of the 19th century. Therefore, it is important to consider some historical circumstances that have helped to create the conditions in which this trend has become established. These are circumstances that have been well highlighted by Daniel Defert in his analysis of the exemplary case of France.

The first of these consists in the fact that the insurance techniques have matured and consolidated themselves at least since the end of the 18th century, when they began to take the human life as their own object and, consequently, adopted the logic of life assurance. This happened above all in the private financial economy[47] in which life assurance became «a new channel for the concentration of capital». Of course, the insurance companies that took this route certainly didn't find their main clientele in the working class. However, the fact remains that «industrial accident insurance was initially framed within the logic of life assurance», which they had elaborated and perfected.[48] In the 19th century these companies openly offered workers exposed to the risk of accidents «a form of benefit no longer drawn from the resources of others but created by the workers themselves out of the product of their own labour».[49]

---

46 Defert, '"Popular life" and insurance technology', p. 211.
47 Here it is appropriate to remember that the first great company of life assurance (*The Equitable Life Assurance Society*) was founded in the United Kingdom in 1762.
48 Defert, '"Popular life" and insurance technology', p. 212.
49 The French company *Sécurité Generale* expressed these terms in the sixties of the 19th century in a document sent to the French Government at the time when it first approved social insurance laws. The company therefore denounced «the unexpected competition of the state with us,

On the other hand, they soon had to face state competition when, not only in France but also in other European countries, especially in the last decades of the century, governments began to approve social insurance legislation. In any case, it is not reckless to assume that the state systems of social insurance – as Defert maintains – were formed first of all through the undertaking by the state of the industrial accident insurance methods developed by private companies.[50]

These methods are based on a form of asset management regulated by a contractual relationship between the individual and a centralized organization. Moreover, unlike what happens in the case of savings banks, they do not leave the individual the possibility of freely manage the money saved. The savings in this case have precise and binding objectives: «[p]rovidence against those defined risks is made the sole purpose of this mode of saving».[51] From this point of view, it can be generally said that the private insurance systems firstly and then the state social security systems, adopting these methods, take life as an object of attention to the extent that it is vulnerable, can be reduced to a state of impairment, weakness, decay or near death. Finally, the insurance methods deeply destabilize the logic according to which, already in the aftermath of the French Revolution, other forms of management of the unpredictability of life had begun to develop. These are, in particular, the numerous and multiform experiences whose protagonists define themselves with a wide variety of names: «Friends of man, philanthropists, associations, mutualists, stockholders, co-operators, phalanstery dwellers, socialists, communists».[52]

A large part of these experiences animate the general phenomenon of *workers' mutualism* which, in its most politically significant forms, tends to combine socio-economic solidarity and political

---

setting itself up as an insurer at expense of a company established (...) with its own approval». The document, available in French Archives Nationales (Manuscrits de la Société Générale, 117 AQ 16), is quoted in Defert, '"Popular life" and insurance technology', pp. 222-3.

50 Defert, '"Popular life" and insurance technology', pp. 211-2 and 214.
51 '"Popular life" and insurance technology', p. 231.
52 '"Popular life" and insurance technology', p. 227.

resistance. In fact, this tends to guarantee, on the one hand, mutual help between workers, in the event of accidents, unemployment or reduced wages; on the other, material support for strikes against the anti-worker behaviour and policies of bosses and governments. The workers' mutualism also tends to create cooperative forms of work, alternative systems of production, distribution, consumption and management of economic resources. In its most radical expressions, it aims at the «reduction of the exploitation of man by man» and the socialist transformation of society. At the same time, it promotes forms of social relations that cannot be reduced to the dimension of private and family relationships, mostly in the context of the neighbourhood rather than the factory. Cooperation and reciprocity are the ideal principles that workers' mutualism seeks to apply. And it is also on these principles that it has historically based the creation of «a system of insurance that will cover the whole of life».[53]

As Defert says, «[w]orking-class mutualism constituted the precise point of interchange between traditional tactics of financial solidarity and the elaboration of new systems of sociability».[54] From an economic point of view, it tended to keep the control of the solidarity funds in the hands of workers, so that their use served to guarantee life, health and decent living conditions for the employed and unemployed on the one hand, and political resistance during the struggles on the other.[55] Evidently, due to these characteristics, this

---

53 This was expressed in 1848 in the working-class newspaper *L'Atelier* which added: «then, we would all mutually serve each other». See Defert, '"Popular life" and insurance technology', p. 229. A useful overview of the revolutionary newspapers of the period 1848-1851 is proposed in: *I giornali del triennio democratico (1848–1851)*, ed. by David Bidussa (Milan: Fondazione Giangiacomo Feltrinelli, 2018): http://fondazionefeltrinelli.it/app/uploads/2018/09/I-periodici-del-1848-David-Bidussa.pdf.

54 '"Popular life" and insurance technology', p. 228. For a useful historical reconstruction of the phenomenon of the workers' mutualism see Maria Grazia Meriggi, *Cooperazione e mutualismo. Esperienze di integrazione e conflitto sociale in Europa fra Ottocento e Novecento* (Milan: Franco Angeli, 2005).

55 Also Marx in the *Capital*, albeit implicitly, refers to these goals of the workers' mutualism writing: «As soon (..) as the labourers learn the

form of mutualism was clearly distinguished from the paternalism of philanthropic organizations. However – according to Defert's analysis – it was precisely these organizations not only to oppose it, but also to assume their organizational models and impoverish their goals by favouring

> the format of provident associations whose funds, exclusively earmarked for relief of sickness, infirmity and old age, were kept under the control of the employer who, on that condition, was also prepared to contribute.[56]

In this way philanthropism contributed not only to the neutralization of the political potentialities of workers' mutualism, but also to the advantage of the insurance technique organized according to the model developed by private companies, as a financially more powerful and effective instrument than both mutualism and philanthropism itself in facing the problems of life reduced to their most elementary biopolitical content.[57]

In any case, it is because of historical circumstances such as these that the state, proposing itself as an active subject in the insurance management of these problems, in the second half of the 19th century created the foundations for «a modern

---

secret, how it comes to pass that in the same measure as they work more, as they produce more wealth for others, and as the productive power of their labour increases, so in the same measure even their function as a means of the self-expansion of capital becomes more and more precarious for them, as soon as they discover that the degree of intensity of the competition among themselves depends wholly on the pressure of the relative surplus population; as soon as, by Trades' Unions, &c, they try to organise a regular co-operation between employed and unemployed in order to destroy or to weaken the ruinous effects of this natural law of capitalistic production on their class, so soon capital and its sycophant, political economy, cry out at the infringement of the "eternal" and so to say "sacred" law of supply and demand. Every combination of employed and unemployed disturbs the "harmonious" action of this law». *Capital Volume I*, p. 634.

56   Defert, '"Popular life" and insurance technology', p. 230.
57   See '"Popular life" and insurance technology', pp. 228-32. For an accurate reconstruction of the historical processes that led to these results, see Henri Hatzfeld, *Du Pauperisme à la Sécurité sociale* (Paris: Armand Colin, 1971).

state of security, guaranteeing the citizen against old age and misfortune, redistributing resources, where security comes now to signify (...) that modern idea which enfolds in itself the lives of each and all».[58]

2.3 *Solidarity as an invention*

To focus precisely on this evolution of the government of the state as a biopolitical actor, we must consider the substantial incapacity which it had shown in the aftermath of the French Revolution in making the practice by all of the rights that had been proclaimed as universal with the said Revolution effective. For a long period, the post-revolutionary state was not able to "keep the promise" of the Revolution, not only for the substantial unwillingness of most of its political class to act in this sense, but also for its dramatic lack of adequate tools for this purpose.

In this regard Jacques Donzelot argues that in post-revolutionary France, particularly after the February 1848 uprising, the modernization of society through the full extension of the legal sovereignty of the state to all citizens appeared dramatically impossible. One of the main achievements of that insurrection was the extension of the right to vote with the establishment of the universal male vote. This was indeed a fundamental act of extending legal sovereignty to a large number of social subjects; but – argues Donzelot – just as this conquest was realized, the conditions were also created for the extended sovereignty of the state to rapidly enter into crisis.[59] The Republican Assembly, directly elected by the people (in its male constituent), immediately found itself under the pressure of the Parisian proletariat – the part of the electorate that most of all wanted to see the equality of law transformed in the suppression of the de facto inequality in which it existed. Applying pressure on the Assembly the people of Paris claimed and also obtained the proclamation of the right to work. In a sense, this was precisely the most important

---

58   '"Popular life" and insurance technology', p. 232.
59   Jacques Donzelot, *L'invention du social: essai sur le déclin des passions politiques* (Paris: Fayard, 1984), p. 21.

result of the insurrection; but the Parisian people expected that right to be put into practice as quickly as the feudal privileges had been suppressed by the 1789 Revolution. Any delay in this implementation placed the Assembly under suspicion of wanting to keep the people in a state of submission.[60] Therefore the *Ateliers nationaux* were established, factories that in a few months gave work to around one hundred thousand people. The result was the rapid growth of the state deficit and the profound political contrasts within and outside the institutions, followed by a second wave of street riots and the massacre with which the state repressed them in June 1848.[61]

According to Donzelot, the social revolts, the insurrectional uprisings, the great political conflicts of the 19th century – as well as the repressions and restorations that followed – had tragic consequences above all because the state remained unable for a long time to activate organizational systems of the social coexistence and management of collective progress more effective than those based simply on the extension of sovereignty and law.[62] The first important steps in this sense were made only when the instrument of the law was no longer used simply for the creation of new representative institutions or to identify and assert new rights, duties, responsibilities, injunctions, sanctions and punishments, but also to define and activate social security strategies and techniques. It was from that moment that the great problems raised by the claim to universal rights began to be transformed into a series of individual questions (accidents, illnesses, unemployment, old age, etc.) and to be dealt with case by case with specific solutions.[63]

Certainly, in this way the ruling classes triggered a great system of "ruses" that allowed them to retain power. However, the fact remains that in this way they largely overcame the limits and the abstractness of the instruments of political and juridical sovereignty, no longer simply proposing judicial and penal solutions of conflicts between workers and entrepreneurs, but

---

60   *L'invention du social*, p. 70.
61   *L'invention du social*, pp. 36-9.
62   *L'invention du social*, p. 122.
63   *L'invention du social*, pp. 121-77.

above all of an administrative and welfare nature. It was on this basis that – according to Donzelot – the "social"' was formed, understood as a specific dimension and different both from the political-juridical sphere and from the economic one. In France, in particular, the conditions for a clear change in this sense was created by the political class of the Republicans who, especially in the nineties of the 19th century, began to govern «building bridges, compromises» between the liberal-conservative alliance, which tended to favour market mechanisms, and the revolutionary-socialist one, which aimed at extending political sovereignty.[64]

On a theoretical level, moreover, an important factor of this change was offered by the theory of social solidarity, developed by Émile Durkheim, according to which not only traditional societies, but also modern society is characterized by solidarity mechanisms that reproduce its cohesion; passing from its traditional forms to modern and complex ones, society simply passes from a form of «mechanical solidarity», founded on the similarity of conditions and on the homogeneity of values, to a form of «organic solidarity», founded on the social division of labour, which increases the interdependence of the individuals that make up society. Solidarity, therefore, while changing nature, remains the constitutive law of society. In modern industrial societies, solidarity represents a cohesive force similar to that which animates the parts of a biological organism, that cooperate to guarantee its survival.[65]

Ultimately, this theory – as claimed by Donzelot – made it possible to maintain that society lives and evolves according to its own laws. Therefore, from this point of view, to solve its problems it was neither a question of destroying or overturning it, nor of blocking its dynamism to restore the alleged lost equilibria. Instead, it was necessary to favour and regulate the functioning of its mechanisms so that it could continue to reproduce according to its logic and its laws.[66] Furthermore, an important implication of

---

64 *L'invention du social*, pp. 78-9.
65 Émile Durkheim, *The Division of Labor in Society*, trans. by W.D. Halls, (New York: The Free Press, 1997), pp. 31-87.
66 *L'invention du social*, p. 83.

this view was the possibility of arguing that, in reality, there are no rights that come before duties; everyone is indebted to everyone; furthermore, no one can be considered self-sufficient, since society survives and functions if the division of tasks that each performs functions. The debt to society is a priority and its collection through taxes and contributions cannot but be in turn. There is no one who can be considered absolutely in credit to society. The credit must be established from time to time according to the different conditions in which each one finds himself or, in fact, the «de facto situations» rather than the «a priori legal claims».[67] In short, the lack of functioning of society must be compensated, rather than the whole society having to be demolished and re-founded.

The theory of social solidarity found a translation in terms of political perspective. To implement it – notes Donzelot – was particularly Léon Bourgeois, a French politician and prime minister in the years 1895-1896. He transformed Durkheim's theory into "solidarism", that is, into a theoretical vision and political strategy that could be contrasted both with liberalism and with socialism in their most radical forms.[68]

According to Donzelot, it is based on a vision like this that in France the insurance and social security logic of the society's government is historically affirmed: the damage will be repaired, the deficiencies will be filled, the people will be assured against the risks that they run in the activities with which they contribute to the cohesion of society. This approach to state action produces a real turning point in the use of the legislative instrument: alongside constitutional law, civil and criminal law a real *social right* is born: laws on working conditions, against the risk of unemployment, accidents, diseases, the problems of old age, for the protection of health, for education, and even for social morality.[69]

67   *L'invention du social*, p. 111.
68   See Léon Bourgeois, *Solidarité* (Paris: Armand Colin, 1896). See also: J. E. S. Hayward, 'The Official Social Philosophy of the French Third Republic: Léon Bourgeois and Solidarism', *International Review of Social History*, 6 (1961), 19-48; Daniel Béland, 'Back to Bourgeois? French social policy and the idea of solidarity', *International Journal of Sociology and Social Policy*, 9/10, 29 (2009), 445-56.
69   *L'invention du social*, pp. 123-5. See also Jacques Donzelot, 'The

A problem with which the insurance logic immediately gave convincing results was that of accidents at work. In this field it allowed first of all to reduce the importance of legal conceptions linked to the idea of individual responsibility. Previously many of the disputes concerning accidents found no solution, since often there was no way to establish who was to blame at a judicial level: the employer or the worker? With regard to this question, the insurance technique constituted a sort of *escamotage* based on reasoning such as the following: it is not said that one should always look for a culprit of the accidents; apart from the obvious cases of intentionality and negligence, generally an accident must be considered an occasional, casual result of the work process which is always a collective matter. Therefore, all those who participate in this process are involved in what happens to you. All, therefore, must contribute as far as possible to the compensation of damages that people may suffer. So how will this problem be addressed? Firstly, by replacing the notion of guilt with that of "professional risk"; secondly, by collecting contributions in advance and creating a social security fund; finally, using the insurance calculation method to determine the amount of compensation for damages. In this way, a procedure is formed that to some extent solves a problem, avoids or reduces a conflict and can be applied to many other similar issues.[70]

2.4 *Protection and marginalization*

As Donzelot himself observes, in reality, those who first achieved an historic success in promoting this type of policy were not the French rulers, but German Chancellor Otto von Bismarck.[71] As is known, he was the aristocratic and authoritarian politician who had the so-called Anti-Socialist Laws (1878) approved in Germany, with which the German Social Democratic party was subjected to heavy forms of discrimination and repression; on

---

promotion of the social', *Economy and Society*, 17, 3 (1988) , 395-427.
70   *L'invention du social*, pp. 129-33.
71   *L'invention du social*, p. 128.

the other hand, between 1883 and 1889 he was the first to create a system with a certain degree of organic state insurance against illness, accidents, old age and invalidity.[72]

This system has taken on such historical importance that it is generally considered to be the first form of welfare state. However, it must be said that it is precisely from the history of welfare policies promoted by Bismarck that a very problematic consequence of the insurance strategies inaugurated in the 19th century clearly emerges. This is a consequence that Donzelot, for his part, does not bother to highlight, thus risking offering us a totally positive and substantially uncritical view of these strategies. It is true that they allowed a substantial part of the labouring population to reduce the scope of a series of dangers that this ran; however, those strategies left without any protection a large part of precarious, underpaid and unemployed workers, which the same industrial development produced: these workers were not in the contractual and economic conditions that could allow them to contribute to the state insurance system and benefit from it.[73] In this regard the *Sozialpolitk* inaugurated by

---

72   For a reconstruction of the birth of social policies in Germany see Eckart
      Reidegeld, *Staatliche Sozialpolitik in Deutschland, Band I: Von den
      Ursprüngen bis zum Untergang des Kaiserreiches 1918* (Wiesbaden: VS
      Verlag für Sozialwissenschaften, 2006), pp. 133-235, especially pp. 193-227.
73   Donzelot rightly highlights the importance that the political recognition
      of professional unions had for the birth of "social policies" as a specific
      area of governance of the risks to which life was exposed; this recognition,
      in fact, strengthened the corporate ties in the various productive sectors
      and weakened the influence of revolutionary workers' organizations
      (*L'invention du social*, pp. 79 and 85). It should be added, however, that
      in this way the designation of skilled workers permanently employed as
      the main beneficiaries of the protections provided by the Bismarckian
      Sozialstaat was achieved; vice versa, a large mass of temporary and
      unskilled workers were left out of the sphere of social protection. In
      this regard see Nicola Massimo De Feo, *Riformismo, razionalizzazione,
      autonomia operaia. Il "Verein fur Sozialpolitik", 1872-1933* (Manduria:
      Lacaita,1992). As can be deduced from the subtitle of this last book,
      the author insists (very appropriately) on the fundamental role played
      by the debate and sociological studies, of which Max Weber was the
      protagonist, promoted in Germany by the "Verein fur Sozialpolitik"
      (Association for social policy) in the consolidation and continuation of
      this type of social policy even after the Bismarckian period.

Bismarck had an exemplary meaning. In fact, it was an essential expression of his *Realpolitik* and political opportunism, the main purpose of which was the co-optation of the most skilled, stable and organized part of the industrial working class to weaken its revolutionary impulses and converge their energies in building the economic, imperial and colonial power of Germany.[74] The flip side of this strategy was, inevitably, the radically different treatment reserved for economically and politically marginal social figures such as the unemployed, unskilled and temporary workers. As Nicola Massimo De Feo observes,

> the Bismarckian *Sozialpolitik* institutionalizing, through an organic and unitary legislative body, the sparse corporate, entrepreneurial and trade union measures of support, defence and assistance to the living and working conditions of mostly skilled and professional workers, establishes the juridical as well as economic and technical division between skilled and unskilled labour, entrusting the former to public assistance, and the latter to the disciplinary control of the poor.[75]

In reality, for a long time no effective remedy was put in place for this kind of consequences of the social policies inaugurated in the 19th century. On the contrary, it can be said that the absence or lack of protections for the lives of the great masses of the poor will continue to reproduce even when social policies – with the American New Deal and with the various versions of the welfare state established after the Second World War – will assume dimensions and organicity far greater than those achieved in the 19th century. Also, for this reason, in various contemporary capitalist societies, the poor, temporary workers, unskilled workers, immigrants or unemployed have often given rise to very radical forms of struggle that have

---

74   See Marcel van Meerhaeghe, 'Bismarck and the social question', *Journal of Economic Studies*, 33, 4 (2006), 284-301; Patricia Owens, 'From Bismarck to Petraeus: The question of the social and the Social Question in counterinsurgency', *European Journal of International Relations*, 19, 1 (2011), 139-61.

75   De Feo, *Riformismo, razionalizzazione, autonomia operaia*, p. 66.

found a strong motivation in their exclusion or marginalization from the social security systems.[76]

All this, in any case, does not change the overall meaning that can be attributed to the "invention of the social" as a specific sphere of government, which implies the consideration of life as a fundamental object of political attention. From this point of view, it can be said that the formation of this area of government represents a decisive step towards the disappearance of any clear distinction between *polis* and *oikos*, between the public sphere of politics and the private sphere of the conservation and reproduction of life. As Hannah Arendt says when talking about the historical phase of modernity in which the birth of the "social" is set,

> society became the subject of the new life process, as the family had been its subject before. Membership in a social class replaced the protection previously offered by membership in a family, and social solidarity became a very efficient substitute for the earlier, natural solidarity ruling the family unit.[77]

That which, on the other hand, cannot be overlooked is that the contemporary policies of social protection of life have been intertwined since the beginning with power strengthening policies not only economic but also military and imperial of the state, as in the case of Bismarckian Germany. In short, biopolitics also in this case establishes a clear relationship with thanatopolitics. This is a relationship that – as we know – will become blatantly evident with Nazism as a regime of protection and biopolitical and thanatopolitical affirmation of the "German race" to the detriment of the other "races". Less obvious, but far from irrelevant, is the fact that the biopolitics of social security have

---

76 A useful analysis in this regard is proposed in Frances Fox Piven and Richard A. Cloward, *Poor People's Movements. Why They Succeed, How They Fail* (New York: Vintage Books, 1979). Furthermore, on the political radicality of the unskilled and casual workers' struggles, one can see Karl Heinz Roth, *Die "andere" Arbeiterbewegung und die Entwicklung der kapitalistischen Repression von 1880 bis zur Gegenwart* (Munchen: Trikont Verlag, 1974).

77 *The Human Condition*, p. 256.

intertwined with more or less evident forms of thanatopolitics precisely when they reached – so to speak – their maturity with the contemporary welfare state.

2.5 *War as an opportunity, the Beveridge Plan as a paradigm*

What we have just asserted can be verified if we consider the context in which the so-called *Beveridge Plan* (1942) was developed and proposed, that is the programmatic document commissioned by the British government during the Second World War, universally considered as the first and the most organic project of welfare state systems implemented from 1945 onwards.[78] This is a project at the centre of which was the organization of a National Insurance and a National Health Service, actually initiated by the British Labour government in the years immediately following the war. Focusing on the historical coincidence between the elaboration of the *Beveridge Plan* and the enormous war effort to which the British government summoned citizens in the same period, Foucault highlighted the paradoxical relationship between life policies and death policies which established itself in this way: «At a time when the War was causing large-scale destruction, society assumed the explicit task of ensuring its members not only life, but also a healthy life».[79] «One could symbolize such a coincidence – supports Foucault – by a slogan: Go get slaughtered and we promise you a long and pleasant life. Life insurance is connected with a death command».[80] These apparently "provocative" observations of the French philosopher do not constitute a forced interpretation; in this sense it will be enough to consider what Beveridge said on the opportunity to elaborate a vast plan of social protection during the war so that it could add a decisive motivation to the pursuit of military victory by all citizens:

---

78 William Beveridge, *Social Insurance and Allied Services* (London: His Majesty's Stationery Office, 1942). This work – as is known – is also referred to as the *Beveridge Report* or *Beveridge Program*.

79 'The Crisis of Medicine or the Crisis of Antimedicine?', p. 6.

80 'The Political Technologies of Individuals', p. 147. On the *Beveridge Plan* Foucault expressed himself in similar terms also in *The Birth of Biopolitics*, p. 216.

the purpose of victory is to live into a better world than the old world; each individual citizen is more likely to concentrate upon his war effort if he feels that his Government will be ready in time with plans for that better world; that, if these plans are to be ready in time, they must be made now.[81]

Richard M. Titmuss, an authoritative scholar of social problems and a supporter of the system designed by Beveridge, also insists on the relationship between the state of war and the birth of the contemporary welfare state. He very clearly highlights in particular the fact that modern warfare, in the forms it took on in the 20th century, could not fail to involve the organization and development of vast strategies of attention towards «the biological characteristics», «the quantity and quality of population».[82] According to this author, it can be substantially said that after the Second World War the promotion of the British welfare and, in particular, the creation of the National Health Service were based largely on the techniques and intervention systems already activated during the war in this sense. In that period, in fact, the state had understood as problems of great importance the satisfaction of primary needs for all, the attention to the demographic processes and the state of health of the population as a military force, as a labour force for war production, as a totality of individuals affected by the debilitating and deadly effects of the conflict or of persons in need of assistance because they were dependent on «husbands and fathers (...) serving in the Forces».[83]

Rosanvallon also gives great importance to the connection that was created between the Second World War and the birth of the contemporary welfare state not only in Great Britain, but elsewhere also. According to him, the said connection demonstrates that historically it is moments of crisis (social, political, international) that provoke the mobilization of the social energies which feed the consensus, the compromise and the social contract on which the various forms of the protective state are founded. From this point

---

81   Beveridge, *Social Insurance and Allied Services*, p. 171.
82   Richard M. Titmuss, *Essays on 'The Welfare State'* (London: George Allen & Unwin, 1976 3th edn), p. 78.
83   Titmuss, *Essays on 'The Welfare State'*, p. 84; see also pp. 78-86.

of view, the Second World War created a situation from which the policies, which – in one way or another – were inspired by the *Beveridge Plan,* responded to the profound need to regenerate the social contract radically undermined by the war itself.

> If the welfare state reaffirms itself and extends into the experience of armed conflict, it is because in this circumstance it really seems that society returns to its imaginary origins, to the formulation of the social pact. The symbolic stipulation of the original contract between individuals and the state is reaffirmed in such periods. The debt of protection contracted by the state finds a more visible statement.[84]

What, on the other hand, Rosanvallon clearly highlights is that the welfare state, as an updated form of the modern protector state, appears exposed to its own crisis since its foundation. While claiming that this form of state responds to the need to regenerate the «social bond»[85] that risks dissolving in moments of crisis, the French author cannot help but consider that the same welfare state actually fails, and perhaps it cannot succeed, to really be a social state: precisely as a contemporary version of the protector state, in reality, it still continues to be based on the privileged relationship between state and individual, which is the basis of that protective pact that Hobbes and Locke believed indispensable: «[the] protector state is unthinkable and impossible without the emergence of the individual as a political and juridical category», says Rosanvallon. It isolates the individual from the relationships in which he is immersed because it cannot accept to share with other forms of power present in society the task of protection that it has assumed, if not at the price of sharing with them its own sovereignty which cannot be such if it is not exclusive. Moreover – according to the author – the protector state,

> as a fiscal state, cannot be built unless it increasingly frees individuals from real social groups (patriarchal family, neighbourhood relations based on barter, etc.) in which the economic exchanges that elude it are founded. The wealth and exchanges must be made visible (...). The modern state cannot exist, in short, without economy and market

---

84 Rosanvallon, *La crise de l'État-providence*, p. 30.
85 *La crise de l'État-providence*, p. 31.

society, that is without affirming the individual as a central economic category.[86]

Equally clearly Rosanvallon claims that

the welfare state only continues and expands this process of protecting the individual as a figure of social reality. Its goal is to free him from the ties of constrictive and precarious solidarity in which he is still included: the *welfare state wants to free the individual simplifying the social reality*.[87]

If it is therefore true that the welfare state responds to the need to reconstitute social ties threatened by wars and crises, it is also true that it recognizes and betrays this need at the same time. In fact, sooner or later it becomes a bureaucratic mechanism, far from the development of concrete social relations. «Isolated from the real relationships that structure it, the organization of solidarity implemented by this welfare state becomes more abstract. The welfare state mechanically proceeds to a real suppression of social relations».[88]

Rosanvallon proposes his theses at a time (1981) in which the growing success of neoliberalism and its welfare state dismantling policies is clearly emerging. He is extremely aware of this situation; however, he also seems convinced that the profound crisis in which the welfare state has entered can be resolved by responding to the persistent need of sociality in ways different from those – according to him, substantially counterproductive – with which the welfare state itself has historically responded to. In a nutshell, according to him, this is a question of activating or reactivating forms of autonomous social solidarity with respect to the state as well as to the market, without claiming to do without one or the other, but certainly trying to reappraise the importance that the individual, as an isolated and abstract figure, plays in the functioning of both; this is above all a matter of promoting and enhancing the initiatives that society assumes directly to tackle

---

86   *La crise de l'État-providence*, p. 44.
87   *La crise de l'État-providence*, pp. 44-5.
88   *La crise de l'État-providence*, p. 41.

the problems of assistance to life and social solidarity: formal and informal associations, neighbourhood relations, volunteering, etc. All of this, in general, should be part of «a triple process of *reducing the demand of the state, of re-establishing solidarity in society and of producing greater social visibility*».[89]

It can be said, in any case, that – according to Rosanvallon's point of view – the crisis in which the welfare state has entered since the end of the seventies concerns the social compromise (between capital and labour, entrepreneurs and employees, rich and poor) on which it was built, but does not affect the need for sociality recognized and, at the same time, betrayed by the welfare state itself; it is a need to which neoliberalism – according to the French author – will never succeed in responding adequately, since it is an updated and radicalized expression of liberal individualism.[90]

These theses, in reality, lead us to think that Rosanvallon underestimates the profound effects that the prolonged promotion of individualism – in its "Hobbesian", "Lockian", liberal, neoliberal or welfarist forms – may have had in the formation of the personal and social *ethos* of contemporary man. In this sense, it is significant what he claims after recognizing that, in any case, the welfare state crisis «also corresponds to a *crisis of solidarity*», as witnessed by the «tendency to social corporatism» or the «development of narrowly sectorial reactions in the field of taxes or social contributions»; in fact, he adds to this acknowledgement:

> Obviously, it is not considering the evolution of individual behaviours that one acquires the possibility of grasping the meaning of this phenomenon: individuals have not become more selfish or less generous. It is in sociological terms that one must try to understand this social fact.[91]

What one can oppose instead to a consideration like this is that precisely «considering the evolution of individual behaviours»

---

89 *La crise de l'État-providence*, p. 112; also see pp. 113-38. Donzelot also outlines a perspective quite similar to this one in *L'invention du social*, pp. 179-263.

90 See *La crise de l'État-providence*, pp. 97-106.

91 *La crise de l'État-providence*, p. 41.

we can grasp at least some of the most profound effects that the political, economic and biopolitical promotion of individualism may have had on the *ethos* of contemporary people, pushing them to actively contribute to the crisis not only of the welfare state, but also of solidarity and sociality in general. If the sociological analysis of this crisis remains necessary, it must nevertheless be freed from the risk of considering the social dimension or the need for sociality as metahistorical realities that would remain substantially immune to the influence of political and biopolitical government technologies and the resulting transformations of the behavioural models.

2.6 *Unresolved problems*

To clarify the issue, first of all, we can try to develop some results of the survey carried out in this chapter.

Firstly, the "social", as a sphere of life security management and as a representation of the collective dimension, is an historical "invention" that the contemporary welfare state inherits from the insurance strategies of the 19th century and perfects in its complementary or alternative function toward two other historically determined "inventions": 1) the "free market" as a mechanism endowed with its "natural" functioning which would allow society to reproduce and progress indefinitely; 2) the "class struggle" as a tool for undermining capitalism and producing a "just society" through the political victory of labour over capital (Donzelot).

Secondly, despite what their historical promoters claimed, the centrality that insurance techniques have assumed both in the contemporary welfare state and in previous social security policies is a factor of radical desolidarization, anything but casual, of life care; in fact, these techniques – as we have seen – contribute to resizing or supplanting with impersonal and abstract forms of mutuality the experiences of mutualism, developed above all in the 19th century, and managed directly and autonomously by their beneficiaries (Defert). Ultimately, if – as Rosanvallon himself says – the welfare state produces «irresponsibility and social reflux», these outcomes do not constitute «perverse social effects» of its function,[92] but the result of an inevitable transformation of the citizen into the subject of an insurance contract or, in any case, simple tax payer and user of life protection services. Therefore, the idea that social insurance «provides a form of association which combines a maximum of socialization with a maximum of individualization» is credible, inasmuch as «[i]t allows people to enjoy the advantages of association while still leaving them free to exist as individuals».[93]

If it is true, moreover, that – as Beveridge writes in 1942 about his project – «[t]he main feature of the Plan for Social Security is a scheme of social insurance against interruption and destruction of earning power»,[94] this means that a fundamental purpose of the policies inaugurated or relaunched by that plan is to protect life as a productive capacity of citizens as economic entities. In other words, these policies must ensure that citizens continue, as far as possible, to relate to their society as a market society. What they tend to guarantee with the protection of their lives is above all the preservation of their work potential. This consideration may appear "dubious" only if one disregards what has characterized, from the outset, the insurance logic that the welfare state recuperates from the history that precedes it and adapts to its policies. This logic, in reality, never effectively "ensures" a life or a body: these – in case of injury, illness or death – are affected or compromised in a more or less serious, but generally irreversible way; and it is precisely because the insurance logic deals with the irreversible or with the irreparable that it cannot aspire to truly remedy them; therefore, it adopts criteria of simple compensation for the sufferings of life based on economic calculations, rather than on "inaccurate" evaluations of other kinds. And this can only contribute to the transformation of those who benefit from an insurance (no matter whether private or managed by the state) into a holder of *human capital* that must be quantified to some extent to be compensated in some way if it is compromised or lost.[95] After all, in a capitalist

---

92 *La crise de l'État-providence*, p. 41.
93 Ewald, 'Insurance and Risk', p. 204.
94 Beveridge, *Social Insurance and Allied Services*, p. 9.
95 In this regard Ewald is particularly convincing in 'Insurance and risk', pp. 204-5. See also Defert, ''Popular life' and insurance technology', p. 212.

society precisely the economic, or rather work and production related, misadventures of life are among the major causes of the sufferings of the individual.

Furthermore, particular attention should be paid to the fact that the main figure of the social scenario to which the welfare state refers until the 1970s is the wage labourer.[96] This also certainly means that the affirmation of its policies is a result, direct or indirect, of the great struggles of which the working class – as the nucleus of wage labour particularly active on the political level – has been a protagonist since the 19th century. On the other hand, the fundamental role that was assigned to Keynesian economic policies in the promotion of the welfare state in the 20th century can be reliably interpreted as a strategic response to the political force that the labour movement has assumed worldwide with the revolutionary establishment of a socialist regime in Russia aimed at overcoming capitalism.[97] All this, in any case, does not prevent us from arguing that, through the welfare state, the mechanisms of social security and care of life have not been placed in the hands of wage labourers, or those who have directly or indirectly contributed to determining its formation; these mechanisms – as Rosanvallon himself shows – were socialized on an economic level and at the same time centralized on a political level, thus preventing this involvement of labourers from being realized. This is also the reason why their substantial reduction to simple taxpayers and users of a life insurance or social assistance system has resulted.

In any case, the contemporary welfare state, from a biopolitical point of view adds something decidedly new to the previous protective strategies, namely a radicalization of the processes of

---

96   See Robert Castel, *From Manual Workers to Wage Laborers: Transformation of the Social Question*, trans. and ed. by Richard Boyd (New Brunswick, USA, and London: Transaction Publishers, 2003), pp. 303-66.

97   In this sense, see Antonio Negri, 'Keynes and the Capitalist Theory of the State', in Michael Hardt and Antonio Negri, *Labor of Dionysus: A Critique of the State-Form* (Minneapolis: University of Minnesota Press, 1994), pp. 25-32. See also the considerations of Foucault in *The Birth of Biopolitics*, pp. 68-9.

medicalization of the existence of the individual, which passes through a sort of reversal of their previous relationship with the state. As Foucault says, up until the time of the Beveridge Plan, the attention of the state to the life of the individual was aimed above all at «the preservation of national physical strength, the work force and its capacity of production, and military force». Instead, from that moment, «the terms of the problem were reversed: the concept of the healthy individual in the service of the state was replaced by that of the state in the service of the healthy individual».[98] This does not mean that in this way the link between political attention to life and economic rationality is subdued or reduced. This, rather, means that the state is moving towards an incorporation of the insurance and welfare logic into a broader perspective of redistribution of wealth. The very aspiration of the welfare state to guarantee health for all falls within this perspective.

> Through the avenue of health – Foucault says in this sense –, illnesses and the need to ensure the necessities of health led to a certain economic redistribution. (...) This redistribution did not, however, depend on taxes, but on the system of regulation and economic coverage of health and illnesses. In ensuring for all the same opportunities for receiving treatment, there was an attempt to correct inequalities in income.[99]

In this regard, however, it should be noted that the prospect of wealth redistribution establishes a close relationship with Keynesian economic policies and, in particular, with the full employment policies tending to favour a large presence of wage incomes in society, the development of consumption and a widespread possibility of contributing to the financing of the structures and services of the welfare state.[100] Certainly the welfare state in this way does not achieve the "social justice" that it somehow promises. It does nothing but try to compensate for a lack of well-being also by guaranteeing a minimum of health to

---

98   'The Crisis of Medicine or the Crisis of Antimedicine?', p. 6.
99   'The Crisis of Medicine or the Crisis of Antimedicine?', pp. 6-7.
100   See William Beveridge, *Full Employment in a Free Society* (London: George Allen & Unwin, 1960, 2nd edn).

all. Nevertheless, its function cannot be fulfilled satisfactorily for various reasons.

In particular, it establishes public healthcare services, but does not abolish private medicine, since its inextricable relationship with the market economy does not allow it. Private medical care, on the other hand, remains an opportunity to which the social classes able to economically afford it do not intend to give up; furthermore, under certain conditions, private medicine tends to develop by providing services that the public medical systems cannot satisfactorily provide. This will go hand in hand with the reproduction of a profound inequality of possibilities of accessing the "right to healt" by figures with too little economic resources to be able to adequately contribute to the financing of the welfare state and therefore to fully benefit from its protection, for example, by receiving decent pensions during old age. On the other hand, it is true that in many cases public medical services tend to break free from the strictly insurance logic to try to guarantee equal services for all, financed with general taxation; however, even in the cases of "universal health care systems" the marginal social figures suffer the limits, the territorial differences and the inefficiencies of such services without being able to resort to private medicine, due to the lack of economic resources.[101]

---

101 Here, with the phrase "universal health care systems" we intend to refer to the first of the two models in which health care systems are generally distinguished: 1) the *Beveridge model* that would tend to guarantee all citizens equal medical services financed by general taxation; 2) the *Bismarck model* that would offer individual health assistance financed by compulsory insurance contributions drawn from the income of individual workers. In this case, there is the possibility that the unemployed are not guaranteed health care, unless the state finances it with appropriate funds. Furthermore, this classification is usually completed with the model corresponding to systems in which the financing of medical care is based on voluntary insurance contracts. What is certain is that this categorization does not consider the complex intertwining between different methods of financing and supplying of services that characterizes the various health care systems. Not surprisingly, a distinction of seven different models has recently been proposed, applied to 24 OECD countries «with reference to the following dimensions: who pays for and who benefits from the system; the number of insurers, and the public or private nature of the coverage

Of the presence of these figures, Richard M. Titmuss clearly observes the consistency a few years after the creation of the contemporary welfare state in Great Britain, indicating it with definitions such as «the politically obscure minorities; the powerless groups; the dependent poor, the disabled, the deprived and the rejected».[102] Ultimately, it can be assumed that the welfare state will not be able to fulfil its task of guaranteeing the equitable protection of life also because contemporary capitalism does not put an end to the periodic marginalization or expulsion from the economic system of substantial quotas of the population, which in general we can indicate with the definition of «relative overpopulation» used at the time by Marx or with that of «supernumeraries» used by Castel most recently when referring to the «"unemployable", unemployed or employed only precariously and intermittently».[103]

In conclusion, the structure of the welfare state does not nullify either economic inequality and social exclusion or the discriminatory effects they produce on the level of effective protection of life.

---

scheme; the contribution method; users' freedom of choice; the arrangements between insurers and providers; the role of the State». The seven models are therefore indicated in the following ways: «1) direct market; 2) voluntary private insurance; 3) social health insurance; 4) residual programs; 5) compulsory national health insurance; 6) universal single-payer system; 7) national health service». Federico Toth, 'Non solo Bismarck contro Beveridge: sette modelli di sistema sanitario', in *Rivista Italiana di Politiche Pubbliche*, 2 (2016), 279-305 (p. 279). More generally, it must be said that it is very difficult to maintain that "universal systems" capable of guaranteeing all citizens the right to health truly exist. The reasons are many and certainly cannot be listed and discussed here; but it can be agreed, at least, with those who maintain that in the field of health care systems «universal approaches do not automatically guarantee access to individuals in vulnerable situations (...). [R]educed mobility, age, geographic remoteness, unemployment, low income, an unstable housing situation and being deprived of liberty can all pose obstacles to accessing services». European Commission, *Thematic session 1: Universal approaches to healthcare Concept, Paper*, Written by ICF Consulting Services Ltd, October 2017: https://eurohealthnet.eu/sites/eurohealthnet.eu/files/Thematic%20session%201%20concept%20paper.pdf (accessed October 13, 2019).

102 Titmuss, *Essays on 'The Welfare State'*, p. 217.
103 Castel, *From Manual Workers to Wage Laborers*, p. XIII.

This is easily understood if one considers what the Beveridge Plan already envisaged, namely that «social insurance» should pursue its objectives «in combination with national assistance and voluntary insurance as subsidiary methods».[104] In fact, in countries where the welfare state has become established, social insurance is generally accompanied by a system of assistance, mostly uncertain and residual, destined to individuals in need; furthermore, in these same countries the presence of a private insurance sector, intended for those who can economically afford to benefit from it, has never been questioned.[105]

3. *Social policies and* ethos *variations: towards neoliberal biopolitics*

3.1 *Wage labour: an unlikely ethical model*

The insufficiency of protection in which the life of a large number of "marginal" figures is usually found, can be considered a sort of "omen" of that crisis to which the welfare state seems destined since its conception.[106] Foucault himself – in an interview in 1983 – recognizes, in the substantial exclusion from social security of a whole set of figures, one of the aspects of the crisis, in progress at that time, of this state system and its promise to guarantee to all the "right to health". What is interesting about his considerations is that, according to him, the crisis of this promise coincides with the emergence in society of two forms of dependence: one of these derives from «*integration*», that is to say that «[a] whole machinery of social coverage (...) fully benefits the individual if

---

104 Beveridge, *Social Insurance and Allied Services*, p. 9; see also pp. 11 and 12.

105 For a further theoretical and historical study of the welfare state, refer to: Gøsta Esping-Andersen, *The Three Worlds of Welfare Capitalism* (Princeton: Princeton University Press, 1990); Fiorenzo Girotti, *Welfare state. Storia, modelli e critica* (Rome: Carocci, 1998). See also: Anna Salfi and Fiorenza Tarozzi, *Dalle società di mutuo soccorso alle conquiste del welfare state* (Rome: Ediesse, 2014).

106 In this sense it is expressed not only by Rosanvallon *(La crise de l'État providence,* pp. 41-45), but also by Castel, *L'insecurité social*, pp. 5-9.

that individual is *integrated*, whether in terms of family, work place, or geographical area».[107] The other form of dependence instead derives from the «*marginalization or exclusion*», or rather from the danger of substantial abandonment to which, according to him, not only those marginalized by the economic system are exposed, but also – or above all – those who do not adhere to «a particular way of life»; so «any person or group that, for one reason or another, will not be able to embrace that way of life is marginalized by the operation of the institutions».[108]

Indicating, on the one hand, the relationship between dependence and integration and, on the other, the relationship between dependence and marginalization, Foucault evidently invites us to critically examine the welfare state policies. However, what must be kept in mind is that he proposes his considerations a few years after the Course (*The Birth of Biopolitics*) in which he carried out his most extensive analysis of liberal and neoliberal governmentality: as we shall see later, in that analysis he undeniably places the neoliberal criticisms of the welfare state under discussion, criticisms with which therefore the considerations we have just mentioned cannot be confused.[109] In any case, in his 1983 interview, the French philosopher urges us to criticize the welfare state not simply in economic and sociological terms, but rather by questioning first the forms of the individual and social *ethos* that its policies tend to favour.[110] As we have seen,

---

107 Michel Foucault, 'Social Security', in *Politics, Philosophy, Culture: Interviews and other Writings-1977-1984*, trans. by Alan Seridan, ed. by Lawence D. Kritizman (New York-London: Routledge, Chapman & Hall, 1990), p. 162.

108 Foucault, 'Social Security', pp. 164-5.

109 *The Birth of Biopolitics*, pp. 186-92.

110 In this sense it is important what he states in a passage of his interview, in which he indicates the need for «a subtle analysis of the present situation»: «By "present situation" I don't mean the totality of economic and social mechanisms (...): I'm speaking rather of the kind of interface between, on the one hand, people's feelings, their moral choices, their relationship with themselves, and, on the other hand, the institutions that surround them. It is here that malfunctionings, malaise, and, perhaps, crises are born». Similarly, he expresses himself in another passage of the interview by saying: «taking the situation as a whole, there are good

speaking in particular of marginalization, he identifies possible victims not only in those who remain outside the main circuits of the production of wealth, but also in those who adhere to ways of life, or rather forms of *ethos*, different from those prevailing in society. So, considering Foucault's observations from this point of view, we can firstly try to clarify which are the privileged ways of life of the welfare state, thus also trying to remedy the scarcity of indications that the French philosopher offers us in this regard.

Put in a nutshell, it is entirely plausible that these ways of life have as their main model the behaviour that is generally expected – not only economically but also on an ethical level – by the wage labourer;[111] moreover, if we want to develop Foucaultian suggestions on the two forms of dependency that would have been created with the welfare state, we can say in the first place that the dependency deriving from *integration* («in terms of family, work place, or geographical area») is above all that caused by the need to be permanently employed workers to fully benefit from the various forms of "welfarist" protection of life. This is obviously a necessity that requires adherence to a precise work ethic, which – so to speak – will be rewarded by the systems created by the welfare state for the protection from accidents, disability, old age, for «the maintenance of employment and prevention of mass unemployment», as well as «for prevention and for cure of disease and disability by medical treatment» which «covers rehabilitation and fitting for employment».[112]

Thus far it seems clear in what sense Foucault's idea can be understood, according to which the dependency deriving from integration is expressed «in terms of work place»; on the other hand, one can understand equally clearly why we can say that this dependency is also expressed «in terms of family»

grounds for elucidating the relations that exist between the functioning of social security and lifestyles. (...) it's a study that would require much further research, and yet avoid a strict "sociologism," divorced from certain ethical problems». 'Social Security', pp. 161-2 and 165.

111 In this regard, the following are essential: Castel, *L'insecurité sociale* and *From Manual Workers to Wage Laborers*.
112 Beveridge, *Social Insurance and Allied Services*, pp. 163 and 158. See also pp. 158-65.

and «geographical area». In fact, the welfare state attributes primary importance to the family and to the ethical models that can mature within it, first of all by organizing what is defined in the Beveridge Plan as «a general scheme of children's allowances».[113] Furthermore, it is not difficult to guess that the «geographical area» in which one lives and works cannot fail to influence the various possibilities of taking advantage from the benefits and services of the welfare state, in particular those of its most qualified and equipped medical facilities, mostly located in the more important urban areas. As regards, instead, dependency – or the absence of autonomy – deriving from *marginalization*, it can be said that this is certainly created if one is «"unemployable", unemployed or employed only precariously and intermittently», as Castel would say; but – on the basis of what Foucault allows us to hypothesize – it must be added that this can be created even if one does not unequivocally adhere to the ways of life and the forms of *ethos* corresponding to the social importance that the welfare state attributes to wage labour and the family.

In any case, considering the attention that the welfare state addresses to wage labour, it cannot be overlooked that in reality this form of work certainly cannot be identified only with that of the factory worker. The wage labourer, of course, is also the person employed in an office, who generally believes that he is in a social position of greater "respectability" than the factory worker and, for the most part, manages to improve his position more easily than the worker in this sense.[114] The worker, on the other hand, throughout the history of the welfare state, lives in a sort of division between two conditions: on the one hand, that determined by the massified character of his work which is often also generally subjected to the rigid Fordist-type organization of industrial production; on the other hand, that caused by a series of growing demands not only

---

113 *Social Insurance and Allied Services*, p. 154. See also pp. 54-158. This indication by Beveridge will have its legislative formalization in the *Family Allowance Act* (1945).

114 On this type of dynamics and on the extreme variety of figures and social conditions that has developed within wage labour in contemporary society, see Castel, *From Manual Workers to Wage Laborers*, pp. 303-66.

economic, but also of recognition and social respect, which mature outside the factory, particularly in the family. In this sense Titmuss argues that, the male worker, in his relationship with the family finds himself having to consider that «to win a bare level of subsistence is no longer (...) a sufficient reason by itself alone to be accorded – and expect to be accorded – respect by one's fellows and by one one's wife and children».[115] This basically implies that the relationship between the economic role of wage labour and the biopolitical role of the family, from an ethical point of view, constantly risks going into crisis in advanced industrial societies.

In other words, it can be said that social integration based on the link between the work place and family does not arise spontaneously from the historical, economic and social context in which the welfare state occurs; this must be produced and actively supported, especially if – as in the case of the massified worker of the large factory – such integration cannot generally be founded either on a satisfactory economic condition or on a secure status or on a socially recognized and respected "professional" role. This seems to be the reason why Titmuss, after about a decade from the creation of the British welfare state, observes that neither the care of the so-called «human relations in industry» nor the optimistic trust in the socially stabilizing role of the family can be enough to compensate for the difficulties of social integration that the growing industrial development of contemporary societies produces. The family in particular – according to him – seems to require special attention on the part of social services to the extent that it is, at the same time, «benefited and damaged» by «the forces of industrialization». Ultimately, family risks being the situation where all the economic, social and psychological frustrations of the industrial worker end up spilling over, compromising both the stability and the integrational function it should perform. Therefore, says the author,

> we need to see the social services in a variety of stabilizing, preventive, and protective roles. Interpreted in this way, and not as the modern equivalent of Bismarckian benevolence, the social services become an ally – not an enemy – of industrial and technological progress.[116]

---

115 Titmuss, *Essays on 'The Welfare State'*, p. 114.
116 *Essays on 'The Welfare State'*, pp. 117-8.

Evidently, according to Titmuss, it is a matter of going beyond the merely economic support of the family based on "children's allowances", by also guaranteeing services aimed at the direct improvement of the quality of life, from the physical and biological one to the housing, urban and educational one of its members. In this way, among others, the problems and frustrations that industrialization causes, especially to the worker, will be able to find satisfactory compensation in the family. This – according to the author – is what is perhaps happening in Britain at the end of the nineteen-fifties for the quality that the social services promoted by the state have already achieved, unlike in other countries like Germany.

> One has only to notice the way in which husbands now do the shopping, take the laundry to the laundrette (perhaps because the wife has been out to work), play with the children, and unashamedly push prams, to realize that family life in industrialized Britain is changing. Do husbands now push prams in Germany? Should they?[117]

Whether this representation of the family life of the nineteen-fifties in Britain is reliable or not, Titmuss's reasoning clearly brings out one of the most important purpose that the welfare state pursues by placing the relationship between wage labour and family dimension at the centre of its attention: to ensure that the private sphere of the family is sufficiently stable to strengthen the economic and ethical role of wage labour.

3.2 *Paradoxes of emancipation*

In any event, it is of great interest what Titmuss points out concerning the evolution that the family and the condition of women in their relationship with procreation have undergone in the advanced industrial societies since the late 19th century. In particular, the author notes that in the early 20th century – when the Women's Suffrage Movement fought hard to increase the personal, legal and political freedoms of the female population – it was widely believed that «to release women from the domination of men, exercised through, what John Stuart Mill called, "the foul

---

117 *Essays on 'The Welfare State'*, p. 117.

means of marriage" would lead to fewer marriages in the future».[118] This, at least in certain industrialized countries like Great Britain and the USA, will not happen until the 1950s: undoubtedly, many results will be achieved in terms of equality and individual freedom of women; but, at the same time, the number of marriages will tend to grow. «Paradoxically, therefore, fewer social and legal restraints and more equality and freedom for women have been accompanied by an increase in the popularity of the marriage institution».[119]

This sort of unexpected side effect of women's emancipation can be explained if one considers, from a biopolitical point of view, the changes in the ways of living family life which – according to Titmuss – have become established in the most dynamic industrial societies. What the author particularly insists on in this regard is the clear reduction in the number of pregnancies and the consequent decrease in the size of families, processes that have occurred to a remarkable extent not only within the middle class, but also in that of the working class. It is a profound change in the marital *ethos* that – according to him – could lead to this evolution; this, in fact, can be interpreted «as a desired change within the working-class family rather than as a revolt by women against the authority of men on the analogy of the campaign for political emancipation».[120]

> [M]utual relationships of husband and wife – adds Titmuss – are very different today from the picture of married life which emerges from the literature and social investigations of Edwardian times. The extent to which fertility has come under control by married couples is evidence of this. New patterns in the psychological management of married life have been slowly evolving; the idea of companionship in marriage is being substituted for the more sharply defined roles and codes of behaviour set by the Victorian patriarchal system.[121]

What is important to note in the changes reported by Titmuss is not so much the trend in the number of marriages that, in fact, will tend to decline after the 1950s; rather one must grasp their

---

118 *Essays on 'The Welfare State'*, p. 98.
119 *Essays on 'The Welfare State'*, p. 101.
120 *Essays on 'The Welfare State'*, p. 91.
121 *Essays on 'The Welfare State'*, p. 98.

precise biopolitical implications to which the author himself seems to allude by stating: «The fall in the birth rate in Western societies is one of the dominating biological facts of the twentieth century».[122] The changes in the female and marital *ethos* that give rise to transformations of family life are in fact linked to biological, medical and demographic processes – among which stand out, together with the decrease of the birth rate, the improvement of health conditions and reduction of female and child mortality – to which social policies inaugurated in the 19th century and developed by the welfare state have certainly contributed.[123]

As we will try to show, the relationship that seems to have been created between certain changes in the ways of life and these biopolitical transformations, also seems to constitute in reality a premise of the crisis of the welfare state's social policies and, at the same time, the birth of post-welfarist and neoliberal forms of biopolitics.

3.3 *The welfare state between crisis and criticism*

As we have seen, the welfare state policies confirm the central role that economic rationality plays in the prevailing forms of government of modern society. In this case this centrality is expressed above all through the Keynesian attention to industrial development, full employment and consumption. On the other hand, it is well known that the political centrality of economic rationality will be expressed even more clearly in the neoliberal forms of government through the clear privilege of free market mechanisms, with which neoliberalism has managed to take over the welfare state since the end of the 1970s.

---

122 *Essays on 'The Welfare State'*, p. 89.
123 For a broad overview of the issues of motherhood and the family in relation to the birth of the welfare state, see: Gisela Bock, 'Poverty and Mothers' Rights in the Emerging Welfare State', in Georges Duby, Michelle Perrot, Françoise Thebaud (ed. by), *A History of Women in the West*, vol. 5, *Toward a Cultural Identity in the Twentieth Century* (Cambridge, UK: Belknap, 1994), pp. 402-31; Nadine Lefaucheur, 'Maternity, Family, and the State', trans. by Arthur Goldhammer, in *A History of Women in the West*, vol. 5, pp. 433-52.

With regard to neoliberalism, in *The Birth of Biopolitics*, Foucault himself constantly insists on the radical nature of the economic declination of its governmental rationality. He also offers us the possibility of understanding that a serious criticism of welfare state policies and biopolitics certainly cannot find its primary reference in the criticism that neoliberalism generally addresses to this form of state.[124] According to his reconstruction, this criticism began to develop from the very moment in which the welfare state strategies were outlined with the American New Deal and the British *Beveridge Plan*. For most neoliberal theorists, the simple aspiration expressed in these strategies to guarantee a minimum of "social justice" or a certain redistribution of wealth is a sufficient reason to criticize them harshly and reject them. According to Friedrich von Hayek, in particular, the state cannot take on such tasks unless it risks seriously compromising the free economic initiative which is the foundation of a true free society:

> the recognition of a claim by every citizen or inhabitant of a country to a certain minimum standard, dependent upon the average level of wealth of that country, involves, however, the recognition of a kind of collective ownership of the resources of the country which is not compatible with the idea of an open society and which raises serious problems.[125]

From this point of view, the most dangerous consequence of welfarist policies is that they entail the planning by the state as an indispensable tool of its government action: this orientation cannot fail to extend the intervention without limits of the state over society, thus creating the conditions of totalitarianism. This is a kind of criticism that neoliberalism has never stopped proposing before and after the emergence of its political hegemony at a global level. This criticism, of course, does not call into question the fundamental link that welfare state policies establish with

---

124 *The Birth of Biopolitics*, pp. 186-92.
125 Friedrich von Hayek, *Law, Legislation and Liberty: A new statement of the liberal principles of justice and political economy* (London: Routledge & Kegan Paul, 1982), vol. III, pp. 55-6. See also the relentless criticism of the concept of «'social' or distributive justice», developed in this same work, vol., II, pp. 62-100.

economic rationality; rather, it tends to show that this rationality is applied in a completely incorrect way. Therefore, neoliberalism proposes to regenerate it by minimizing state intervention on the economy and assigning it, rather, the role of guarantor of competition and the proper functioning of the free market.[126]

Foucault, for his part, in his Course – held at the same time as neoliberalism powerfully imposed itself both in Europe, with Margaret Thatcher (1979), and in the USA, with Ronald Reagan (1981) – does not limit himself to showing the unacceptability of the neoliberal idea according to which there is a continuity between the economic interventionism of the welfare state and totalitarianism;[127] he also offers us useful elements to grasp the intensity that the relationship between economics and biopolitics can achieve within the framework of neoliberal governmentality. From this point of view, we can say that the ratio of continuity that should be brought out is not so much what could be created between the welfare state and totalitarianism, but what could be established historically between the welfare state and neoliberalism itself. It is

---

126 Exemplary texts of the formulation of this criticism of the welfare state and of "government activism" in general are: Friedrich A. von Hayek, *The Road to Serfdom* (London and New York: Routledge, 2001); Wilhelm Röpke, *Civitas Humana: A Humane Order of Society* (London, Edinburgh, Glasgow: William Hodge and Company, 1948). The *Beveridge Plan*, in particular, has been the subject of radical criticism in: Henry C. Simon, 'The Beveridge Program: An Unsympathetic Interpretation', *Journal of Political Economy*, 3 (1945), 212-3, article republished in *Economic Policy for a Free Society* (Chicago: Chicago University Press, 1948), chap. 5; Wilhelm Röpke, 'Das Beveridgeplan', *Schweizerische Monatshefte für Politik und Kultur*, 3/4 (1943), 159-78. The latter author took up the terms of his criticism in *Civitas Humana*, pp. 142-9. A very interesting read is also Paul Matzko, 'Hayek vs. Beveridge on the Welfare State', June 13-September 11 (2019), https://www.libertarianism.org/columns/hayek-vs-beveridge-welfare-state. For an overall theoretical framework of the neoliberal criticism of the welfare state, see Rosanvallon, *La crise de l'État-providence*, pp. 59-106 and 174-9.

127 What to Foucault seems unacceptable of the neoliberal criticisms of the welfare state is above all «the idea that the state possesses in itself (...) an endogenous imperialism constantly pushing it to spread its surface and increase in extent, depth, and subtlety to the point that it will come to take over entirely that which is at the same time its other, its outside,

in this sense that we can try to develop the consideration proposed in the previous pages, according to which certain changes in the ways of life that occurred with the emergence of the welfare state may have favoured both its crisis and the emergence of post-welfarist and neoliberal biopolitical forms; which can result from the analysis of the role that the family seems to play in a neoliberal society while at the same time prolonging and changing the role it has already assumed in the welfare state.

To try to verify this hypothesis, we will refer to the studies on the family by Gary S. Becker – one of the major supporters of the neoliberal theory of human capital –, also considering some suggestions proposed by Foucault on this theory.[128]

3.4 *Birth of the neoliberal family*

In his research on the fertility of marriages, Becker argues that Malthus's pessimism about the relationship between the evolution of the economy and population growth has historically

---

its target, and its object, namely: civil society». Deeply questionable to him is the idea implicit in these criticisms «that there is a kinship, a sort of genetic continuity or evolutionary implication between different forms of the state, with the administrative state, the welfare state, the bureaucratic state, the fascist state, and the totalitarian state». (*The Birth of Biopolitics*, p. 187). In this regard Foucault does not limit himself to objecting that «the welfare state has neither the same form, of course, nor (...) the same root or origin as the totalitarian state, as the Nazi, fascist, or Stalinist state». (p. 190); in reality – according to him – totalitarianism is the result of one of the two forms of weakening of the state, which are affirmed in the 20th century: the first derives from «a governmentality of the party» that produced totalitarian regimes by subjecting state institutions to the iron supremacy of political organizations; the second, instead, derives exactly from the «neoliberal governmentality» that destabilizes the role of the state, limiting its action and denouncing it constantly as the source of the "totalitarian danger" (pp. 190-2). This position of Foucault clearly denies the thesis according to which, in his Course of 1978-1979, the French philosopher would have suffered an unconfessed fascination by neoliberalism. In this regard see Daniel Zamora and Michael C. Behrent (ed. by), *Foucault and Neoliberalism* (Cambridge, UK: Polity, 2015).

128 See *The Birth of Biopolitics*, pp. 227-30; On the relationship between Foucault and Becker see: Gary S. Becker, François Ewald, Bernard

been denied, at least in the most developed countries. The limit of Malthus's analysis – according to him – does not consist in placing demographic phenomena in too close a relationship with economic development; this limit consists rather in the fact that Malthus, as well as his followers, have failed to identify other important economic variables that intervene in this relationship and negatively affect the fertility of the couples. In any case, in contemporary society the widespread knowledge and the growing availability of contraceptive techniques requires research to identify and carefully analyse the influence of the reasons why parents decide to procreate or not, reasons that are not considered in the Malthusian analytical framework. There is a precise historical fact that makes this broader articulation of the analysis particularly appropriate, according to Becker: the fact that since the end of the 19th century in Europe, the United States, Japan and other developed countries the average income of the population has risen, but the fertility of couples has decreased. In this regard – the author maintains – the economic analysis of the parents' decisions on procreation is effective and much more convincing than other sociological or psychological analyses.[129]

The American author, in this sense, strives above all to show the influence that such variables as the following exercise in the decisions of couples: the *price of children* (the cost of the goods and the time needed for their upbringing); the *"quality" of children* (education, learning, health, etc.); *mortality*. The increase in the average income that normally occurs with economic development establishes, according to Becker, an important relationship with these variables especially in the sense of inducing parents to consider

---

E. Harcourt, 'Becker on Ewald on Foucault on Becker American Neoliberalism and Michel Foucault's 1979 *Birth of Biopolitics* Lectures', *Chicago Institute for Law and Economics Working Paper,* 614 (2012): http://www.law.uchicago.edu/Lawecon/index.html; Miguel Vatter, 'Foucault and Becker: a biopolitical approach to human capital and the stability of preferences', in Ben Golder and Daniel McLoughlin (ed. by), *The Politics of Legality in a Neoliberal Age* (London and New York: Routledge, 2018), pp. 64-82.

129 See Gary S. Becker, 'An Economic Analysis of Fertility', in *The Economic Approach to Human Behaviour* (Chicago and London: University of Chicago Press, 1976), pp. 171-2.

it convenient to have fewer children in order to raise them better. Generally they are steered in this direction for precise reasons: in a developed and urbanized society the cost of goods useful for raising children is generally higher than that which must be sustained in a rural society; the time parents can subtract from the production of their income to dedicate it to raising children cannot go beyond certain limits; as yields of certain intellectual abilities grow, parents renounce less and less on investments in education, learning and, of course, in the health of their children; therefore, they are willing to increase the expenses for the formation of such skills for each individual child, if their income grows; the decrease in mortality, finally, reduces the need to "diversify risks" of procreation through a large family and further convinces parents that it is more convenient to have fewer children and intensify investments in their quality, bearing in mind that they are mostly destined to survive longer.[130]

Becker's position evidently refers to a tendency (the fall in the birth rate in economically more developed societies) that we have already seen appear in the analysis of a supporter of welfare state policies like Titmuss. This author also highlights the fact that in industrialized countries the size of families tends to decrease as marital behaviour changes profoundly. From his point of view, the typical family of societies that have a welfare state is a family in which female emancipation produces its effects also by reducing the number of children. However – for our part – we can add that this type of family certainly inspires its procreative choices also with the economic rationality which permeates the society in which it lives, although the dominance of this rationality can be – so to speak – mitigated by the social services and protection policies of the welfare state. Ultimately, one can reliably hypothesize that the ways in which couples of welfarist societies behave would be compatible also with neoliberal policies tending to give an increasing significance to the calculation of the costs and benefits of the choices one makes: from this point of view, after all, it is a matter of considering that for these couples making

---

130 See Gary S. Becker, 'Fertility and the Economy', *Journal of Population Economics*, 3, 5 (1992), 185-201. See also Becker, 'An Economic Analysis of Fertility', pp. 171-9.

a few more children can only be worth if there is a welfare state that is particularly generous with subsidies or services; otherwise, it is more convenient to avoid it.

Going back to Becker, we must observe that – according to him – the economic analysis of family life and of marriage itself can be extended far beyond the sphere of procreation, starting from the idea that «persons marrying (or their parents) can be assumed to expect to raise their utility level above what it would be were there to remain single». Furthermore, «since many men and women compete as they seek mates, a *market* in marriages can be presumed to exist. Each person tries to find the best mate, subject to the restrictions imposed by market conditions».[131] On this basis – according to the author – one can succeed in proving that a man and a woman choose each other, marry and remain together because they find the «compatibility» and «complementarity» that they can achieve between their personal resources (time, income, intelligence, beauty, education, property, etc.) advantageous in the production of their own and children's goods and abilities usable on the market, in the same family or in other areas not strictly economic, but in ways that are nevertheless convenient.[132] In any case, the «quality of own children» in Becker's analysis is presented as the main advantage that – together with other economic benefits – is pursued through marriage, «since children are a major source of the gain from marriage».[133]

The fundamental concept that is at the base of this type of analysis is that of *human capital* which – as mentioned – is the cornerstone of the neoliberal theory of which Becker is a supporter.[134] What the authors who elaborated this theory insist on is that the value of human capital derives from the specific characteristics and abilities that allow each individual to obtain and increase their income. Human capital therefore appears to be

---

131 Gary S. Becker, 'A Theory of Marriage: Part I', *The Journal of Political Economy*, 4, 81 (1973), 813-46 (p.814). See also Gary S. Becker, 'A Theory of Marriage: Part II', *The Journal of Political Economy*, 2, 82 (1974), Part 2, S11-S26.

132 Becker, 'A Theory of Marriage: Part I', pp. 815-22.

133 Becker, 'A Theory of Marriage: Part I', p. 834.

134 See Gary S. Becker, *Human Capital: A Theoretical and Empirical*

inseparable from individuals and their actual attitudes and skills. This theory considers the workforce of an individual not simply as a counterpart of capital possibly held by someone else, but as an immediate embodiment of capital; therefore this theory regards the individual as an *entrepreneur of himself* whose capacities, as capital, will have to be the object of continuous investments so that they can produce and increase profits in material and immaterial, monetary and intellectual terms. From this point of view, the marked preference for quality rather than the quantity of children, which – according to Becker – parents express in developed societies, is nothing other than a consequence of the growing importance that investments in human capital assume in these societies through education, training and improvement of the mental and physical abilities of individuals.[135]

This theory does not represent only a vision of which scientific validity must simply be ascertained or disproved; rather, this must be considered first of all as a description of an evolution of the ways of life, that has been widely accomplished in richer societies, including those that have benefited or still benefit from welfare state services; on the other hand, it can be interpreted as focusing on the results that neoliberal policies can still achieve in shaping the *ethos* of contemporary individual in an economic and privatistic sense, having a good chance of achieving their goals.

Analysis, with Special Reference to Education, (Chicago and London: University of Chicago Press, 1993, 3th edn).

135 The theory of human capital has been developed by some US economists since the 1950s. It presents itself as the first systematic attempt to remedy the alleged inability of classical economic thought to adequately consider the "intangible resources" corresponding to human capacities (education, experience, skills, health, etc.) among the most important factors of development. According to its supporters, in fact, it is these resources that are decisive in explaining the great advantage acquired historically in the economic competition from some countries, like the United States, over others. Among the most important works by the authors who formulated this theory – apart from those already mentioned by Becker – it is appropriate to point out: Jacob Mincer, *Schooling, Experience and Earnings* (New York: Columbia University Press, 1974); Theodore W. Schultz, *Investment in Human Capital: The Role of Education and Research* (New York: Free Press, 1971).

3.5 *Human capital as bio-capital*

It is important to underline that Becker's analyses of the family allows us to grasp the biopolitical implications of its behavioural models by insistently relating «fertility to the economy through the education and other human capital of the labour force».[136] It can be said, in particular, that by explaining the tendency of couples from rich countries to have fewer children with the considerable costs involved in raising and educating them, Becker indirectly proposes a sort of "neoliberal improvement" of biopolitics that historically have been possible starting from analyses such as those of Malthus and from the campaigns of the philanthropic organizations, developing then through the various insurance and social policies of the contemporary state.

Extremely important from this point of view is the fact that Becker, although he insists above all on *acquired abilities* – that is on the abilities that children learn through education and other formative activities –, does not fail to consider also their *inheritable traits* as elements of their human capital. Referring to «race, intelligence and height», he argues:

> An important result in population genetics is that positive assortive mating of inheritable traits, like race, intelligence, or height, increases the correlation of these traits among siblings; the increase would be greater the more inheritable the trait is and the greater the assortive mating (...). Therefore, inheritable traits of M and F [married *Male* and *Female*] can be said to be complements in reducing the uncertainty [in quality] about one's children. Positive assortive mating of inheritable traits would increase the utility of total output if more certainty about the "quality" of children is desirable.[137]

One might think that Becker with this cold description of procreative relations simply intends to "scientifically" formalize the consequences of the spontaneous propensity of people to choose their partners based on the characteristics they positively

---

136 Becker, 'Fertility and the Economy', p. 189; See also Gary S. Becker, 'Nobel Lecture: the Economic Way of Looking at Behaviour', *Journal of Political Economy*, 3, 101 (1993), 385-409 (especially pp. 395-401).

137 Becker, 'A Theory of Marriage: Part I', p. 834.

value. But to the extent that he traces these characteristics, on the one hand, to genetic criteria and, on the other, to an evaluation of profitability («the utility of total output») of procreation, his speech cannot fail to have precise biopolitical implications, evidently marked by economic rationality.

In his analyses devoted to American neoliberalism, Foucault does not let some of these implications escape, considering in particular that the development of genetic research «makes it possible to establish for any given individual the probabilities of their contracting this or that type of disease at a given age, during a given period of life, or in any way at any moment of life».[138] Which, obviously, will also allow to identify «what the risks are of a union of individuals at risk producing an individual with a particular characteristic that makes him or her the carrier of a risk». What, however, must be avoided in this regard – according to Foucault – is to simply denounce the dangers of new forms of racism that, evidently, may derive from the combination between the human capital theory and the results of genetic research. As we have seen in the third chapter, to him it seems much more worthy of reflection the possibility that «good genetic make-ups» may enter into «economic circuits or calculations». In fact, these hypothesis points to realistic scenarios of the tendencies that both biopolitics and economic government or self-government of individuals can assume within the framework of a society permeated by neoliberal governmentality. To the extent that genetics can become part of government techniques based on the idea of human capital, it can also become an essential factor in strategies that are not only economic, but also bio-political, of the «control, screening, and improvement of the human capital of individuals, as a function of unions and consequent reproduction».[139]

However we evaluate this type of scenario, what is certain is that the concept of human capital has long been – explicitly or implicitly – one of the main references not only of individual training and ability and skill building practices, but also of the

---

138 Foucault, *The Birth of Biopolitics*, p. 227.
139 Foucault, *The Birth of Biopolitics*, p. 228.

general political strategies developed in this sense at a national and international, local and global level.[140] In any case, the interest of Becker's analyses on the family lies above all in the fact that he assumes as their premise the link that has historically been created in certain societies between the growing industrial development and the rooting of behaviour patterns permeated by economic rationality in the family. Therefore, the vast application of economic analysis to family life, which this author manages to exercise, can be understood as a "proof" of the fulfilment of the said economic moralization of the behaviour of individuals, which was advocated by Malthus and pursued by the philanthropists of the 19th century. The same tendency of Becker to extend the economic approach to every aspect of human behaviour can be interpreted as an indication of the extreme degree of economic governability of the contemporary man's *ethos*, which neoliberalism can succeed in achieving by relying on the relationship between the individual as an entrepreneur of himself and the family as an aggregation of bio-economic resources.

What should not be taken for granted, however, is that the welfare state has succeeded in promoting models of behaviour and forms of *ethos* capable of escaping the consideration of the individual as the holder of a human bio-capital.

---

140 In this regard see: Theodore W. Schultz, *Investing in People: The Economics of Population Quality* (Berkeley, Los Angeles, London: University of California Press, 1982).

CHAPTER FIVE
MOLECULAR BIOPOWER
AND GLOBAL CAPITALISM

1. *From the welfare state to the bioeconomy*

1.1 *Transitions*

Wishing to indicate some important implications of the trends that we identified in the previous chapter, we can start from the hypothesis that, in the historical context of the welfare state, the medicalization processes have become more pronounced. In this sense some ideas that Foucault proposes in the interview already referred to can also be construed. There he shows the indeterminate character that the concept of "right to health" has assumed in recent history and the decisive role that this indeterminacy has ended up playing as a crisis factor of the welfare state. According to the French philosopher, when the social security system was established, «there was a sort of more or less explicit and largely silent consensus» on what were the «"health needs"» to which this system had to respond. «In short, it was the need to remedy "accidents", that is to say, incapacities caused by illness and handicaps, congenital or acquired». Subsequently, however, the boundaries of this idea of health to be guaranteed politically – according to him – were decidedly questioned by two processes:

> Firstly, a technical acceleration of medicine, which has increased its theoretical power, but even more quickly its capacity for examination and analysis. Secondly, a growth in the demand for health that has demonstrated the fact that the need for health (as experienced) has no internal principle of limitation.

> Consequently, it is not possible to lay down objectively a theoretical, practical threshold, valid for all, on the basis of which it might be said that health needs are entirely and definitively satisfied.[1]

These theses of Foucault appear reliable and seem to confirm the idea that a growing medicalization of the approach to life has found particularly favourable conditions in the history of the welfare state: it is credible, in fact, that the health care systems of the welfare state have stimulated the growth of the potential of medicine and its intervention techniques, placing it in a relationship of mutual strengthening with the development of needs and the demand for medical services in society. Therefore, it is reasonable to think that, in a situation like this, «if those needs [for health] are likely to increase indefinitely», to «try to satisfy by collective means individuals' need for health» sooner or later becomes very difficult.[2]

However, a scenario like this can also be interpreted as the result of a growing capacity of the social subjects who contested the dominant structures of power, to increasingly assert the "right to well-being" and to impose the "duty" on the state to guarantee it without subjecting it to the logic of the market. In countries such as Italy, for example, the welfarist response to "needs for health" reached remarkable levels in the late seventies, that is, after a period of extreme political vigour of the social movements established around 1968, animated by young people, women, industrial workers and medical workers themselves. It was in 1978, in fact, that an actual National Health Service was created in this country, important laws were approved such as that which imposed the closure of asylums and established public mental health services, and that which decriminalized and regulated abortion, allowing women who resorted to it to be assisted by state medical institutions.[3]

---

1   'Social Security', p. 169.
2   'Social Security', p. 170.
3   See: Saverio Luzzi, *Salute e sanità nell'Italia repubblicana* (Rome: Donzelli, 2004), pp. 289-318; John Foot, *La "Repubblica dei Matti". Franco Basaglia e la psichiatria radicale in Italia, 1961-1978* (Milan: Feltrinelli, 2014); Giambattista Sciré, *L'aborto in Italia. Storia di una*

On the other hand, the criticisms that neoliberalism generally addresses to welfarist policies to propose their rejection or drastic downsizing, have found fertile ground in situations of this type. In fact, already in the mid-seventies, both the growing demands of social movements and the policies promoted by the welfare state appeared intolerable to certain political, economic and intellectual elites of the more developed countries. In 1975, the well known *Report on Governability of Democracy to the Trilateral Commission* denounced «the overloading of government», namely «the expansion of the demands on government from individual and groups», which takes the form of «an increasing expectation (...) that government has responsibility to meet their needs», and «an escalation in what they conceive those needs to be».[4] The authors of the *Report*, hence, argued that it was necessary to overcome or downsize the «democratic idea that government should be responsive to the people» since this idea «creates the expectation that government should meet the needs and correct the evils affecting particular groups in society».[5]

These arguments resumed and brought about the extreme consequences the criticisms that neoliberal culture had addressed for decades to the political interventionism of the state, criticisms according to which – as we have seen – the very idea of recognizing «a claim by every citizen or inhabitant of a country to a certain minimum standard (...) raises serious problems».[6] Consequently, the possibility that the state could respond to a demand for an increasing socialization of health costs could only appear unacceptable from this point of view. It appeared unacceptable above all because it was seen as the result of a dangerous "excess"

---

legge (Milan: Bruno Mondadori, 2008). See also the collection of writings by the founder of the "Medicina Democratica" (Democratic Medicine) movement: Giulio A. Maccacaro, *Per una medicina da rinnovare: scritti 1966-1976* (Milan: Feltrinelli, 1981).

4   Michel J. Crozier, Samuel P. Huntington, Joji Watanuki, *The Crisis of Democracy: Report on Governability of Democracy to the Trilateral Commission* (New York: New York University Press, 1975), pp. 163-4.

5   Crozier, Huntington, Watanuki, *The Crisis of Democracy*, p. 164.

6   Hayek, *Law, Legislation and Liberty*, III vol., pp. 55-6.

of democracy; secondly, because the welfare state, having made health care systems available to society, presented itself as an indeterminate mechanism for the multiplication of the health needs to be met, inevitably destined to become economically unsustainable. It is certain, however, that the public health care systems themselves, in the late 1970s, found reasons to begin to seriously select the needs to respond to, in order to avoid the uncontrollable growth of their costs.

> A machinery set up to give people a certain security in the area of health – says Foucault – has (...) reached a point in its development at which we will have to decide what illness, what type of pain, will no longer receive coverage – a point at which, in certain cases, life itself will be at risk. This poses a political and moral problem not unrelated, all things considered, to the question of the right enjoyed by a state to ask an individual to go and get himself killed in war. (...) The question that now arises is how people are going to accept being exposed to certain risks without being protected by the all-providing state.[7]

In such a situation, new forms of discrimination or unequal treatment have added to those which the welfare state has not been able to avoid throughout its history. Many citizens ended up being excluded from certain medical services without having the economic possibility of obtaining them through private medicine; therefore, they found themselves realising their irremediable dependence on public health care services; which happened and can still happen, in fact, «when the authorities declare "You no longer have a right to that," or "You will no longer be covered for such operations," or "You have to pay a proportion of the hospital costs," and even "It wouldn't be any use extending your life by three months, so we're going to let you die"».[8]

Obviously, all this must be seen in the context of societies increasingly dominated by the capitalist economy. Already in the early eighties, the globalization of this economy and the radicalization of the logic of the free market became the

---

7   'Social Security', pp. 171-2.
8   'Social Security', p. 163.

main coordinates within which contemporary societies were urged to reorganize their ways of governing themselves. It can therefore be said that from that moment neoliberalism managed to become the prevailing form of governmentality based on the progressive and general political acceptance of global capitalism as an insurmountable economic regime.[9] This situation, of course, became an additional obstacle for any political strategy aimed at socializing the costs of treating and improving the health of each and every one.

What, however, should be asked in this regard is whether today, with the consolidation of this scenario, the crisis of public health care systems and the difficulties of reproducing and extending their services are still due to the "impracticability" of the welfare state project to guarantee everyone the same opportunities for care and assistance; it is quite probable, in fact, that in the context of globalization and neoliberal hegemony, the ability of medical sciences and technologies to develop and expand their influence indefinitely have become a determining factor in the growing difficulty of socializing the costs of their services. More precisely, it can be assumed that in this scenario the developments of medicine have acquired a completely new strength, due above all to their pressing convergence with the private logic of the market. Consequently, the growing demand for health that the welfare state itself seems to have historically generated may have merged into a process of further and indefinite medicalization of the existence of each and every one, also assuming the character of a progressive privatization of the approach to the care for life. If this hypothesis is credible, it can also be assumed that this privatization has been based above

---

9   Very interesting in this sense are the theses proposed in Quinn Slobodian, *Globalists: The End of Empire and the Birth of Neoliberalism* (Cambridge, Mass.: Harvard University Press, 2018). According to the author, neoliberalism represents the «philosophy of global ordering» and its history consists of continuous attempts to impose the supremacy of the "world economy" on the policies of States, attempts that in our time would have «isolated market actors from democratic pressures in a series of institutions from the IMF and the World Bank to port authorities and central banks worldwide», etc.. (p. 4).

all on three general trends: 1) the prevalence of a medicine increasingly dominated by molecular biology and genetics; 2) the growing intertwining of research in these areas with its financialization and the commercialization of its results; 3) the progressive affirmation of people's attitudes towards individualization and familiarization of their relationship with physical and mental well-being, attitudes largely encouraged by the other two trends indicated.

1.2 *The era of biomedicalization*

Ever since the debate on biopolitics began to intensely unfold, it is mainly social science scholars who have insisted on the biopolitical implications of developments in molecular medicine and genetic research. Generally, they argue that the growing importance that medicine today attaches to the molecular and genetic micro-factors of health, birth rate, mortality, ability and spread of diseases, drastically reduces the possibility that a deterministic vision of people's biological destinies will reaffirm itself. Genetic diagnostics and biotechnology create the conditions for conceiving the fate of the individual, his family members, his current and potential descendants, not as fatally "predetermined" by their genetic heritage, but as timely foreseeable and therefore governable, self-governable and modifiable through appropriate decisions, medical interventions and lifestyles. In short, contemporary genetics must be considered as inseparable from its purposes of technical transformation of the biological material it investigates; its main meaning lies in the fact that it defines a completely new field of active and transformative intervention on life. Consequently, even the forms of biopolitics that are based on this type of medicine are not necessarily characterized by biological determinism.[10]

---

10   See Paul Rabinow, 'Artificiality and Enlightenment: From Sociobiology to Biosociality', in *Essays on the Anthropology of Reason* (Princeton: Princeton University Press, 1996), pp. 91-111; Nikolas Rose, *The Politics of Life Itself: Biomedicine, Power, and Subjectivity in the Twenty-First Century* (Princeton: Princeton University Press, 2007). See also: Thomas Lemke, 'From Eugenics to the Government of

In light of these analyses, the idea is entirely reliable that the period between the mid-seventies and mid-eighties was also the moment from which the medicalization of the existence of people tends increasingly to assume the characteristics of a *biomedicalization* intended as an approach to life problems dominated by investigation and intervention techniques on bio-genetic material. This seems to have entailed, in particular, that diseases are no longer identified and treated simply on the basis of their symptoms, but that their very possibility or probability has become the object of attention and treatment. Hence the new and fundamental importance that the notion of risk has assumed as the primary criterion for the definition of health and for the decisions that tend to guarantee it; hence the importance attributed to the improvement and enhancement of the biological capacities of bodies.[11]

From this point of view, there is a concept that tends to take on great importance: that of genetic responsibility; the individual, being able to know the risks of which he appears intrinsically the bearer through genetic tests and checks, and persuading himself to be able to intervene on them, takes on new tasks and obligations towards himself and towards his partners, relatives, descendants. Research developments, in fact, seem to place the individual in front of new moral duties such as informing himself about the genetic risks that he and his descendants and family members run; to inform the latter too; to act on his own behaviour; to try to influence those of one's relatives, etc.. This means, among other things, that the family – as a social group whose members share a set of genetic characteristics – becomes

Genetic Risks', in Robin Bunton and Alan Petersen (ed. by), *Genetic Governance: Health, Risk and Ethics in the Biotech Era* (London and New York: Routledge, 2005), pp. 95-105; Thomas Lemke, 'Genetic Responsibility and Neo-Liberal Governmentality: Medical Diagnosis as Moral Technology', in Alain Beaulieu and David Gabbard (ed. by), *Michel Foucault & Power Today: International Multidisciplinary Studies on the History of our Present* (Lanham, MD: Lexington Books, 2006), pp. 83-91.

11 On these issues see, in particular, Adele Clarke and others (ed. by), *Biomedicalization: Technoscience, Health, and Illness in the U.S.* (Durham: Duke University Press, 2010).

a privileged area of a certain type of assumption of responsibility by the individual;[12] on the other hand, one can guess how this assumption of responsibility can take on both the traits of a traditional morality tending to emphasize the sacredness of life, and those of an attentiveness to the good use of life itself as a factor of well-being not only physical, but also economical. In any case, – as Thomas Lemke claims –

> [w]e might see a time when it will be more and more problematic to opt against genetic information and the transmission of this knowledge, when a refusal of this knowledge will constitute objective evidence of one's moral incompetence or irrational behaviour.[13]

It is important to underline in this regard that the idea of genetic responsibility, «as a political and moral technology», begins to take shape precisely in the historical phase which coincides with the crisis and the overcoming, in a neoliberal sense, of the welfare state policies; a phase which is also the one in which scientific privilege and the economic support of genetic research tend to impose themselves more and more.

> One condition of existence for the discourse of genetic responsibility – writes Lemke to this regard – is the crisis of the Keynesian state and the successful implementation of neo-liberal policies from the mid-1970s on. As the "active management of responsible choice in risk taking is at the core of neo-liberal governance," the massive financial support and public acceptance of human genetic research could be conceived as part of a comprehensive political transformation that is increasingly individualizing and privatizing the responsibility for social risks. (...) The retreat of the state goes hand in hand with an appeal to personal responsibility, self-care and the promotion of self-regulatory competencies among individual and collective subjects.

---

12 Lemke, 'Genetic Responsibility and Neo-Liberal Governmentality', pp. 86-9.
13 Lemke, 'Genetic Responsibility and Neo-Liberal Governmentality', p. 91. See also Thomas Lemke, 'Biopolitica e neoliberalismo. Rischio, salute e malattia nell'epoca post-genomica', in *Biopolitica, bioeconomia e processi di soggettivazione*, ed. by Adalgiso Amendola and others (Macerata: Quodlibet, 2008), pp. 295-309.

> Within this more global political conjuncture, the idea of a personal responsibility for health takes shape. From the mid-1970s, we have observed an increasing individualization of conditions for disease.[14]

We are therefore faced with the formation of an ethical attitude of the individual perfectly in tune with the neoliberal strategies that tend to reduce the guarantees of assistance and treatment of the disease understood as an individual "accident" whose costs must be socialized. Here it is no longer the simple current disease to be subject to treatment or compensation; it is also and above all the statistical probability of an "eventual pathology" that immediately creates a need for ethical and private self-government through which the individual will reduce his "dependence" on the assistance of public institutions.

An assessment of this perspective simply in terms of new freedoms, new opportunities, new possibilities and new rights seems largely insufficient for its full understanding. In fact, the increased diagnostic accessibility and the idea of a technical modifiability of the genetic factors of diseases and health compared to their more complex social, economic and environmental factors, seem to lead to a progressive transformation of freedoms and rights into personal, family and private duties: the individual as such will increasingly feel obliged to intensify examinations and controls, prevent risks and, ultimately, rely on new forms of biopower that are based on developments in molecular medicine.

Endeavouring to investigate these issues, in the following pages we will refer above all – but not only – to the work of Nikolas Rose and Melinda Cooper, two scholars who more than others have acutely grasped the biopolitical implications of the molecularization of contemporary medicine.

---

14 Lemke, 'Genetic Responsibility and Neo-Liberal Governmentality', p. 83. The internal quotation in this passage is taken from Richard Ericson, Dean Barry, Aaron Doyle, 'The Moral Hazards of Neo-Liberalism: Lessons From the Private Insurance Industry', *Economy & Society*, 29, 4 (2000), 532-58 (p. 553).

2. *Nikolas Rose and the biomedical government of the self*

2.1 *Genetics as liberal discipline*

Nikolas Rose is an author who considers the critical approach to be generally inadequate for the analysis of the current biopolitical scenario. According to him, to take strength away from this approach today is the fact that it can no longer rely heavily on the denunciation of the deterministic tendencies of biology-related visions of life: «new life sciences (...) open up a space of uncertainty, not certainty»; therefore, now biopolitics itself «operates in practices of uncertainty and possibility».[15] Research into contemporary molecular biology – according to Rose – shows that the «causal chains» of what happens at a cellular level are not simple, linear and direct, but «complex»: «the relations here (...) are stochastic, open and not closed, and hence probabilistic»;[16] similarly, «at levels above the cell, the knowledges produced by the new biology are also probabilistic rather than deterministic».[17]

By insisting on these arguments Rose concludes that the historical normalizing, eugenic and racist tendencies of biopolitics are clearly reduced by the current overcoming of traditional biological determinism. Therefore, according to him,

---

15 Rose, *The Politics of Life Itself*, p. 52.
16 *The Politics of Life Itself*, p. 51. In this regard the author claims: «While causal chains can be traced, between a coding sequence and a protein for example, the actual cellular mechanisms involved in the creation of that protein in vivo depend on interactions between multiple events at different levels, involving the regulation of gene expression by factors in the cellular environment. And the mode of action of that protein, once synthetized, involves a nexus of activations and terminations, cascades, feedback loops, regulatory mechanisms, epigenic processes, interactions with other pathways, and much more». (Ibid.).
17 *The Politics of Life Itself*, p. 51. «Even in the very simplest and starkest example, of a condition long believed to be caused by a mutation in a single gene – Huntington's Disease – which has been localized to the short arm of Chromosome 4, and identified as an expanded CAG repeat – the test that enumerates the numbers of repeats does not tell the affected individual or their family when will become ill, or how rapidly the condition will progress, let alone when they will die». (pp. 51-2).

the condemnation of the danger that these tendencies may renew through contemporary genetics appears largely unfounded; in this sense he emphasizes the aspects of molecular medicine which weaken the connection between the life of the individual body and that of the collective body. The molecularization of research and medical practice – according to Rose – makes the same unitary idea of the body problematic, radicalizing its "fragmentation" which has already been triggered for some time with the possibility of transferring blood, organs, eggs, sperm, embryos, etc. from one body to another:

> now tissues, cells, and DNA fragments can be rendered visible, isolated, decomposed, stabilized, stored in "biobanks", commoditized, transported between laboratories and factories, re-engineered by molecular manipulation, their properties transformed, their ties to a particular individual living organism, type, or species suppressed or removed. (...) [M]olecularization is conferring a new mobility on the elements of life, enabling them to enter new circuits – organic, interpersonal, geographical, and financial.[18]

All this – according to Rose – clearly reduces the possibility that contemporary biopolitics continue to have, as a prime reference, the relationship between the individual body and the collective body of the population, on which the possibility of a eugenic and racist exercise of biopower by the states of the 19th and 20th centuries was based. Historically – argues the author – this exercise has been possible through the interaction between two factors: on the one hand, the Darwinian evolutionary vision of life, in which the concept of inheritance understood in substantially fatalistic terms occupies a central position; on the other, the strategic concern of the nation states to safeguard and strengthen the health of their collective bodies.[19]

> Thus eugenic responsibilities fell upon states, or statesmen, to act both negatively – to prevent the excessive breeding of those of worst quality, or the dilution of the quality of the population by an influx of those less fit from outside through immigration – and positively – to

---

18   *The Politics of Life Itself*, pp. 14-5.
19   *The Politics of Life Itself*, pp. 54-62.

Biopolitics for Beginners

encourage those who were fittest to reproduce for the good of the nation as a whole.[20]

While in Nazi Germany this type of biopolitics produced extreme forms of thanatopolitics, many other states – even democratic ones – have, until a few decades ago, nevertheless dedicated eugenic political attention to the problem of reproduction. For example, in the 1920s and 1930s, laws of coercive sterilization «of those considered threats to the quality of the population» were passed in the USA, Europe and Latin America, and in countries such as Sweden this practice was continued until the 1970s. However, – according to Rose – after the Second World War «the links between concerns about genetic health of individuals and concerns about the quality of the population en masse» have been progressively dissolved. «Genetics was to transform itself into a liberal discipline (...). The norm of individual health replaced that of the quality of the population».[21]

The author does not deny that in recent times genetics have still been used politically in the context of eugenic strategies, for example, in countries such as China: here the regime has promoted, at least until early 2000, demographic policies that did not simply tend to control the quantity of the population with the well-known "one child policy", but also its quality; in particular, the sterilization of people believed to be carriers of hereditary diseases or genetic defects seems to have been widely practiced together with other forms of discouragement or penalization of procreation by certain individuals, until a less "questionable" approach to demographic problems began to prevail.[22]

In the «advanced liberal societies», however, according to Rose, things have been going very differently for some time.

---

20 *The Politics of Life Itself*, p. 56. For a very useful overview on the subject of eugenics see Patrica Chiantera-Stutte, 'Eugenetica', in *Lessico di biopolitica*, pp. 138-43.

21 *The Politics of Life Itself*, p. 62.

22 *The Politics of Life Itself*, pp. 66-8. Rose's most important reference in this regard is Frank Dikötter, *Imperfect Conception: Medical Knowledge, Birth Defects, and Eugenics in China* (New York: Columbia University Press, 1998).

Reproductive techniques are used within the context of «styles of biological and biomedical thinking» that have nothing to do with «the quality of the race and the survival of the fittest». Therefore, in these realities it is not eugenics that develops, but rather some biopolitics in which the individual and their entourage become central, or rather «forms of self-government imposed by the obligations of choice, the desire for self-fulfilment, and the wish of parents for the best lives for their children».[23]

As we have seen, a decisive factor of this type of change – according to the author – consists in the fact that the progress of biology highlights the complexity and uncertainty of the mechanisms of life. What, however, does not seem problematic to Rose is that the "discovery" of this complexity does not induce contemporary medicine to adopt greater prudence in its interventions on living matter, but – on the contrary – pushes it to consider technically modifiable and improvable the mechanisms of life itself. Which – at least in theory – could also lead to an increase in the danger of regulatory and normalizing use of biomedical techniques. But, from Rose's point of view, since the end of the 20th century in advanced liberal societies this danger has actually been reduced to the minimum since these societies have now overcome the relationship with political power based on the unitary and totalizing ideas of the national state and collective political body.

> The idea of "society" as a single, if heterogeneous, domain with a national culture, a national population, a national destiny, coextensive with a national territory and the powers of a national political government has entered a crisis. The idea of a "national culture" has given way to that of "cultures", national identity to a complex array of identity politics, "community" to communities. In this new

---

23 *The Politics of Life Itself*, p. 69. Rose does not actually consider the theses of authors who speak explicitly, and without scandal, of "liberal eugenics" regarding a certain use of genetics and reproductive medicine. Nicholas Agar, for example, argues that what distinguishes liberal from Nazi eugenics is the fact that it does not tend to favour a single genome over others; moreover, it is entrusted to the freedom of the individual and is therefore not mandatory. See Nicholas Agar, *Liberal Eugenics: In Defence of Human Enhancement* (Oxford: Blackwell, 2004).

configuration, the political meaning and salience of health and disease have changed.[24]

In reality, as we know, our era is now characterized by ever more numerous forms of nationalism, mostly authoritarian; therefore, we can consider that the vision expressed by Rose in his 2007 book is largely "optimistic".[25]

2.2 *A post-racist race?*

Rose does not seem unaware of the fact that in contemporary societies, however, «programmers of preventive medicine, health promotion, and health education still take, as their object, "the nation's health"». According to him, in any case, the political interest in the health of the community «is no longer framed in terms of the consequences of population unfitness as an organic whole for the struggle between nations»; rather this political interest is justified on economic grounds, with «the costs of ill health in terms of days lost from work or rising insurance contributions», or with moral reasons like «the imperative to reduce inequalities in health».[26]

Be that as it may, Rose cannot fail to recognize – both in *The Politics of Life Itself* and in an article published with Paul Rabinow – that in our age the concept of race still somehow performs an important political function. In fact, in recent historical moments it has been taken as a crucial reference in various situations: for example, in the USA, «as a marker of belonging and the basis of a claim to disadvantage»; or during the «murderous racist wars

---

24   *The Politics of Life Itself*, pp. 62-3. On the decline of the unitary concept of "society" see also the interview with the author: 'Nikolas Rose: "Governing the Social"'', in Nicholas Gane (ed. by), *The Future of Social Theory* (London: Continuum, 2004), pp. 167-85.

25   In this regard, see the articles of Susan B. Glasser, Richard McGregor, Kaya Genc, Paul Lendvai, Chad P. Bown and Douglas A. Irwin proposed in 'Autocracy Now', ed. by Gideon Rose, *Foreign Affairs*, 98, 5 (2019). The authors examine the political figures and strategies of Wladimir Putin, Xi Jinping, Recep Tayyip Erdogan, Viktor Orban, Donald Trump.

26   *The Politics of Life Itself*, p. 63.

that spread across the Europe in the wake of the demise of the Soviet empire, from Armenia to the Balkans», when appealing to «racial identities to ground the elimination of other groups»; or even in the case of the genocide of the Tutsis by the Hutus in Rwanda, in 1994. However – according to Rabinow and Rose – in none of these cases was it sought the «justification in the truth discourse of biology».[27] And this, from their point of view, confirms that eugenic racism is no longer an essential feature of contemporary biopolitics.[28]

Unfortunately, a thesis like this is not enough to downscale the fact that in particular the "ethnic cleansing" practiced in the Balkans and the genocide of the Tutsis are terrible examples of forms of biopolitical purification of the collective body, which can still come true even in an era like ours.[29] Rabinow and Rose, on the other hand, risk corroborating the idea that today racist biopolitics can be recognized effectively as such only if they refer precisely and explicitly to the biological sciences; in short, the two authors tend to underestimate the possibility that in our age the imposition of the economic and political models of "advanced liberal societies" indirectly contributes to provoking the re-emergence of forms of racist discrimination in states that have difficulty making space in the scenario of globalization, dominated precisely by advanced liberal societies; which may be true even if these forms of discrimination are not immediately based on biological theories. Be that as it may, it is precisely in these terms that one can interpret what happened in a catastrophic way in the 1990s, particularly in the Balkan countries «in the

---

27 Paul Rabinow and Nikolas Rose, 'Biopower Today', in Vernon W. Cisney and Nicolae Morar (ed. by), *Biopower: Foucault and Beyond* (Chicago and London: The University of Chicago Press, 2016), p. 310.

28 Rabinow and Rose, 'Biopower Today', pp. 309-10. For useful critical evaluations of Rose's point of view in this regard, see Antonio Tucci, *Dispositivi della normatività* (Turin: Giappichelli, 2018), pp. 76-9.

29 In this sense, for example, consider the case of persecutions against the Rohingya people, which have become particularly serious since 2017: 'Myanmar: "Caged without a Rooof": Apartheid in Myanmar's Rakhine State', *Amnesty International Report*, November 2017, Index: ASA 16/7484/2017: https://www.amnesty.org/en/documents/asa16/7484/2017/en/ (accessed January 23, 2020).

wake of the demise of the Soviet empire». Furthermore, it cannot be ignored that in our era the rulers of various countries consider the rights and values of liberal democracy as obstacles for their participation in the international economic competition that globalization imposes; therefore they deliberately adopt or reinforce authoritarian, illiberal, sovereign and nationalist policies that often produce forms of substantial racial and ethnic discrimination.[30]

Apparently correcting their theses, however, Rabinow and Rose admit that, since the beginning of the 21st century, «race is once again re-entering the domain of biological truth, viewed now through a molecular gaze».[31] In this sense – according to them – the research carried out within the framework of the *Human Genome Project* played a fundamental role: based on this,

> many population geneticists were convinced that the mapping of the human genome has confirmed that the world population can be divided into five major groups – Africans, Caucasians, Pacific Islanders, East Asians, and Native Americans – defined by their "out of Africa" date.[32]

Therefore, many researchers today think that genome mapping is a particularly useful basis for pinpointing «the relations of ethnicity and disease», as well as the «differences in morbidity and mortality between groups defined in terms of ethnicity».[33]

---

30 An exemplary case of the current authoritarian tendencies which produce forms of racist discrimination, in particular towards immigrants, is examined in Paul Lendvai, 'The Transformer: Orban's Evolution and Hungary's Demise', *Foreign Affairs*, 98, 5 (2019), 44-54. An example of substantial ethnic regime discrimination is, moreover, that of contemporary China's policies towards the minority of the Uighurs. See: 'China: "Where are They?". Time for Answers about Mass Detentions in the Xinjiang Uighur Autonomous Region', *Amnesty International Report*, September 2018, Index: ASA   17/9113/2018:   https://www.amnesty.org/en/documents/asa17/9113/2018/en/ (accessed January 23, 2020).

31 'Biopower Today', p. 310.

32 *The Politics of Life Itself*, p. 156.

33 *The Politics of Life Itself*, p. 157. The main references of Rose to this

Although these conceptions are often criticized, according to Rose, they are still placed

> in the context of well-established and relatively uncontentious arguments that some single gene disorders do occur in different frequencies in different population groups delineated in terms of race or ethnicity, and these have clinically significant implications.[34]

According to the author, both in countries «outside "the West"» (China, Japan, Vietnam, India) and in western countries such as the USA, biomedical research generally takes into account the diversity and genomic specificity of populations.[35] Even in contexts in which the idea that racial categories have no scientific basis prevails, these same categories are still used since it is believed that they can serve to reduce the severity of certain diseases of genetic origin that seem frequent in certain ethnic groups.[36]

Rose's main thesis in this regard is that «the resurgence of interest in race and ethnicity in contemporary genomic medicine» cannot be interpreted as «the most recent incarnation of the biogenetic legitimation of social inequality and discrimination».[37] While taking into account that, in recent times, in countries such as China the medical practices of reducing "genetic disorders" have been placed in «an explicit eugenic population policy», the author

---

regard are: Neil J. Risch and others, 'Categorization of Humans in Biomedical Research: Genes, Race and Disease', *Genome Biology*, 3, 7 (2002), comment 2007.1-comment2007.12; Esteban G. Burchard and others, 'The Importance of Race and Ethnic Background in Biomedical Research and Clinical Practice', *New England Journal of Medicine*, 348, 12 (2003), 1170-5; Joanna L. Mountain and Neil J. Risch, 'Assessing Genetic Contribution to Phenotypic Differences among "Racial" and "Ethnic" Groups', *Nature Genetics*, 36, 11 (2004), suppl., S48–S53 .

34   *The Politics of Life Itself*, p. 158. Rose here refers in particular to cases of cystic fibrosis and haemoglobinopathies such as sickle-cell anemia and thalassemia. In this regard, see Melbourne Tapper, *In the Blood: Sickle Cell Anemia and the Politics of Race* (Philadelphia, Penn.: Pennsylvania University Press, 1999).
35   *The Politics of Life Itself*, pp. 158 and 172.
36   *The Politics of Life Itself*, pp. 171-4.
37   *The Politics of Life Itself*, p. 160.

claims however that «the biopolitical implications of the framing of genomic knowledge in the categories of race or ethnicity are not inherent in the biotechnology itself: they take their character from national cultures and politics». In any case, according to him, the «advanced liberal societies of the West» are more capable than others of avoiding the risk of using new knowledge of genomics to promote racism and eugenic policies:

> in advanced liberal societies – he writes – (...) the forms of collectivization being shaped in the links of ethnicity with medicine are not those of racial science but those of biosociality and active biological citizenship.[38]

Rose attributes fundamental importance to the notions of "biosociality" and "biological citizenship" not only with regard to what he indicates as a tendential surmounting of the eugenic and racist declinations of biopolitics, but also with regard to the overall changes that the latter – according to him – is undergoing in our age. We will return to this later; here, for now, it is appropriate to consider that Rose is not willing to give the deserved importance to the fact that the weakening of the unitary visions of "society" and of the "nation" does not exclude that they continually become important references also for advanced liberal societies.

2.3 *The caring nation*

What Rose calls "advanced liberal societies" don't really exist in their pure state; they are intersected and conditioned by influences of various kinds. These influences can be "progressive", "liberal", "secular", "cosmopolitan" or "conservative", "authoritarian", "fundamentalist", "nationalist", and often the latter are the ones that win the most consensus. The political hegemony that neoliberalism has exercised for several decades on the richer contemporary societies does not imply the dissolution of the "backward" political models, but rather the general interchangeability of the models, according to a logic similar to that of the free market,

---

38   *The Politics of Life Itself*, p. 176.

for which what matters most is the game of supply and demand. For this reason, what appears "backward" can always return in updated forms to constitute a "supply" that finds its "demand" on the political "market". Ultimately, it can be said that even in advanced liberal countries the biopolitical reference to the "nation" or "society" ideas does not occur marginally or – as Rose argues – only for economic reasons (the collective costs of diseases) and moral reasons (the social injustice of inequalities in health care); explicitly or implicitly, ideas such as these can return to being used when the political market – for occasional or strategic reasons – requires, for example, to combat immigration by inducing rulers to strengthen border controls and even build walls to make advanced liberal countries inaccessible to migrants.[39] On the other hand, contemporary medicine itself can once again find, in the reference to the nation, support to extend and strengthen its biopower. And this can happen, for example, when it comes to dealing with serious and increasingly widespread diseases in richer societies such as cancer, over which molecular medicine now has a solid control.

Miguel Benasayag in this regard maintains that cancer is a disease with which medicine today is confronted, at the same time, with successes and failures. It undoubtedly achieves increasingly satisfactory results in individual care by using an increasingly sophisticated knowledge of the genetic aspects of the pathology and an increasingly precise therapeutic approach. However, medicine can no longer hide the fact that it cannot fulfil the promise of "eradicating the disease"; the number of tumours – Benasayag observes – mostly tends to increase in spite of the progress of medical research.[40] One might think, therefore, that for this reason medicine risks going into crisis, but in reality – according to the author – it is its biopower that can be compromised. Therefore, it seeks to regenerate it by relaunching the combination between the individual discipline

---

39 See Giulia Maria Labriola, 'Muros y confines: Una reflexión sobre el renacimiento de la idea de límite', *Soft Power*, 5, 1 (2017), 121-37.

40 Miguel Benasayag, *La santé à tout prix. Médecine et biopouvoir* (Paris: Bayard, 2008), p. 48. In this regard, see Geneviève Barbier and Armand Farrachi, *La société cancérigène. Lutte-t-on vraiment contre le cancer?* (Paris: Éditions de la Martinière, 2004).

and the government of the population, transforming cancer into an enemy to be fought with the contribution of each and every one. Undoubtedly, in liberal societies, the medical biopower can only maintain the individual as its preferred object of reference and intervention. As Rose himself shows us, the molecular matrix of contemporary medicine (and in this case, of oncology) requires this privilege, and personal assumption of responsibility is a fundamental condition of this. It is the individual, in fact, who has to worry about his health in the first person, regulating his own behaviour, reducing the risks of getting sick through diagnostic tests, proper nutrition, physical activity, etc.. However, if for a disease like cancer the growth of investments in medical research is accompanied by an increase in the number of cases, it becomes difficult to deny that it depends largely on environmental causes related to the development of industry, consumption, and the economy in general. Consequently, the decisive importance that is attached to individual responsibility and discipline can only be confirmed if it is strengthened by collective mobilization. Which – Benasayag says – can happen above all by turning cancer into a "national cause".

> What makes discipline always work so well, even when it seems that the promise to eradicate the disease, the promise that was supposed to accompany it, can no longer be kept? (...) If the promise to eradicate the disease fails (...), then "it is necessary" (here we are, of course, in the context of strategies without strategists) to manufacture a new one, which is expressed in terms of population safety (of the social body). (...).
>
> When cancer becomes a "national cause", it is as if we were witnessing a counter-offensive of power against the crisis of progress, in particular medical; (...). Unlike what is presented in the slogans, the counter-offensive in question does not concern research in the first instance, but rather the regulatory power. From this follows the development of national prevention and screening programs, connected with the meticulous definition of "treatment protocols", which will participate in the ever-increasing responsibility and normalization of our behaviour.[41]

---

41   Benasayag, *La santé à tout prix*, pp. 48-9.

2.4 *Is criticism still needed?*

Returning to Rose, the impression obtained from his analyses is that they are too conditioned by the idea that the molecularization of medicine weakens the link between the individual body and the collective body and progressively reduces the supremacy of the national and state dimension over that individual. The author argues that in order to fully grasp the originality of 21st century biopolitics, it is necessary to renounce reconstructing the conditions of its advent through the genealogical approach, thus avoiding placing it within the context of «a linear story».[42] In this way, however, the author risks making us believe that the genealogical approach necessarily implies the adoption of a linear vision of history; but his intention, in reality, is to reduce the influence that Foucault's genealogy exerts on the analyses of contemporary biopower, to the extent that it seems linked to the idea that biopolitics implies a subordination of the individual's life to that of the population, which can have discriminatory and racist consequences.[43]

Rose, on the other hand, while arguing that with the current forms of biopolitics «a threshold has been crossed», nevertheless places these forms within the context of a progressive vision of biopower transformations: the dominant thesis of his reasoning remains that according to which these forms lead us towards a future increasingly unbound from the discriminatory and thanatopolitical effects of biopower. Furthermore, while stating that the originality of the situation created by molecular medicine requires the search for «new critical tools to analyse it», he in fact ends up giving up not only on the genealogical approach, but on the criticism itself, perhaps fearing that it could hide the medical and political benefits of this situation. Indeed, at the end of his 2007 book, the author empowers the reader to think that there is «too much description, too little analysis, too little criticism». And, referring to Max Weber, claims to have wanted to «avoid judgment, merely to sketch out a preliminary cartography of an emergent form of life and the possible

---

42   *The Politics of Life Itself*, p. 167.
43   See *The Politics of Life Itself*, pp. 162.

futures it embodies».[44] Rose's reasoning, in any case, is guided from beginning to end by mistrust towards those who consider the prevailing patterns of the social critique, that is, towards «the pessimism of most sociological critics, who suggest that we are seeing the rise of a new biological and genetic determinism».[45]

In reality, it is not a question of choosing between critical pessimism and realistic optimism. Rather, it is a question of taking seriously the idea that current biopolitical scenarios cannot be framed entirely in the perspective of overcoming the normalizing and discriminatory forms of biopower.[46] As we have seen, in fact, in the geopolitical context of globalization there are many situations in which normalizing, discriminatory and racist forms of this power continue to reproduce, despite the "beneficial" function that science and the molecular vision of life should play, becoming increasingly influential. We have also seen that even in the "advanced liberal societies" the idea of the nation can still play an important role in guiding biopolitical strategies.

---

44   *The Politics of Life Itself*, p. 258.
45   *The Politics of Life Itself*, p. 8.
46   Rose himself offers many issues in favour of the hypothesis that the old forms of biopolitics today can be renewed, even if partially, through the results of biomedical research, for example, in the field of «biological criminology». While insisting on the idea that in this field there is no tendency to elaborate «neither a new eugenics nor a genetic determinism», the author finds «the emergence of a new human kind – the person "genetically at risk" of an antisocial conduct»; also, he can not help but show that «contemporary biocriminology» interacts with a social and political environment that feels exposed to an «"epidemic" of antisocial, aggressive, and violent conduct». It is no coincidence, therefore, that «the new biological criminology intersects with (...) the new centrality accorded in many jurisdictions, notably in the United States and United Kingdom, Australia, and New Zealand, to social and public protection». (*The Politics of Life Itself*, p. 241; see also, pp. 226-51). So we can say that, if this scenario is no longer influenced by deterministic biology and criminology, it is in any case not very different from the one in which the theories and practices of *social defence* were established between the 19th and 20th centuries. What is really different is the willingness of advanced liberal societies to practice various forms of control (biological, pharmacological or other) of behaviours according to the logic of immediate convenience, typical of the economic rationality of the free market.

Worthy of being discussed, on the other hand, is the way Rose proposes the idea that the individual is the true centre of contemporary biopolitics. The author, on the one hand, insists on this centrality, on the other, he is not willing to consider that it can also produce exasperated forms of individualism. Indeed, he argues that today the individual is placed in a context of new social relationships – of biosociality – which free him both from the risk of closing in on himself and from that of enduring totalizing forms of biopower like those of the past. In this way, however, Rose manages to avoid indulging in the "pessimistic critique" of the dangers of individualism, but overlooks the possibility of considering privatization processes, linked to those of individualization, as a key for the critical understanding of the trends he describes.

To clarify the terms of the role that the individual assumes, Rose insists in particular on the importance that the concepts of *susceptibility* and *enhancement* are taking on in medical practices today. As regards the first concept, he recognizes that an idea similar to it, such as that of «inherited predisposition to certain illnesses», had already established itself in the past; but – according to him – the notion of susceptibility opens up a much wider field of medical intervention than that linked to the idea of inherited predisposition: the precision of genome analyses, the availability of genetic screening techniques, the fervent aspiration of medicine to reduce the severity of certain foreseeable pathologies today radically transform the relationship between the life of the individual and medicine itself; it is not only an increasingly effective preventive medicine that is emerging, but also a personalized medicine.[47] This perspective is based on the assumption that – according to research on the human genome – a relatively limited number of the DNA variations that distinguish individuals, predispose a certain number of them to certain pathologies. Therefore scientific research can be considered to allow, and will allow more and more, to identify «hundreds, if not thousands of genes that predispose to disease» and to intervene in advance on

---

47   *The Politics of Life Itself*, pp. 85-8.

them:[48] these research trends, in fact, create the possibility of «presymptomatic diagnosis and preventive interventions on a scale previously unimaginable»;[49] on the other hand, even the farmacogenomics moves in the same direction, in the hope «that the efficacy of drugs can be increased by individualizing drug prescribing on the basis of a genetic test».[50]

Rose does not fail to highlight that the greatest progress in these areas concerns the «susceptibility to relatively rare single gene disorders» and that the results obtained in the field of «common complex diseases» are much less significant. Nonetheless, according to him, the great dynamism of the research on susceptibility represents the proof of a general change that can now be considered irreversible.

Even though genetic tests do not produce certainties, but uncertainties and probabilities, the growing importance they are taking on shows that «something is happening, not so much in clinical practice, perhaps, but in the form of life that is emerging».[51] In this sense Rose considers anything but problematic the fact that,

> once diagnosed with susceptibilities, the responsible asymptomatic individual is enrolled for a life sentence in the world of medicine – of tests, of drugs, of self-examination and self-definition as a "prepatient" suffering from a protosickness.

Indeed, he believes that the individual, precisely by accepting more and more to undergo forms of control of his own susceptibility, finds himself establishing «a new ethical relation to the self».[52] Ultimately, the biopolitical perspective opened up by this type of medicine – according to Rose – places us in front of «new forms of subjectification taking shape, new self-technologies whose "ethical

---

48   *The Politics of Life Itself*, p. 87. Rose takes the quote from the website of the Institute for Systems Biology. This Institute is a reality of global importance and is increasingly active both in the field of biomedical research and in that of the economic investment activities connected to it. See https://isbscience.org (accessed January 23, 2020).
49   *The Politics of Life Itself*, p. 89.
50   *The Politics of Life Itself*, p. 91.
51   *The Politics of Life Itself*, pp. 93-4.
52   *The Politics of Life Itself*, p. 94.

substance," to use Foucault's term, is soma, and whose telos is the prolonging of healthy life». It is these forms of subjectification, on the other hand, that extend and express themselves in biosociality and biological citizenship practices, that is, in new experiences of aggregation and political mobilization, which also have a sort of "molecular" character; in fact, they tend to escape the "molar" dimension of society and population, dominated by the state; rather they give birth to

> new biosocial communities assembling around these somatic identities – parents and families raising money, funding research, lobbying politicians, enacting their biological citizenship by demanding their rights for attention to their particular disorder.[53]

2.5 *Risk as an opportunity*

Rose intensely emphasizes the fact that the figure privileged by these tendencies is the individual «genetically at risk», that is, a person who cannot fail to be conditioned and beset by anxiety. This individual, however, seems to save himself from the apparent negativity of his destiny by taking on without hesitation the new responsibilities that research and new diagnostic and intervention techniques impose on him today: the new medicine places its life prospects along a «genetic axis» that «does not generate fatalism», but «creates an obligation to act in the present in relation to the potential futures that now come into view».[54] In this regard too, Rose claims that the individual tends to go beyond his strictly personal sphere.

> When an illness or pathology is thought of as genetic, it is no longer an individual matter. It has become familial, a matter both of family histories and potential family future. In this way genetic thought induces "genetic responsibility": it reshapes prudence and obligation, in relation to marriage, having children, pursuing career, and organizing ones financial affairs.[55]

---

53   *The Politics of Life Itself,* p. 95.
54   *The Politics of Life Itself,* p. 107.
55   *The Politics of Life Itself,* p. 108.

It is in a context like this that the new forms of subjectivity and responsibility – according to the author – find the most favourable conditions for development. Here, on the other hand, according to him it is evident that the centrality assigned to the individual by the new medicine does not imply at all his retreating on himself and his isolation, since it is the same genetic approach that pushes him to relate to others. It is equally evident, however, that these relationships are dominated by the family, by the relationships between partners and current or potential blood relatives. It is easy to note, on the other hand, that the family management of genetic problems, which underlies this scenario, is very similar to the economic governance of one's own human capital, practiced by the family-enterprise of which Becker speaks. In fact, as we have seen, the forms of responsibility that emerge from Rose's analysis concern – as well as the destinies of the individual – both future marriages and procreation, and careers and financial affairs.

Certainly it must be added that these forms of empowerment – as Rose argues – induce the individual to make his choices by referring to a set of interpersonal relationships that do not only include «actual and potential kin, past and present, but also genetic professionals and biomedical researchers»;[56] these relationships may extend to include associations and movements animated by actual or potential patients and their relatives, who – for example – interact with medical institutions and biotechnological or pharmaceutical companies to develop research, technologies and therapies in certain directions. The experiences of biosociality and biological citizenship mentioned by Rose are also, or above all, of this type.[57]

The author, therefore, is right to oppose the critical analyses according to which the genetization of biopolitics produces the self-referential isolation of the individual or his reduction to a state of passivity towards medical knowledge.[58] It is not in these terms, in fact, that the scenario he designs must be problematized.

---

56   *The Politics of Life Itself*, p. 109.
57   See *The Politics of Life Itself*, pp. 131-54, in particular pp. 144-7. Rose takes up the concept of biosociality from Rabinow, 'Artificiality and Enlightenment: From Sociobiology to Biosociality', pp. 91-111.
58   *The Politics of Life Itself*, pp. 109-11.

Critically questioning the individualizing implications of contemporary medicine does not necessarily mean to maintain that it «leads to a focus on the individual as an isolate». Rather, in this sense, the importance it deserves must be given to the fact that the individual, as the main reference of the new medicine, becomes an actor of a general tendency towards the privatization of scientific, political and economic attention to life. And it is also in this context that he finds in genetic medicine decisive reasons for privileging the sphere of relations between his own self and his family; in fact – as Rose himself observes –, medical genetics

> has been one of the key sites for the fabrication of the contemporary self – free yet responsible, enterprising yet prudent, conducting life in a calculative manner by making choices with an eye to the future and with the aspiration of maintaining and increasing his or her own well-being and that of their family.[59]

Evidently, the tendency of the individual to privatize his relationships and his attention to life is something that Rose is fully aware of; however, he does not focus on it critically, since he considers it an obvious and necessary fact, as a favourable condition for an entrepreneurial and positive evolution of the biopolitical subjectivities that he theorises. One can understand, therefore, why in this scenario the concept of enhancement to the author appears as important as that of susceptibility.

In this regard, the subject of particular attention on his part is the growing use of neuro-psychiatric drugs, on which – as he observes – many bioethicists express themselves critically, claiming that the contemporary individual through this use tends to guarantee himself a superficial and deresponsibilizing "happiness".[60] According to Rose, instead, these drugs generally respond to the desire to alleviate and transform states of «crippling misery into

---

59 *The Politics of Life Itself*, p. 111.
60 *The Politics of Life Itself*, pp. 98-9. The bioethical debate on the general theme of *genetic enhancement* is actually very rich and varied. For a broad survey of this, see: Julian Savulescu, 'Genetic Enhancement', in Helga Kuhse and Peter Singer (ed. by), *A Companion to Bioethics: Second Edition* (Oxford: Blackwell, 2009), pp. 216-34.

everyday unhappiness»;[61] in this sense, he appropriately correlates the consumption of drugs that treat social anxiety disorder, depression, and panic disorder with the competitiveness of the social relationships in which the individual is forced to live today, while considering it essentially inevitable.

> In a regime of the self that stresses self-fulfilment and the need for each individual to become the actor at the centre of his or her life, these drugs, which are often used to complement rather than to substitute for other therapies, do not promise a new self, but a return to the real self, or a realization of the true self.[62]

However, his reasoning on the improper use that is often made voluntarily of drugs intended for the treatment of sleep disorders, attention deficits, memory loss resulting from age or mild forms of Alzheimer, etc. is different. In reality, this use – according to Rose – is in tune with the production and commercial strategies of large pharmaceutical companies whose purpose is to develop and propose drugs aimed at «cognitive enhancement».[63] Well, the author believes that it does not make much sense today to oppose these trends, as if the «distinction between treatment and enhancement grounded in a postulate of a natural vital order of the human body and soul» was still valid. In this, as in many other cases, new biomedical and pharmacological trends can push us to ask ourselves about life, about «who we are as human beings, what we should fear, and what we might hope for»; but one need to realize that these issues «will be worked out only in the messy interactions of science, technology, commerce, and consumption that are the territory of contemporary vital politics».[64]

---

61   *The Politics of Life Itself*, pp. 99.
62   *The Politics of Life Itself*, p. 100. Rose has always paid close attention to the relationship between medical sciences and "mental health", and its political implications. Among the latest results of this commitment see: Nikolas Rose, *Our Psychiatric Future: The Politics of Mental Health* (Cambridge, UK: Polity Press, 2019); Nikolas Rose, Joelle M. Abi-Rached, *Neuro: The New Brain Sciences and the Management of the Mind* (Princeton and Oxford: Princeton University Press, 2013).
63   *The Politics of Life Itself*, pp. 101-4.
64   *The Politics of Life Itself*, p. 104.

In short, according to Rose, in advanced liberal societies we must now go beyond the idea that medicine can still limit itself to restoring the conditions of "natural" normalcy of life and health; furthermore, it is necessary to overcome the belief that ethical and political attention to life can be expressed outside the intertwining of new representations of the body, market dynamics, career ambitions, financial flows, political strategies for economic development: in these societies the new paths of subjectification

> are energized by the illimitable demands of those who possess the financial and cultural wherewithal to their rights as consumers to medical resources in the name of the maximization of their somatic selves and those of their families.

The main innovation that derives from these tendencies is that life itself in its bodily and biological materiality (the soma, the flesh, the organs, the tissues, the cells, the gene sequences, the molecular corporeality) has unquestionably become the centre around which people elaborate their forms of existence and their aspirations as human beings.[65]

From this point of view, a distinction that definitively fades – according to Rose – is that between the spheres of *zoé* and *bios*. *Bios* understood as an ethically qualified way of life is now gradually absorbed into the sphere of *zoé* as biological life. It is the growing attention to the *zoé* as an object not only of care, but also of investigation, control, transformation and empowerment, to increasingly qualify both the ethical elaboration of our *bios* and our relationships with politics.[66]

---

65 *The Politics of Life Itself*, p. 105.

66 *The Politics of Life Itself*, p. 83. Rose, of course, has the foresight to consider that the trends towards a new preventive and personalized medicine allow not only more or less free forms of "self-government", but also coercive and discriminatory ways of "government of others". This is the case, for example, of attempts by insurance companies to request susceptibility tests from their customers to decide the conditions to be applied to their contracts; or proposals for «testing for susceptibilities in the serotonin system linked with inability to control conduct», concerning disruptive school children and prisoners for violent crimes, to be able to administer psychiatric drugs to them in

2.6 Ethos *and economy: an inevitable intertwining*

Evidently, the *ethos* and identity of the individual, their
formation and their self-government are particularly important
in the processes described by Rose. According to him, in richer
contemporary societies «genes themselves have been constituted
as an "ethical substance"» on which the individual tends to carry
out an «ethical work» by placing himself «in relation to the self
(genetic identity, reproduction, health) and in relation to others
(siblings, kin, marriage, children)». The importance of this ethical
work consists in the fact that it

> intersects with, and becomes allied with, a more general style of work
> on the self in contemporary advanced liberal democracies that
> construes life as a project, framed in terms of the values of autonomy,
> self-actualization, prudence, responsibility, and choice.[67]

According to Rose, in these democracies also the prevalent
forms of biopolitics largely coincide with the ethical attention of
the individual to life. In this sense, biopolitics falls into a more
general «ethopolitics» in which

> the ethos of human existence – the sentiments, moral nature, or
> guiding beliefs of persons, groups, or institutions – has come to
> provide the "medium" within which the self-government of the
> autonomous individual can be connected up with the imperatives of
> good government.[68]

Set in these terms, biopolitics appears as a «biomedical
government of somatic selves», led not only by doctors or by the
traditional figures of social workers, therapists, personnel managers,
but also by the new and ever more numerous «somatic experts»:
psychological therapists, speech therapists, physiotherapists,

---

advance. So Rose himself highlights that «new potentials are emerging
for "governing through susceptibilities"» (p. 95), new potentials which
complicate the picture of "vitalism" of the 21st century biopolitics,
which he talks about.

67   *The Politics of Life Itself*, p. 125.
68   *The Politics of Life Itself*, p. 27.

nutritionists, dieticians, remedial gymnasts; addiction, sex, family, relationship, mental health, educational counsellors; «and, of course, genetic, family planning, fertility, and reproduction counsellors».[69] In this framework, genetic counsellors constitute the most significant figures of «the new kinds of "pastoral powers"» that, for example, with genetic analysis combined with brain scan, that is, through their "premonitory" knowledge, «may indicate risk of future disease or (...) undesirable behaviour traits such impulsivity».[70]

Insisting on this perspective, Rose seems to suggest that today there are not many possibilities better than contemporary medicine offers, to actively train our subjectivity, to autonomously elaborate our life strategies, to ethically practice our freedom, taking into account the limits of our existence.[71] The ethical quality of the processes to which Rose refers proves to be an important aspect even when the considerable economic profits that derive from them are totally evident. There is no doubt, in any case, that the intertwining of economics, research, medicine and biopolitics is a fundamental element of the framework in which these processes are placed. Today, in particular, information on health, genomic inheritance, genetic susceptibility, medical records, blood samples or biological tissues enters a dimension in which disease is no longer simply a dangerous eventuality, physical damage, or a social cost to be reduced; in addition to being important for the pursuit of individual and collective well-being, this information has now become

---

69   *The Politics of Life Itself*, p. 28.
70   *The Politics of Life Itself*, p. 29.
71   See *The Politics of Life Itself*, pp. 125-9. In Rose's viewpoint, among other things, there is no room for questioning the exasperated "healthism" that can derive from the behaviors to which it refers. On this issue see: Mauro Turrini, 'A genealogy of "healthism": Healthy subjectivities between individual autonomy and disciplinary control', *eä Journal*, 7, 1 (2015), 11-27; Irving Kenneth Zola, 'Healthism and Disabling Medicalization', in Ivan Illich and others, *Disabling Professions* (London, New York: Marion Boyars, 1977), pp. 41–6; Robert Crawford, 'Healthism and the medicalization of everyday life', *Health*, 10, 3 (1980), 365-88; of this same author see also: 'Health as a meaningful social practice', *Health*, 10, 4 (2006), 401-20.

a potential resource for the generation of wealth and health, and one that provides great economic opportunities for the novel alliances of states and commerce taking shape within contemporary circuits of biovalue.[72]

It is therefore almost inevitable that the intertwining of ethical paths, biopolitical practices and economic strategies also manifests itself in the experiences of biological citizenship promoted from below by patients' organizations. In these experiences, in fact, it can happen that particularly capable organizations and activists engage in the collection and storage of blood and tissue to promote biotechnological research on them, and economically manage the intellectual property of the results of such research.[73] In these cases it is particularly clear – according to Rose – not only that «the vitality of biological processes can be bought and sold», but also that «ethics becomes both a marketable commodity and a service in its own right». Ethical and economic decisions therefore tend to meet «contributing to the commercial values of products through demonstrating a commitment to the ethical values of the biocitizen-consumer of health and his or her requirements for trust».[74]

Ultimately, it is a question of acknowledging – according to the author – that in contemporary societies the production of health and the production of wealth are increasingly connected to each other; therefore, from this point of view, the ethical motivations of economic choices become necessary and, in the same way, the redefinition of ethical values in relation to economic choices is always possible.

The fact that all these trends are closely related to neoliberal governmentality emerges clearly from Rose's discourse when she

---

72   *The Politics of Life Itself*, p. 151.
73   *The Politics of Life Itself*, pp. 151-2. The case to which Rose pays special attention is that of the PXE International foundation, established in 1996 by Sharon Terry and Patrick Terry, parents of two boys who had been diagnosed with the rare disease of *pseudoxanthoma elasticum*.
     An important study on similar experiences and their biopolitical and economic implications is that of Carlos Novas, 'Patient Activism and Biopolitics: Thinking through Rare Diseases and Orphan Drugs', in *Biopower: Foucault and Beyond*, pp. 183-98.
74   *The Politics of Life Itself*, pp. 152 and 153.

says that «[t]his shift from implacable abnormalities to manageable susceptibilities is entirely consistent with the wider reshaping in contemporary practices for the government of persons». Contemporary individuals, as biological citizens, feel urged to actively deal with their genetic susceptibilities by evaluating their way of life, regulating their lifestyles and the use of drugs in relation to the changing needs of their susceptible body, in the same way in which as citizens of neoliberal societies, in general, they feel called to be flexible, update their skills, be available to buy new goods, manage economic risks. What distinguishes the experiences of biological citizens – according to Rose – is that they «are redefining what it means to be human today».[75]

Here too, therefore, the British author shows that he wants to avoid critically considering the scenarios he outlines. It is much more important for him to try to demonstrate that the most interesting and innovative consequences of contemporary biopolitics derive from the interactions between the experiences of biological citizenship, the changes in the exercise of power, the developments of scientific knowledge and the transformations of capitalism. Therefore, his position proves impermeable to the possibility of also considering other perspectives of the ethical-political relationship of contemporary man with the sphere of life.

In this sense, the way in which he frames the experience of the people who in Ukraine have tried to deal with the radioactive effects of the explosion of the Chernobyl nuclear reactor is significant. For him, it is important to note that this experience also represents a case of biological citizenship, insofar as those people have claimed health services and social support «in their damaged biological bodies».[76] From his point of view, however, this is a limited and regressive experience, since it still falls within the context of «the residual social states in the post-Soviet era». It has nothing to do with «the West novel practices of biological choice», of which the citizen of advanced liberal societies is the protagonist:

---

75 *The Politics of Life Itself*, p. 154.
76 *The Politics of Life Itself*, p. 133.

a prudent yet enterprising individual, actively shaping his or her life course through acts of choice, activities that extend to the search for health in the face of the fear of illness, and management of risks – now genetic risk – of disease.[77]

The fact that the Chernobyl disaster, as well as the requests for assistance addressed to the state by Ukrainian citizens, are linked to the decline of Soviet socialism does not make Rose suspect that that disaster also alludes to the political and ethical limits of modern industrialism that the same advanced liberal societies and capitalism in all its forms seem incapable of questioning. A suspicion of this kind, in fact, would require hypothesizing the existence, or to indicate the need, of forms of ecosystemic, terrestrial and worldly – more than merely biological – citizenship.

In short, it would be a matter of not excluding a priori that biopolitics is a problematic terrain on which other political and ethical tasks can be set, in addition to avoiding the risks that are run in the context of one's own genetic heritage and that of one's family.

3. *Melinda Cooper and biocapitalism*

3.1 *A post-Fordist life*

A hardly debatable historical fact is that the take-off of molecular medicine, genetic research and their applications found particularly favourable conditions in the USA in the late 1970s and early 1980s. In this sense, Melinda Cooper's thesis is reliable, according to which in that context the promotion of research in the biological sciences and biotechnologies was one of the strategic choices that were made to unlock the economic system in crisis in the USA at the same time as neoliberalism was emerging as the main form of government.[78]

---

77   *The Politics of Life Itself*, p. 154.
78   Melinda Cooper, *Life as Surplus: Biotechnology & Capitalism in the Neoliberal Era* (Seattle: University of Washington Press, 2008).

The heavy increases in the price of oil that occurred in 1973 and 1979 on the international market had contributed to the crisis in the American economy, but many others had also been the causes. According to Cooper, the petrochemical and pharmaceutical industries were among the economic sectors most affected by that crisis: the first one mainly due to the decline in profits deriving from the export to developing countries of mass monoculture agriculture based on the use of pesticides, herbicides and chemical fertilizers, also due to the multiplication of protests against the heavy environmental effects of that agriculture and the increase of government controls on it; the pharmaceutical industry, on the other hand, had entered a crisis mainly due to the growing attention of society and political institutions towards the toxicity of various drugs, and the lack of regulation of clinical trials, etc.[79] It was these two sectors – according to Cooper – that took on the promotion of biological research and investments in biotechnologies as strategies for exiting the crisis through the radical change of their production policies; thus they inaugurated a real bioeconomic capitalism.

For this purpose, a direct and continuous link was activated between scientific experimentation, production activity and large-scale investments, a link that became a decisive reason for assuming «the financial markets» as «the very generative condition of production». It is true, on the other hand, that the dominant presence of financial capital has since characterized this form of economy with an intensity and extension similar to that which generally characterizes the so-called post-Fordist capitalism. In the latter – Cooper says – the «promise», that is the constant postponement of the economic results of the productive, scientific and technological choices to an indeterminate future,

> is what enables production to remain in a permanent state of self-transformation, arming it with a capacity to respond to the most unpredictable of circumstances, to anticipate and escape the possible "limit" to its growth long before it has even actualized.[80]

---

79   Cooper, *Life as Surplus*, pp.21- 2.
80   *Life as Surplus*, p. 24.

To focus on the importance that "biological production" has assumed in this context – according to Cooper – it must be considered that the neoliberal era, which definitively opened with the Reagan administration, coincides with the assumption by the state of a role very important in supporting life sciences research and the economic exploitation of its results with reforms and funding; these sciences, in fact, «would become the most heavily funded of basic science research in the United States, apart from defence».[81] Certainly, it could be observed that this active role assumed by the state is in contradiction with the usual neoliberal exaltation of the free market; but what needs to be kept in mind, in reality, is that the governmental strategies of neoliberalism do not necessarily tend to be "coherent" with presumed mandatory principles; in their concrete applications these strategies are often characterized by unscrupulousness, and therefore also by "incoherence", as attitudes necessary to decisively promote the freedom of private economic initiative. And this is, in fact, the aim that the Reagan policies have achieved with regard to biological production.

As Cooper writes, «this focus on the life sciences has gone hand in hand with a redistribution of funds away from public health and non-profit medical services toward commercially oriented research, health services, and for-profit applications». In this sense, the reform of intellectual property laws, already carried out in 1980 – a few weeks before Reagan's rise to the presidency – with the Trademark Amendments Act, was of fundamental importance. By authorizing and encouraging state-funded scientific institutions and organizations to patent and market the results of their research, this law (known as the Bayh-Dole Act) allowed the economic exploitation of these results to become one of the main purposes of the research itself.[82]

---

81   *Life as Surplus*, p. 27.
82   It is important to remember that, «by its own terms, the Bayh-Dole Act applies only to nonprofit organizations (including universities) and small businesses. However, in a February 1983 memorandum concerning the vesting of title to inventions made under federal funding, then-President Ronald Reagan ordered all agencies to treat, as allowable by law, all contractors within the Bayh-Dole Act framework regardless of

> [The] initially public-funded patents could then be privately exploited by the patent holders, who might choose to issue exclusive licenses to large private companies, enter into joint ventures, or create their own start-up companies.[83]

The immediate involvement of scientific research in economic strategies and the public-private alliance, which was promoted for this purpose, found decisive support in the amplitude and largely deregulated dynamism of the US financial market whose flows of various origins (highly liquid stock market, pension funds, savings of workers, etc.) converge towards forms of investment in emerging high-risk ventures.[84] Furthermore, the financialization of the economy in general and of biological production in particular may have found a decisive condition for developing and becoming a fundamental element of the American and world economic system in the fact that the US in 1971 had abandoned the Gold Standard. From that abandonment, in fact, had arisen the almost unavoidable need for foreign countries in possession of surplus dollars that could no longer be exchanged for gold, to buy US Treasury bonds and to continuously increase their loans to the US which thus became an economic power based essentially on debt.[85]

In a framework like this, debt and the speculative use of money ended up becoming fundamental elements of contemporary capitalism; in this same context – according to Cooper – the bioeconomy was able to establish itself as a form of production based on continuous financial investment in experimentation, in the promise of future profit, in the economic valorisation of variable life forms and in their constant renewal.[86] Thus –

---

their size». John R. Thomas, 'March-In Rights Under the Bayh-Dole Act', *Congressional Research Service*, August 22, 2006, p. 6. https://fas.org/sgp/crs/misc/R44597.pdf (accessed January 23, 2020). See also 'Memorandum on Government Patent Policy from President Ronald Reagan, to Heads of Executive Departments and Agencies', February 18, 1983: https://www.presidency.ucsb.edu/documents/memorandum-government-patent-policy (accessed January 23, 2020).

83   *Life as Surplus*, p. 27.
84   *Life as Surplus*, pp. 27-8.
85   *Life as Surplus*, p. 29.
86   *Life as Surplus*, pp. 29-31.

according to the author – the «delirium» and the «megalomania» also became essential aspects of this economy: since then it has not simply tended to overcome the limits of the production models of the past historical phases; it aspires to overcome the very limits of life just as this has been done so far on our planet, trying to produce it in ever new forms.[87] Biocapitalism, however, cannot be simply «promissory»; its delirium – according to Cooper – would not be such if it did not attempt to materialize its promises by «recapturing the reproduction of life itself within the promissory accumulation of the debt form». In other words, «[i]t dreams of reproducing the self valorisation of debt in the form of biological autopoiesis».[88]

3.2 *Regenerate or reproduce?*

Among the expressions of the new biomedical technologies that seem to correspond more than others to the perspective indicated by Cooper, those of regenerative medicine, concerning stem cells and tissue engineering, are particularly significant. These are clearly distinguished from other medical technologies tending to "body reconstruction", such as organ transplantation and prosthetics; the latter, in fact, are based on a "mechanistic" and "architectural" vision of the organism, since they presuppose a stable shape of the body that must be reconstituted or completed from the outside with the grafting of parts or organs equally stable in their forms. The regenerative medicine, instead, implies a "morphogenetic" conception of life processes;[89] it «works with and exploits the active responsiveness of living tissue, its power to affect and to be affected and thus to change in time». In short, this medicine does not tend to reconstitute a predefined form of the body, but «to determine the threshold conditions under which an ensemble of cells, defined by certain relations, will *self-assemble* into a particular form and tissue, with particular qualities».[90]

---

87   *Life as Surplus*, pp. 30-1.
88   *Life as Surplus*, p. 31.
89   *Life as Surplus*, pp. 103-11.
90   *Life as Surplus*, p. 113.

From this point of view, regenerative medicine corresponds to a conception of matter and space that can be defined as "non metric" and "topological", that is to say a vision radically different from the rigid and metric one which is the basis of medicine of transplant and prostheses.[91] Regenerative medicine implies that the structural stability of a shape does not depend on the rigidity of its parts, but on its ability to transform itself without changing nature.[92] From this point of view, the space-physical forms are not only characterized by their morphological variety, but also and above all by their intrinsic transformability.

The main theoretical-scientific references of this medicine include the studies on morphogenesis of René Thom who – as Cooper observes – uses the theory of topological transformations «to give mathematical sense to the embryological concept of the morphogenetic field».[93] Embryology, in fact, is the most important field of research both on the scientific and technological level of regenerative medicine. By studying and manipulating embryonic cells, it tends to make the most transformable and plastic of the space-physical forms of living matter technically usable, with respect to which the adult body is only the most rigid form of this matter. The main technological aspiration of regenerative medicine is «to reproduce the topological space of the early embryo in order to then regenerate the successive geometries of the body otherwise».[94] Therefore, it is important to consider the role that a device such as the bioreactor plays in this area: in addition to being an incubator used to store and transport a tissue construct, it is a manufacturing tool whose purpose «is also to provide the conditions under which a tissue can be modulated, deformed, continuously remoulded».[95]

---

91   *Life as Surplus*, pp. 115-21.
92   *Life as Surplus*, pp. 114-5.
93   *Life as Surplus*, p. 119. Here Cooper refers to the well-known study of René Thom, *Structural Stability and Morphogenesis: An Outline of as General Theory of Models*, trans. by D. H. Fowler (Reading, Mass.: W. A. Benjamin Inc, 1975).
94   *Life as Surplus*, p. 120.
95   *Life as Surplus*, p. 123.

In short, it can be said that regenerative medicine has the ambition to produce and reproduce tissues capable of transforming and growing in relation to the tissues in which they are implanted. It actually aspires to immortalize the potential of stem cells by making them available not so much for the reproduction of specific forms of organs or parts of the body, but to make the process of transformation itself perpetually possible. «What regenerative medicine wants to elicit – says Cooper – is the generative moment from which all possible forms can be regenerated – the moment of emergence, considered independently of its actualizations».[96]

For these characteristics, regenerative medicine – according to the author – distinguishes itself from another important sector of research and contemporary biomedical technology, with which it is appropriate to compare it because it also deals with living matter in its "elementary" forms (embryos, sperm, eggs, etc.). This is reproductive medicine, developed mainly through in vitro fertilization (IVF) and assisted reproductive technologies (ARTs). Reproductive medicine, in particular, tends «to culture the fertilized egg cell to term – in other words, to actualize its biological promise in the form of the future individual organism». Differently, regenerative medicine, based on the stem cell science, does not aim to produce a particular organism or a specific type of differentiated cell; rather, its purpose – as we have seen – is to reproduce the «*biological promise itself, in a state of nascent transformability*»; in short, it tends to perpetually regenerate the potential of the embryonic stem cells «in the form of a not-yet realized surplus of life».[97]

According to Cooper, the respective characteristics of these sectors of biotechnological research also allow us to understand

---

96   *Life as Surplus*, p. 127. For an in-depth study of the relationship between research on cell regenerative capacities, economic investments and ethical concerns of society, see Sarah Franklin, 'Ethical Biocapital: New Strategies of Cell Culture', in Sarah Franklin and Margaret Lock (ed. by), *Remaking Life and Death: Toward an Anthropology of the Biosciences* (Oxford and Santa Fe, NM: School of American Research Press, 2003), pp. 97-128.

97   *Life as Surplus*, p. 140.

the different ways in which they relate to the economy.[98] Reproductive medicine is involved in economization processes that undoubtedly differ from those that historically characterize animal reproductive medicine developed in the field of industrial livestock breeding. This apparently obvious clarification is however necessary since – as the author claims – «there is a shared history of technical developments» between these two forms of medicine, but it cannot be said that there is a common tendency to commercialize their "products".[99] In the USA in particular, despite the lack of homogeneous legislation regarding reproductive techniques, human embryos are generally considered worthy of being preserved or as objects of property, but not as goods freely tradable on the market. Also for this reason human reproductive medicine relates to the economy above all as a set of private services provided to the family; its various aspects are «contracted out to service providers (sperm and egg donors, surrogate mothers, and so on) in the same way that domestic labour and child care are now increasingly available as commercial services». On the other hand, the sourcing of human eggs in this field is increasingly based on «underpaid, unregulated labour of various female underclasses» and, therefore, does not seem to distinguish much from «the brute commodification of labour and tissues that prevails in the agricultural industry».[100] In any case, here in general the importance of the family model is paradoxically confirmed by means of medical technology which tends, instead, to transfer the reproductive process from the sphere of conjugal relations to that of the laboratory and the clinic.[101]

---

98 For an overall analysis of this question see Melinda Cooper and Catherine Waldby, *Clinical Labor: Tissue Donors and Research Subjects in the Global Economy* (Durham: Duke University Press, 2014).

99 *Life as Surplus*, p. 135. See also pp. 131-6.

100 *Life as Surplus*, p. 135-6.

101 In this regard, see the interview with Cooper in the Italian edition of *Life as Surplus*: 'Conversazione con l'autrice', ed. by Angela Balzano, in Melinda Cooper, *La vita come plusvalore,* trans. by Angela Balzano (Verona: Ombre corte, 2013), pp. 13-21.

Things are different in the case of regenerative medicine. Through stem cell science, first of all, it destabilizes the legal tradition that connects the protection of living matter to the protection of the integrity and dignity of the person; it tends to affirm the idea that the embryonic stem cell is not equivalent to a potential person, but rather an indeterminate generative and regenerative potential that can perpetuate itself indefinitely and translate into the most varied forms of life; for this reason, its patenting is seen as legitimate to the extent that, conceived in these terms, it seems to correspond to the existing legal definitions of invention.[102] This, however, does not mean that regenerative medicine simply tends to the commodification of biological life.[103] It goes far beyond this possibility by placing itself in clear harmony with the markedly financial and speculative character of contemporary capitalism. In fact, as Cooper claims referring to «the burgeoning U.S. stem cell market», the latter

> is one instance in which the logic of speculative accumulation – the production of promise from promise – comes together with the particular generativity of the immortalized embryonic stem cell line, an experimental life form that also promises to regenerate its own potential for surplus, indefinitely.[104]

The different relationship that, according to these indications, regenerative and reproductive medicine establish with the economy lead us to think that the second, unlike the first, is in some way conditioned by the influence that conservative morality of a religious nature exerts on society insisting on the sacredness of the person's life, of which the embryo would already be the embodiment, and on the social centrality of the family. Admitting this possibility, Cooper also argues that conservative culture plays a role apparently contrary to the "unscrupulous" choices that prevail in regenerative medicine. According to her, on the level of concrete political decisions, neoliberal open-mindedness and conservative moralism are

---

102 *Life as Surplus*, pp. 145-7.
103 *Life as Surplus*, p. 148.
104 *Life as Surplus*, p. 142.

far from irreconcilable. In fact, it may happen that a President like George W. Bush during his presidency, on the one hand, proclaims himself a defender of the sacredness of human life inherent in "unborn children"; on the other, let the patenting of the unmodified embryonic stem cell lines be approved, after having promoted the research on the available ones, justifying with the argument that «life and death decisions "had already been taken by scientists"».[105]

Beyond this specific question, we have already seen that the political hegemony gained by neoliberalism since the late 1970s does not in any way imply a downsizing of the importance of the family;[106] this importance, in fact, can be attributed to the family not only if it is respectful of traditional moral values, but also if it is not. In these terms, in particular, the relevance that both Becker and Rose attribute to the family as a favourable context for the emergence of forms of genetic self-government oriented by economic choices can be considered. Indeed, not only education and intellectual abilities, but also the biological characteristics of parents and children can play an important role in the investments through which the family relates to contemporary society as permeated by the rationality of the free market. In any case, the genetic microcosm of the individual and his relationship with that of his family become fundamental points of reference of the forms that biopolitics takes in the context of societies permeated by neoliberal governmentality.

---

105 *Life as Surplus*, p. 153; see also pp. 152-4. As Cooper observes, «[i]n making this concession to stem cell research», Bush «claimed, the U.S. government was not condoning the destruction of the unborn. (...). By intervening after the fact, the state was ensuring that life would nevertheless be promoted, in this case not the life of the potential person but the utopia of perpetually renewed life promised by stem cell research». (p. 153)

106 Melinda Cooper proposes an interesting analysis of the convergence between neoliberalism and conservatism in the attribution of a political, social and moral centrality to family in *Family Values: Between Neoliberalism and the New Social Conservatism* (New York: Zone Books, 2017).

3.3 *Biopower epidemic*

Returning to what Rose claims about biological citizenship, it is interesting to note that he indicates in the «campaigning groups that arouse around AIDS» an example of the «moral pioneers» who from the beginning of the 1980s would have contributed to establishing this form of citizenship. These groups of activists would have performed very important functions, for example, in disseminating information about the disease, in supporting those affected, in claiming rights for them, in fighting stigma, etc. Furthermore, especially in the English-speaking world, they have often agreed to form an alliance with the health establishment «in promoting the message of safe(r) sex», thus obtaining the opportunity to express themselves «in the organization and deployment of social resources, and indeed gain the resources necessary for their activities».[107] All this evidently implies that with regard to the AIDS epidemic, at least in some of the wealthiest countries, state institutions have not given up playing a role similar to that played historically by the welfare state, even without going beyond the limits of neoliberal governmentality. However, if you look at the issue from a supranational point of view, there are other considerations too.

In this regard, it is Cooper who allows us to complicate the context of the analysis. According to her, AIDS is only one example of the unexpected re-explosion of infectious diseases in our age, «despite the long-held belief that the modern pharmaceutical industry would see to the near total elimination of infection-related deaths by the beginning of the millennium»;[108] the explosion of the epidemic of this disease, in any case, has been an event from which there have been shocking changes in biopolitics worldwide. These changes mainly concerned poor countries and, in particular, those of sub-Saharan Africa. If – according to Rose's analysis – in the richest countries the AIDS activists have been able to negotiate at least the partial socialization of costs and responsibilities of prevention and treatment with the health

---

107 *The Politics of Life Itself*, p. 144.
108 *Life as Surplus*, p. 52.

establishment, in Africa the epidemic was used as an opportunity to counteract the realization of such possibilities; more precisely, it was not possible to obtain in a timely manner the therapeutic results achieved on a large scale in rich countries with the use of antiretroviral therapies. The legal action promoted in 1998 by the large pharmaceutical companies, with the support of the US government, against the South African government represented a decisive obstacle in this sense: that action, in fact, prevented South Africa from using the emergency clause «that would allow it to override the World Trade Organization (WTO) rules on the importing of low cost generic drugs». In this sense, in 1997 the South African Medicines Act was approved in that country, which referred to article 31 of the Agreement on Trade Related Aspects of Intellectual Property Rights (known as TRIPs) signed by the WTO member States: according to this article the use of patented drugs may be authorized «in the case of a national emergency or other circumstances of extreme urgency».[109] But – according to Cooper – in the long period that was necessary for the complete application of this Agreement (from 1996 to 2005), the US innovation industries – and the pharmaceutical one in particular – had the opportunity to develop in a condition of growing "privatization" of knowledge.[110] In fact, the neoliberal policies promoted since the 1980s by the International Monetary Fund (IMF) and the World Bank definitely guaranteed the protection of the rights of rich countries to economically exploit patents on research results; therefore these policies also allowed the economic dominance of the US over poor countries to be strengthened significantly.[111]

For this reason, therefore, AIDS in Africa was only partially treated as a public health problem that governments could deal with as quickly as necessary using state resources without getting heavily indebted and worsening the economic conditions of their countries. Rather, the spread of the disease – according to Cooper – has gradually been transformed into a global humanitarian

---

109 *Life as Surplus*, pp. 52-3.
110 *Life as Surplus*, pp. 55-7.
111 *Life as Surplus*, pp. 58-9.

emergency.[112] Furthermore, in the case of South Africa, the government led by Thabo Mbeki from 1999 to 2008 contributed to aggravating the epidemic by contesting the therapeutic validity of antiretroviral drugs and considering them an instrument of imperialism of wealthiest countries; in any case, after the victory in the legal battle against the drug consortium (2001), the said government, paradoxically refused to declare AIDS a national health emergency and only in 2003 did it undertake to make antiretrovirals available.[113]

Overall, for Cooper, the way AIDS has been addressed globally is part of a broader strategy of «deliberate demolition of the keynesian nation-state centred regime of growth established in the post-World War II period».[114] According to her, since the 1980s no state can any longer aspire to truly guarantee general protection of the lives of its citizens; in poor countries, in particular, the most serious problems to which life is exposed are projected into a supranational dimension in which the character of humanitarian emergencies is increasingly attributed to them, to be eventually dealt with as a war and its consequences would be dealt with; on

---

112 *Life as Surplus*, p. 51.

113 *Life as Surplus*, p. 54. Here it should be remembered that a fundamental role in the legal battle against pharmaceutical companies was played by the association Treatment Action Campaign (TAC), which for a long time also opposed the policies of the Mbeki government. For an in-depth analysis of the whole question, see Michael Vittori, *La sfida dell'AIDS: la risposta politica nel Sudafrica post-Apartheid*, Tesi di laurea in Storia moderna e contemporanea dell'Africa, Università di Bologna (Italy), 2007: https://www.michaelvittori.it/storia/aids-sudafrica/ (accessed January 6, 2020). It is also important to consider the different trend of the epidemic in Uganda, where the spread of AIDS would have been substantially halted through policies and campaigns aimed at changing people's sexual behaviours. In this regard, see 'UNAIDS/WHO Epidemiological Fact Sheets on HIV and AIDS – Core data on epidemiology and response – Uganda – 2008 Update': http://d35brb9zkkbdsd.cloudfront.net/wp-content/uploads/2014/09/AIDS-Epidemiological-Fact-Sheet-on-Uganda.pdf (accessed January 7, 2020). For a critical approach to this case see: Elaine M. Murphy and others, 'Was the "ABC" Approach (Abstinence, Being Faithful, Using Condoms) Responsible for Uganda's Decline in HIV?', *PLoS Medicine*, 3, 9 (2006), 1443-7.

114 *Life as Surplus*, p. 61.

the other hand, these problems are often intertwined with war or with «civil strife, ethnic violence, guerrilla rebellions, coups d'état» or «ethnic cleansing».[115]

The author strongly proposes these theses, tending to attribute a paradigmatic value to the military approach to emergencies with regard to new forms of biopolitics. In fact, she considers exemplary in this sense the strategies promoted by the Bush administration to counter the "biological threats" that occurred with the terrorist attacks carried out using anthrax, after the 2001 attack on the Twin Towers. Those strategies – according to the author – have inaugurated a biopolitics which consists in treating bioterrorism and infectious diseases as similar, inasmuch microbiological threats; this resulted in a reorganization and a new conceptualization of «the very nature of warfare, security, and military threat (...) at the interface between public health and security, the biotech industry, and military research».[116] Ultimately, it is in a context like this that the biopolitical strategies concerning the great epidemics are placed as «complex humanitarian emergencies».[117]

3.4 *Humanitarian reason*

Framing the issue of major epidemics in these terms, in reality, the author focuses only in part on the importance that humanitarianism as such – beyond the concept of emergency and military approach – has assumed in the forms of biopolitics established between the nineties and the 2000s. The "humanitarian reason", in fact, since then presents itself more and more often as a general way of reorganizing life policies not only on a global

---

115 *Life as Surplus*, pp. 64-5. This trend became completely evident – according to Cooper – in 2000 when the UN Security Council dedicated its inaugural meeting of the millennium to the growing impact of AIDS in Africa, and the US National Intelligence Council, in its report, warned that «new and re-emerging infectious disease [would] pose a rising global health threat». (ibid., pp. 51). Cooper here refers to National Intelligence Council, *National Intelligence Estimate: The Global Infectious Disease Threat and Its Implications for the United States* (Washington, DC: National Intelligence Council, 2000). p. 1.

116 *Life as Surplus*, p. 75.

117 *Life as Surplus*, pp. 51-2, 63-7, 92-100.

level, but also on a local level. It is true in fact, that today the exposure of life to emergencies of supranational dimensions – epidemics, wars, ethnic violence, climate change – has become an important condition of the application of biopower in an era when the state is no longer its main player; but it is equally reliable that the humanitarian characterization of the government of life today allows it to be exercised in all those situations in which life itself can be treated as worthy of compassion, as it is exposed to precariousness and not necessarily to catastrophic or global emergencies. As Didier Fassin claims, it is precisely between the end of the 20th and the beginning of the 21st century that humanitarianism has become a real model of government of "precarious lives", a model that can be applied towards the unemployed, asylum seekers, sick immigrants, people with AIDS, as well as people involved in disasters and conflicts, through the action of states and nongovernmental organizations, international bodies and local communities.[118] The main consequence of this type of government is an overall decontextualization of the issues that are addressed, which is achieved through the translation of social inequalities, the violence of relations of domination and exploitation in terms of suffering, trauma, marginalization or misery of individuals generally considered to be "victims".[119] Precisely in the case of the AIDS epidemic in South Africa – according to Fassin – humanitarianism has been able to clearly express itself as a compassionate government of life, which goes beyond the limits of traditional forms of power, in particular, through the dramatization of the problem of childhood. Inasmuch affected directly or indirectly by the infection, and innocent victims of the irresponsibility of adults, the figures of the sick child, the abused child and the orphan child have become the privileged

---

118 Didier Fassin, *Humanitarian Reason: A Moral History of the Present*, trans. by Rachel Gomme (Berkeley, Los Angeles, London: University of California Press, 2012). By the same author, see also *Life: A Critical User's Manual* (Cambridge, UK: Polity Press, 2018).

119 On the problematic nature of the notion of victim see: Philippe Mesnard, *La victime écran: La représentation humanitaire en question* (Paris: Textuel, 2002); Daniele Giglioli, *Critica della vittima* (Rome: Nottetempo, 2014).

object of media attention and of the aid programs of national and international humanitarian organizations. However, claims the author,

> the affective emphasis reifies children as victims in a way that removes them far from social reality in which they live. The weight of poverty and the role of exploitation in the spread of HIV/AIDS among disadvantaged communities, the ordinary violence in social relations, the permanence of traditional forms of family solidarity – all these things that constitute the life context of these children – disappear. By eluding this complex reality, which makes moral judgments less certain and solutions less univocal, compassion may paradoxically prove to be an emotion that spares those feeling it from having to take more demanding action.[120]

Indeed, if the problems to be addressed are simplified through a compassionate vision, it can also happen that certain governments invoke «the humanitarian argument as a ground for their armed interventions»,[121] treating the lives of some as worthy of being protected more than others, as it happened – for example – with the NATO bombing during the Kosovo war in 1999 or in Afghanistan in 2001.

By supporting a view like this, Fassin also affirms that humanitarian practice certainly constitutes a biopolitics in the Foucaultian sense of the term; in fact, it – precisely in the case of international conflicts – is expressed through forms of «management of populations», managed mostly by humanitarian organizations and based, for example, on the setting up of refugee camps and on «epidemiological studies of infectious diseases, malnutrition, trauma», etc.. However, – says the author – humanitarian action must also be distinguished to some extent from biopolitics and rather defined as «politics of life» in the sense that «it takes as its object saving lives, which presupposes not only risking others, but also selecting those that have priority for being saved (for example, when drug supplies are insufficient)»; moreover, it is a politics of life also in the sense that «it champions causes

---

120 *Humanitarian Reason*, p. 180. See also pp. 161-80.
121 *Humanitarian Reason*, p. 7.

publicly, which implies not only neglecting other ones but also constructing them by choosing the best way of representing the populations assisted (for instance, as victims rather than resistance fighters)».[122] Ultimately, the presence of victims, or the possibility of representing certain figures rather than others as victims, seems to be a decisive condition for the transformation of biopolitics into a politics of life in which moral judgment and compassion become fundamental factors of its legitimacy.

3.5 *Global dangers*

The last considerations, in reality, serve to integrate rather than to question the analysis carried out by Cooper on the importance that the concept of emergency assumes in contemporary biopolitical strategies. Indeed, the author is right to insist on the exemplary case of the AIDS epidemic; if this represented a shocking biopolitical event, primarily it is because in the historical moment of its explosion they combined together: on the one hand, the end of the dream of modern medicine to definitively win its war against major epidemic diseases; on the other, the emergence of neoliberalism as a hegemonic form of governmentality that excludes considering the protection of life for each and every one as a mandatory task of political institutions. From this point of view, the biopolitical importance of the emergency concept is expressed in two ways: first of all, in the sense that it implies that disaster (health, humanitarian or other) must be considered a realistic possibility and – at the same time – unpredictable in its size and consequences; secondly, in the sense that this concept indicates, in the unpredictability of the disaster, not so much a reason to give up intervening to avoid it or reduce its consequences, but as a reason to conceive and implement new ways of intervening on life, which entail its protection, but not at any cost.

On these bases, in fact, the supranational and global dimension becomes an essential element of the context in which a large part of the dangers and security problems of our era are placed. Therefore Cooper's analysis, from this point of view, remains very useful

---

122 *Humanitarian Reason*, p. 226.

also because it can help us understand the relationship that has developed since the end of the last century between the changes in biopolitics and the increasingly current ecological crisis understood as "global emergency". Returning to the example of the AIDS epidemic, in this sense it can be said in particular that, if it had a huge biopolitical significance, it is also because it represented in some way a proof of the profound crisis of certain balances, that modern man – the western one in particular – in recent centuries had managed to build to his advantage, between his cumbersome presence on the planet and the biological ecosystems in which he lives, through forms of biopolitics based on social security, welfare states and public health care systems. When these state-centred forms of biopolitics were challenged by neoliberalism, on the one hand, the supranational dimension of globalization took them over; on the other, the same crisis of the ecosystem balance between man and the environment has ended up finding in this global dimension the framework of the prevailing perception of the dangers that it entails:

> the new dangers – writes Cooper – no longer originate in the constitutional sphere or arena of international relations, but rather they erupt from below and from within the fabric of social and biological reproduction, or else from above, from the biospheric or ecological level down. (...) Whether human-made or natural, intruding from the outside or within, what distinguishes them is simply their indifference to national, territorial, boundaries.[123]

However, it is evident that an issue such as the ecological one, once it is projected beyond the territorial and local contexts – which do not necessarily coincide with those of the nation-state – acquires only in part, or apparently, the magnitude and complexity more appropriate to its severity. In fact, in this way it is also abstracted by the varied multiplicity of its causes and its natural, historical and political specificities that can be grasped above all at the different levels of its geographical, topological, space-time expression. This perception of the ecological question, on the other hand, becomes possible to the extent that it is reduced

---

123 *Life as Surplus*, p. 64.

to a general and abstract problem of relations between organic and inorganic matter, biological forms of life and energy flows or, in general, to a question concerning the planet considered globally and as a *biosphere*.

Cooper offers us some particularly interesting elements in this regard by highlighting the importance that life sciences have attached to the microbiological sphere for several decades. The author considers in particular theoretical conceptions that are affirmed in the same period in which new infectious diseases such as AIDS spread in a situation that – as we know – has been made increasingly alarming by the malicious return of "old" epidemic diseases (tuberculosis, malaria, yellow fever, etc.), from the onset of new zoonotic diseases such as *Creutzfeld Jakob* disease (or "mad cow") and fears of global pandemics of diseases such as *coronavirus* influences.

According to her analysis, while the dream of defeating deadly epidemic diseases declines, new scientific theories begin to attribute to microbial life the role of protagonist of an inescapable coevolution scenario between the various forms of life (human, animal, plant, microbial) and their geological and atmospheric conditions. From this point of view, the re-explosion of infectious diseases appears as the result of a breakdown of certain balances in the relationships between human life and that of microorganisms such as bacteria and viruses, a breakdown which could be connected, among other things, to climate change.[124] The prospect thus outlined is made even more worrying by theories that insist on the idea that microorganisms evolve and develop much more rapidly and pervasively than other living beings: according to these theories, they interact with environmental changes not simply by random selection of their life forms more capable of adapting and resisting; they react to the conditions in which they live by transferring "horizontally" – that is, from one organism or group of organisms to another – the genetic material that allows

---

124 *Life as Surplus*, pp. 76-7. Cooper's main reference in this regard is Lynn Margulis and Dorion Sagan, *Microcosmos: Four Billion Years of Evolution from our Microbial Ancestors* (Berkeley: University of California, 1997).

the rapid formation and expansion of resistant life forms. This happens because the processes of their evolution do not take place in the lengthy periods of natural selection, within the limits of "vertical" reproduction through sexual relations and the transfer of genetic characteristics from one generation to another. As Cooper notes, certain studies show that «bacteria do not even have to wait around for random mutation to confer resistance; they can share it among themselves. The new microbiology is discovering that for bacteria resistance is literally contagious».[125]

Obviously – as you may guess – this type of theory seems useful to explain enormous problems of our time such as that of the resistance of bacteria to antibiotics, the seriousness of which Foucault had already perceived. According to Cooper nonetheless, these theories also make it possible to place the renewed spread of infectious diseases in relation to the political changes of «ecologies of public health»; in this sense, the growing resistance of certain pathogens to drugs can be seen as a result, albeit indirect, of the prevalence of neoliberal policies: these can involve, for example, a dangerous combination of tendencies laden with negative consequences such as the overuse of antibiotics in rich societies and the underuse of them in poor societies.[126] Similarly, according to the author, it can be considered that certain health emergencies may also be unexpected effects of the applications of genetic research favoured by biocapitalism, such as the use of recombinant DNA technologies: «[t]he production of "transgenic" life forms, after all, hitches a ride on the same vectors of communication that are responsible for resistance – viruses, transposons (mobile genetic elements), and plasmids (extrachromosomal genetic elements».[127]

All this allows us to think that neoliberalism and biocapitalism, on the one hand, tend to increase the possibilities of defence and improvement of human life, and on the other hand, contribute to

---

125 *Life as Surplus*, p. 77. See: Stuart B. Levy and Richard P. Novick (ed. by), *Antibiotic Resistance Genes: Ecology, Transfer and Expression* (New York: Cold Spring Harbor Press, 1986); Stuart B. Levy, *The Antibiotic Paradox: How Miracle Drugs Are Destroying the Miracle* (Berlin: Spring, 1992).

126 *Life as Surplus*, p. 81.

127 *Life as Surplus*, p. 78.

creating a growing unpredictability of its fate. In fact – as Cooper claims – however difficult it is «to asses to what extent the neoliberal dismantling of public health is responsible for accelerating the emergences of new diseases, although it is surely a contributing factor». In any case, – according to the author – the drastic reduction of the protections guaranteed in the past by the state implies that one must be prepared for the most unexpected emergencies; at the same time, it provokes «a general loss of preparedness in relation to the emergent event».[128] Which – according to Cooper – means that «nonpreparedness in the face of the surprise event is a distinguishing feature of the neoliberal politics of risk more generally». This politics encourages us to consider the threats to which we are exposed as less and less predictable and to assume them as inevitable and pervasive; but, «although we are exhorted to feel prepared», they leave us «unprepared for even the mildest of surprises».[129]

By outlining a picture like this, Cooper also argues that this corresponds with an overall change in the conceptions of risk that has occurred since the 1980s. Since then, the idea of risk clearly refers to the possibility of catastrophe. This is a possibility confirmed – so to speak – by the ever more probable event of disasters deriving from global warming, nuclear accidents and «emerging disease and food-borne, transgenic, and biomedical epidemics».[130] In such a scenario, evidently, the ecological crisis and the possibility of the global environment disaster take on an undeniable concrete and symbolic importance; this finding, however, does not necessarily entail questioning what appears to be their determining factor, namely the unlimited growth of capitalist production based on the indefinite development of technology.

As Cooper observes, there are two main postures that are taken in addressing the dangers, in particular those deriving from the unpredictable effects of technological innovations: the first is that which is inspired by the precautionary principle, formalized on the occasion of the Rio de Janeiro Earth Summit (1992), resumed

---

128 *Life as Surplus*, p. 82.
129 *Life as Surplus*, p. 81.
130 *Life as Surplus*, p. 82.

in the context of the Kyoto Protocol (1997) and introduced into European Union legislation; the second is based, instead, on the concept of pre-emption, understood in a sense not entirely compatible with the idea of precaution.

As is known, the precautionary principle, with regard to environmental risks, in the *Rio Declaration* establishes that «[w]here there are threats of serious or irreversible damage, lack of full scientific certainty shall not be used as a reason for postponing cost-effective measures to prevent environmental degradation».[131] This principle naturally lends itself to be applied also to the dangers deriving from the most varied technological applications. However, although it appears to impose a reasonable surveillance obligation over their unpredictable effects, it has remained largely unenforced. In fact – according to Cooper – especially in the USA, there is another posture that generally has prevailed in facing risks, the more they present themselves as potentially catastrophic: that of pre-emption understood as «aggressive counterproliferation, where the point is no longer to halt innovation on the mere suspicion of its incalculable effects but precisely *to mobilize innovation in order to pre-empt its potential fall-out*».[132]

This is an approach that has been widely applied in military strategies designed to counter the danger of terrorism since it has taken on a global dimension and enormous technical capabilities for destruction; therefore, in this same area, biological research aimed at combating bioterrorism has earned a place. In addition, the American military institutions, from the early 2000s, also began to comprehend, in terms of pre-emption, the potential consequences

---

131 *Declaration on Environment and Development, Principle 15*, United Nations Conference on Environment and Development (Rio de Janeiro, 3-14 June 1992). For a more detailed study of the genealogy and of the ethical, political and juridical aspects of the "precautionary principle" see: Renata Brandimarte, 'La scienza incerta e la precauzione', and Luigi Pannarale, 'Il principio di precauzione e i suoi usi giurisprudenziali', both in Ottavio Marzocca (ed. by), *Governare l'ambiente. La crisi ecologica tra poteri, saperi e conflitti*, (Milan: Mimesis, 2010), pp. 197-208 and 241-54.

132 *Life as Surplus*, p. 84.

of abrupt climate change for the security of the country, designing, for example, "geo-engineering" strategies aimed at changing the Earth's climatic conditions «by unleashing various active gases into the atmosphere». The most significant research in this regard however seems to be the pharmacological ones that, using the technique of DNA shuffling, «not only attempt to perfect our defences against existing threats but more ambitiously to create antibiotics and vaccines against infectious diseases that have not yet even emerged».[133]

The ability of microbial life to develop drug-resistant forms of life presents itself in some way as the paradigm of dangers that cannot be predicted with certainty, but which it is impossible not to actively prevent even without knowing them; which leads us to think that the task that pre-emption strategies set themselves can only be unlimited, as the exercise of biopower through them can become potentially unlimited.

4. *Generative Uncertainty*

Evidently, various trends in research applied to the fate of life show that in the context of neoliberal governmentality and biocapitalism, the growth of uncertainty and dangers – or even simply the intensification of their perception – does not at all involve a conversion to caution in the use of technologies. Rather, uncertainties and dangers are transformed into conditions that, on the one hand, the players of research, technological development, economic growth and political government contribute to create, and on the other hand, use as decisive reasons to continue to intervene on biophysical materiality. More generally, the uncertainty and unpredictability of events no longer represent the limits against

---

133 *Life as Surplus*, p. 91. Cooper illustrates these research trends by referring, among others, to the activities carried out since the early 2000s by Defense Advanced Research Projects Agency (DARPA) and to the studies by: Judith Miller and others, *Germs: The ultimate Weapon* (New York: Simon and Schuster, 2001); Jamie Bacher and others, 'Anticipatory Evolution and DNA Shuffling', *Genome Biology*, 3, 8 (2002), 1021-5.

which it would be necessary to hesitate or stop; they are taken as essential data of reality, on which – because of their continuous reproduction – one cannot help but intervene trying to prevent them or actively stem them through continuous technological innovation.

In this sense, Luigi Pellizzoni reliably maintains that a new relationship with uncertainty and unpredictability has now developed in societies dominated by neoliberal government, which goes beyond the idea that they simply correspond to the contingent limits of human knowledge. Rather, they are taken as ontological characteristics of our world, regardless of whether they also present themselves as a temporary lack of information or as results of society's action on nature. According to this view,

> [t]he nature-society compound is essentially unpredictable; the limits to knowledge are permanent and not contingent, hence no proper planning is possible. However, this is not problematic as long as the human agent adopts a purposive attitude toward contingency: as long as the agent is able to apply a 'both/and' logic, where the difference between epistemic uncertainty and ontological indeterminacy loses meaning, and as long as the market, as a blind mechanism of co-ordination, ensures ex-post the overall soundness of choices.[134]

The transformations that the relationship between society and risk has undergone with respect to the past seem to have contributed decisively to this change in the concept of uncertainty. As we have seen, Cooper offers us important elements for the comprehension of these transformations. Her main reference in this regard are the studies of François Ewald.[135] It should be added, however, that it is

---

134 Luigi Pellizzoni, *Ontological Politics in a Disposable World: The New Mastery of Nature* (Farnham, UK: Ashgate, 2015), pp. 66-7.Other important studies by this author in this regard are: 'Fabbricare la natura. Crisi ecologica, critica sociale e governamentalità', in *Governare l'ambiente. La crisi ecologica tra poteri, saperi e conflitti*, pp. 175-96; 'New Materialism and Runaway Capitalism: A Critical Assessment', *Soft Power*, 5, 1 (2017), 63-80. See also Luigi Pellizzoni and Marja Ylönen, 'Hegemonic contingencies: Neoliberalized techoscience and neorationality', in Luigi Pellizzoni and MarjaYlönen (ed. by), *Neoliberalism and Technoscience: Critical Assessments* (Farnham, UK: Ashgate, 2012), pp. 47-74.

135 See: François Ewald, 'Two Infinities of Risk', in Brian Massumi

Ulrich Beck who describes the change we are talking about in very clear terms, starting from the 1980's. He does so also by claiming that the new scenario results in a progressive increase of mistrust towards science, technology, experts and political decision-makers. The German author describes contemporary society as a society in which risks (technological and environmental risks in particular) tend to become incalculable and global: they are now irreducible to the historical state strategies of government, prevention and insurance compensation of damages that may ensue. From this point of view, our time, as an age of incalculable risks, is the result of the passage from a "first" to a "second modernity" in which damages – unlike in the past – tend to become unmanageable.[136]

Beck's vision has been the subject of precise criticism from authors who have contributed to the so-called *governmentality studies*. Mitchell Dean, in particular, challenges Beck's claim to describe the risk in itself, losing sight of the fact that it is a technical-conceptual tool linked to variable forms of knowledge, political strategy and representation of society. Furthermore, Dean argues that, speaking of our time as an age of incalculable risk and as a result of the passage from a "first" to a "second modernity", Beck tends to construct a totalizing vision, totally inadequate to recognize the multiplicity and empirical character of risk governance strategies. According to Dean, the incalculable risk theory assumes the crisis of insurance calculation, social security and *welfare state* as indisputable proof of the general crisis of calculability; but, in reality, there are no calculable or incalculable risks; there are only different, more or less effective ways of using the notion of risk according to different ways of conceiving its

---

(ed. by), *The Politics of Everyday Fear* (Minneapolis: University of Minnesota Press, 1993), pp. 221-8; François Ewald, 'The Return of Descartes's Malicious Demon: An Outline of a Philosophy of Precaution', in Tom Baker and Jonathon Simon (ed. by), *Embracing Risk: The Changing Culture of Insurance and Responsibility* (Chicago: University of Chicago Press, 2002), pp. 273-301.

136 See Ulrich Beck: *Risk Society: Towards a New Modernity*, trans. by Mark Ritter (London: Sage, 1992); *World Risk Society* (Cambridge, UK: Polity Press, 1999); *World at Risk*, trans. by Ciaran Cronin (Cambridge, UK: Polity Press, 2008).

calculability. It is therefore necessary to hypothesize that forms of risk calculation and governance different from insurance or welfarist ones are possible. The *welfare state* crisis, on the other hand, does not necessarily imply the decline of the social dimension of this government, but must be seen in the context of a *post-welfarist* transformation of social security. In this sense, the main trend that Dean indicates is that of general encouragement to autonomy, to the direct responsibility of individuals and groups in risk management. The campaigns against harmful lifestyles, the incitement to diagnose predispositions and risk factors, to follow diets, to exercise, etc., would only be the most evident consequences of a set of strategies, institutional and non-institutional, through which today the governance of risk reproduces itself in a social context dominated by neoliberal culture.[137]

Ultimately, comprehending in these terms the increasingly intense relationship of our society with danger, it can be considered that the tendency not to retreat in the face of uncertainty and risk finds extremely fertile ground in the subjectivities that are formed in the context of neoliberal governmentality. The importance assumed by the figure of entrepreneur of himself can but be significant proof of this hypothesis. Furthermore, the willingness of the contemporary individual to consider himself a potential bearer of genetic risks is a paradigmatic example of an increasingly widespread attitude to positively relate to the risk.

If these indications are reliable, it can therefore be said that an important result that neoliberal governmentality achieves is that of transforming the social dimension into an aggregate fluid of individuals and groups aimed at recognizing the risk first of all in themselves; in this way it fragments the all-encompassing picture that results from the discourses on the global or incalculable nature of the risks we run. It is difficult to deny, on the other hand, that the latter appear increasingly reliable especially in light of the multiplication of ecological problems. Nevertheless, in this regard, certain changes that have occurred since environmental problems have become unquestionable should not be overlooked.

---

137 Mitchell Dean, *Governmentality. Power and Rule in Modern Society* (London: Sage, 1999), pp. 176-97; see also pp. 166-7.

According to Dean and Lemke, for example, the change in the risk approach that US chemical companies promoted after the Bhopal disaster (1984) is very significant: since they could no longer simply rely on insurance logic, they elaborated «comprehensive risk-management strategies that recognize worst case scenarios». These strategies are not based on the preventive quantification of possible damage, but on an articulated instrumentation made of emergency procedures, evacuation plans, risk education, «participation of those previously excluded by a scientific-technological rationality of risk assessment, such as workers and local communities», etc.[138]

Obviously, it is not easy to establish whether and to what extent this type of risk approach has established itself in industrial production and technology management. Nevertheless, it can be recognized that it indicates the possibility of effectively reactivating the calculated government of risk precisely in situations where it would seem impractical. It can also be observed that this approach is very close to the forms of institutional government that deal with dangers and disasters through *Emergency management systems*, based on territorial plans, voluntary involvement, empowering citizens, etc. All this does not prevent the occurrence of disasters and catastrophes, but nevertheless pushes individuals and societies to accept as their ethical, political and existential perspective a kind of active self-government of the inevitable.

---

138   See: Dean, *Governmentality*, pp. 190-1; Thomas Lemke, 'Neoliberalismus, Staat und Selbsttechnologien', *Politische Vierteljahresschrift*, 41, 1 (2000), 31-47. See also Fant Pearce and Steve Tombs, 'Hegemony, risk and governance: "social regulation" and the American chemical industry', *Economy and Society*, 25, 3 (1996), 428-54.

CHAPTER SIX
BIOPOLITICS BETWEEN ECOLOGY
AND ECONOMY

1. *A lack of biopolitics*

1.1 *Milieu*

In *Security, Territory, Population* Foucault connects three specific forms of spatiality to the forms of power which, according to him, have prevailed in modernity since the seventeenth century. The expressions he uses to indicate them are: *territory, architectural module, milieu.* According to his analysis, the *territory* is the spatiality corresponding to sovereignty: in it there is the relationship focused on the city-capital between the sovereign and the geographical distribution of the social groups that perform the essential functions of the life of the state. The ideal structure of this distribution would involve, in particular, the displacement of farm workers in the countryside, of artisans in small towns, and of the sovereign's officers in the capital. From this point of view, the fundamental problem of power is that of guaranteeing the best exercise of sovereignty through the application of the laws to a centralized distribution of subjects, the specific area of which is precisely the geographical territory as a whole.[1]

On the other hand, it is a spatiality defined by its architectural structure that corresponds to disciplinary power. The latter tends to organize the multiplicity of people and their activities by hierarchically and functionally arranging them in space. In this case, therefore, the privileged spatial form is not territorial globality, but an elementary, empty and abstract geometric unit (an *architectural module*) which, reproduced in variable dimensions,

---

1   *Security, Territory, Population*, pp. 13-5.

allows the power to circumscribe in a certain way the areas in which men and women can be monitored. In the city, in particular, disciplinary power thus tends to distribute and control precisely the areas intended for housing, businesses, crafts, etc.[2]

Finally, a third form of the space of power is that indicated with the term *milieu* that Foucault associates with biopower. This is configured as a complex and dynamic dimension in which natural and artificial elements, events and processes interact, which must be governed without setting out to control them in a rigid and complete manner; in fact, it is a matter of exercising power guaranteeing a general fluidity of the relationships and phenomena that take place. The milieu, in any case, is the spatiality within which men can be governed as a population, that is to say as «a multiplicity of individuals who are and fundamentally and essentially only exist biologically bound to the materiality within which they live».[3] Within this spatial configuration, biopower tends to ensure that the circulation of things and people, the occurrence of events and the relationships between the elements are compatible with hygiene and health, the effective conduct of commercial traffic, the necessary development of the city. Therefore, security is the general principle that guides the exercise of power within this spatiality:

> security will try to plan a milieu in terms of events or series of events or possible elements, of series that will have to be regulated within a multivalent and transformable framework. The specific space of security refers then to a series of possible events; it refers to the temporal and the uncertain, which have to be inserted within a given space. The space in which a series of uncertain elements unfold is (...) roughly what one can call milieu.[4]

As outlined by Foucault, the notion of milieu appears similar to that of environment that we use today to refer to the ecosystem contexts affected by the ecological crisis. This is a similarity which, however, must be clarified and limited within specific boundaries.

---

2   *Security, Territory, Population*, pp. 15-7.
3   *Security, Territory, Population*, p. 21.
4   *Security, Territory, Population*, p. 20; see also pp. 17-23.

It must be considered, first of all, that – as claimed by Georges Canguilhem to which Foucault himself refers – the concept of milieu, even before the term, asserts itself in the mechanical sciences with Newton to be accepted later by the life sciences at the beginning of the 19th century through Lamarck. Starting from the latter, biology largely matures around the analysis of the relationship between living beings and the environmental circumstances in which they live. From the Lamarck's point of view, there is a complex relationship between these circumstances and the organisms, in which, however, the former seems to exert a deterministic influence on the latter. With Darwin, attention to environmental conditions is definitively imposed, but among these conditions the presence of other living beings exerts a greater influence on organisms than that of merely physical circumstances. It is in this context that the importance that the Darwinian theory attaches to the «struggle for existence» and to «natural selection» is placed. As Canguilhem notes, «[t]he first milieu an organism lives in is an entourage of living beings, which are for it enemies or allies, prey or predators».[5] Furthermore, in this same framework is the centrality that Darwin assigns to the living species, that is to the population of which the organisms are part of. Foucault, in this sense, claims that for the author of *The Origin of Species* «the population (...) was the element through which the milieu produces its effects on the organism»; in other words, «population was the medium between the milieu and the organism, with all the specific effects of population: mutations, eliminations, and so forth».[6] Therefore, it can be considered that the attention that evolutionary biology gives to the milieu also indirectly confirms the fundamental importance that biopower assigns to the population. Historically the population, and not the physical milieu, is the object around which the totalisation of the exercise of biopower takes place, while the individual organism is the object of the individualization of this exercise;

---

5   Georges Canguilhem, 'The Living and its Milieu', in *Knowledge of Life*, trans. by Stefanos Geroulanos and Daniela Ginsburg (New York: Fordham University Press, 2008), p. 105; see also pp. 98-120.
6   *Security, Territory, Population*, p. 78.

the milieu, on the other hand, is above all the context of the living conditions of the multiplicity of people to be governed biopolitically.

As we saw in the first chapter, according to Foucault, to be reconsidered from a perspective of this type, already from the second half of the 18th century, it is above all the urban space from the moment in which the growth and dynamism of the cities impose specific security needs such as: circulating the air, the miasmas, the waters; avoid accumulation, stagnation, crowding; avoid contamination; control the traffic of goods without hindering them; regulate the mobility and presence of people. The main biopolitical purpose of this kind of attention is to guarantee the salubrity of the urban environment and public hygiene. Foucault makes us understand, on the other hand, that the influence of this biopolitical approach to the concept of environment has not gone beyond certain limits, despite the remarkable quality that it has achieved. It basically limited itself to guaranteeing a sort of asepsis of the relationship between the population and the environment. The urban medicine that gave it substance has failed to make it prevail over other forms of biopolitics, nor has it ever had a stronger power than that of the private interests with which it came into conflict. In addition, it has been gradually overtaken by other expressions of social medicine tending to favour the assistance and control of the poor, the immune prevention of the most common pathologies and to guarantee the division of therapeutic roles between public medicine and private medicine.[7] On the other hand, 19th century hygienism has undoubtedly re-proposed the concerns of urban medicine, but – as we saw in the first chapter – through psychiatry it ended up freeing them from the attention to the material environment of the city and applying them directly to the bodies and behaviours deemed dangerous to individuals.

It can be said, therefore, that in this evolution of biopolitics the problem of the consumption and productive abuse of environmental resources does not take on any particular importance. If in the Darwinian theory the physical conditions of the environment remain, in a certain sense, in the background of competitive

---

7   'The Birth of Social Medicine', pp. 142-51.

relations between living beings, the overall natural context of the budding industrial society appears destined to remain in the "external world" condition available for its indefinite use. There is no other way to grasp the environmental implications of supremacy that the market economy attains in this historical context with the affirmation of liberal governmentality. It is almost trivial, on the other hand, to say that the "struggle for existence", which characterizes the relationships between living beings according to Darwin, places his vision of the relationship between organisms and the biological and physical environment in harmony with the liberal theories of social competition based on market economy and unlimited industrial development.[8]

The condition of "externality" in which the natural environment of life is destined to be found with the emergence of liberal governmentality emerges clearly, albeit implicitly, from Adam Smith's most famous work. Here the city, developing its manufacturing and commercial economy, tends to establish a relationship of substantial indifference with the environment that surrounds it and with the agriculture that takes place there as an activity to sustain the natural life of citizens. Indeed, Smith insists that the development of this activity depends almost entirely on the growth of the urban economy: it is the latter that represents the main market for agricultural products, while certainly it cannot be said that the agricultural economy constitutes the main market for manufacturing and urban trade.[9] However, according to him, in order to develop the "wealth of nations", the development of these latter activities is far more important than that of agriculture, since «the revenue of a trading and manufacturing country»

---

8   Although Darwin's thought cannot be reduced to a biological prefiguration of the so-called social Darwinism, it is however significant that, in the sixth edition of his main work, he claims that «the expression often used by Mr. Herbert Spencer of the Survival of the Fittest (...) is more accurate, and (...) sometimes equally convenient» in respect to the expression «Natural Selection». Charles Darwin, *On the Origin of Species by Means of Natural Selection, or the Preservation of Favoured Races in the Struggle for Life* (London: John Murray, 1872), p. 49.

9   Adam Smith, *An Inquiry into the Nature and Causes of the Wealth of Nations*, ed. by Edwin Cannan (London: Methuen & Co., 1904), vol. II, pp. 183-4.

cannot fail to be «much greater than that of one without trade or manufactures». Therefore, a nation capable of developing the urban economy first of all can also avoid worrying about the fate of its agriculture; in short, the city can also take no interest in the goods that the surrounding natural environment provides them through the main activity that takes place there, since it can easily obtain them elsewhere.

> The inhabitants of a town, though they frequently possess no lands of their own, yet draw to themselves by their industry such a quantity of the rude produce of the lands of other people as supplies them, not only with the materials of their work, but with the fund of their subsistence. (...) A small quantity of manufactured produce purchases a great quantity of rude produce. A trading and manufacturing country, therefore, naturally purchases with a small part of its manufactured produce a great part of the rude produce of other countries.[10]

This view is indirectly explained with Smith's assurance in the free market's ability to spontaneously produce the well-being of each and every one. Although the author in his work shows to be aware of the importance that agricultural production has for a nation, he also believes that the ability of the latter to produce wealth through manufacturing can easily remedy its possible shortage of agricultural goods; this wealth can obtain in abundance the nutritional goods necessary for the life of the inhabitants of the nation from the countryside of other countries, rather than from one's own rural environment.

If the free market can spontaneously guarantee this result, it must therefore be observed that the "naturalness" of its functioning does not imply a privileged relationship with the "nature" of the environment surrounding the city, let alone an imperative attitude to its care. Foucault in this sense opportunely points out – as we saw in the first chapter – that it is not «the naturalness of processes of nature itself, as the nature of the world»; it is in fact «a naturalness specific to relations between men, to what happens

---

10   Smith, *An Inquiry into the Nature and Causes of the Wealth of Nations*, p. 175.

spontaneously when they cohabit, come together, exchange, work, and produce».[11] Indeed, the same unlimited action of men on the natural environment is part of the naturalness of the economic processes which must be left free to unfold and spontaneously produce their positive effects.

Returning to the Foucaultian reasoning on the forms of spatiality of power, it can certainly be recognized that the biopolitical attention to the life of the population as a collective body and economic resource of society is placed in the context of an environmental spatiality different from those of the territory of sovereignty and disciplinary architectures; but, if it is true that it is above all the city that is reconfigured in these terms, this means that, «with this technical problem posed by the town (...) we see the sudden emergence of the problem of the "naturalness" of the human species within an artificial milieu».[12]

The external character of the natural environment with respect to the life of society will remain confirmed even when trust in the beneficial functioning of the free market, already in the 19th century, will be questioned and compensated with the launch of social security policies. As we saw in the fourth chapter, these policies will mainly deal with the suffering and individual damage caused to workers by the activities in which they are involved, in terms of insurance and social security. No effective possibility will open instead for the management of environmental hazards deriving from the abuse of natural resources. These will not be perceived either as essential risks or as indemnifiable risks according to an insurance calculation. Their outsourcing will also be confirmed by Marxism with the identification of the main source of wealth and the primary object of exploitation with the labour. Such a vision will evidently hinder the possibility of recognizing the consequences of the extensive and intensive exploitation of the environment, which will therefore continue to take place even in situations where capitalism will give way to socialism or communism.

All this happens despite a very relevant development of the natural sciences in an ecological sense, which has taken place

---

11   *Security, Territory, Population*, p. 349.
12   *Security, Territory, Population*, p. 21-2.

since the beginning of the 19th century. From the botanical geography studies by Alexander von Humboldt to the ecosystem ecology – developed by Arthur Tansley and Raymond Lindeman between the 1930s and 1940s – through the scientific elaboration of concepts such as *habitat, biotope, biosphere, biocenosis* and *biotic community*, the specification of the relationships between physical contexts and living species remains a fundamental standpoint of these sciences.[13] At least apparently, therefore, for a very long historical phase we are faced with a sort of failed-meeting on a practical level between government strategies, on the one hand, and scientific ecology, on the other. This, however, does not exclude that ecological knowledge has established a relationship of assonance with political visions since the government of people has stably assumed its economic and biopolitical characteristics with the attention, on the one hand, to productive mechanisms of society and, on the other, to the reproductive processes of the population. Indeed, perhaps it can be said that if the bio-economic government of society has not been particularly influenced by ecological knowledge for a long time, the latter have instead been sensitive from the outset to the need to economically and biopolitically govern the society-environment relationship.

Significant traces of this kind of sensitivity can be found in fundamental expressions of the maturation of scientific ecology, such as botanical geography, evolutionary theory, population ecology and ecosystem ecology.

1.2 *Bio-ecological knowledge*

1. In the first decades of the 19th century, *botanical geography* – through the works of authors such as Alexander von Humboldt, Augustin and Alphonse de Candolle – creates the essential conditions of ecological knowledge going beyond the typical formats of the natural sciences of the 18th

---

13   See Jean-Marc Drouin, *L'écologie et son histoire* (Paris: Flammarion, 1993), chapts 2-3, and Jean-Paul Deléage, *Histoire de l'écologie* (Paris: La Découverte, 1991), chapts 2-6.

century, based especially on the classification of living beings. This geography in fact turns its attention to the relationships between plant species and their geo-climatic contexts, directing its research in an *ante litteram* eco-systemic sense. What is evident, on the other hand, is that the investigations of botanical geography are developing close to the pressing need to improve agricultural production at a time when, on the one hand, the expansion of the market economy strengthens the idea that the progress of society passes through the increase of production, and on the other, population growth increases the demand for land products. This research, in fact, does not only concern spontaneous plants, but also those that are cultivated or can be cultivated. Furthermore, since this research is carried out largely in the colonies, it entail a flourishing of both scientific and productive experiments with the introduction of exotic plants in Europe, many of which will prove suitable for cultivation on this continent.[14]

The proto-ecological knowledge of botanical geography, therefore, is not only affirmed as a more adequate approach than the previous ones to the complexity of the relationships between plant life and the surrounding world, but also responds to precise economic urgencies (improvement of agricultural production) and biopolitical urgencies (to increase availability of food for the population). In this sense, what Achille Bruni (Professor of Agriculture of the Royal University of Naples) writes in 1857 is interesting. After paying tribute to Alphonse de Candolle, he regrets that research on botanical geography in the Neapolitan Kingdom is still poorly practiced and signals the absolute «need for strict studies» in this field, «without which – he says – not only can we not understand the real causes for which certain given crops do not move forward in agriculture; but we won't

---

14   Alexander von Humboldt, *Essay on the Geography of Plants*, trans. by Silvie Romenowski (Chicago: University of Chicago Press, 2009); Augustin-Pyramus de Candolle, *Essai élémentaire de géographie botanique*, Extrait du 18° volume du *Dictionnaire des sciences naturelles* (Strasbourgh: Levrault, 1820); Alphonse de Candolle, *Géographie botanique raisonnée* (Paris: Librairie Masson, 1855).

even be able to find the true path to the positive progress of agricultural science».[15]

2. With *biological evolutionism*, the conditions are created for the first explicit definition of ecology as a science, developed – as is known – by the Darwinian zoologist Ernest Haeckel.

> By ecology – writes the author – we mean the science of the relationships between the organism and the outside world, in which we can more widely recognize the factors of the struggle for existence. These are partly organic in nature and partly inorganic in nature; they are also (…) of the utmost importance for the form to which organisms are forced by themselves to adapt. Among the conditions of existence of an inorganic nature to which each organism must submit, firstly come the physical and chemical characteristics of the place it inhabits, the climate (light, temperature, humidity and electricity conditions of the atmosphere), the chemical nature of the means of nourishment, the quality of water and soil etc.
>
> As conditions of existence of an organic nature we consider the reciprocal relationships that the organism maintains with all the other organisms with which it enters into a relationship and that contribute to its well-being or damage it. Each organism has among others friendly and enemy organisms, some of which favour its existence and others affect it.
>
> Organisms that serve others as organic means of nutrition or that live at their expense as parasites, also fall into the category of organic conditions of existence.[16]

This definition of ecology is made possible because evolutionary theory assumes the relationship between the *demographic variations* of species and their *material conditions of survival* as an essential object of study. According to Darwin, in fact, the numerical consistency of the species tends to grow according to a geometrical ratio, if it does not find limits in the environmental conditions among which the more or less wide availability of means of nourishment must firstly be considered, that is above

---

15   Achille Bruni, *Descrizione botanica delle campagne di Barletta* (Naples: Stamperia e Cartiere del Fibreno, 1857), pp. 8-9.

16   Ernest Haeckel, *Generelle Morphologie der Organismen* (Berlin: Reimer, 1866), vol. II, p. 286.

all other edible living beings. Next to this element, the greater or lesser "compatibility" of the physical and climatic characteristics of the environment with the biological structure of organisms must be considered. This set of conditions will never be so favourable to the individual species as to guarantee an unlimited demographic growth, since growing too much they – among other things – can no longer find enough to feed on and therefore also have difficulty reproducing. Therefore – according to Darwin – organisms and species in order to survive, to grow, to reproduce or to avoid extinction, participate in the "struggle for existence" on which the mechanism of "natural selection" is based. In short, the survival, consistency or quantitative growth of the species depend on their ability and on that of the organisms that compose them to win this fight and to adapt to the more or less favourable environmental conditions in which they live.[17]

In this regard, it is very important that Darwin acknowledges in his *Autobiography* that he was inspired by the *Essay on the Principle of Population* by Thomas R. Malthus for the elaboration of his theory. In that political economy classic – as we saw in the fourth chapter – the analysis of economic problems is clearly intertwined with the examination of a question that, so to speak, could not be more biopolitical. As Malthus claims, the human population tends to increase according to a geometrical ratio unlike the production of means of subsistence, which instead grows according to an arithmetical ratio. Due to the disproportion that derives from this, the population periodically exposes itself to hunger, diseases and the danger of a ruinous decrease. It is easy to understand why, while reading Malthus' work, an idea such as that of "struggle for existence" could have flashed in Darwin's mind.

> A struggle for existence inevitably follows from the high rate at which all organic beings tend to increase. Every being, which during its natural lifetime produces several eggs or seeds, must suffer destruction during some period of its life, and during some season or occasional year, otherwise, on the principle of geometrical increase, its numbers would quickly become so inordinately great that no country could support the product. Hence, as more individuals are

---

17   See Darwin, *On the Origin of Species*, chapts 3-4.

produced than can possibly survive, there must in every case be a struggle for existence, either one individual with another of the same species, or with the individuals of distinct species, or with the physical conditions of life. It is the doctrine of Malthus applied with manifold force to the whole animal and vegetable kingdoms; for in this case there can be no artificial increase of food, and no prudential restraint from marriage. Although some species may be now increasing, more or less rapidly, in numbers, all cannot do so, for the world would not hold them.[18]

It is important, on the other hand, to remember precisely the general question that – from his point of view – Malthus had asked himself. It can be summarized in the following terms: "how can the development of subsistence goods production be prevented from causing population growth that exceeds the limits of this development?" In fact, in this way the author of the *Essay* became an interpreter of concerns that – in a very different way – will be re-proposed by the ecological culture of the 20th century, which in essence will ask itself: "how can we avoid that the mutual strengthening relationship between productive development and population growth compromises the natural resources and environmental conditions on which both depend?" This is the big question that the ecological debate stirs above all since the early 1970s, when the famous Report for the Club of Rome, *The Limits to Growth*, was published worldwide.[19] What should be noted in this regard is precisely that in Malthus' discourse the same intertwining, which is found in ecological discourse, was already present – albeit differently set – between the economic problem of production development and the biopolitical question of population growth.[20] But in Malthus's reasoning the ecological question of the limits of natural resources and environmental degradation does not arise at all; instead, in the ecological discourse – already in

---

18   *On the Origin of Species*, pp. 63-4.
19   Donella H. Meadows and others, *The Limits to Growth. A Report for the Club of Rome's Project on the Predicament of Mankind* (New York: Universe Books, 1972).
20   Giorgio Nebbia, *Introduzione* a Thomas R. Malthus, *Primo saggio sulla popolazione* (1798), trans. by Gabriella Menozzi Nebbia (Bari: Laterza, 1976) pp. XV-XVI.

its Darwinian version – the bio-economic scheme of Malthusian reasoning is presented as fundamental.

3. Well before the seventies of the last century, the attention to the relationship between demographic variations and material conditions of survival was taken up and strengthened by the *population ecology*, which developed mainly starting from the 1920s. This deals with both the relationships between the demographic cycles of the various species and their environments and the economic implications of these relationships. This is what is found, for example, in studies on the populations of parasitic insects that invade the countryside and damage the crops, or in the research on the alterations that the increases and decreases in fishing activities cause in the relationships between populations of fish-prey and predatory fish influencing the fate of their economic sector. In short, the population ecology does not simply tend to avert the alteration of the balance between living beings and the environment; it also aims to rationalize the relationship between the economy and the consistency of the various species, paying both economic and biopolitical attention to their reproductive cycles. In these kinds of studies, the mathematical approach tending to predict the quantitative variations of species in relation to their environmental conditions is decidedly established. In this way, a "law" of population growth (defined as *logistic curve*), already formulated in the 19th century by a Belgian mathematician (Pierre François Verhulst), also influenced by Malthus, was re-proposed and updated. According to this "law", generally the consistency of a population-species, after a certain period of growth, first moderate and then accentuated, reaches its limit and remains stable on a certain level. Its main supporter – the American biologist Raymond Pearl – in the 1920s strives hard to demonstrate that it can be applied to all species, including the human one.[21]

---

21   Raymond Pearl, *The Biology of Population Growth* (New York: Alfred A. Knopf, 1930). See also Sharon E. Kingsland, *Modeling Nature. Episodes in the History of Population Ecology* (Chicago: The Chicago University Press, 1995), pp. 56-97.

Despite the disputes it has been subject to, this "law" has been an important reference point for much of the scientific ecology. In fact, it has been the touchstone of the scenarios designed by the authors of *The Limits to Growth* even in their most recent research. In these scenarios, however, it now presents itself as a law that the human population should, but is no longer able to respect. Humanity can but try to reconcile with it only by implementing systematic policies of demographic limitation or regulation, which must be associated with strategies for reducing the consumption of environmental resources.[22]

4. With the birth of the *ecosystem ecology*, the need to go beyond the attention that previous theories dedicate to organisms is imposed. As Arthur Tansley stated, «[t]hough the organisms may claim our primary interest, when we are trying to think fundamentally we cannot separate them from their special environment, with which they form one physical system».[23] In the developments of this ecology, the bio-evolutionary approach will be reconnected and, in a certain sense, subordinated to the physical and chemical sciences among which thermodynamics will assume a fundamental role.[24] The relations between the biological sphere and the physical world will be described above all in terms of flows, circulation and transformation of energy and matter. The biosphere will be seen as a gigantic mechanism of accumulation, consumption and conversion of energy, which produces and reproduces living matter by drawing from the environment both energy and the organic and inorganic matter necessary for this purpose. The importance that energy flows assume in this context clearly emerges if we consider

22   See Sabine Höhler, 'The Law of Growth: How Ecology Accounted for World Population in the 20th Century', *Distinktion: Scandinavian Journal of Social Theory*, 14 (2007), 45-64 (pp. 54-6).

23   Arthur G. Tansley, 'The Use and Abuse of Vegetational Concepts and Terms', *Ecology*, 16, 3 (1935), 284-307 (p. 299).

24   See Raymond Lindeman, 'TheTrophic-Dynamic Aspect of Ecology', *Ecology*, 23, 4 (1942), 399-417; Eugene P. Odum, *Fundamentals of ecology* (Philadelphia: Saunders, 1959); Eugene P. Odum, *Ecology* (New York: Holt, Rinehart and Winston, 1975, 2nd edn); Howard T. Odum, *Environment, Power and Society* (New York: Wiley & Sons,1971).

the main process by which – according to this ecology – the life of an ecosystem takes place; it is a process, generally indicated with expressions such as *food-cycle* and *food chain*, which is substantially expressed in these terms: plants capture solar energy and, by combining it with inorganic materials (minerals) through photosynthesis, transform it into organic matter; in this form they transfer energy to herbivores which in turn reproduce it as organic matter and transfer it to carnivores, and so on. During this cycle, energy dispersions occur, and residues are released which, especially through the decomposition caused by microorganisms, can be included among the mineral substances making themselves available for a new trophic cycle.

Among those who have given greater impetus to this form of knowledge, three American scholars must certainly be remembered: Raymond Lindeman, who is considered to be its true founder, and the brothers Eugene P. and Howard T. Odum, that have led to extreme consequences the energy declination of the relationship between life and the environment, laying the foundations to place the relationships between societies and their bio-physical contexts in similar terms. For Eugene P. Odum, in particular, ecological science must study the conditions in which energy, chemical and biological processes manage to interact and combine so that the ecosystems in which they take place guarantee a constant production of organic matter. According to him, the evolution of ecosystems tends to become «mature in the developmental sense, that is, in steady-state timewise».[25] And it is through their tendency to maintain this state of balance that ecosystems function best. Therefore, in studying them, one must first check whether within them «[o]ne kind of ecological "steady-state" exists», that is «if the annual production of organic matters equals total consumption (...) and if exports and imports of organic matter are either non-existent or equal».[26] In this case it will be necessary to make sure that they are not «subject to severe stress or other disrupting forcing functions».[27]

---

25   E. P. Odum, *Ecology*, p. 54.
26   E. P. Odum, *Ecology*, p. 69.
27   E. P. Odum, *Ecology*, p. 54.

The fact that – according to this ecology – ecosystems have an ability to achieve and maintain a state of equilibrium by making good use of their resources, makes clear the negative influence that humanity exercises by behaving «as a separate unit that strives only to exploit nature for his immediate needs or temporary gain».[28] Indeed, man is generally not aware of the fact that

> [t]he strategy of nature is to diversify, but not to the extent of reducing energetic efficiency. Since this is, to some extent at least, contrary to the current strategy of man, we need to inquire into possible reasons for this conflict between man and nature, and to ask to what extent it is necessary or desirable.[29]

Even in the case of ecosystem ecology, therefore, it can be said that ecological knowledge tends to frame the environmental question in both economic and biopolitical terms: its purpose is to ensure that in an ecosystem the efficiency criteria and the balance according to which biological reproduction must take place are not "violated". On the other hand, in this context the economic vision ends up prevailing over the biopolitical one. As Paul Rutherford states, this knowledge defines a «bio-economic paradigm» of ecology and an «energy economic model of the environment». In other words, it tends to propose itself as a form of economic rationality superior to that in force in the current economy of human society or as «the rationale behind a *new form of political economy*».[30] It is, in fact, in terms of a *bionomics* – of an economy of life – that, according to Odum, the functioning of ecosystems can be analysed, starting from those of which human societies are part. The efficiency with which these ecosystems guarantee the quantitative and qualitative reproduction of life can be assessed in terms of both productivity and monetary value.

---

28   E. P. Odum, *Ecology*, p. 142.
29   E. P. Odum, *Ecology*, p. 54.
30   Paul Rutherford, 'The Entry of Life into History', in *Discourses of the Environment*, ed. by Éric Darier (Oxford: Blackwell, 1999), pp. 53 and 54.

Since "productivity" is a measure of a natural system's capacity to do all kinds of useful work, such as waste treatment, CO_2 absorption, O_2 production, seafood production, wildlife habitat maintenance, protecting cities from storms, transportation, and so on, then converting work energy to money is a convenient way of making a bionomic evaluation.[31]

Ultimately, from this point of view, the application of the ecosystem approach is an indispensable condition for reconciling the human economy with the functioning of nature on which it depends. Therefore, it is no coincidence that this approach will become an essential reference for *ecological economics* and "sustainable development" strategies. Starting from the last decades of the 20th century, these strategies will try to answer questions such as the following: "how many energy and material resources are consumed by the economy and how many of them is the ecosystem capable of regenerating in a given period? How many and what residues of economic activities can the environment afford to welcome and reintegrate without damage in the cycle of its ecosystem reproduction? How many humans can the environment sustain without compromising the survival of the ecosystems they depend on?" On the basis of these questions, "sustainable development" will occur if the activities and the numerical consistency of men do not cause consumption of resources and emissions of polluting substances which exceed the capacity of the environment to regenerate the former and absorb the latter without irreversible damage. The environmental issue will thus tend to become a problem of rational reorganization of the economy and of "conservation" of nature as a "natural capital".[32]

---

31 Odum, *Ecology*, p. 217.
32 See: Robert Costanza (ed. by), *Ecological Economics. The Science and Management of Sustainability* (New York: Columbia University Press, 1991); Herman Daly, *Steady-State Economics* (Washington, DC: Island Press, 1991); Enzo Tiezzi and Nadia Marchettini, *Che cos'è lo sviluppo sostenibile? Le basi scientifiche della sostenibilità e i guasti del pensiero unico* (Rome: Donzelli1999); See also Nicola Russo, *Filosofia ed ecologia* (Naples: Guida, 2000), pp. 141-97.

1.3 *The environment, life and economic government*

On the basis of a recognition like the one just made, it is natural to ask why, despite the assonances and kinships that link scientific ecology to the economic and biopolitical government of society, the former has never managed to exert an effective and lasting influence on the second.

For a possible answer to a similar question, it is necessary first of all to place it within the framework of some noteworthy "historical circumstances" that have contributed to defining the modern forms of governmentality. They can be summarized in the following terms: 1) between the biopolitical and the economic direction, it was the second to assume the main role in defining the dominant governmentality in the last two centuries; 2) the "political regime" historically prevalent in this area has been liberalism which in recent times – as we know – has strengthened and radicalized in the form of neoliberalism; 3) in this context, security policies have played a major role, around which biopolitical attention to life and the safeguarding of the functioning of the economy tend to combine with each other; 4) finally, the transformations in a radically economic sense of the individual and social *ethos* have had a fundamental importance, transformations determined above all by the exercise of liberal and neoliberal governmentality.

With regard to the first circumstance, it is not simply a question of pointing out that ours is a society dominated by capitalism. Above all, it is a question of considering that the birth of modern governmentality has responded first of all to the need of most states to treat their social body as an economic entity, a requirement from which that of giving biopolitical attention to health and to the physical well-being of the population and individuals is also derived. Therefore, it can be said that the essential nucleus of modern government rationality is the political economy and that the life sciences constitute a sort of indispensable complement. In this sense, one can read what Foucault says when he claims that modern governmentality «has the population as its target, political economy as its major form of knowledge, and apparatuses of security as its essential technical instruments».[33] In the same way, we must also interpret what he claims when he says that

> the analysis of biopolitics can only get under way when we have understood the general regime of this governmental reason (...), this general regime that we can call the question of truth, of economic truth in the first place, within governmental reason (...). Consequently (...) it is only when we understand what is at stake in this regime of liberalism (...) will we be able to grasp what biopolitics is.[34]

These clarifications contain elements that also refer to the second "historical circumstance" which we have mentioned, or to the hegemonic role that liberalism has managed to gain in the context of the governmentality of the last centuries. In fact, it is the imposition of the liberal political economy that establishes the supremacy of the economic approach to the government of the modern state, a supremacy that was already prepared by Mercantilism at the time of absolutism. But, if it is true that in this way the predominantly economic character of modern governmentality is fully affirmed, it is equally true that its aims can be effectively pursued only if it is declined in terms not only economic, but also biopolitical: if the population is to be treated as an essential part and as a source of state wealth, for this same reason it must also be taken as a living species, that is to say, by facing the set of biological problems that condition its potential and economic capacity. This clearly emerges if we consider the third "historical circumstance" that we have indicated, or the importance that the "apparatuses of security" have assumed as instruments of government.

From this point of view, the most direct link between economics and biopolitics has historically been created around the problem of *scarcity*, which affects both the productive activities and the reproductive processes of the population.[35] As Malthus' discourse shows, a fundamental question that the political economy poses in this regard is that of the risk of a shortage of subsistence

---

33   *Security, Territory, Population*, p. 108.
34   *The Birth of Biopolitics*, pp. 21-2.
35   *Security, Territory, Population*, pp. 29-49.

goods; therefore it is necessary to avoid the possibility that the population grows beyond the production levels of said goods.[36] In this context, as we have already seen, the question of the limits of natural resources does not find space to be addressed in terms of the ecological sustainability of economic activities. For the political economy, the problem of scarcity arises as a need to match the development of production to the growth of the needs of the population and vice versa. The fundamental assumption of this vision is that the main means for satisfying the needs of a nation is nothing other than the development of production, that is, the increase in labour productivity and the exploitation of natural resources in the best technically possible way. The problems arising from the fact that the land proves less and less productive as the crops are extended to less fertile parts of the ground, seem to depend on the short-sightedness of those who have too many children and on the uncertainty of human destinies, rather than on the abuse to which humanity submits the earth itself. What matters, in fact, is to produce more and more and, at the same time, to be proactive towards the future. For these reasons, therefore, it is difficult to believe that the general question of scarcity is a field of possible encounter between political economy and ecological sensitivity.

On the other hand, it cannot be ignored that modern economic rationality would not have established itself so widely if it had simply been based on the need to avoid the danger of scarcity. It also managed to establish itself because, becoming a governmental rationality, it was able to influence the *ethos* of the modern individual, thus creating the "fourth historical circumstance" we mentioned. Of course, also from this point of view – as we saw in the fourth chapter – the dramatization of the risks of scarcity and poverty has played a significant role, especially in promoting the ethics of savings and prudence among the poorest classes. Historically, modern economic rationality however has not only encouraged prudential attitudes dictated by fear of the future; it has also or above all promoted the aspirations of the individual to self-realization by assuming the risks. In this sense, two processes

36   Malthus, *An Essay on the Principle of Population*, pp. 337-9.

have undoubtedly had great importance: the secularization of Protestant morality with the affirmation of the human figure of man who seeks the sign of predestination in his ability to produce and reinvest wealth; and the emergence of utilitarian ethics that evaluates actions based on the interests they realize and the amount of pleasure they produce.[37] Thus the same (domesticated) promotion of desire as a creative and productive impulse ended up playing an essential role in favouring the economic declination of the individual and social approach not only to work, but also to relationships, consumption, leisure, communication and life itself.[38] All this, of course, cannot fail to have had serious ecological consequences.

We will return to the modern forms of *ethos* and their ecological implications. For the moment, we shall dwell again on the crucial question of security, considering both its particular biopolitical importance and the topicality that it reveals with the succession of ecological emergencies.

1.4 *Ecology, security and society of uncertainty*

There was an historical moment in which the conversion of the dominant governmentality in an ecological sense seemed to become an unavoidable urgency: the early seventies of the 20th century when – as we have seen – analyses such as that of the Report for the Club of Rome presented the relationship between production development and population growth as a planetary ecological degradation factor that imposed to run for cover. Since those years, the environmental issue has been increasingly portrayed as a global problem by definition, as a danger that the planet's ecosystem limits will be

---

37   See: Max Weber, *The Protestant Ethic and the Spirit of Capitalism*, trans. by Talcott Parsons (Abingdon, UK: Routledge, 2001); Jeremy Bentham, *Deontology together with a Table of the Springs of Action and Article on Utilitarianism*, ed. by Amnon Goldworth (Oxford: Clarendon Press, 1983).

38   See: Jean Baudrillard, *The Consumer Society: Myths and Structures*, trans. by C. T. (London: Sage Publications, 1998); Laura Bazzicalupo, *Il governo delle vite. Biopolitica ed economia*, (Rome-Bari: Laterza, 2006), pp. 57-95.

overcome, producing catastrophic consequences. Since then, global alarms and strategies regarding the *carrying capacity* of the earth have gradually multiplied through references to the "ozone hole", to the reduction of biodiversity, to deforestation, to desertification, to climate change and so on; these are, in fact, "global changes" analysed and generally addressed in terms of increases or reductions in ecological risk factors of global importance.[39] Since the seventies, a series of Summits, World Conferences and International Protocols on the various aspects of the ecological crisis were triggered: from the Conference on the Human Environment in Stockholm (1972) to the most recent on climate, via the Rio de Janeiro Earth Summit (1992) and the Kyoto Protocol (1997), a real globalization of environmental policy strategies has unfolded.

In short, in a certain sense it can be argued that the "political-ecological globalization" started well before the "economic globalization" that developed mainly since the eighties. In reality, however, this chronological advantage was quickly cancelled, turning into a sort of desperate pursuit of the second globalization by the first. In fact, when in the eighties the prospect of "sustainable development" was officially placed at the centre of global ecological government strategies,[40] it was quite clear that the *deregulation* of the market and neoliberalism were now taking over the planetary dimension that the global "solution" strategies of the ecological crisis had given the impression of being able to dominate or condition. All of this depended largely on the radical changes in the prevailing forms of governmentality that had occurred since the seventies. In that context, profound changes had taken place regarding the issue of security, which would have influenced the perception and political treatment of the ecological crisis.

As we know, a progressive reorganization of social security policies had started in that period, which – as Robert Castel claims – contributed to creating a general climate of insecurity concerning not only the spheres of individual existence, but also

---

39 Daniele Guastini, 'Cambiamenti globali', in Roberto Della Seta and Daniele Guastini, *Dizionario del pensiero ecologico. Da Pitagora ai No-Global*, (Rome: Carocci, 2007), pp. 90-2.

40 World Commission on Environment and Development, *Our Common Future*, (Oxford: Oxford University Press, 1987).

civil coexistence, translating into forms of intolerance, racism, demonization of marginal social figures and in claims of "return to law and order". More generally, it can be said that since then the problem of insecurity has expanded and accentuated, for objective and subjective reasons, to the point that it has been possible to speak of a *world risk society*.[41]

As we saw, Ulrich Beck describes this situation as the context in which the development of society now produces incalculable global risks:«[i]t is the accumulation of risks – ecological, terrorist, military, financial, biomedical and informational – that has an overwhelming presence in our world today».[42] The risks of our time – according to the author – do not correspond to those which "early modernity" governed through insurance calculations and prevention. Current risks are characterized by three features:

> (1) *De-localisation*: Their causes and consequences are not limited to one geographical location or space, but are in principle omnipresent.
> (2) *Incalculableness*: Their consequences are in principle incalculable; at bottom it is a matter of "hypothetical" or "virtual" risks which, not least, are based on scientifically induced not-knowing and normative dissent.
> (3) *Non-compensability*: (...). If the climate has changed irreversibly, if progress in human genetics makes irreversible interventions in human existence possible, if terrorist groups already have weapons of mass destruction available to them, then it is too late. Given the new quality of threats to humanity, the logic of compensation breaks down.[43]

The threats that arise from this type of risk – according to Beck – make us all members of a world risk society. This society is largely willing to politically take charge of its new condition. Globalization, in fact, does not simply imply the triumph of the market economy and the crisis of politics; it also favours the birth of a new cosmopolitanism that manifests itself through the forms of

---

41   Castel, *L'insécurité sociale*, pp. 39-62; see Ulrich Beck, *World Risk Society* and *World at Risk*.
42   Ulrich Beck, 'World Risk Society and Manufactured Uncertainties', *Iris*, 1, 2 (2009), 291-9 (p. 291).
43   Beck, 'World Risk Society and Manufactured Uncertainties', p. 294.

politicization practiced by the new transnational actors, in particular by non-governmental organizations and by the movements that give rise to experiences of global citizenship based on the commitment to deal with planetary risks and their causes.[44]

Undoubtedly, both the consideration of the ecological crisis as an essential context of the world risk society, as well as the possibility that promising forms of supranational ecological politics may emerge in this scenario, cannot be overlooked. However, in this analytical framework, trends linked to the political predominance that neoliberalism has achieved not only on social problems but also on the governance of global ecological risks remain substantially unexplored. In this regard, just think of the strategy adopted against global warming and climate change with the signing of the Kyoto Protocol by setting percentages of reduction of "greenhouse gas" emissions to be implemented within certain deadlines. As is well known, *Emission Trading* was promoted on this basis, that is, the trading of emission allowances between different countries and economic subjects. In particular, «if a company reduces its emissions, it can keep the spare allowances to cover its future needs or else sell them to another company that is short of allowances»; moreover, the richest countries can obtain "on their own" or share *international credits* (corresponding to certain quantities of CO_2 removed or reduced from the atmosphere), in the event that they carry out economic development projects with effects of reducing emissions in the less wealthy countries (*Clean Development Mechanism*); or if they carry out emission reduction interventions in countries in economic conditions similar to their own (*Joint Implementation*). Ultimately, what one is trying to do in these ways is to make the active policies for reducing emissions and the defaults of the countries that find it more convenient not to reduce them, functional to the further expansion of the global market economy.[45]

---

44   See Ulrich Beck: 'World Risk Society as Cosmopolitan Society? Ecological Questions in a Framework of Manufactured Uncertainties', *Theory, Culture & Society*, 13, 4 (1996), 1-32; 'The Cosmopolitan Society and its Enemies', *Theory Culture & Society*, 19, 1-2 (2002), 17-44; 'Critical Theory of World Risk Society: A Cosmopolitan Vision', *Constellations*, 16, 1 (2009), 3-22.

45   'EU Emissions Trading System (EU ETS)', https://ec.europa.eu/clima/

That the economism of neoliberal governmentality thus ends up becoming a sort of insurmountable pattern also for the great ecological-political strategies is demonstrated by the fact that this system of marketing the reductions of "greenhouse gases" is still considered valid, despite its failures and despite the global amount of emissions has not decreased since the Kyoto Protocol was signed (1997).[46]

However, other forms of neoliberal governmentality of environmental risks increasingly coexist with those of this type: for example, the one that can be traced back to the *polluter pays principle* or the one that can be linked to the so-called *disaster capitalism*. In both cases, it is accepted that our society inevitably produces environmental damage and dangers. In the first, neoliberalism only leads to a sort of economic accounting of pollution problems which, in reality, in terms of size and complexity, it is increasingly difficult to quantify in monetary terms and increasingly difficult to attribute to individual offenders only;[47] in the second, instead, the traumas and social alarms that derive from environmental disasters – such as that of Hurricane Katrina – can become the condition for drastically simplifying, in a possibly authoritarian sense, the role of the state, reducing it to merely emergency tasks.[48]

What, however, a picture like this should lead us to think is that the globalization of risks and their acute social perception are not

---

policies/ets_en (accessed March 10, 2020). See also: Nicholas Stern, *A Blueprint for a Safer Planet: How to Manage Climate Change and Create a New Era of Progress and Prosperity* (London: The Bodley Head, 2009), chap. 6; see also Razmid Keucheyan, *Nature is a Battlefield*, trans. by David Broder (Cambridge, UK: Polity Press, 2016), pp. 55-103.

46 For a very critical analysis of the prevailing approaches to the issue of climate change, see Lisa Heinzerling, 'Climate Change, Human Health, and the Post-Cautionary Principle', *O'Neill Institute Papers*, 4(2007): http://scholarship.law.georgetown.edu/ois_papers/4 (accessed March 10, 2020). See also Kevin Grove, 'Biopolitics and Adaptation: Governing Socio-Ecological Contingency Through Climate Change and Disaster Studies', *Geography Compass*, 8, 3 (2014), 198–210.

47 Daniele Ungaro, *Democrazia ecologica. L'ambiente e la crisi delle istituzioni liberali*, (Rome-Bari: Laterza, 2004), pp. 33-6.

48 See: Naomi Klein, *The Shock Doctrine: The Rise of Disaster Capitalism* (New York: Metropolitan Books, 2007); Cooper. *Life as Surplus*, pp. 94-5.

a guarantee that it is precisely the ecological dangers that assume an indisputable urgency or greater importance than other dangers. In fact, it can be assumed that, in a world context dominated by neoliberalism, the logic of the interchangeability of investment sectors ends up extending from the sphere of economic and financial choices to that of political decisions concerning global risks: many of these can be tackled or neglected depending on the profits not only economic, but also political that they can produce, or on the basis of the degree of dramatization, more or less instrumental, of which they can be the object from time to time. If this hypothesis is reliable, the continuous variation of the focuses of attention of the world media system – now increasingly controlled by the so-called *neoliberal digital capitalism*[49] – certainly plays a very important role. So if contemporary society – as Beck himself claims – perceives ecological problems as well as economic crises, financial storms, terrorist attacks, etc. as global risks, it is quite likely that global alarms for climate change, deforestation or the reduction of biodiversity will be continually overcome – for example – by the global panic created by the disruption of the stock exchanges or by the risks of default by the states that are too indebted.

2. *Life against the environment?*

2.1 *A matter of flows*

The context outlined in the previous paragraphs suggests that in our era the growth of sensitivity to environmental problems clashes with a persistent dualism of the conception of the society-environment relationship, due to a sort of deep-rooted unwillingness of the dominant culture to take the ecological crisis seriously. This is an entirely reliable impression; however, it certainly does not imply the idea of an absolute indifference of the

---

49   Paula Chakravartty and Dan Schiller, 'Neoliberal Newspeak and Digital Capitalism in Crisis', *International Journal of Communication*, 4 (2010), 670-92.

main political, economic and techno-scientific systems towards environmental degradation and the fate of life in the multiplicity of its natural forms. In fact, attempts to tackle these problems are made, although they are often highly questionable and do not involve overall conversions of the current relationship between society and the environment.[50] In any case, we we can say that these attempts are carried out mainly through the articulation or the combination, in different measures and with different intensities, of two variations of environmental problems: one of a thermodynamic type, in which attention to flows of energy and material resources prevails; the other biological, in which greater attention is paid to the reproduction of life.

To recognize and appraise the two declinations it is appropriate to relate to the last historical form of ecological knowledge to which we referred, that is to the ecosystem ecology; in fact, in it, the two declinations are clearly delineated: more precisely, the difference and the interaction between the circulation of energy and matter, on the one hand, and biological production and reproduction, on the other, appear particularly clear. At the same time, however, in this theory – as we have seen – the trend of energy flows tends to assume a decisive importance: biological processes and ecosystems themselves work mainly by feeding on these flows, transforming them into organized structures of organic matter and contrasting the universal tendency towards entropy through its own self-regulation capacity. From this point of view, the ecological crisis presents itself as a potentially uncontrollable acceleration of entropic degradation, mainly caused by the human abuse of physical-energy resources, a trend which the ecosystems under normal conditions would instead be able to counteract by regulating themselves. Consequently, to remedy this acceleration it would be necessary to reconstitute the natural capacity of the systems to maintain its overall stability by regulating the quantity and speed of resource consumption.

---

50 A particularly significant example of rejection of environmentalism as a political approach necessary to face the ecological crisis is that of Ted Nordhaus and Michael Shellenberg, *Break Through: From the Death of Environmentalism to the Politics of Possibility* (New York: Houghton Mifflin Company, 2007).

This type of vision – as Nicola Russo observes – links the idea of the environment to a form of "mechanicism" whose cornerstones are thermodynamics and cybernetics; based on this, an ecosystem is normally capable of operating as a sort of boiler equipped with a thermostat which, in certain conditions, fails and therefore "allows" the dissipative abuse of the resources that feed it; it would therefore be necessary to repair it so that the abuse is eliminated or reduced to a minimum. Here, moreover, the environment appears to be structurally destined, from the outset, for "use": it is ultimately a matter of "using it" so that its further usability is not compromised. Therefore, from this point of view, "sustainable development" represents the obligatory solution of the ecological crisis, not so much because it is the remedy for this crisis, but because it would be able to regenerate the essential usability of the environment by adapting economic development to the alleged thermodynamic and cybernetic functioning of ecosystems.[51]

A recent attempt to revitalize the idea of sustainable development in terms very close to the classical vision of ecosystems is that of the *biomimicry theory*. The unsustainable levels of pollution and consumption of resources in this theory are indicated as causes of the inevitable crisis to which the industrial system is destined due to its indifference regarding the rules («laws, strategies, and principles») that nature proposes with its functioning. Among these rules, those deriving from nature's ability to make a measured use of energy, to recycle the residual matter of its processes, to activate cooperation relationships between its components, to develop the diversity of its forms, to reduce waste, and to respect the limits of the conditions in which its processes take place would be particularly important.[52] Production systems, therefore, should "imitate" nature by adapting to the cyclical character of its activities, overcoming development models based on the constant

---

51   See Russo, *Filosofia ed ecologia*, pp. 21-197.
52   Janine Benyus, *Biomimicry: Innovation Inspired by Nature* (New York: HarperCollins, 1997): «Nature runs on sunlight. Nature uses only the energy it needs. Nature fits form to function. Nature recycles everything. Nature rewards cooperation. Nature banks on diversity. Nature demands local expertise. Nature curbs excesses from within. Nature taps the power of limits» (p. 7).

extraction of resources, abandoning the very idea that production must result in unusable waste and rather adopting the perspective of circularity and renewability.[53]

Again, one cannot help but determine that, despite this type of foresight presents itself as an economic rationality, the dominant forms of economy and governmentality do not seem at all willing to adopt its perspective of conjugation between production and environmental protection. The dominant forms of economy and government often try to modify and adapt ecological strategies so as to exclude that environmental degradation may be a sufficient reason to question the economic development that causes it. Changes in this sense, in fact, are outlined precisely on the subject of the thermodynamic concepts of the environmental issue. An important example in this regard seems to be that of *geo-engineering* projects that tend to develop carbon dioxide removal techniques (systems for transferring greenhouse gases from the atmosphere to the subsoil, the bottom of the oceans or, possibly, beyond the atmosphere) or solar radiation management techniques by causing the Earth to absorb less solar radiation.[54] These projects, in fact, re-evaluate the importance of strategies that address climate change by trying to reduce the consumption of fossil energy; indirectly they also weaken the general idea that the progressive consumption of energy and non-energy resources inevitably leads to the collapse or irreversible degradation of the relationship between society and the environment: if – in

---

53 In addition to Benyus, *Biomimicry*, see also Henry Dicks, 'The Philosophy of Biomimicry', in *Philosophy and Technology*, 29, 3 (2016), 223-43. For a useful critical analysis of the biomimicry theory, see also Emanuele Leonardi, 'For a Critique of Neoliberal Green Economy: A Foucauldian Perspective on Ecological Crisis and Biomimicry', *Soft Power*, 5, 1 (2017), 169-85.

54 On this topic see John Shepherd and others, *Geoengineering the climate: science, governance and uncertainty* (London: The Royal Society, 2009). See also Matthias Honegger, Axel Michaelowa, Sonja Butzengeiger-Geyer, 'Climate Engineering Avoiding Pandora's Box through Research and Governance', *FNI Climate Policy Perspectives*, 5 (2012),1-8: https://www.fni.no/getfile.php/132218-1470209742/Filer/Publikasjoner/FNI-Climate-Policy-Perspectives-5.pdf (accessed February 24, 2020).

a relevant case such as that of climate change – we can try to "remove" the degrading and polluting effects of resource abuse, we can also accept the idea that such abuse can continue, as its negative consequences could be "swept away", even if they seem irreversible.

2.2 *Creative Dissipations*

Of course, the risk of oversimplifying the analysis of the scenarios we are considering must be avoided. However, at least from a general point of view, it should be borne in mind that for some decades scientific theories have been elaborated which render the idea that the ecological issue must be addressed by trying to limit the quantity and moderate the speed of resource consumption questionable. And in this regard it is very significant that one of the most important of these theories is based on the reassessing of the prevailing view of thermodynamic processes.

This is the *theory of dissipative structures*, according to which in nature there are open systems capable of contrasting the entropy foreseen by the second principle of thermodynamics by organizing themselves into complex structures that evolve creatively by drawing energy and matter from the external world; these structures are characterized by their ability to place themselves in low entropy situations, i.e. far from equilibrium. Which means that they find in instability the conditions not only to survive, but also to evolve in directions and forms that cannot be predetermined and that in any case subtract them from the trend towards degradation. In short, in their case, the consumption of resources leads to the growth of their complexity and, therefore, does not involve the progressive reduction of their opportunities for further evolution, but rather the increase and improvement of these opportunities. In this theory – the main author of which, as is well known, is Ilya Prigogine – the thermodynamic law according to which entropic processes constitute a universal and irreversible trend is valid only for closed systems that must essentially use limited reserves of resources. If we consider instead the behaviour of open systems towards an indefinite external world, the idea that the dissipation of resources leads to their disintegration must be radically questioned. What matters most here however is that biological life forms represent the most important expressions of such systems. The extreme importance that this theory attaches to thermodynamics, from this point of view, is functional to the classification of biological phenomena as essentially negentropic. Indeed, proponents of this theory identify a fundamental reason «to develop thermodynamics beyond the equilibrium range» in «the need for a physico-chemical basis of biological order». In other words, their theory not only tends «to explain the maintenance of low entropy situations and subtle metabolic regulation processes, but also (...) to provide a physico-chemical basis of evolution towards structures of increased complexity».[55] On these foundations even the planet earth can be conceived as an open dissipative system which, with its ability to keep away from the tendencies towards degradation, makes life possible.

> The earth as a whole is an open system subject to the constant flow of energy from the sun. This influx of energy provides the driving force for the maintenance of life and is ultimately responsible for maintaining an atmosphere out of thermodynamic equilibrium (...). Every living cell lives through the flow of matter and energy.[56]

A theory such as this allows us to conceive the evolutionary logic of life as substantially free from the limits and constraints that the material conditions of existence seem to impose on it. It outlines a perspective in which the forms of life succeed in establishing themselves because they are capable of reversing their dependence on material contexts and, in a certain sense, of freeing themselves from this dependence by transforming it into the possibility of evolution. This type of theory, on the other hand, superimposes on the predictability and temporal linearity of entropic processes an essential discontinuity of time and a substantial unpredictability

---

55 Ilya Prigogine and Rene Lefever, 'Theory of Dissipative Structures', in *Synergetics. Cooperative Phenomena in Multi-Component Systems*, ed. by Hermann Haken (Wiesbaden: Springer Fachmedien, 1973), p. 124.

56 Ilya Prigogine and Dilip Kondepuli, *Modern Thermodynamics: From Heat Engines to Dissipative Structures* (New York: John Wiley &Sons,1998), p. 409.

of the events and the ways in which life escapes trends towards decline and evolves creatively. The evolutionary processes in this context are not conceived as the results of a progressive succession of events but, rather, are considered on the basis of the idea of an «"order through fluctuations"» that implies «an unstable world where small causes can have large effects».[57]

From a point of view like this it may be possible to exclude that the ecological crisis is truly a problem or that it is a problem that can be solved only by renouncing the unlimited consumption of resources: if we understand the ecological crisis as a situation that endangers life, we can say that this danger is substantially averted from the beginning by the ability of life to transform the consumption of energy and matter into a decisive factor of evolution; in a sense, the ecological crisis would only be truly such if life's ability to evolve into increasingly complex and creative forms were compromised; and it is precisely to avoid this possibility that life consumes resources and can only continue to do so.

Unfortunately, however, it is impossible to ignore that in a scenario like this, life can also continue to assert itself, but only in its forms that do not become extinct and certainly to the detriment of others that end up becoming extinct. This may seem "normal", but only if an elementary question like this does not arise: is there at least a speed and size threshold beyond which the decline of this or the other form of life becomes an ecological problem – so to speak – not to be underestimated?

2.3 *Vital pollution*

If – as we have seen – the theory developed by Prigogine assumes thermodynamics as a starting point in order to consider biological processes as factors of profound reduction of the implications of the law of entropy, other visions oriented in a similar sense have

---

57   Ilya Prigogine and Isabelle Stengers, *Order Out Of Chaos: Man's New Dialogue with Nature* (Toronto, New York, London, Sidney: Bantam Books, 1984), p. 206. Ultimately, this kind of vision creates the possibility of conceiving the catastrophes as inevitable and substantially necessary events for life to move towards growing ability to assert itself. In this regard, see Cooper, *Life as surplus*, pp. 38-9.

been elaborated more directly emphasizing the prominence of biological life compared to its physical conditions. Among these visions, the theory known as *Gaia hypothesis* has a decidedly exemplary meaning with respect to the possibility of reappraising the importance of the ecological crisis. This theory is largely based on assumptions and concepts developed by Vladimir I. Vernadsky, such as that of the *biosphere*. According to this author, life does not just adapt to the geochemical conditions of the environment, but reproduces itself by constantly transforming solar radiation into new chemical compounds and accumulating quantities of energy that go beyond the limits of that already available on the planet. Therefore, the fate of life is not the entropic decline, but the growth of its complexity. In any case, all living beings that make up the biosphere continually alter the geological, chemical and atmospheric structures of the earth, since life is essentially autopoietic and expansive, rather than adaptive.[58]

This vision is taken up and radicalized by the supporters of Gaia hypothesis, who insist on the idea that evolutionary processes involve pollution as an «inevitable consequence of life at work».[59] These scholars also argue that the production and accumulation of waste products can be destructive for certain forms of life, but will never reach a size that blocks biological evolution in general. Environmental crises occur periodically in the history of life, but the latter responds to them with «evolutionary innovations» that allow it to overcome them and continue to evolve.[60] In the biosphere context, moreover, these authors attribute crucial importance to the microbial life in which – according to them – the most important evolutionary processes take place: in essence, microbes represent the most powerful forms of life, since their reproductive capacity is indifferent to the limits that condition the sexual reproduction of

---

58 Vladimir I. Vernadsky, *The Biosphere*, trans. by David B. Lagmuir, rev. by Mark A. S. McMenamin (New York: Copernicus-Springer Verlag, 1998), pp. 50-60.

59 James E. Lovelock, *Gaia: A New Look at Life on Earth* (Oxford: Oxford University Press, 1987), p. 27.

60 Lynn Margulis and Dorion Sagan, *Microcosmos: Four Billion Years of Evolution from Our Microbial Ancestors* (Berkeley: University of California Press, 1997), pp. 236-7.

microorganisms. Bacteria, in particular, are capable of reproducing and multiplying dramatically by duplication of single organisms, and their genome can diversify by "horizontal" transfer of genes from one organism or from one strain to another.[61]

Among the many implications of this importance that biosphere theorists attribute to microbial forms of life, there is one that gives a good idea of the influence that their vision can exert on technological, economic and biopolitical approaches to environmental problems: it is the ability of microorganisms to metabolize and transform matter. Ultimately, the theory of the Gaia hypothesis leads us to believe that in these forms life can even "feed" on toxic waste products and convert them into ecologically harmless matter. In this sense, in fact, the research and promotion of bioremediation technologies are oriented today, around which an important articulation of the bioeconomy is developing. In general, it can be said that the emphasis on the transformative capacities of microbial life represents a fundamental assumption of the tendency to face ecological problems avoiding to limit the development of industrial production and consumption. In this sense, in fact, not only bioremediation activities, but also productions such as biofuels and bioplastics, based on the use of microorganisms, can be interpreted.

Therefore, considering the theories of dissipative structures and the biosphere as a whole, it could be said that they constitute the basis of a "post-ecological knowledge" based on a sort of reassessment of the thermodynamic mechanism that seems to characterize the ecosystem ecology; this knowledge allows us to search in biological life the conceptual tools for framing environmental problems without questioning the indefinite

---

61   In this regard, see: Robert V. Miller and Martin J. Day, 'Horizontal Gene Transfer and the Real World', in Robert V. Miller and Martin J. Day (ed. by), *Microbial Evolution: Gene Establishment, Survival, and Exchange* (Washington, DC: American Society of Microbiology Press, 2004), pp. 173-7. See also Todd A. Gray and others, 'Distributive Conjugal Transfer in Mycobacteria Generates Progeny with Meiotic-Like Genome-Wide Mosaicism, Allowing Mapping of a Mating Identity Locus', *PLoS Biol*, 11, 7 (2013): e1001602: https://doi.org/10.1371/journal.pbio.1001602 (accessed February 12, 2020).

production development to which contemporary society is linked.[62] It is important to underline in this sense that the main reference of this knowledge is neither "nature" nor "environment" in the general sense of the terms, but "life", to the extent that it can be considered a productive and reproductive power capable of creating, on the one hand, complexity (and wealth for those who are able to benefit from it) and, on the other, real or presumed solutions of the individual problems of environmental degradation that may arise from time to time. It can be said that in a context such as this the ecological question is reassessed above all because here a "bio-centric" rather than "eco-centric" vision of the environmental question is outlined: the world as asset of material and immaterial elements and relationships that cannot be totalised is regarded from the beginning as the background of an undisputed supremacy of biological life. In this same sense, it can be said that here a sort of necessary alienation from the world is what allows life, in the most capable of evolving forms, to assert itself creatively by leveraging on the uncertainty and unpredictability of its fate.

It is therefore legitimate to think that, in the light of a post-ecological knowledge of this kind, the very dynamism of contemporary society can be considered a fundamental part of the overall dynamism of life and its ability to impose itself on the conditions of the world. More precisely, it is possible that in this context the prevalence in society of certain forms of the *ethos* that we encountered in the previous chapters finds support and a decisive justification: ways of being and acting that enhance the productive "vitality" of the individual, his entrepreneurial creativity, his willingness to deal with risks and transform them into opportunities or possibly monetizable sources of benefits.[63] In general, therefore, one can share the idea that the theories that underlie the post-ecological knowledge of which we speak, «may well have their origins in essentially revolutionary histories of

---

62 See Cooper, *Life as surplus*, pp. 34-45.
63 In this sense – in addition to the texts already cited by this author – see Luigi Pellizzoni, 'Governing through disorder: Neoliberal environmental governance and social theory', *Global Environmental Change*, 21 (2011), 795–803.

the earth, but in the current context they are more likely to lend themselves to a distinctly neoliberal antienvironmentalism».[64]

2.4 *Neoliberalism and environmental subjects*

Returning to the question of the currently prevailing forms of *ethos*, what in fact cannot be underestimated is the profound conditioning that neoliberal governmentality exerts on the ethical relationship of our society with the ecosystemic extent of the world. In this regard there is an aspect of the same governmentality concept, that has a fundamental importance: this way of exercising power – as we have seen several times in this book – is characterized by the fact that it does not only concern bio-economic resources and potential of the social body; it also affects the "conduct" of individuals, that is their *ethos*, their attitudes towards themselves, towards others and towards the world.[65] From this point of view, therefore, the political and biopolitical analysis of environmental problems essentially requires consideration of the relationship that is established between government strategies, behaviours and their transformations. It is no coincidence that, in recent years, studies have been carried out that examine the ecological question in these terms, that is, considering the individual and social *ethos* as the fundamental stake of the relationships that are created between the rulers and the ruled when the environmental problems are addressed politically. These are studies that, inspired by Foucault, analyse said problems as issues of *environmentality*, or rather, *environmental governmentality*.

In this context, Arun Agrawal's research on the profound transformation that the political-economic management of forests has undergone in the last one hundred and fifty years in India's Kumaon division, have been exemplary in a certain sense. This management has passed from the initial authoritarian centralism to the involvement of villagers in the administration of forest resources. According to the author, the contestation by the inhabitants – first with "passive resistance" and then

---

64   Cooper, *Life as surplus*, p. 41.
65   See Foucault, *Security, Territory, Population*,191-232.

with forest fires – of the intensive industrial exploitation of tree vegetation, practiced by British colonialism, played a fundamental role in this transformation; furthermore, it was also very important the questioning of the scientific forest management based on the statistical and quantitative approach that is independent of the relationships between varieties of plant and animal species, human presence, traditional peasants' use rights, local economies and knowledge. The main political outcome of this lengthy event was the creation in the 1930s of decentralized and participatory government institutions (*forest councils*). In relation to these – according to Agrawal – *subjectivities* have emerged in the villages, capable of both actively animating these institutions and making an effective critical use of political participation.[66]

In short, according to this author, the historical passage of the local communities from the clash with the institutions to the involvement in the "environmental government" cannot be reduced to a simple political integration of the villagers: in fact, many of them still remain unrelated to participatory practices; to animate the latter, however, is above all the figure of an individual who relates to them by adopting «new ways of understanding the world», that is, by combining an increasingly marked ecosystemic vision of forests with a clear ethical and political redefinition of himself as an «environmental subject». Agrawal proposes this notion by making it consciously oscillate

---

66 See Arun Agrawal, *Environmentality: Technologies of Government and the Making of Subjects*, (Durham and London: Duke University Press, 2005); Arun Agrawal, 'Environmentality: Community, Intimate Government, and the Making of Environmental Subjects in Kumaon, India', *Current Anthropology*, 46, 2 (2005), 161-90. Among the other studies on *environmentality* here is the case to quote the essays included in Éric Darier (ed. by), *Discourses of the Environment* (Oxford: Blackwell, 1999), especially those of Paul Rutherford, Timothy W. Luke, Éric Darier. Also see: Stephanie Rutherford, 'Green Governmentality: Insights and Opportunities in the Study of Nature's Rule', *Progress in Human Geography*, 31, 3 (2007), 291-307; Tracey Heatherington, 'The Changing Terrain of Environmentality: EIONET and the New Landscapes of Europe', *Anthropological Quarterly*, 85, 2 (2012), 555-79.

between the meaning of "agent" subject and that of "subordinate" subject. According to him, the governmental dimension cannot be analysed assuming that the processes of *subjection*, on the one hand, and those of *subjectivation*, on the other, are constantly and unilaterally controlled by those who implement them; the condition of governed, in particular, never excludes the possibility of radically problematizing and transforming the prevailing ways of governing. In Foucaultian terms, therefore, with regard to *environmentality*, it is necessary to highlight the interactions between the *technologies of power* with which one tries to determine the conduct of men and the *technologies of the self* by which individuals try to govern and transform themselves independently.[67]

Of course, this general indication cannot fail to be accepted. However, it easily risks translating into a generic formula suitable for all uses. In short, we must always keep in mind the specific governmental context to which it applies. More precisely, it must be said that, in our age, it is difficult for the predominance of liberal and neoliberal governmentality to inevitably allow, sooner or later, to establish a positive interactive relationship between the economic government of people and their eco-sustainable self-government. The more the latter opens up to the ecosystemic and common dimension of the world, the more it creates breaches that are difficult to remedy within the context of such governmentality. This is what seems to have demonstrated for some time the experience of the *Chipko* movement, animated by women who, in recent decades, have engaged themselves exactly in the defence of Indian forests from their persistent intensive and extensive exploitation.[68] Furthermore, something similar

---

67   Agrawal, 'Environmentality: Community, Intimate Government', pp. 162, 163 and 165; Foucault, *Technologies of the Self,* pp. 17-9. Also see Orazio Irrera, 'Environmentality and Colonial Biopolitics: Towards a Postcolonial Genealogy of Environmental Subjectivities', in Sophie Fuggle, Yari Lanci, MartinaTazzioli (ed. by), *Foucault and the History of our Present* (London and New York: Palgrave Macmillan, 2015), pp. 179-94.

68   See Vandana Shiva, *Staying Alive: Women, Ecology and Survival in India* (New Delhi: Kali for Women / London: Zed Books, 1988), pp.

seems to demonstrate more generally contemporary movements that oppose recurring attempts to privatise common ecosystemic goods such as water.[69]

It can certainly be seen, on the other hand, that various efforts are being made today to adapt contemporary government practices in an ecological sense, to which the affirmation of *ecologically correct* behaviour in society corresponds (separate collection and composting of waste, reduction of energy consumption and use of cars, purchase of goods produced with recycled materials, etc.). In general, therefore, it can be considered that today the ecological adaptation efforts of the dominant governmentality often interact with individual and social behaviours sensitive to environmental problems.[70] It is true, on the other hand, that when this convergence between the rulers and the ruled in the promotion of eco-friendly attitudes occurs, it nonetheless takes place within the context of a governmentality that assigns indisputable priority to economic growth and to the competitive logics of the global market; in fact, this promotion often ends up being contextualised in new forms of economic calculation that include the environmental effects and costs of activities and behaviours, as variables which are noteworthy to improve the competitiveness of the various market players. This promotion, therefore, is also based on the individual's willingness to change their personal and private habits by referring to their own interest: the individual may be motivated to correct their polluting behaviours since they can negatively affect their economic situation or the one in which he lives.[71]

55-95, especially pp. 67-77.

69   In this regard see, in particular, Oscar Oliveira, in collaboration with Tom Lewis, *Cochabamba: Water War in Bolivia* (Cambridge, Mass.: South End Press, 2004).

70   See Timothy W. Luke, 'Environmentality as Green Governmentality', in *Discourses of the Environment*, pp. 121-151.

71   On these issues, see: Angela Oels, 'Rendering Climate Change Governable: From Biopower to Advanced Liberal Government?', *Journal of Environmental Policy Planning*, 7, 3 (2005), 185-207; Matthew Paterson and Johannes Stripple, 'My space: governing individuals' carbon emissions', *Environment and Planning D: Society and Space*, 28, (2010), 342-62; Martin Letell, Göran Sundqvist, Mark

All this can be appreciated or criticized, but in any case it requires attention to the possibility that a large part of the responsibilities of the economic and political powers that promote unlimited industrial development is transferred to the shoulders of the individual consumer.[72] However, in the context of neoliberal governmentality, the models of ecologically correct behaviour must necessarily confront and compete with other models that correspond more directly to the prevailing logic of the market economy. In this sense, once again, the theory of *human capital* can help us understand the issue, to the extent that this theory effectively describes the tendency of the average individual of neoliberal societies to behave as "entrepreneur of himself".

In this regard, it is extremely interesting the evolution that in the economic analysis of the supporters of this theory has a problem that historically has been at the centre of attention of both the economic and biopolitical government of society and ecological knowledge: population growth. As we saw in the fourth chapter, Becker insists that the parent couples of the richer contemporary societies ward off the dangers denounced by Malthus at the time by deliberately reducing their prolificacy. These couples are oriented in this direction precisely because they take the economic calculation of costs and benefits as the decisive criterion of their behaviour: having few children is the necessary condition to concentrate and make more profitable the investments of their income in the human capital of their offspring (as well as in one's own) through education, training, formation of psychophysical skills etc. If we also take into account Rose's analyses considered in the fifth chapter, we can say that the *ethos* that underlies these behaviours is strengthened by the possibility that contemporary biomedicine offers individuals to consider the genetic risks and susceptibilities of which they are bearers as fundamental elements for making procreative decisions also

Elam, 'Steering through the neighborhood: towards an advanced liberal risk society?', *Environment and Planning A*, 43 (2011), 106-25.

72   Stephanie   Rutherford,   'Green   Governmentality: Insights   and Opportunities in the Study of Nature's Rule', p. 299.

adhering to criteria of economic rationality and remaining within the precise boundaries of the administration of their private and family interests.

This type of analysis highlits behaviours that are now widespread in advanced liberal societies; in any case, it does not seem that these behaviours produce appreciable reductions in the abuse of environmental resources, although they contribute to a decrease in population growth. If this is true, as it seems, the main reason for this situation can be indicated in the following terms: through the radicalization of the private and economic character of the individuals' conduct, the neoliberal governmentality conveys the classic question of the scarcity of resources from the macro-economic context outlined by Malthus or by the planetary dimension of the ecological crisis illustrated in the Report for the Club of Rome to the micro-economic context of individual and family existences. This question thus becomes a problem of "rational allocation" of the limited resources that the individual has in his private life (time, skills, abilities, money, etc.) to increase the psycho-physical qualities of their human capital and of their children. It follows that these same resources must be constantly maintained and increased by accessing any opportunity of income, created by productive or financial activities, and any kind of reproductive consumption that allows the "enhancement" of the human capital in question. Conversely, ecologically correct conduct, having to deal with this strictly economic attitude – sometime even in the existence of the same person – is constantly subjected to "competition" and prevalence of this same attitude. Therefore, generally, ecologically correct conduct often end up playing a minor and scarcely influential role on the overall tendencies of the economy, the government of society and the self-government of individuals. And it is also for this reason that the logic of the global market and unlimited development take precedence over the possibility of promoting credible, broad and effective forms of ecological governmentality and social ethics.

3. *Beyond bioenergetic ecology*

3.1 *"Physicalism" and "ecology of mind"*

Returning to the scientific theories considered in the previous paragraphs of this chapter, it remains to be elaborated the fact that both those more sensitive to environmental problems and those that seem to constitute post-ecological knowledge are characterized by a marked attention to consumption that biological processes make of energetic and physical resources. This means that those who want to understand environmental problems on the basis of these theories will not easily escape the idea that they can be taken seriously or reassessed especially by focusing on this consumption and determining if and how serious its consequences are. There is, however, an ecological theory which, while not neglecting this question, tends to go beyond the limits of the analytical scheme in which it is posed. Taking this theory into consideration can be useful in identifying possibilities other than those that have emerged so far, to set up the examination of the relationship between government, self-government, life, environment and *ethos*.

This is the *ecology of mind* by Gregory Bateson, which already with its name alludes to the need to analyse the relationship between life and the environment without reducing it to a question of resource consumption: in light of this theory, in fact, this relationship should be understood above all as a mental relationship in a sense that we can try to clarify here. For now, however, it is fundamental to consider first of all that the ecology of mind is proposed as a vision, at the same time, integrative and alternative towards traditional scientific ecology: it is based on the same bio-evolutionary foundations on which most of the ecological (and post-ecological) sciences was built, but at the same time it goes beyond the "physicalism" of these sciences: on the one hand, Batesonian ecology overcomes their tendency to consider the "survival" or "health" of specific individuals, groups and populations as the main criteria for assessing their relationship with the environment; on the other hand, it reassess the importance of the bioenergetic paradigm that prevails in ecological and post-ecological theories, giving space to an «informational ecology».

More precisely, Bateson's vision implies above all a concept of «unit of survival» different from that which emerges from the bio-evolutionistic tradition. According to the author, in fact,

> Darwinian evolutionary theory contained a very great error in its identification of the unit of survival under natural selection. The unit which was believed to be crucial and around which the theory was set up was either the breeding individual or the family line or the sub-species or some similar homogeneous set of conspecifics.[73]

This led «to think of units bounded at the cell membrane, or at the skin; or of units composed of sets of conspecific individuals».[74] From this point of view, the concept of struggle for existence implies a vision of the relationship between living beings and the environment, which is substantially dualistic and antagonistic. Indeed, Darwin's concern was to understand how and why certain individuals and groups of individuals manage or fail to survive, thrive, evolve in certain environmental conditions. According to Bateson, you have to realize instead that, «if an organism or aggregate of organisms sets to work with a focus on its own survival and thinks that that is the way to select its adaptive moves, its "progress" ends up with a destroyed environment».[75] In short, we must consider that «[t]he unit of survival is not the breeding organism, or the family line, or the society. (...) The unit of survival is a flexible organism-in-its-environment».[76]

Bateson believes that ecological science is still deeply influenced by the Darwinian view. The centrality that this science assigns to the bioenergetic paradigm in the analysis of ecosystems makes this conditioning particularly clear. According to him, here the "boundaries" that delimit individuals or their groups are «the frontiers at which measurements can be made to determine the additive-subtractive budget of energy for the given unit».[77] While

---

73 Gregory Bateson, *Steps to an Ecology of Mind* (Northvale, NJ, and London: Jason Aronson, 1987), p. 457.
74 *Steps to an Ecology of Mind*, p. 467.
75 *Steps to an Ecology of Mind*, p. 457.
76 *Steps to an Ecology of Mind*, pp. 457-8.
77 *Steps to an Ecology of Mind*, p. 467.

acknowledging the importance of this type of analysis, the author shows that it does not allow to respond to a crucial need that necessarily arises: to understand – or at least get a glimpse of – how large and complex the ecosystemic aggregate and the series of interactions that contribute to the vitality of the relationship of an individual or a set of organisms with their environment are. Therefore he focuses above all the *relations* between living beings and between them and the environment: it is not simply a question of asking what is the *substance*, the "material composition" of elements and processes that are given in an environment, but above all to ask what is the *form* that a set of elements and processes assumes based on the relationships between them to which we give importance.[78] This approach, according to the author, becomes possible and proves fruitful if you shift your gaze from the circulation of energy to communication, from the distinction between matter and thought to the recognition of the "mental" character, as well as material, of the processes that take place between living beings and between them and the world. From this point of view, overcoming attention to the "borders" of individuals and their groups is necessary since it is much more important to consider the unit of survival as «flexible organism-in-its-environment» and, above all, as «unit of mind»,[79] rather than as a simple biophysical aggregate.

Obviously in this regard it is necessary to understand well what the author calls *mind* (or *mental system*).

3.2 *Minds, sub-minds, differences*

According to Bateson, the concept of mind is irreducible to that of individual consciousness. For him «[a] mind is an aggregate of interacting parts or components».[80] From this point of view, the definition of a mental system does not depend so much on its delimitation, as on the development of relationships, of variable

78   *Steps to an Ecology of Mind*, pp. 455-6.
79   *Steps to an Ecology of Mind*, p. 498.
80   Gregory Bateson, *Mind and Nature: A Necessary Unity* (New York: E. P. Dutton, 1979), p. 92.

interactions between its parts and between these and the context "external" to the system, a context that therefore ends up proving not to be truly "external". Indeed, to define a mind «there is no requirement of a clear boundary»;[81] in this sense, there is a difference in size and complexity between a mental system and its ecosystem, but there are no boundaries, even if there may be discontinuities and obscurities which, however, do not exclude the interplay of relationships at all. Therefore, what we generally call the environmental ecosystem is only a mental system of greater size and complexity than what it contains.

An essential characterization of the mental system is what Bateson indicates by saying that it «shall operate with and upon *differences*».[82] The *difference* is the type of "disturbance" that most activates the mental systems; it is difficult to define, but in any case it "differs" profoundly from merely physical things and events, even though it can derive from them, from their relationships and comparisons.

> A difference is a very peculiar and obscure concept. It is certainly not a thing or an event. This piece of paper is different from the wood of this lectern. There are many differences between them – of colour, texture, shape, etc. But if we start to ask about the localization of those differences, we get into trouble. Obviously the difference between the paper and the wood is not in the paper; it is obviously not in the wood; it is obviously not in the space between them, and it is obviously not in the time between them. (Difference which occurs across time is what we call "change.") A difference, then, is an abstract matter.
>
> In the hard sciences, effects are, in general, caused by rather concrete conditions or events – impacts, forces, and so forth. But when you enter the world of communication, organization, etc., you leave behind that whole world in which effects are brought about by forces and impacts and energy exchange. You enter a world in which "effects" – and I am not sure one should still use the same word – are brought about by *differences*.[83]

---

81 Gregory Bateson and Mary Catherine Bateson, *Angels Fear: Towards an Epistemology of the Sacred* (New York: Macmillan, 1987), p. 19.

82 *Steps to an Ecology of Mind*, p. 488.

83 *Steps to an Ecology of Mind*, pp. 458-9. See also *Mind and Nature*, pp. 94-100.

Sensitivity to differences distinguishes minds from merely physical entities. Therefore Bateson proposes the distinction between the world of living beings (*creatura*) and that of inorganic objects (*pleroma*): only the former are activated by the difference both on a cognitive and behavioural, and biological level, as well as by «concrete conditions or events»; on the other hand, inorganic objects react only to these events, according to a mechanical game of causes and material effects, based on thrusts, forces, impacts, energy flows.[84] A mind can be activated by a difference even in the absence of physical events and energy flows. In fact, even this lack can "make a difference". «In the world of mind, nothing – that which is *not* – *can* be a cause. (...) The letter which you do not write can get an angry reply (...). The letter which never existed is no source of energy».[85]

Living beings are therefore certainly "minds", but they must also be considered as "sub-minds" of larger mental systems, while inorganic objects are mostly non-mental parts of mental systems in which at least one living entity is present which, as such, can take them as sources of differences. What must be clearly emphasized in this regard is that, in the context of mental processes, it is not the differences as such that are transmitted to the minds but are the latter to translate the differences into "information" when they perceive them. Therefore, the main "effects" of the differences is the information itself «as transforms (i. e., coded versions) of the difference which preceded them».[86]

The fact that mental systems do not have a "priority" relationship with physical events obviously does not mean that these are irrelevant to them. Rather it means that these events, even if they convey energy or produce physical changes, are not the main cause of the "reactions" of a mind; rather, the "cause" is the difference that these same events can produce for a mental system. In this sense, the Batesonian characterization of the mental system must be understood, according to which the behaviour of the latter depends largely on the energy already available inside it, rather than on that coming from outside.[87]

---

84   *Steps to an Ecology of Mind*, pp. 462-4 and 486-7.
85   *Steps to an Ecology of Mind*, p. 459.
86   *Mind and Nature*, p. 109.
87   *Steps to an Ecology of Mind*, p. 487; see also *Mind and Nature*, pp. 101-2.

Two other fundamental aspects of Batesonian mental systems must also be highlighted: *circular causality* and the possibility of *self-correction*. With regard to the former, it can be said that, since a mental system is necessarily made up of interacting parts, «effects of events at any point in the circuit can be carried all around to produce changes at that point of origin».[88] When the interactions or reciprocal "reactions" of the parts of the system always follow the same logic (when, for example, one part attacks and another always responds with a counter-aggression or always with submission), the relationships are «subject to progressive escalation», up to the «*schismogenesis*», that is, up to the disintegration of the system.[89] However, mental systems generally manage to ensure long-term survival. This allows us to think that the risks of schismogenesis deriving from circular causality are mostly countered by *self-correction* capabilities. These abilities have to do with what we call feed-back in cybernetic terms and can give life – according to Bateson – to learning processes, so systems and their parts can also "correct" their mistakes, "learn" to creatively vary their responses to disturbances to avoid the risk of disintegration deriving from maximizing a certain type of interaction.[90]

3.3 *Habits without a world and cosmic learning*

The concept of *learning* plays a very important role in Bateson's thinking. The author uses it in reference to two types of phenomena: *behavioural* and *biological-evolutionary*.[91] However, for him, it is above all with regard to the sphere of *behaviour* that this concept is particularly appropriate and fruitful. The ecological implications of the use he makes of it become intuitively evident as his discourse on it proceeds.

In this regard, his intent is to go beyond the analytical arrangement that explains the *behaviour* of organisms as the outcome of stimulus-

---

88   *Mind and Nature*, p. 104.
89   *Mind and Nature*, p. 105; see also *Steps to an Ecology of Mind*, pp. 71-136.
90   *Steps to an Ecology of Mind*, p. 466 and 284-314; see also *Mind and Nature*, p. 103-6.
91   See *Steps to an Ecology of Mind*, pp. 258-63.

response relationships. This is the reason why Bateson, inspired by Russell and Whitehead's theory of logical types, proposes a hierarchy of learning levels, based in turn on «the hierarchic series – stimulus, context of stimulus, context of context of stimulus, etc.»[92] On this basis Bateson elaborates, in fact, a sequence of forms of learning, ranging from a level zero to level IV.[93]

Zero learning is what consists in simply sticking to immediate stimuli by giving them the answer that immediately presents itself as the only appropriate one. As Bateson says, this learning is characterized by the *specificity of response*.

In *learning I*, on the other hand, the "trial and error" approach appears, which implies the possibility of correcting a previous behaviour. It is in this case that the organism also considers the context of the stimuli which therefore will no longer be taken as individual presuppositions of "obligatory" responses, but as elements of a more complex scenario which however is not immediately evident.

Learning II, on the other hand, consists in the intervention of the organism itself on the context: the organism learns to "segment", or to contextualize its experiences on the basis of what it has previously experienced. For example, the "success" achieved with learning I may induce him to "segment" a new experience contextualizing it in terms similar to the previous one, so that answers similar to those already given can be (or seem) adequate. Therefore, a consequence of this learning is that it can help to form habits. In this case, therefore,

> [w]hat we term "con-text" includes the subject's behaviour as well as the external events. But this behaviour (...) will be of such a kind as to mould the total context to fit the expected punctuation. In sum, this self-validating characteristic of the content of Learning II has the effect that such learning is almost ineradicable.[94]

---

92   *Steps to an Ecology of Mind*, pp. 293-4.
93   *Steps to an Ecology of Mind*, pp. 287-314.
94   *Steps to an Ecology of Mind*, p. 306.

Sooner or later, however, new problems, "contradictions", experiences that are irreducible to habitual segmentations can impose on the individual the effort to overcome them, to no longer adapt experiences to these segmentations. In this endeavour, the difficult and risky possibility of entering into an intense relationship with larger and more indeterminate contextual dimensions, with the "cosmos" or with what we call ecosystem will be played. The possible transition to *learning III* consists in something of this type. According to Bateson, this is a passage which men generally prove incapable of and which, however, can lead to a loss of their psychic cohesion:

> any freedom from the bondage of habit must also denote a profound redefinition of the self. (...) Selfhood is a product or aggregate of Learning II. To the degree that a man achieves Learning III, and learns to perceive and act in terms of the contexts of contexts, his "self" will take on a sort of irrelevance. The concept of "self" will no longer function as a nodal argument in the punctuation of experience.

Finally, *learning IV* is – in a sense – only theoretical. It would consist in acquiring the ability not only to transcend one's subjectivity, but even to overcome behavioural inclinations that seem to be inscribed in one's genetic heritage. Therefore, it is a "learning" that can eventually take place at a level that includes the history of the organism and that of its species.[95] As Bateson says, «[t]he problem in regard to any behaviour is clearly not "Is it learned or is it innate?" but "[u]p to what logical level is learning effective and down to what level does genetics play a determinative or partly effective role?"».[96]

It is with this type of question that Bateson implicitly indicates to us also the possibility of comparing and, within certain limits, liken the biological-evolutionary processes with those of behavioural learning. Both the elements of similitude and the profound differences that exist between each other have very important ecological implications.

---

95 *Steps to an Ecology of Mind*, p. 298.
96 *Steps to an Ecology of Mind*, p. 312.

3.4 *Evolution and technical consciousness*

According to Bateson, there are essentially two similarities between behavioural learning and biological evolution. The first is their common *describability in terms of logical levels or types*. From his point of view, even bio-evolutionary changes can be distinguished and ordered according to different levels which, in turn, are essentially two: that of *somatic (or phenotypic) change* affecting single *individual organisms*; that of *genotypic change* affecting the *genetic heritage* of a population and a certain number of its generations; on the other hand, it is essential that these changes interact with *environmental conditions and changes* that are placed on a further contextual level. What must be considered, in any case, is that this description according to a hierarchy of levels does not at all exclude forms of both communication and discontinuity between the various levels.

A somatic change is what a man undergoes, who adapts to environmental conditions through a certain physical activity from which the development, for example, of biceps of considerable size may derive after some time. Nonetheless, while this happens at the somatic level, what happens at the genotypic level? Can we say that those biceps will sooner or later become part of the genetic heritage of that man's descendants? The answer is – or should be – no. Jean-Baptiste Lamarck however believed that somatic change, under certain conditions, can be hereditary. In reality – according to Bateson – this idea is only plausible but does not consider the discontinuity that occurs between the somatic and genotypic levels. It is a discontinuity, a "barrier", theorized by the German embryologist August Weismann who argued that the somatic change does not affect the "germ plasm" and therefore cannot be transmitted to the descendants of an individual. On the other hand – observes Bateson –, the empirical controls in this field are extremely difficult. But if the "hereditary transmission" hypothesis of somatic change were the only valid or prevailing possibility, the evolution would run serious risks; for example, in the evolution of a population it could be lost the possibility that individuals genetically capable of both enlarging and reducing their biceps, by doing or not doing physical exercise, reproduce. In short, the Lamarckian inheritance hypothesis may imply that the genetic capacity to obtain reversible somatic modifications is compromised.[97]

The second similarity between behavioural learning and biological evolution is their common stochastic character, that is, their development by "trial and error": both behavioural learning and bio-evolutionary change can be examined first of all as the results of random responses to "stimuli" or, better, as answers to environmental influences, among which selections are made through attempts, errors and corrections.[98]

Finally, if we consider the differences between behavioural learning forms and bio-evolutionary changes, from Bateson's point of view, one must highlight an absolutely essential one, starting from one observation: behavioural learning primarily concerns individuals and therefore it can be compared to somatic change; but, especially in the case of men, it is clear that the results and habits deriving from individual learning can be easily extended to the community. Particularly in contemporary societies nothing prevents – indeed, it can be said that everything favours – that certain outcomes of individual experience are easily transferred or propagated on a communal level, in the immediate and from one generation to the next. What is certain is that there is no "Weismann barrier" here.[99] In short, here things go as if a sort of Lamarckian inheritance really worked, in a synchronic and diachronic way. According to Bateson, two problems make this situation particularly alarming: the first consists in the fact that man tends to "segment" his experiences in a very selective manner, that is, to relate to the world above all through that limited part of his mind that it is consciousness; the second consists in the development of the technique, which has now become almost uncontrollable in our society.

The first problem lies mainly in the fact that «the contents of the "screen" of consciousness are determined by considerations of purpose».[100] In other words, man tends to set suitable goals and

---

97 *Mind and Nature*, p. 151.
98 *Mind and Nature*, pp. 145-85.
99 *Mind and Nature*, p. 222.
100 *Steps to an Ecology of Mind*, pp. 451-2.

to use consciousness to identify the tools that, rightly or wrongly, appear to him to be most effective in achieving them. This approach, if systematically privileged, tends to block the learning and evolution processes of the relationship between man and the world. This ends up producing ineradicable habits, so that man will give the same type of answers to problems that instead require variable and creative answers.

This trend constitutes a serious problem above all because with modern technology man has now created a mechanism that relentlessly strengthens and reproduces it. In particular, advanced technologies now unlimitedly extend and generalize purposeful choices of which one almost never has the way and the time to verify the opportunity for the existence of the individual, societies, species or ecosystems. In short, in the context of contemporary societies, man now constantly operates that direct transfer of individual changes or acquisitions from the individual level to the general level, which instead does not normally occur in the context of his biological evolution and that of many other living beings. On the other hand, it is quite clear that today man does not intend to stop even in the face of this "difficulty": through biotechnology, he aims to intervene also on the level of the genetic heritage of the species.

To understand more precisely the biological and ecosystemic implications of these trends, according to Bateson, one must first consider «man's habit of changing his environment rather than changing himself».[101]

> In. a few cases organisms other than man have achieved the creation of modified microenvironments around themselves, e.g., the nests of hymenoptera and birds, concentrated forests of conifers, fungal colonies, etc. (...) Man, the outstanding modifier of environment, similarly achieves single-species ecosystems in his cities, but he goes one step further, establishing special environments for his symbionts. These, likewise, become single-species ecosystems: fields of corn, cultures of bacteria, batteries of fowls, colonies of laboratory rats, and the like.[102]

---

101 *Steps to an Ecology of Mind*, p. 452.
102 *Steps to an Ecology of Mind*, pp. 452-3.

What makes the role of modern technology particularly problematic in this scenario is not only the progressive systematic nature of its intervention on life and the world, but also the *speed* it gives to change of «the power ratio between purposive consciousness and the environment. (...) Conscious man, as a changer of his environment, is now fully able to wreck himself and that environment – with the very best of conscious intentions».[103]

Another circumstance that – according to Bateson – makes this scenario dramatic is, in short, the fact that in our society «a large number of selfmaximizing entities», or organizations that consciously, systematically and indefinitely pursue their ends, is constantly being formed and strengthened: «trusts, companies, political parties, unions, commercial and financial agencies, nations, and the like».[104] The continuous technical and "conscious" enhancement of the maximizing behaviour of these entities can produce exponential growth both of immediate advantages and of unexpected and uncontrollable effects on the ecosystem in which they live.

4. *Living, dwelling, acting*

4.1 *Bios, ethos, kosmos*

According to what we have been able to obtain from the examination of the ecological and post-ecological theories of the life-environment relationship, we can generally say that they lend themselves easily to represent references for both economic and biopolitical forms of government of the environmental question; this can be maintained regardless of the willingness of governments to "use" them in this sense or the fact that these theories consider or do not consider the ecological question as an urgent problem. For example, ecosystem ecology seems immediately available to function as a source of inspiration for the bio-economic government of the relationships between flows of

---

103 *Steps to an Ecology of Mind*, p. 453.
104 Ibid.

resources, biological processes and production activities; a post-ecological theory such as that of the Gaia hypothesis, on the other hand, seems to be able to legitimize in particular the industrial use of microbial life forms for the degradation of polluting substances or for the production of biofuels and bioplastics, without this entailing the questioning of the dominant economic, political and biopolitical models.

It is somewhat difficult, instead, to sustain that the ecology of mind can certainly be mobilized as a knowledge for the biopolitical or bio-economic government of the environmental question; this can be said at least to the extent that it radically distances itself from a certain bioenergetic cult of efficiency of scientific ecology. More generally, one has the impression that Batesonian ecology is not particularly suitable for "functioning" either as a tool for bio-economic rationalization of the life-society-environment relationship or as a reference for an affirmative and liberating biopolitics, based on exaltation of the "power" of life. Rather, the ecology of mind, attributing extreme importance to behavioural processes and their interactions, similarities and differences with biological and ecosystem processes, leads us to recognize the crucial value that the transformations of the individual and social *ethos* should assume in addressing the ecological question.

By reconnecting to Foucault, we could say that Bateson indirectly invites us to grasp and develop the implications of that sort of transition to a higher level of learning that took place between 1977 and 1979 during the path of research that the French philosopher intended to dedicate to the genealogy of biopolitics. As we know, in fact, in that period there was a kind of transition of the Foucaultian path from this genealogy to that of governmentality, or – in a certain sense – from the analysis of power over life to that of the government of *ethos*.

For Foucault, at that time, the fact that in modernity life has become the object of a bio-power was certainly very important; but this was beginning to be less relevant than the possibility that biopower itself is part of a wider complex of governmental arts, which must be examined in its specificity. In fact – as we saw in the first chapter – trying to focus the knowledge that most influences the general rationality of this complex, Foucault did not find it in *life sciences*, but in the *political economy*.[105] The fact that, on the one hand, he identified one of the main historical models of government in *pastoral power* and, on the other, he defined it as «the way in which one conducts the conduct of men», has a precise meaning: it means that, for him, the main issue at stake in the exercise of governmental power is the *ethos* of each and every one.[106] This is confirmed by the work of his last years in which, studying the subjects of *care of the self* and the *courage of truth (parrêsia)* in the context of Greek and Roman antiquity, he identified exactly in the *ethos* the main reference of self-government. Ultimately, this means that – according to Foucault – it is around the *ethos* that the essential confrontation takes place between those who govern and those who try to self-govern,[107] between the art of governing others and «the art of not being governed, or the art of not being governed like that and at this price».[108]

All this helps us to explain the fact that, until his death, the French philosopher no longer returns to the relationship between power and life, even if he does not rule out being able to deal with it again.[109] However, as we have already seen in the third chapter, in his 1980-1981 course he examines one of the most important themes of the debate that will subsequently develop around biopolitics: that of the Greek distinction between *zoé* and *bios*. What he concludes is that *zoé* for the Greeks is the simple fact of living, while *bios* is not "qualified life" at all, but rather «life that can be qualified», the «course of existence» that one can try to transform and direct in one direction or another.[110]

---

105 See *Security, Territory, Population*, pp. 106-10; *The Birth of Biopolitics*, pp. 21-2.

106 See *The Birth of Biopolitics*, p. 186; *Security, Territory, Population*, pp.115-216.

107 Foucault, *The Hermeneutics of the Subject*, pp. 251-2.

108 Michel Foucault, 'What Is Critique?' trans. by Kevin Paul Geiman, in James Schmidt (ed. by), *What is Enlightenment?: Eighteenth-Century Answers and Twentieth-Century Questions* (Berkeley and Los Angeles: University of California Press, 1996), p.384.

109 Michel Foucault, 'On the Genealogy of Ethics: An Overview of Work in Progress', in Dreyfus and Rabinow, *Michel Foucault: Beyond Structuralism and Hermeneutics*, p. 232.

110 Foucault, *Subjectivity and Truth*, pp. 34.

On these bases, in the reflection of Foucault, *bios* and *ethos*, *existence* and a *way of conducting oneself*, end up referring to each other in a very precise sense: *bios* presents itself as the context of an *ethopoiesis*, that is, as a dimension in which it is possible «to constitute an *ethos*, a way of being and doing things, a way of conducting oneself». The author also notes that in western history *bios* does not present itself as the only dimension of the constitution of an *ethos*; in fact, another dimension of this type is the *psykhê*, the soul. And through the difference between *psykhê* and *bios* Foucault highlights two different ways of conceiving and practicing self-care or self-government, tracing their inaugural or at least exemplary version in the philosophical experiences of Platonism and Cynism: Platonism historically promotes a way of taking care of oneself in which attention to the soul requires an effort of purification and a projection towards «the other world», towards an ontological reality distinct from the body; Cynism instead – assuming *bios* as an object of attention – tends to constitute an *ethos* of freedom in the immediate way of living «in this world against the world».[111]

The radically different relationships that are established with the world in the two philosophical experiences have significant implications. They are first of all reflected in the ways of understanding the *knowledge of the self*, an issue that Foucault insists on in *The Hermeneutics of the Subject*. While Platonism practices self-knowledge by seeking the connection between the soul and the supersensitive world of ideas, Cynism puts it into practice by paying attention to the intraworldly multiplicity of natural and artificial events and processes in which man is invested. For Cynics, the immersion of the self in the complexity of the world is an indispensable condition of self-knowledge, since precisely from it derive consequences regarding the appropriate way of living.[112]

According to Foucault, Cynism will largely share this approach to self-knowledge through knowledge of the world with other great Hellenistic philosophies, in particular with Stoicism and Epicureanism. As Demetrius – Cynic philosopher quoted by

---

111   Foucault, *The Courage of the Truth*, pp. 338 and 341; see also pp. 159-72.
112   Foucault, *The Hermeneutics of the Subject*, pp. 76-8, 209-11, 230-8.

Seneca (Stoic philosopher) who appreciates his ideas – says: it is necessary to dedicate oneself to the knowledge of the world not simply to look for the causes of events and phenomena; however appropriate, this type of knowledge easily translates into pure accumulation of culture, without effects on one's way of life. Instead – says Foucault – Hellenistic philosophies opt for «a relational mode of knowledge that asserts and prescribes at the same time and is capable of producing a change in the subject's mode of being»; it is, in fact, an «"ethopoetic" [or ethopoietic] knowledge (...), that is to say knowledge which provides or forms *ethos*»: this way of knowing considers the whole that includes events, the cosmos, riches, men, gods, death as the «field of the relation between all these things and oneself»; from the attention to the intertwining of relationships between the self and the world, of which this knowledge makes aware, prescriptions for one's own way of life derive, that is, *ethopoietic effects.*[113]

4.2 *Etho-poiesis and eco-poiesis*

The divergence between Cynism and Platonism, which is outlined in this context, does not seem reducible to the contrast between a preference for immanence and a projection towards transcendence. Above all, it presents itself as a divergence between a *cosmicisation of oneself* and a *separation of oneself from the world*. More generally, it can be said that Hellenistic (non-Platonic) philosophies propose an *etho-poiesis* consisting de facto in an *eco-poiesis* or, more precisely, in building a relationship with the world as a context of dwelling. This idea does not represent a free interpretation of Foucault's thought. Rather, it corresponds to what the French philosopher himself urges us to think when – paraphrasing Demetrius – he indicates the general purpose of self-knowledge based on knowledge of the world in these terms: «knowing (...) that the world is a common dwelling-place in which all men are joined together to constitute precisely [a] community».[114]

---

113 *The Hermeneutics of the Subject*, pp. 235-8. More generally see pp. 229-85.
114 *The Hermeneutics of the Subject*, pp. 234-5.

This is an apparently simple indication, however it is not appropriate to underestimate some elementary, but important implications. Highlighting the link between the establishment of an *ethos* and attention to the world as a *common dwelling-place*, Foucault – knowingly or unknowingly – invites us in fact to broaden the meaning of the term *ethos* to its original meaning which refers exactly to the dimension of the dwelling. As is known, in fact, the word *ethos* can be translated both with terms such as *custom, usage, disposition, character, habit*, and with expressions such as *accustomed place*. It is no coincidence that Martin Heidegger identifies the philosophical sense of the *ethos* concept in its "dwelling" sense, referring to the famous fragment of Heraclitus, which reads: «*ethos anthropoi daimon*».

> *Ethos* – says Heidegger – means abode, dwelling place. The word names the open region in which man dwells. The open region of his abode allows what pertains to man's essence, and what in thus arriving resides in nearness to him, to appear.[115]

In this sense, it is very interesting the way in which Nancie Erhard connects the meaning of "behavioural" to that of "dwelling" of the *ethos* concept, proposing the idea of «ethos as moral habitat». The author in this regard recalls, in fact, that from Homer and Hesiod up to Oppianus, passing through Herodotus and Aristotle, the word *ethos* is used to indicate both the homes or accustomed places of animals and humans, as well as the customs, disposition or moral character. This – according to her – allows us to consider environments, including the biotic communities of which men are part, as contexts that influence their moral attitudes.[116] This does not mean that there is a unilateral and deterministic influence relationship between the environment and the individual, habitat and society. This relationship – as well as being necessarily interactive – always takes place in different ways and with different

---

115 Martin Heidegger, 'Letter on Humanism', in *Basic Writings*, from *Being and Time* (1927) to *The Task of Thinking* (1964), ed. by David F. Krell (New York: Harper Collins, 1993, 2nd edn), p. 256.

116 Nancie Erhard, *Moral Habitat. Ethos and Agency for the Sake of Earth* (Albany, NY: State University of New York Press, 2007), pp. 11-34.

intensities, but it does not always correspond to it on the part of men the recognition of its importance and the willingness to let themselves be ethically formed by it. According to the author, this lack of recognition characterizes in particular modern and hyper-modern societies which, in fact, tend to consider themselves essentially independent of their environments.[117] In other contexts, however, men manage to develop lasting forms of agreement with the habitats of their existence, as in the case of the cultures of certain peoples native to North America; the traditional *ethos* of these peoples was formed precisely through attention to the network of relationships between human communities and non-human presences that constitute and share their environments: animals, plants, atmospheric phenomena, material objects, "spiritual entities", etc... According to Erhard, a system of moral obligations based on the cultivation of these same relationships arose out of this attention. This clearly emerges from even the most controversial activity of these peoples: hunting. According to the *Mi'kmaq* vision, in particular, the success of a hunter does not depend only on his ability, but also on his responsibility towards the prey; this, escaping him, tests his "acumen" and his "virtue" and then gives itself or denies itself to him, possibly through the intervention of a spiritual entity. In short, what was formed on this type of basis is an overall *ethos* that expresses in an exemplary way even in the dramatic case of hunting: in this case, in fact, «the need for sustenance involves the giving of life for life, it involves petition, apology, gratitude, and respect for self-sacrifice» and, more generally, towards the life cycles of the presences that share their habitat.[118]

4.3 *Worldly subjectivity beyond biopolitics*

Here it should be reiterated that the ecopoietic elaboration of the Foucaultian concept of ethopoiesis does not imply any forcing of the concept itself; rather, it is based on its declination in a dwelling sense, made possible both by the broad meaning of the term *ethos*

---

117 *Moral Habitat*, pp. 20-1.
118 *Moral Habitat*, p. 39; see also pp. 35-43.

and by the importance of the ethopoietic relationship between self-knowledge and knowledge of the world, highlighted by Foucault himself. This elaboration responds to the need to go beyond the limits of biopolitics, without however ceasing to consider it a terrain of conflict and political action. The sphere of biopolitics is compromised not only by the presence of biopowers of various kinds, but also by mostly uncritical emphasis on life as a force capable of productivity and incoercible creativity or as a mere object of exclusion, killing, immunization, manipulation or extinction. In fact, it is not a question of simply overcoming the historical limits of biopolitics by replacing the bio-anthropocentrism on which its prevalent forms are based, with a naturalism or an ecosystemic biocentrism; it is not even a question of denying a centrality to the concepts of *life* or *nature*; rather, it is a question of giving ethical form in a dwelling, local and cosmic sense to the relationships between our subjectivity and the world in its various artificial and natural, human and non-human dimensions.

A perspective such as this does not at all exclude that a frankly ecological knowledge should play an important role. But this knowledge must not perform this function as a simple "theory of nature" or "science of environmental degradation"; rather it must carry it out as "relational" and "ethopoietic" knowledge of the world, as Foucault would say. In this sense, an ecosystemic approach to the world is necessary above all as an experience and practice of recognition of the "system of relations" between our self and the world, which we cannot demand to master beyond certain limits. Without experience and practice of this modesty, there is neither ecology, nor ecosystemic *ethopoiesis*, nor the possibility of practicing forms of freedom from biopowers and governments of all kinds. The ethopoietic tasks that an approach of this type seems to impose, in any case, are similar to those that can be obtained from the Foucaultian analysis of the care of the self: it is, on the one hand, to try to "govern oneself" more than the world; on the other, to "not get too governed" by those who do not care about the immense margins of ungovernability of the world itself.

In this sense, the ecology of mind by Gregory Bateson can represent an important reference. Indeed, it is an ecosystemic vision which, however, goes beyond the bioenergetic – and potentially biopolitical – physicalism of the ecological sciences. As we have seen, for Bateson the ecosystem is above all a *system of relations between parts*, in which *mental processes* – that is, the conscious or unconscious "communication" with the world and life – count more than exchanges of energy and matter. Furthermore, the Batesonian ecosystem is a mental system that cannot fail to transcend the concept of the mind linked to the individual's conscience and psychic interiority; the unconscious of this mental system itself is irreducible to the (Freudian) idea of secret «cellar or cupboard to which fearful and painful memories are consigned by a process of repression». Here the unconscious – like the mind itself – is what continually escapes us by extending to the "external", but not "separate" dimension of our relationships with the contexts in which we live and with which we communicate consciously or not.[119]

Precisely since it is conceived in these terms, Batesonian ecology can respond to an important need on which Foucault insists: that of releasing the practices of ethical subjectivation from the forms of internalization of one's self; forms that we find, in one way or another, in the Platonic reminiscence of eternal ideas through the soul, in the Christian confession of every hidden thought and impulse and, finally, in the modern search for a «ground of subjectivity» in the ravines of the psyche or in some other ontological container of "human nature".[120]

Another important element of Bateson's thought that needs to be considered is what can be derived from the simple consideration, which we have already encountered, of the «man's habit of changing his environment rather than changing himself».[121] Whether or not it is a spontaneous inclination, this attitude – as "man's habit" – presents itself as an unreflected custom, as a rooted way of living and acting, worthy of being problematized and possibly transformed – as Foucault would say – through ethopoietic practices. But while the French philosopher offers us

119 See *Steps to an Ecology of Mind*, pp, pp. 142-52; 447-54.
120 See Michel Foucault, 'About the Beginning of the Hermeneutics of the Self: Two Lectures at Dartmouth', *Political Theory*, 21, 2 (1993), 198-227 (pp. 198-223).
121 *Steps to an Ecology of Mind*, p. 452.

only indirect suggestions on the ecopoietic direction that these practices should take, Bateson strongly invites us to think about them in relation to the mental ecosystem of which man is part of. We cannot ignore, however, what Foucault allows us to understand in this regard: man – in particular the western one – swings from one pole to another in the same form of *ethopoiesis*: the first pole is that of renouncing to immerse oneself in the world to seek through the soul a truth in the unworldly sphere of ideas or a salvation to be enjoyed in the eternal afterlife; the second is that of affirming one's *self* on the *world* by renouncing to take care of one and the other. A simple question can be asked in this regard: how to avoid this oscillation?

Bateson also offers us some indications on this matter, without hiding from us the extreme difficulty of his "solution". In fact, it is an arduous form of learning that – from his point of view – can put our self on the path of an ecosystemic ethopoiesis. According to him, man can easily pass from a behaviour that responds in predictable ways to immediate stimuli, to the ability to solve complex problems based on his own experiences and skills acquired. Having reached this level, however, he generally tends to face problems by adapting the contexts in which they present themselves to his skills. His behaviour thus ends up creating habits that are increasingly difficult to eradicate.[122] In this sense – according to Bateson – man's inclination to use what he calls «purposive consciousness» plays a crucial role. In fact – as we have seen –, tending to favour «the "screen" of consciousness» as a way of accessing the world and its problems, man «deals only with a skewed sample of the events of the total mind»; furthermore, it must be considered that generally «the contents of the "screen" of consciousness are determined by considerations of purpose»:

> "D is desirable; B leads to C; C leads to D; so D can be achieved by way of B and C." But, if the total mind and the outer world do not, in general, have this lineal structure, (...) [o]ur conscious sampling of data will not disclose whole circuits but only arcs of circuits, cut off from their matrix by our selective attention.[123]

---

122 *Steps to an Ecology of Mind*, p. 306.
123 *Steps to an Ecology of Mind*, pp. 451-2.

Relating to the world as a relational and mental ecosystem therefore means becoming capable of going beyond one's own consolidated self in habits, starting from those of «purposive consciousness». In this difficult endeavour – to which one is driven mostly by traumatic experiences – one exposes oneself to serious existential dangers and even to the loss of one's own self. In fact – according to Bateson – it should be possible to merge with «all the processes of relationship in some vast ecology or aesthetics of cosmic interaction», risking – among other things – «being swept away on oceanic feeling»; but perhaps – says the author – these dangers can also be avoided by becoming modestly capable «to focus in on the minutiae of life», as if «[e]very detail of the universe» could offer us «a view of the whole»; or managing to live in «a simplicity in which hunger leads directly to eating».[124]

In short, in a certain sense, it would be a matter of being inspired by the way of life of the Cynic philosopher who found in frugality and in life freely lived in the open space of the city the best conditions for practicing his philosophical *ethos*.

4.4 *From "cosmo-capital" to the common world*

If the Batesonian perspective perhaps helps us to determine the necessary ethical transformations of the relationship between the self and the world in an ecopoietic sense, it however leaves the political side of the question substantially unexplored. In this regard, the need to re-establish a dwelling and cosmic sense to the relationships between our subjectivity, life and the world does not diminish, but grows; it can be said that this need goes beyond the need to open ourselves to the complex communicative and "mental" relationships that we have with the world, and bring us back to the urgent need to reconnect with the material variety of the forms of the world itself. From this point of view, the problem also arises of placing the biopolitical dimension of our simple fact of living in a wider and more complex context than that defined by the life/death, health/risk, production/dissipation interaction, and so on. All this, on the other hand, implies a willingness to

---

124 *Steps to an Ecology of Mind*, p. 311.

recognize that the world has no «lineal structure», and to renounce ambitions of completeness, clarity and mastery of this "structure".

Here we can try to briefly indicate some paths that could be followed to move in this direction. First of all, we should focus on the fact that today we are involved in processes of "de-worldliness" and reduction of the ecosystemic complexity of existence and life. Pierre Dardot and Christian Laval seem to offer us some useful indications in this regard when they claim that today we are increasingly immersed in «the "world-becoming" of capital», that is, in the «suffocating logic of [a] "cosmo-capitalism"». According to the two authors, the upper hand of neoliberal governmentality over all other forms of government has been and is the determining condition of this trend. More precisely, they argue that neoliberalism produces a radical change in our relationship with the world through the systematic imposition of a «new norm of generalized competition»; in this sense, according to them, the main neoliberal strategies «shape our behaviour such that it conforms with the generalized norm of greater and greater accumulation». The two authors obviously take into account the fact that these strategies are accompanied by large privatization processes of common goods and assets, public activities and services, that is, by forms of expropriation of the society of shared parts of the world; however, they insist that the effectiveness of neoliberal governmentality is primarily based on «the continuous reproduction of the social, cultural, political, and subjective conditions necessary for broadening the accumulation of capital, or the world-becoming of capital». The same capitalist accumulation that neoliberalism favours, in their opinion, does not simply consist in the exploitation and appropriation of collective wealth; it is «a general accumulation» that takes place

> through an expanded and deepened subordination of all elements of the population's existence: consumption, transportation, leisure time, education, health, the use of space and time, social and cultural reproduction, and ultimately subjectivity itself.[125]

---

125 Pierre Dardot and Christian Laval, *Common: On Revolution in the 21st Century*, trans. by Matthew MacLellan (London: Bloomsbury, 2019), pp.87-8.

Indeed, these theses can not only be shared, but can also be radicalized further. In this sense, it is certainly necessary to underline the fact that, referring to the subjection strategies that create subordination by forming behaviours and subjectivities, Dardot and Laval define neoliberal governmentality as a mechanism that produces specific forms of social and individual *ethos*. Ultimately, even these authors urge us to take seriously the idea that *ethos* is a decisive ground of the dominant governmentality in our age. Having said this, however, we must avoid the risk of considering the question of «the world-becoming of capital» in simply metaphorical terms. In other words, we must avoid underestimating the meaning of the material processes of privatization and expropriation that accompany the production of forms of competitive and individualistic *ethos*, of which the two authors speak to us.

The privatization policies that have been applied for several decades to common goods and public services of various kinds are well known; therefore there is no need to insist on them. What should be clearly highlighted, however, is that they fall within a broader set of trends that affect the world both in its material immediacy and in its ecosystemic complexity understood in the broadest sense of the expression. It is also in these terms, in short, that it is necessary to understand the processes, allowed by globalization and neoliberal policies, of appropriation, privatization and capitalization of common goods, public assets, territories, structures, urban spaces and collective services. That these processes weigh heavily on both materiality and the overall relationships between contemporary humanity and its biological, physical and mental cosmos can be easily understood if one of the most macroscopic and, perhaps, most underestimated examples of these processes is considered. This is the phenomenon of the so-called *land grabbing*, meaning «the process of appropriation of arable land (...) by local, national and transnational elites, investors and governments of the developed and wealthy countries».[126] The

---

126 Giulia Franchi, 'Chi mangia la terra?', *Scienze del Territorio*, 1 (2013), 211-7 (p. 217): «Land grabbing is (...) now experiencing an acceleration due to the following factors: the food crisis and the need for food of

effects of phenomena like this, evidently, are primarily of material dispossession and economic expropriation; but they are also – and perhaps above all – dwelling, ecological, existential, mental and ethical, as well as biological, political and biopolitical effects. In short, it must be recognized that these processes, pushing the poorest individuals and societies towards the global dimension of the market, induce them to adhere to competitive, private and individualistic forms of *ethos* by alienating their existence from the world, depriving them of their material and mental relationships with the land, with the production of food and with life itself.

The fact that these relations with the world are a fundamental stake in the current dominant political and economic trends can also be grasped in another set of well-known processes. It concerns the extensive and intensive development of networks and telematic communication technologies. It is difficult to deny that this development produces, in addition to enormous opportunities for information and communication relationships, also a general process of despatialisation, deterritorialization and virtualization of the relationships between individuals, their life and the materiality of the world.[127] In this regard, of course, one

---

insecure countries to secure a steady and low-cost food supply by outsourcing food production; the energy and the climate crisis, with the related need to diversify energy sources and thus with the increase in demand for agro-fuels; the financial crisis and the huge amount of capital flight from the traditional markets in search of more secure and profitable investment, which led to a sharp increase in speculation on land and food. Consequences of land grabbing are local communities' reduced access and control over their lands and other natural resources, the impairment of ecosystems' and environmental balances and the strengthening of inequalities and speculative mechanisms».(ibid.). See also: Shepard Daniel and Anuradha Mittal, *The Great Land Grab. Rush for World's Farmland Threatens Food Security for the Poor* (Oakland: The Oakland Institute, 2009); Philippe Sibaud, *Opening Pandora's Box: The New Wave of Land Grabbing by the Extractive Industries and The Devastating Impact on Earth* (London: The Gaia Foundation, 2012.

127 In this regard, we refer here in general to Paul Virilio's broad reflection on what this author was able to define as «the loss» or «the end of the world», mainly caused by the speed of communication technologies. For an overall picture of his thought, see Paul Virilio, *Politics of the Very Worst. An Interview with Philippe Petit,* trans. by Michael Cavaliere

cannot fail to note that the aims and effects of these strategies are primarily economic, insofar as they strengthen and expand the global market out of all proportion; but it is impossible to overlook, on the other hand, that they produce and are based on a general departure of contemporary man from the world, a de-cosmicization of his life, his existence and his *ethos*, caused by the reassessment of the physical relationships between people and between them and their environments, and by the supremacy that *profiling* and the systematic conditioning of their behaviours exert on their subjectivity. As is known, these are precise strategies that have been rightly defined with the expression: *algorithmic governmentality*.[128]

Another path to explore to try to focus politically on the current forms of de-cosmization of life is what Hannah Arendt offers us when she indicates the different contexts of the human condition in her most important work. They are essentially three and each of the three forms of active life that the author identifies (labour, work, action) relates in particular to one of them. The first is the context defined by the *earth* as a planet and by the *land* as a natural dimension of life and its needs to which *labour* responds; the second is the *world of artificial objects*, a lasting condition of *inhabiting* (or *dwelling*) created by the production of *works*; the third is the *public realm* which allows *political action* and, at the same time, is guaranteed by the free development of the latter.[129]

In this worldly articulation of the human condition, with wich we need to reconnect, natural life – the simple fact of living – is appropriately contextualized in its immediate terrestrial dimension

---

(New York: Semiotext(e), 1999); also see: *The Information Bomb*, trans. by Chris Turner (London: Verso, 2000); *Negative Horizon: An Essay in Dromoscopy*, trans. by Michael Degener (London: Continuum, 2005).

128 In this regard, see: Antoinette Rouvroy and Thomas Berns, 'Gouvernementalité algorithmique et perspectives d'émancipation. Le disparate comme condition d'individuation par la relation?', *Réseaux*, 177, 1 (2013), 163-96; Antoinette Rouvroy, 'The end(s) of critique: data-behaviourism vs. due process', in Mireille Hildebrandt and Katia de Vries (ed. by), *Privacy, Due Process and the Computational Turn: The Philosophy of Law Meets the Philosophy of Technology* (Abingdon, UK: Routledge 2013), pp. 143-67.

129 See *The Human Condition*, pp. 7-11, 50-8, 136-9.

with the identification of «the most necessary and elementary labor of man» with «the tilling of the soil». We also know that, referring to the Greek *polis*, Arendt identifies the main area of labour – as a life conservation activity – with the private sphere of the *oikos*. But today we can say that our problem is not that of further enclosing life-care activities in the dimension of family and private affairs; our problem, rather, is to reconnect them to the materiality and care of the terrestrial environments that nourish life, starting from the most tangible and closest places of our worldly existence.

CHAPTER SEVEN
THE WORLD AS A PANDEMIC ECOSYSTEM
Biopolitics in the Age of
Global Reproduction of Viruses

> Before 12 years ago, anybody could get on a plane anywhere
> in the world carrying a pocket knife. Now it's unthinkable
> that you would get on a plane carrying a pocket knife. But
> you can still get on a plane carrying a virus.
> (David Quammen, 2013)[1]

1. *A planetary zoonosis*

1.1 *Spillover*

In the days when this book was about to be completed, the
SARS-COV2 (or COVID-19) pandemic exploded, affecting
primarily some of the most economically developed societies –
from China to South Korea, from Italy to Spain, from France to
Germany, from the UK to the USA – to subsequently spread to
many other areas of the world. The aggressiveness, the rapidity
and the vastness of the spread of the coronavirus have placed
medicine at the forefront of the urgency not only to understand
and cure a substantially unknown pathology, but also to counter
its exponential spread;[2] at the same time, the pressing needs

---

1   David Quammen, Interview with Abdul-Kareem Ahmed in his book
     review of 'David Quammen, *Spillover: Animal Infections and the Next
     Human Pandemic* (New York: W.W. Norton & Company, 2012)', *Yale
     Journal of Biology and Medicine*, 86 (2013), 107-14.
2   For «a picture of the state of the art» a few days after the declaration
     of the global pandemic, see Francesco Di Gennaro and others,
     'Coronavirus Diseases (COVID-19) Current Status and Future
     Perspectives: A Narrative Review', *International Journal of
     Environmental Research and Public Health*, 17, 690 (2020), 1-11.

imposed by the emergency created the conditions for experts and medical workers to dramatically extend their interventions to protect life and greatly increase their biopolitical role. Contemporary societies, on the other hand, found themselves faced with the possibility of being totally dependent on medical sciences and practices and with the need to radically transform their attitudes, their relationships with life and with the world.

After proposing in the previous chapter a sort of ecological reconfiguration of the discourse on biopolitics, here for many reasons we will try to frame in a similar way the reflection on the topicality of the pandemic problem. In fact, among the needs that both contemporary societies and medicine should experience in order to overcome problems such as those mentioned above, we must certainly consider that of recognizing the ecosystemic framework in which violent epidemic phenomena, potentially pandemic, mature more and more often in our time. Generally, in public discussions about the causes of the SARS-COV2 pandemic only occasionally focus is placed on the decisive role that ecological factors of emergencies such as this can play. Yet it is more than appropriate to hypothesize that the increasingly serious environmental changes caused by contemporary societies are often decisive contributing factors of: cross-species transmissions through which potentially pandemic pathogen agents infect humans; the frequency with which these transmissions seem to occur in our time; the fact that at this time the dangers of a pandemic tend to multiply.

Of course, the studies that fall within the issue in these terms are numerous. They certainly have an influence on the scientific debate, on the perspectives of medicine and on anti-pandemic biopolitics. However, often one has the impression that the need to respond with emergency strategies to the spread of epidemic diseases prevents their ecological factors from being seriously taken into account in biomedical practices, in the analyses and in the political intervention strategies on the problem. It is entirely

---

See also Allan M. Brandt and Alyssa Botelho, 'Not a Perfect Storm – Covid-19 and the Importance of Language', *The New England Journal of Medicine*, 382, 16 (2020), 1493-5.

credible, in any case, that the general context of the matter must be set largely in terms similar to those proposed in the following text.

> The global change that is taking place on Earth (...) is influenced by the so-called *ecological drivers*, elements capable of inducing ecosystemic alterations at a general (such as climate change) or local level (such as the introduction of invasive alien species or the expansion of anthropized areas, in turn possible causes of biodiversity loss and habitat fragmentation). These elements are also able to determine and modulate the emergence of some pathogens (especially viruses) transmitted by animal reservoirs species to other species, evolutionarily not adapted and therefore prone to manifest disease. These events can also involve the human population.[3]

The fact that ecological factors contribute directly or indirectly to creating the conditions of epidemics is a possibility of which, obviously, the terms must be precisely verified by examining the situations, geographic and anthropic contexts in which these events originate and take place on a case-by-case basis. Equally obvious, moreover, is that the consideration of this possibility does not at all imply the downsizing of the importance of the strictly biomedical aspects of epidemic diseases. What cannot be overlooked, however, is an elementary fact: the underestimation of the ecological factors of the possibility of epidemics increases the inability to take them into account analytically, practically and politically, when they prove to be the determinants or accelerants, as can be said about COVID-19.

An important starting point for determining the current dangers of pandemics in ecosystemic terms is certainly the definition of *emerging infectious diseases* in which experts and health organizations, for some decades, have included the potentially

---

3   Maria Alessandra De Marco and others, 'Ecologia dei patogeni emergenti nell'interfaccia uomo-animale: Chirotteri e Coronavirus', *Tavola rotonda*: *Chirotteri e speleologi, un rapporto complesso*, Finale Ligure (Italy), October 18, 2017: https://speleo.it/site/images/doc/dedmarcoispra.pdf; see also: 1044-report-sulla-tavola-rotonda-chirotteri-e-speleologi-un-rapporto-complesso-2 (accessed June 4, 2020).

pandemic diseases of our time.[4] This definition represents an implicit recognition of the growing difficulties that current societies are destined to encounter due to the recurring and unexpected occurrence of new contagious diseases which, combining with the breadth, intensity and speed of the typical processes of globalization, constantly risk to become uncontrollable. With regard to these diseases, there is a concept that has taken on fundamental importance in recent decades: that of *zoonosis*, that is to say the idea that some pathogens that animals carry, under certain conditions, can transfer to human organisms;[5] in this case these pathogens can cause serious epidemic processes and significant levels of mortality, if humans are without effective immune defences against them, having never undergone their infectious action before.[6] The concept of zoonosis, therefore,

---

4   With the phrase "emerging infectious diseases", infectious diseases are defined whose incidence has increased in the last two decades of the 20th century. This definition is generally associated with that of "re-emerging infectious diseases" to indicate the diseases that become frequent again after a longer or shorter period of decrease in their incidence. Within this set of diseases, according to the *World Health Organization,* «at present, the priority diseases are: SARS-COV2; Crimean-Congo hemorrhagic fever; Ebola virus disease and Marburg virus disease; Lassa fever; Middle East Respiratory Syndrome Coronavirus (MERS-COV) and Severe Acute Respiratory Syndrome (SARS); Nipah and Henipaviral diseases; Rift Valley fever; Zika; "Disease X" (Disease X represents the knowledge that a serious international epidemic could be caused by a pathogen currently unknown to cause human disease)». *World Health Organization,* 'Prioritizing diseases for research and development in emergency contexts': https://www.who.int/activities/prioritizing-diseases-for-research-and-development-in-emergency-contexts (accessed April 7, 2020). On this topic, see the publications of the Institute of Medicine (USA): *Emerging Infections: Microbial Threats to Health in the United states*, ed. by Joshua Lederberg, Robert E. Shope, and Stanley C. Oaks (Washington, DC: National Academies Press, 1992); Mark S. Smolinski, Margaret A. Hamburg, Joshua Lederberg (ed. by), *Microbial threats to health. Emergence, detection, and response* (Washington, DC: National Academies Press, 2003). See also: Stephen S. Morse (ed. by), *Emerging Viruses* (New York and Oxford: Oxford University Press, 1993).
5   *Zoonosis* is a term of Greek origin used to indicate any infectious disease of animals propagable to humans.
6   As observed by Frédéric Keck, «[t]he concern for zoonoses, which

implies the need to pay particular attention to the relationships between species and to the possibility that from their human-caused mutations derives not only the interspecific transmission of dangerous diseases, but also their exponential diffusion in human societies.[7]

In fact, these societies – the current ones in particular –, while tending to actively separate from the natural world through the artificialisation of each reality, the industrialization of each production and the dematerialisation of each communication, precisely in this way trigger processes of illusory departure from nature: rather than moving away from the natural world, our societies pursue the alienation of man from the world, to which we have already referred, in the sense that they conceal the impossibility of ignoring natural phenomena; not only do they not produce a "neutralization" of nature, but rather cause alterations of its forms – generally underestimating them –, from which however unpredictable dangers and uncontrollable effects can derive. It is from these alterations that, ultimately, risky changes in the relationships between man and other animal species can arise, the consequence of which may be the epidemic or pandemic spread of emerging infectious diseases of zoonotic origin.

In this regard, it is necessary to insist on an elementary fact: the unexpected transmission from one animal species to another of pathogens unknown to the immune systems of the organisms of the latter is a decisive condition so that the infections that follow can not

---

constitute the main part of emerging infectious diseases, has grown in the last forty years with the fight against Ebola hemorrhagic fever (1976), transmitted from bats to monkeys, mad cow disease (or Bovine Spongiform Encephalopathy, 1996), transmitted from sheep to cows, and SARS (Severe Acute Respiratory Syndrome, 2003), transmitted from bats to civet cats». Frédéric Keck, *Avian Reservoirs: Virus Hunters and Birdwatchers in Chinese Sentinel Posts* (Durham and London: Duke University Press, 2020), p. 2.

7   An important study on the exemplary case of HIV is that of Nuno R. Faria and others, 'The early spread and epidemic ignition of HIV-1 in human populations', *Science* 346, 6205 (2014), 56-61. On the importance of the relationships between species in the case of COVID-19 see Eben Kirksey, 'The Emergence of COVID-19: A Multispecies Story', *Anthropology Now*, 12, 1 (2020), 11-6.

only assume an epidemic character but also become uncontrollable, turn into pandemics and possibly cause high mortality.[8] In the passage from one species to another, pathogens mutate their genetic structure to adapt to organisms of species never frequented previously; they thus often become more capable of being transmitted further and more aggressive than the endemic pathogens with which the infected species coexisted previously. From this point of view, it is important to focus on the concept of *reservoir* with which the animal species or environments in which a pathogen can reproduce for indefinite periods of time – often without causing harmful effects – are indicated; on the other hand, it is appropriate to place this concept in relation to those of: *carrier* which indicates an animal species capable of transmitting a pathogen that can sometimes establish itself in it without causing disease; *mixing vessel* indicating a species in which a pathogen of animal origin can mutate interacting with pathogens of human origin.[9]

Taking all this into account, it can be said that certain epidemics or pandemics can explode if human animals are found to be the arrival point of one or more *spillovers*, that is, a passage from one species to another of infectious agents that in such passages may have undergone dangerous mutations; it is equally justifiable to think that the profound ecosystemic transformations provoked by our societies can favour the spillovers of highly infectious agents and the unfolding of their epidemic consequences.[10] This is a possibility on which it is however necessary to dwell further.

---

8   In this sense, the COVID-19 case appears truly paradigmatic as the study by Roujian Lu and others seems to demonstrate, 'Genomic characterisation and epidemiology of 2019 novel coronavirus: implications for virus origins and receptor binding', *Lancet*, 395 (2020), 565–74. https://www.thelancet.com/journals/lancet/article/PIIS0140-6736(20)30251-8/fulltext (accessed June 1, 2020).

9   On the subject, see the aforementioned Keck, *Avian Reservoirs*, and also: Daniel T. Haydon and others, 'Identifying Reservoirs of Infection: A Conceptual and Practical Challenge', *Emerging Infectious Diseases*, 8, 12 (2002), 1468-73; Richard W. Ashford, 'What it takes to be a reservoir host', *Belgian Journal of Zoology*, 127 (1997), 85-90.

10   See David Quammen, *Spillover: Animal Infections and the Next Human Pandemic* (New York: W.W. Norton & Company, 2012).

1.2 *A postmodern Black Death?*

The idea that certain alterations of the environments in which animal species that are reservoirs or carriers of pathogens live can create the conditions of epidemic processes is believed to be reliable above all with regard to the most classic of epidemics: the plague. As May R. Berenbaum writes, in fact, «[t]hroughout history at intermittent intervals, ecological and environmental conditions change so that plague moves out of its normal circles and enters human society».[11] This idea is considered plausible also with regard to what many consider the most important pandemic event in history: the so-called Black Death, the gigantic plague that struck much of humanity in the 14th century and – between 1347 and 1351 – invested Europe particularly heavily, repeating itself periodically in the following centuries. According to Robert S. Gottfried, the environmental conditions of the Black Death pandemic were created in the Gobi Desert area dominated by the Mongol Empire. The main factors of maturation of those conditions – according to him – were both socio-political and of an immediately natural origin. From the first point of view, the nomadic mobility of the Mongol horsemen, on which a large part of the government of the empire was based, represented the trigger for the diffusion in the most diverse geographical directions of the pathogen (*Yersinia pestis*) that caused the pandemic; but the original source of that pestilence may have been the Chinese region of Yunan, which almost certainly constituted an inveterate focus (a sort of "reservoir site") of that pathogen. From there the Mongol horsemen may have exported *Yersinia pestis* to the Gobi Desert and subsequently to other geographic areas mainly through their caravans laden with goods, after the Yunan had been annexed to their empire. The traffic by sea and by land that took place between East and West may have finally determined the arrival of the plague in Europe, where it had particularly disastrous consequences.[12]

---

11 May R. Berenbaum, *Bugs in the System: Insects and Their Impact on Human Affairs* (New York: Basic Books, 1995), p. 214.
12 Robert S. Gottfried, *The Black Death: Natural and Human Disaster in Medieval Europe* (New York: The Free Press, 1985), pp. 33-4, 36-7, 42-53.

The natural factors of that pandemic, on the other hand, could have been mainly derived from the climate change that occurred since the 13th century, a change that provoked the arrival of increasingly warm and dry winds from Africa to central Asia: it caused in this area an increase in the average temperatures, already normally hot, and an extreme drying of many natural habitats; which may have ended up pushing a whole set of possible carriers of *Yersinia pestis* (from Mongolian shepherds with their flocks to entire populations of rodents, insects and parasites) to head to geographic areas other than the Gobi Desert. According to this hypothesis, the spillovers that could be derived from all this were thus able to multiply and spread their infectious consequences beyond the borders of the Mongol Empire. The pandemic potential of the pathogen, therefore, could only grow progressively.[13] In Europe on the other hand, favourable environmental conditions for the spread of the epidemic could have been created through the other side of climate change that occurred since the 13th century: the so-called "Little Ice Age" which provoked a profound crisis in the predominantly agricultural economy of the continent and – as a consequence – famines, impoverishment and overall weakening of the population.[14]

Although the comparison between this scenario and the one in which the SARS-COV2 epidemic occurred may seem improper, it is not however the case to renounce to some useful suggestion that can derive from it. First of all – having made the necessary distinctions and proportions – it is simply a question of believing that the intertwining of large natural changes and political-economic processes of wide geographical reach is in itself an environmental condition of possible epidemics and pandemics. The case of the Black Death makes us clearly understand how an ecological transformation – beyond the fact that man is or is not primarily responsible for it – can provoke further ecosystem shifts: in particular, a climate change – having an influence on the

---

13 Gottfried, *The Black Death*, p. 34. See also William McNeill, *Plagues and People* (New York: Doubleday, 1976), pp. 149-98

14 Gottfried, *The Black Death*, pp. 22-30. See also: Jonathan D. Chambers, *Population, Economy, and Society in Pre-Industrial England* (Oxford: Oxford University Press, 1972), pp. 9-72.

activity, on the mobility and on the life of men, animals and their symbionts – can determine changes and transfers of presences and life cycles, all the more unpredictably full of consequences the more massive and extensive they are. In other words, large migrations, increased mobility and qualitative and quantitative variations in the presence of organisms of each species can derive from ecosystemic changes and, in turn, cause other changes. Evidently, the epidemic implications of all this cannot be underestimated precisely because they are largely unpredictable.

Of course, if the reflection on the conditions in which the SARS-COV2 pandemic exploded were set in similar terms, it could not be overlooked that the historical situation of our societies is profoundly different from that of medieval societies. However, this observation inevitably implies another very simple consideration: the influence that ecosystemic factors can exert in creating the conditions of an epidemic can only be increased by the environmental impact of the activities of our globalized societies, which is by far greater than that of the activities of medieval societies.

1.3 *Endless alterations*

Today the knowledge and powers that have to do with the care of life do not ignore the epidemic consequences that environmental changes caused by contemporary societies can have. Generally they recognize that the most influential processes in this sense are current climate change and other characteristic trends of our time, which – on the one hand – contribute in turn to climate change and – on the other – make environmental changes ever more profound: focus of attention among these trends are the growing expansion of urbanized and industrialized areas, deforestation, the increasingly intense mining of raw materials, the indefinite development of industrial agriculture, the consequent biological and chemical alteration of land, and the increase and acceleration of the mobility of people and goods, etc.[15] In this

---

15   See: National Research Council (USA), *Under the Weather. Climate, Ecosystems and Infectious Disease* (Washington DC: National

context, moreover, a factor is recognized that directly affects the possibility of triggering zoonotic diseases: the dizzying increase in intensive animal farming; this can only facilitate the occurrence of dangerous spillovers for humans due to their intense relationships with the stock farms.[16]

Beyond the degree of awareness that biomedical sciences and healthcare institutions have about the epidemic potential of this set of factors, it is evident that their consideration makes an observation by Bateson, which we have already met, particularly appropriate.

> Man, the outstanding modifier of environment, (...) achieves single-species ecosystems in his cities, but he goes one step further, establishing special environments for his symbionts. These, likewise, become single-species ecosystems: fields of corn, cultures of bacteria, batteries of fowls, colonies of laboratory rats, and the like.[17]

It is also by forming single-species ecosystems and special environments such as these that contemporary societies are in the condition of being able to be affected by serious epidemic diseases of zoonotic origin. It is entirely plausible, in any case, that increasing urbanization, population growth and concentration, deforestation, acceleration and expansion of mobility, stock farming growth, etc. destroy or deeply transform indefinite quantities of animal habitats; that in this way these processes also increase the intensity and frequency of human relations

---

Academies Press, 2001); Institute of Medicine (USA) – Forum on Microbial Threats, *The Impact of Globalization on Infectious Disease Emergence and Control: Exploring the Consequences and Opportunities*, ed. by Stacey Knobler and others (Washington, DC: National Academies Press, 2006); Gerald C. Nelson and others, 'Anthropogenic Drivers of Ecosystem Change: an Overview', *Ecology and Society*, 11, 2 (2006), art. 29: http://www.ecologyandsociety.org/vol11/iss2/art29/ (accessed May 19, 2020).

16   On this topic see, for example: Yali Si, Willem F. de Boer, Peng Gong, 'Different Environmental Drivers of Highly Pathogenic Avian Influenza H5N1 Outbreaks in Poultry and Wild Birds'. *PLoS ONE*, 8,1, (2013): e53362: https://journals.plos.org/plosone/article?id=10.1371/journal.pone.0053362 (accessed June 3, 2020)

17   *Steps to an Ecology of Mind*, pp. 452-3.

with the most varied species of organisms and microorganisms, also increasing the possibilities of cross-species transmissions of potentially pandemic pathogens.

These possibilities are clear if the changes just mentioned are related to a wider transformation of the relationships between animal species, which has been taking place for several decades: this is the enormous dispersion of organisms and microorganisms in ecosystems other than those of origin, caused by global warming. The results are, among others, profound alterations of specific local ecosystems and, in particular, the reduction of their biodiversity, caused by the fact that many of the "invading" organisms can compromise, until extinction, the survival of native species precisely introducing new pathogens.[18] Obviously, the spread of new diseases that derives from it, in certain conditions, can involve man also or above all in an epidemic form.

In a general context like this, four of the processes of intense anthropization of the environment that we have mentioned seem to play a particularly important role: deforestation, the spread of increasingly large industrial stock farms, the growing urbanization of the territories, the increase in the mobility of large human masses, other living beings and goods between the most varied places on the planet. In the first case, we are faced with one of the main processes of devastation of ecosystems inhabited by wild animals, possibly reservoirs and carriers of potentially pandemic pathogens. In the second we are dealing with very powerful attraction poles of pathogens coming from wild species that – through farm animals – can easily be transmitted to humans. In the third we are faced – as well as with one of the major processes of ecosystem alteration – with one of the main conditions in which an infectious disease can take on a pandemic dimension: a metropolis or a megacity that

---

18 Among the various possible examples, we can mention the case of allochthonous mosquitoes which, invading the Hawaiian islands, have in recent years caused the extinction of some species of native birds introducing avian malaria and a particular type of poxvirus. For a useful understanding of this subject, see Javier Diéguez Uribeondo, 'Un cóctel explosivo para la biodiversidad', *El Diario del Jardin Botanico*, 12 (2018), 6-7.

is caught by surprise by an infection, can transform immediately in a determining factor of its exponential diffusion and of the uncontrollable consequences that derive from it. In the fourth case we are dealing with a pathogen export factor far more efficient than the Mongol horsemen and the European merchants of the fourteenth century. By placing it in a "transversal" position with respect to these four processes, the phenomenon – traditional and more and more flourishing at the same time – of intense trade in wild animals for food or as pets can be added to them: in our globalized world this phenomenon finds in the anthropization processes that we have highlighted, the conditions – direct or indirect – of strengthening, expanding and accelerating its zoonotic and possibly pandemic implications.[19]

---

19   As is known, one of the most accepted hypotheses regarding the explosion of the COVID-19 pandemic is «that the virus has some connections with the wet markets of Wuhan province of China where it possibly was transmitted from a wild animal such as a bat or pangolin to a human being». What, more generally, seems reliable is that «wild, domesticated and captive being traded in various forms in these markets. These markets facilitated a congregation of viruses and bacteria across the world – from primates, pangolins, bats and rodents. These open laboratories provided variables and catalysts to trigger mutations and adaptations of viruses into new hosts and different living conditions and produced upgraded versions of the virus – with COVID-19 suspected as one among them». That this type of animal trade is anything but a traditional endangered phenomenon seems to be demonstrated by the fact that «these markets are controlled by international wildlife trafficking syndicates with well-established procurement, transportation, distribution networks across the globe and the money involved runs into billions. The illegal wildlife trade is an estimated 23 billion industry». Jose Louies (chief of Enforcement, Wildlife Trust of India), 'Of Markets, Wet & Pet & case for One World, One Health', May 5, 2020: https://www.daijiworld.com/chan/exclusiveDisplay.aspx?articlesID=5193 (accessed May 31, 2020). An interesting urge not to focus attention exclusively on the trade of wildanimals in the study of pandemics is that of Evan A. Eskew and Colin J. Carlson, 'Overselling wildlife trade bans will not bolster conservation or pandemic preparedness', *Lancet Planet Health,* June 1 (2020), 1-2: https://www.thelancet.com/journals/lanplh/article/PIIS2542-5196(20)30123-6/fulltext (accessed June 1, 2020).

2. *Global surveillance and impossible normality*

2.1 *World biopolitics*

At this point it is appropriate to make the question that stands in the background of this discussion explicit: what forms does biopolitics take today in the face of the problem of pandemics? Of course, we have to abandon at the outset to think of responding satisfactorily to it: the first real pandemic of the 21st century is still ongoing as we write; therefore, only after its exhaustion can the conditions be given for some sensible answer to the question. Here, however, we can look for tracks to follow in view of answers to be developed in the future.

A first indication in this sense can be given referring again to the importance that the relationship between man and animals assumes with respect to the possibility of epidemics. Drawing on what Frédéric Keck claims, one could say that man's relationship with other animal species as possible pathogen vectors has been and still is at the centre of at least three forms of biopolitics. The first tends towards *prevention* (or "securitization") and consists in treating animals simply as a threat to human health in the event of an epidemic risk, often ending up subjecting them to mass culling. This is what happened, for example, in China when the explosion of the "bird flu" was sufficient reason for the extermination of several million farmed chickens. The second form is, instead, that in which animal species affected by infectious diseases become the object of research and experimentation with vaccines or other medical remedies; in this case, man's relationship with these species is purely instrumental and tends to implement *precautionary strategies*: vaccinations have definitely become part of the state's biopolitics after Louis Pasteur rationally explained their immunizing effects by testing them on animals. Finally, the third form pays greater attention to the complexity of the relationships between species; in this case the animals become a sort of ally in *preparedness* (or "mitigating") *strategies* aimed at avoiding the risk of epidemics in advance or at reducing their damage: they are not necessarily killed because they are dangerous and the researchers study the pathogens of which they are carriers to identify their types and mutations, to prefigure the forms that such pathogens could have if a spillover occurred. Biopolitical strategies based on research concerning wild and farmed birds, often conducted through the collaboration between virologists and birdwatchers in countries bordering People's Republic of China such as Hong Kong, Taiwan and Singapore, have been oriented in this direction in order to face the eventuality of avian flu epidemics.[20]

Of course, in order to recognize the main trends of anti-pandemic biopolitics of our time, it is necessary above all to take into account the guidelines of international organizations that deal with health and well-being. In an era of globalization, the very idea of a pandemic seems to necessarily require that international institutions propose the strategic policies to be implemented in this regard. It is evident, in any case, that institutions such as the World Health Organization (WHO), the Food and Agriculture Organization (FAO) and the World Organization for Animal Health (OIE) have for some decades found in the concept of *emerging infectious diseases* a fundamental reference to strengthen their role as planetary organizations actively committed to protecting life.[21] The great AIDS epidemic of the 1980s had already offered decisive reasons for promoting this strengthening. Further impulses in this sense are then derived from other very relevant events and processes: the re-emergence of old infectious diseases such as tuberculosis and the succession of epidemics – some of which have been declared pandemic by the WHO – such as those of SARS of 2003, "bird flu" between 2003 and 2004, "swine flu" between 2009 and 2010, MERS in 2012, Ebola in 2014, etc.

As observed by Muriel Figuié, from the end of the nineties, WHO in particular started a renewal of its policies trying to overcome their merely international dimension and projecting its role in a supranational and global perspective.[22] Until then, the Organization's policies tended above all to ensure coordination

---

20   See Keck, *Avian Reservoirs*, pp. 11-28 and 69-172.
21   Muriel Figuié, 'Towards a Global Governance of Risks: International Health Organisations and the Surveillance of Emerging Infectious Diseases', *Journal of Risk Research*, 17, 4 (2014), 469-83 (p. 473).
22   Figuié, 'Towards a Global Governance of Risks', p. 473.

between the epidemiological surveillance activities of the various states, without limiting their autonomy; instead, from that moment and especially after the explosion of the SARS epidemic, WHO first of all asks the member states to commit themselves to provide in a transparent and timely way any information on potentially epidemic events that occur within their borders; moreover, on the basis of this information it elaborates guidelines for risk prevention and management of possible emergencies, trying to adapt them to the global scenario in which emerging infectious diseases can unfold their pandemic effects.[23] Finally, this evolution of WHO strategies has found a sort of crowning glory in the convergence of intentions that has taken place around the idea of "One World, One Health" between the policies of WHO itself and those of FAO and OIE, as well as other world organizations such as UNSIC (United Nations System Influenza Coordination), UNICEF (United Nations Children's Fund) and World Bank.[24]

In this context, in principle, great importance is attached to the need «to enhance the collaboration between the public health, animal health and wildlife institutions» or to that of «[a]dapting medical and veterinary curricula to strengthen initial and continuing training of officials for human and animal health services, including appropriate ecosystems health studies».[25] These are needs to which, however, contemporary medicine seems largely unprepared to respond, being deeply conditioned by its sectorial specialties. In any case, to indicate the general orientation that knowledge and medical practices should take in this sense, it will suffice to recall some suggestions proposed by David Quammen, an author who – while being extraneous to the circle of experts – gave importance,

---

23   See World Health Organization, *International Health Regulations (2005), Third Edition* (Geneva, Sw: WHO Press, 2016).
24   See: FAO, OIE, WHO, UNSIC, UNICEF, WB, *Contributing to One World, One Health: A Strategic Framework for Reducing Risks of Infectious Diseases at the Animal–Human–Ecosystems Interface*, https://www.oie.int/doc/ged/D5720.PDF (accessed April 17, 2020); Figuié, 'Towards a Global Governance of Risks', pp. 473-7.
25   *Contributing to One World, One Health*, p. 36.

first and foremost, to the ecosystemic alterations that create the conditions of the potentially pandemic spillovers of our time.

> Medical doctors and public health professionals should be very much involved, and not just back in the hospitals. (...) There's this new professional (...) who has this synergy of skills and training. They maybe start with a degree in veterinary medicine and then add a doctorate in ecology or perhaps a master's in public health. That's somebody who can be out there, in the forest, in the villages, observing and helping to influence what is done to reduce the risk of spillovers and to contain spillovers when they occur. Add to those human physicians and virologists. I think it would be great if more people with both medical degrees and degrees in virology move into field work on zoonotic spillovers. That kind of training is essential to this field. I do know a few of these kinds of professionals. (...) We need (...) more people with that kind of training, with a medical degree and an understanding of the ecology of viruses, and how something can come out of a rodent in the rural landscape of Bolivia and cause a hemorrhagic fever in people.[26]

These types of paths are not really completely marginal in the context of contemporary medical knowledge and strategies. They gave rise, among others, to the scientific and practical approach defined "One Health", which – by paying attention to interspecific relationships and ecological contexts – reduces the essential anthropocentrism of historical forms of medicine.[27] In general, however, it can be said that approaches of this type often find obstacles in the realization of their objectives also due to a certain conflict between different epistemological visions that are expressed in the biomedical field, such as that which often transpires from the comparison between epidemiologists and virologists.[28] It is entirely plausible, in any case, that political

---

26   Quammen, Interview with Abdul-Kareem Ahmed, pp. 110-1.
27   See in particular the web sites of: One Health Commission: https://www.onehealthcommission.org/ (accessed May 21, 2020); EcoHealth Alliance: https://www.ecohealthalliance.org/ (accessed May 21, 2020); One Health Center of Excellence – University of Florida: https://onehealth.ifas.ufl.edu/about/ (accessed May 21, 2020); FAO, 'One Health', http://www.fao.org/asiapacific/perspectives/one-health/en/ (accessed April 17, 2020).
28   As Keck points out, the former favour the management and containment

institutions and economic subjects operating in the biomedical field are generally not available to adequately support the research and strategies that tend to too freely cross the boundaries between scientific sectors.[29] Such research and strategies, on the other hand, having to depend on funding from institutions and companies generally not very sensitive to ecological problems, seem far from being based on radically critical attitudes towards the dominant forms of social and economic development, through which our societies will continue to create pandemic dangers for a long time to come.

2.2 *Fire-fighters and smoke-detectors*

As we have seen, the adoption of the "One World, One Health" concept by world organizations attentive to the care of life has led to the strengthening of the planetary dimension as a privileged area to face the epidemic pathologies of globalized humanity. In this perspective, among the main aspirations of the WHO in particular emerges that of remedying the general unpreparedness of the national states to face the risks deriving from emerging infectious diseases. This unpreparedness would primarily consist of the inadequacy of states to address the global nature of threats from new infectious diseases; furthermore, it would consist of the fact that many nations lack health care systems large and robust enough to face the new health dangers. Hence the importance that the Organization attaches to the constant collection and processing of information on pathogens and epidemic risks, as fundamental tools of a global policy to be based above all on preventive surveillance and the use for this purpose of the most advanced technologies. The WHO favours the global surveillance approach since it considers «to prepare for the inevitable»

---

of ongoing contagion situations, while the latter tend to develop and implement strategies for preparing for contagion, to reduce their impact. Keck, *Avian Reservoir*, pp. 34-5.

29   See Jennifer Kahn, 'How Scientists Could Stop the Next Pandemic Before It Starts', *The New York Time Magazine*, April 21, 2020: https://www.nytimes.com/2020/04/21/magazine/pandemic-vaccine.html (accessed May 21, 2020).

fundamental, believing that now «what is uncertain is what and when».[30] The willingness of states to collaborate in this policy and to respect the indications of the Organization thus becomes an indispensable condition for implementing effective strategies for anticipating epidemic risks and for the timely management of possible emergencies.

The need to tackle the problem of pandemics above all in terms of global surveillance is therefore presented as fundamental and unavoidable. This also conditions aspects of life protection strategies regarding the ecosystemic factors of new diseases. In fact, these aspects are placed in an overall emergency concept, in a perspective of permanent surveillance, which ends up jeopardizing broader approaches. The same general purpose of «reducing risks of infectious diseases at the animal-human-ecosystems interface» is placed in this perspective, since it is in fact subordinated to the priorities: to «develop surveillance capacity, including the development of standards, tools and monitoring processes at national, regional and global levels»; to «strengthen national emergency response capability, including a global rapid response support capacity».[31] Of course, in the context of strategic framework of "One world, One Health", «the critical role that ecosystems play in originating new zoonotic diseases» is recognized; but, in any case, the preferred approach is that of monitoring and surveillance; at the same time, it comes to light that «[u]nder some circumstances, comprehensive wildlife monitoring could require resources that would exceed the total estimated for all other priority areas combined».

The large uncertainty surrounding this area calls for careful consideration of the risk factors and, since it is unlikely that there will be sufficient resources to undertake an intensive global strategy, a decision must be taken as to what constitutes an

---

30   WHO, *Anticipating Emerging Infectious Disease Epidemics*, (Geneva, SW, WHO Press, 2016), p. 50. In this regard, see above all: Institute of Medicine (USA) – Forum on Microbial Threats, *The Impact of Globalization on Infectious Disease Emergence and Control*, pp. 125-74.

31   *Contributing to One World, One Health*, pp. 23-4.

acceptable level of risk. Surveillance activities should strictly follow a risk-based approach.[32]

Be that as it may, the reference to the animal-human-ecosystems interface clearly indicates the importance that the World Organizations attach to the ecological context in which essential factors of most of the current potentially pandemic diseases occur. As we have seen, some of these factors can be recognized, on the one hand, in the changes of certain natural mechanisms and, on the other, in some consequences of the development of human societies: on the first side, the ecosystem character of the problem is evident above all through the fundamental role that relationships between human and non-human animals play in the eventuality of a sudden passage of pathogens from the second to the first; on the other side, the ecosystem character of the matter lies above all in the triggering role that the growing anthropization of the environment plays in creating favourable conditions for cross-species transmissions of pathogens and for their exponential diffusion. Well, both on the natural and anthropic side it is easy to find elements of complexity which are particularly difficult to consider in the predominantly emergency framework in which the world biopolitical organizations tend to face the problem of new and old infectious diseases.

In the context of natural mechanisms, some of these elements of complexity emerge clearly considering an elementary fact: if an animal species is identified as a reservoir of a pathogen, this does not imply that the interruption of relations between man and this species – admitted that it is truly possible – is the most effective choice to avoid epidemic and pandemic risks. In this regard, it must first be noted that the attribution of the definition of reservoir to a single animal species is totally reckless: if, for example, this definition is limited to a species that presents itself as the "original location" of a pathogen (such as, probably, bats in the case of COVID-19), we in fact refuse to recognise other species that could play the same role of reservoir. Furthermore, in this way there is the risk of neglecting the need to identify other

---

32 *Contributing to One World, One Health*, p. 46.

species that could play very important roles: for example, healthy carriers of the pathogen, intermediaries between the reservoir species and humans or between the first and other species that maintain relationships with humans. All in all, moreover, it must be added that the definition of reservoir can also be attributed to environmental contexts or to their elements such as water, soil, etc.[33]

Even in the case of the growing anthropization of the environment, the elements of complexity of the ecosystemic factors of pandemics, difficult to treat in a logic of global surveillance, emerge from the consideration of an elementary fact on which we have already focused: the pathogenic relationships between animal species and the human one are facilitated by the alterations of the discontinuities between the first and the second, which the incessant anthropization of the environment causes. From this point of view it can also be said that the interruption of interspecific relations is far from easily practicable. Think, for example, of three anthropic factors particularly powerful in creating favourable conditions for the occurrence of spillovers: increasing urbanization, the indefinite expansion of industrial farms, the global increase in the mobility of people, animals and goods. A straight question could be asked about all this: are contemporary societies, productive organizations, economic and political systems, individuals willing to renounce – or drastically reduce – in reasonably quick times pandemic danger factors such as ways of living, the patterns of activity, coexistence and social relationship that require or cause the growth of urbanization, industrial farms and the mobility of men, things, and living beings of all kinds?

The answer to this question appears to be inevitably negative. However, to exclude that questions such as this should be asked as they indicate problems that cannot be resolved quickly, means immediately placing oneself in submission; meaning adapting to the presumed comfort of living day by day, which is also the best condition for a biopolitics of surveillance and permanent

---

33   See: Haydon and others, 'Identifying Reservoirs of Infection'; Ashford, 'What it takes to be a reservoir host'.

emergencies to overwhelm our freedoms, reduce the possibility of practicing them politically and ethically rather than simply trying to survive. It is evident, in any case, that asking questions of this type also means trying not to be imprisoned in the framework of biopolitics, even if it is inevitable that one must confront it.

2.3 *An algorithmic biopower?*

The centrality that above all WHO attaches to global surveillance based primarily on the collection and timely processing of information is a fact that needs to be considered further. It is superfluous to remember that real global giants – from Google to Twitter – are moving on this terrain, whose technological ability to process information and practice surveillance appears to be superior to that of the states and the international institutions. The substantial domination that these global players exert on the information and telematic technologies scene does not only entail the accentuation of the privatization processes – in place for some time – of the production and management of common goods such as information and knowledge; it implies also or above all a profound change in the ways of conceiving, collecting and processing information data concerning the life – as well as the activities, relationships and behaviours – of individuals and collectivities. According to some scholars, this radical change is mainly due to the use of algorithmic technologies that these subjects favour in the management of huge and constantly growing masses of data of all kinds; according to these authors, these technologies represent the basis of that algorithmic governmentality which we have already referred to, which goes beyond the classic ways of governing people:[34] the logic that inspires this governmentality is not so much as that of identifying the limits of normality within which it would be a matter of maintaining individual behaviour and collective phenomena to guarantee and administer the security of society; the latter is the typical logic of traditional political institutions

---

34 See the aforementioned: Rouvroy and Berns, 'Gouvernementalité algorithmique et perspectives d'émancipation'; Rouvroy, 'The end(s) of critique: data-behaviourism vs. due process'.

that favour the statistical approach in collecting and analysing information; these institutions pursue normalization based above all on the identification of an average level of performance of social phenomena, to be taken as a reference of the security that must be guaranteed.[35] Algorithmic governmentality scholars argue that, unlike the use of the statistical approach, that of the algorithmic approach – while not excluding normalization purposes at all – tends above all to neutralize in advance the unexpected: here, the timely prefiguration of potentially ungovernable events and behaviours is the main aim pursued to reduce their disruptive reach and make them compatible with the functioning of the market, crime prevention or collective health management.[36]

Whatever the case, the enormous importance that algorithmic technologies have assumed in the management of data collected via telematic networks has inspired the creation of various *syndromic surveillance systems* whose main focus is precisely the danger of epidemics and pandemics. The creation of these systems has been promoted – in addition to the economic giants of the web – above all by large international organizations often structured according to the models of the NGOs. On the other hand, as we will see later, even the most institutional world organizations such as the WHO tend to take advantage of the algorithmic approach of these systems and integrate in this way their more traditional procedures for acquiring information useful for the surveillance and prevention of health hazards and emergencies.

Among the main purposes of syndromic surveillance systems is that of overcoming the limits that condition the collection and processing of information data on emerging infectious diseases by political institutions officially responsible for governing public health. In fact, the information on which the surveillance that these systems aspire to guarantee is based are not only that

---

35   In this regard, the studies on algorithmic governmentality refer to the analyses proposed by Foucault especially in *Security, Territory, Population*.

36   For an analysis in these terms of the issue of new epidemic diseases, see Stephen L. Roberts and Stefan Elbe, 'Catching the flu: Syndromic surveillance, algorithmic governmentality and global health security', *Security Dialogue*, 48,1(2017), 46-62.

officially communicated by national health services, governments or biomedical research laboratories; these systems – at least in their most advanced forms – deal with algorithmic technologies especially the "non-diagnostic" information obtained, for example, from the behaviours that web users make known through the use of their telematic devices when doing certain searches, they buy certain therapeutic remedies, they frequent or do not frequent certain places, and so on.

> The main idea behind the use of such 'proxy' data is that if a novel infectious disease breaks out, then informal signals of unusual clusters of illnesses may surface before any official clinical and laboratory analysis can be undertaken. For example, people suddenly becoming ill may start to search for unusual symptoms on internet search engines, may begin to purchase over the counter remedies, or may decide to stay home from work or school. Through closely and continuously monitoring these early, preclinical signals it may become possible to considerably speed up the process of outbreak detection – thus gaining vital time for preparing a government response.[37]

Obviously, the multiplicity of data that can be examined and processed through this surveillance model is vastly greater than that of information that directly refers to the state of health of people and populations; this multiplicity, in fact, can include

> a wide range of more indirect data – such as reports from hospital emergency departments, hospital admissions, sales of medicines from pharmacies, telephone calls to health advice providers, levels of absenteeism at school and/or workplaces, etc.[38]

Among the syndromic surveillance systems that have been created for the monitoring and processing of any information apparently useful to report the dangers of pandemics, we can mention the Global Public Health Intelligence Network (GPHIN) and HealthMap, both of which make intensive and systematic use of the so-called Big Data by extracting indications and scenarios

---

37 Roberts and Elbe, 'Catching the flu', p. 48.
38 'Catching the flu', p. 47.

of possible pandemic threats with algorithmic procedures. The WHO participates in the GPHIN; in this way, the Organization adds a powerful tool for processing information obtained from the media around the world to its own institutional surveillance system (Global Outbreak Alert Response Network – GOARN) in which the information systems of the participating states are officially involved. The GPHIN demonstrated remarkable efficiency when, in late 2002, it managed to derive the first signs of a "strange flu" from the Chinese local media, which was subsequently defined as SARS and declared pandemic. HealthMap, on the other hand, is the system that probably makes the most intense use of the algorithmic approach to any information that can be extracted from the most varied of sources. It showed its capabilities when it managed to report, before the official institutions, the most serious Ebola epidemic, erupted in Guinea in 2014.[39]

A significant example of a syndromic surveillance system is also that of Google Flu Trends, whose activities started in 2008-2009 and were discontinued in 2014. Based mainly on the research that network users carried out through the same google engine on topics apparently related to initial states of flu, in the 2012-2013 winter season it found itself repeatedly overestimating the signs of a possible epidemic in the USA. In this case, the algorithmic treatment of the Big Data has shown aspects of considerable unreliability of the predictions based on alleged correlations between certain user searches and the onset of infectious diseases. These searches, in fact, can have the most contrasting motivations and therefore they can push the algorithmic calculation systems to "misunderstand" the meaning and scope of certain behaviours recorded randomly on the network. As has been observed, the *correlation* says almost nothing about *causation*. In fact, «[f]iguring out what causes what is hard (impossible, some say). Figuring out what is correlated with what is much cheaper and easier».[40]

---

39   'Catching the flu', pp. 52-3.
40   Tim Harford, 'Big data: are we making a big mistake?', *Financial Times Magazine*, March 28, 2014, https://www.ft.com/content/21a6e7d8-b479-11e3-a09a-00144feabdc0 (accessed May 23, 2020).

This incident has been considered by many to be a failure of Google Flu Trends predictive claims.[41] But, in reality, the problem that this case brings up may not only be that of the questionable degree of reliability of the predictions based on indistinct masses of Big Data. Of course, one can share the idea that algorithmic investigations produce «knowledge without truth» – according to Rouvroy's statement.[42] But there are at least two other considerations to make in this regard. The first is of a general nature: it consists in observing – as in fact Rouvroy invites us to do – that, whatever the reliability of the algorithmic technologies applied to Big Data are, the main purpose for which they are used is not at all that of building scientifically verifiable knowledge, but inevitably inaccurately elaborating the "profiles" of network users and "speculating" their preferences for above all – even if not only – commercial purposes.[43]

The other consideration is a consequence of the one just made and directly concerns the issue of new infectious diseases. In this regard, if we can speak of "failure" of Google Flu Trends or – more generally – of poor reliability of algorithmic technologies, it can be done to the extent that it is believed that they are actually destined to discover truths; if a syndromic surveillance system, overestimating the "signals" extracted from Big Data, launches alarms that turn out to be unfounded, it is because what

41   See, for example: Declan Butler, 'When Google got flu wrong', *Nature,* 494, 7436 (2013), 155-6; Hal Hodson, 'Google Flu Trends gets it wrong three years running', *New Scientist,* 2961 (2014): https://www. newscientist.com/article/dn25217-google-flu-trends-gets-it-wrong-three-years-running/#ixzz6Kc1E1CQN (accessed April 25, 2020); David Lazer and others, 'The parable of Google flu: Traps in big data analysis', *Science,* 343, 6176 (2014), 1203-5. See also: Alexis C. Madrigal, 'In Defense of Google Flu Trend: If the system failed, it did so only in the outsize dreams of Big Data acolytes', March 24 (2014), https://www.theatlantic.com/technology/archive/2014/03/in-defense-of-google-flu-trends/359688/ (accessed April 25, 2020).

42   Rouvroy, 'The end(s) of critique: data-behaviourism vs. due process', p. 151.

43   See Antoinette Rouvroy, 'Algorithmic governmentality: radicalisation and immune strategy of capitalism and neoliberalism?', trans. by Benoît Dillet, *La Deleuziana – Rivista online di Filosofia,* 3 (2016), 30-6: http://www.ladeleuziana.org/wp-content/uploads/2016/12/Rouvroy2eng.pdf (accessed May 23, 2020).

is overestimated or overrated is the type of knowledge that the algorithmic approach to Big Data can produce. From this point of view, the algorithmic surveillance systems of emerging infectious diseases can try to dodge the risk of making gross forecast errors if they agree to compare the conjectural results of their investigations with those statistically based on the analyses of strictly healthcare institutions. It is in this sense, in fact, that the WHO is oriented by combining the use of the algorithmic system of the GPHIN with that of the GOARN, based above all on the collection of data from the states.[44] Precisely in this regard, however, problems arise which cannot be overlooked. The first is contingent, but nonetheless important: the collaboration of states, their ability or willingness to provide complete and timely information on health hazards are inevitably uncertain for various reasons. In particular, it is not irrelevant that not all states adhere to organizations such as the WHO; on the other hand, those who adhere to them may lack effective tools or structures to collect, process and communicate information on epidemic risks in the best ways; moreover, many of them may always have an interest – economic, political or otherwise – in avoiding or delaying the communication and sharing of information on their health problems.

If, therefore, we take into account both these problems and those concerning the predictive use of algorithmic technologies, we have further reasons to consider disputable the idea that a question such as that of pandemics can be adequately addressed through policies based above all on global surveillance. The momentary reticence of a nation state, the overconfidence in the surveillance and decision-making abilities of a world organization or the occasional inefficiency of technological forecasting systems – algorithmic or otherwise – may be enough to provoke a pandemic such as that which exploded in 2020. It is difficult, in fact, to say that among the determining factors of the planetary diffusion of SARS-COV2 there has not been at least one of those just listed. If it is true that immediate political responsibilities for the explosion of this

---

44   'Catching the flu', p. 59; see also Institute of Medicine (USA) – Forum on Microbial Threats, *The Impact of Globalization on Infectious Disease Emergence and Control,* pp. 121-2.

pandemic can be identified, it is also true that even this possibility contributes to confirming a fact: unpredictable and potentially pandemic diseases by definition can make the consequences of the inefficiency – accidental or malicious – of the global surveillance systems aimed to prevent them, irreparable.[45]

On the other hand, an anti-pandemic policy based mainly on surveillance is not questionable only for elementary reasons such as these which, moreover, seem to be generally underestimated; it is also questionable because its implicit assumption is that it should now be considered obvious that the ecosystem, political and economic factors of contemporary epidemics – even if they are clearly highlighted in official documents – cannot be effectively thwarted or reduced, as this would require the implementation of radical and "expensive" wide-ranging strategies. Ultimately, placing global technological surveillance at the centre of anti-pandemic policies creates the conditions to consider secondary, for example, the fact that the situation of public health systems in many countries is very precarious or tends to be so. This situation, however, can be a determining condition for the spread of an epidemic, as has happened in 2020 in various countries.[46]

The SARS-COV2 pandemic has clearly revealed the widespread health vulnerability that the previous forty years of neoliberal policies has created in many countries, starting with the richest ones where the contagion has caused extremely heavy effects (take for example USA, UK, Italy, Spain). Therefore, if it is true that nation states are inadequate to face the pandemic risks of new infectious diseases, the reason for their inadequacy does not lie

---

45   We saw it with what happened between the end of January and the beginning of March 2020: the WHO in late January declared the epidemic of COVID-19 "*Public Health Emergency of International Concern* (PHEIC)" and only on March 11 did they declare it pandemic. This certainly contributed to delaying the interventions necessary to prevent it from spreading. As far as was known before the completion of this book, another delay factor may have been some "hesitation" by the Chinese government to quickly provide information on the outbreak from which the pandemic originated.

46   In this regard, see Pierre Dardot and Christian Laval, 'The Pandemic as a Political Trial', trans. by Matthew MacLellan: https://www.academia.edu/42356180/The_Pandemic_as_political_trial.

only in their difficulty in intervening on health problems whose size exceeds their territorial boundaries; their "unpreparedness" is also explained by the downsizing policies of their health care systems created during the development of the welfare state: decrease in public spending destined for these systems, progressive reduction of their territorial articulations, privatization of most of their services, etc.[47] To all this must be added, moreover, the growing importance gained in the last decades by biomedicine which turns its attention above all to the genetic microcosm of the individual and which, therefore, is unsuitable to manage collective and potentially global health problems.

Of course, if such observations apply to wealthy countries, to an even greater extent they apply to poor countries. The main difference between them is that historically poor countries have never had a great chance of acquiring public health facilities comparable to what many of the rich countries have managed to achieve in the 20th century with welfare state policies. This obviously places the first in conditions of particular danger in the face of emerging infectious diseases: these, in fact, often affect their inhabitants in very serious epidemics without spreading to the richer countries, as happened in 2014 with the Ebola epidemic.

3. *Novelties and historical recurrences*

3.1 *A jump back and a leap in the dark*

The anti-pandemic biopolitics promoted by WHO are part of a perspective of overcoming the typical strategies of past eras. In a publication of the Organization, this perspective is outlined in a

---

47   See the exemplary case of Lombardy, an Italian region in which, in the early months of the pandemic, around 50 percent of the infected and dead that it had caused in Italy was concentrated: Ben Munster, 'What made Italy's wealthiest region so vulnerable to coronavirus? Did private healthcare hamper Lombardy's response to the pandemic?', *New Statesman*, 19 April 2020: https://www.newstatesman.com/politics/health/2020/04/coronavirus-italy-lombardy-private-healthcare-response (accessed May 23, 2020).

scheme which also indicates the essential aspects of the policies that should be overcome and updated. According to the proposed framework, in the 19th and much of the 20th century it was mainly national governments that faced the threats of long-known infectious diseases (cholera, plague, yellow fever, smallpox, typhus, relapsing fever) by imposing quarantine measures and limit restrictions to trade and travel; from the end of the 20th century, however, new threats of epidemic diseases tending to take on global dimensions are emerging: these, together with the danger of bioterrorism, have changed the context of the health risks to be faced and have raised the need to increase capacities for the collection and effective communication of information on eventualities to be kept under control. According to the publication, new technologies have begun to favour these capacities and, in addition, partial forms of global governance have also been promoted with the involvement of organizations other than states; all this, however, has remained firm at a stage of fragmentation and multilateralism of the responses to the dangers of new diseases; but today we must go beyond this state of affairs. The 21st century is the time when the global framework of International Health Security must prevail: «All public health emergencies, including climate change, emerging infections, antimicrobial resistance, and synthetic biology» must be subject to attention and surveillance. «Prevention and preparedness at national level» are the main aims that must be pursued in this global context; the «knowledge infrastructure» must be strengthened and the integration between the strategies of the various players is the condition that must be promoted and maintained for this purpose. Particularly significant, finally, is a sort of summary slogan proposed in the WHO document, which goes like this: «Fire-fighters and smoke-detectors – one and all, we are in the prevention business».[48]

---

48   WHO, *Anticipating Emerging Infectious Disease Epidemics*, pp. 45 6. The key expressions with which the tools to be adopted and the objectives to be pursued in this perspective are also very significant: *Shared Information Response*; *Global Response Teams; Response Contingency Fund*; *Global Fund for Health Security*; *Predict and Prevent*; *Managing Uncertainty*; *Global Health Security Preparedness Index*.

The reconstruction – proposed by the WHO – of the historical phases and anti-epidemic policies that should be overcome today is worthy of being considered in the light of some indications that we can derive from Foucault. Particularly important is to highlight the historical moment in which – according to him – the quarantine model seems to assume a sort of inaugural function with respect to modernity. This is the moment that the author indicates in *Discipline and Punish* referring to «an order published at the end of the seventeenth century», with which the precautions to be taken to deal with the plague in a city are established. This order imposes the strict closure and control of the urban space through the precise surveillance exercised by intendants, mayors and magistrates who have the power to impose sanctions, including the putting to death of those who violate the rules:

> the closing of the town and its outlying districts, a prohibition to leave the town on pain of death, the killing of all stray animals; the division of the town into distinct quarters, each governed by an intendant. Each street is placed under the authority of a syndic, who keeps it under surveillance; if he leaves the street, he will be condemned to death. On the appointed day, everyone is ordered to stay indoors: it is forbidden to leave on pain of death. (...) If it is absolutely necessary to leave the house, it will be done in turn, avoiding any meeting. (...) Each individual is fixed in his place. And, if he moves, he does so at the risk of his life, contagion or punishment.
>
> Inspection functions ceaselessly. The gaze is alert everywhere: (...) guards at the gates, at the town hall and in every quarter to ensure the prompt obedience of the people and the most absolute authority of the magistrates (...). At each of the town gates there will be an observation post; at the end of each street sentinels. Every day, the intendant visits the quarter in his charge (...). Every day, too, the syndic goes into the street for which he is responsible; stops before each house: gets all the inhabitants to appear at the windows (...). Everyone locked up in his cage, everyone at his window, answering to his name and showing himself when asked – it is the great review of the living and the dead.[49]

---

49   Foucault, *Discipline and Punish*, pp. 195-6.

The plague and the danger of spreading the contagion present themselves here as conditions for establishing an order that involves an extreme individualization of each of the social figures subjected to quarantine.

> The plague is met by order (...). It lays down for each individual his place, his body, his disease and his death, his well-being, by means of an omnipresent and omniscient power that subdivides itself in a regular, uninterrupted way even to the ultimate determination of the individual, of what characterizes him, of what belongs to him, of what happens to him. Against the plague, which is a mixture, discipline brings into play its power, which is one of analysis.[50]

This scenario characterized by the strict application of the rules and the detailed articulation of surveillance on each individual, is not the only solution that the forms of power of the first centuries of modernity have adopted to face epidemic emergencies. They soon – according to Foucault – began to move towards more dynamic and fluid approaches. The launch of inoculation (or variolisation) campaigns in the first decades of the 18th century and then of vaccination campaigns in the 19th century represent decisive breakthroughs in this regard. These treatments of epidemic diseases, combined with the statistical calculation that the arts of government use more and more, allow to face the problem of epidemics by breaking down the massive form with which it presented itself previously. It is no longer simply a question of imposing a block on all movements. The problem of epidemics can be addressed by means of differentiated prevention, taking not only the individual, but also the population as a whole and its various components as the object of attention. The population thus becomes statistical matter: it is analysed in its various segments – age, condition, city, environment, profession, etc. – who have different degrees of exposure to infection, mortality or probability of recovery.

Inoculation and vaccination practices are fundamental elements of this statistical and probabilistic approach to epidemic diseases. In turn, these practices find in this approach a

---

50 *Discipline and Punish*, pp. 197.

fundamental condition of their application; they themselves are subject to calculation and probabilistic analysis, to the extent that they too create a risk for those subjected to them. If vaccination, in particular, will become more and more widespread, it is because – so to speak – it promises, in exchange for a certain risk of getting sick and suffering from it, a greater chance of avoiding the danger of being infected and dying, if one is part of the population most exposed to infection and the most serious forms of the disease.[51] Furthermore, the statistical approach allows to determine the contagion phenomenon considering the possibility of «sudden worsening, acceleration, and increase of the disease». Finally, through statistical analysis it can be taken into account that «its spread at a particular time and place carries the risk (...) of multiplying cases that multiply other cases in an unstoppable tendency or gradient until the phenomenon is effectively checked by either an artificial or an enigmatic natural mechanism».[52]

The difference between the quarantine approach and the inoculation and vaccination approach corresponds to the difference between the disciplinary system and the security mechanisms. In both cases what one want to achieve is not simply overcoming or preventing an epidemic, but also or above all the normalization of a potentially ungovernable situation; however, the disciplinary blockade of quarantine pursues normalization by «seeking purely and simply to nullify the disease in all the subject in which it appears, or to prevent contact between the seek and the healthy», imposing for this purpose not a law, but the specific and rigid norms of a set of rules;[53] therefore – according to Foucault – here in reality we have «a normation, rather than a normalization».[54] Instead, it is the security mechanism based on inoculation or vaccination that tends to normalize in the most precise sense of the term.

---

51   *Security, Territory, Population*, pp. 57-61.
52   *Security, Territory, Population*, p. 61.
53   *Security, Territory, Population*, p. 62.
54   *Security, Territory, Population*, p. 57.

> What does the apparatus that appears with variolisation-vaccination consist in? It is not the division between those who are sick and those who are not. It takes all who are sick and all who are not as a whole, that is to say, in short, the population, and identifies the coefficient of probable morbidity, or probable mortality, in this population, that is to say the normal expectation in the population of being affected by the disease and of death linked to the disease. (...) Thus we get the idea of a "normal" morbidity or mortality.[55]

It is not superfluous to note that, according to Foucault, this dynamic approach to the problem of epidemics corresponds to the progressive emergence of liberal governmentality and the attention it pays to the market economy, that is to the circulation of people and goods, so that it does not stop and – at the same time – does not translate into uncontrollable mobility, «in such a way that the inherent dangers of this circulation are canceled out».[56]

Drawing inspiration from these indications, some considerations on our present-day can now be made. In 2020, global strategies for overcoming old anti-epidemic policies have largely failed. The inefficiency of global surveillance by world organizations and the explosion of the SARS-COV2 pandemic have forced many of the contemporary societies to adopt the quarantine model as their first intervention; in this way they took a step back in the history of biopolitics at least until the 17th century. On the other hand, most of these societies have not only failed to approach within a reasonable time something like an arrest of the pandemic, but have also largely missed the goal of affirming the problematic «idea of a "normal" morbidity or mortality». Rather, they have come very close to considering the contagion of millions and the consequent death of hundreds of thousands of people in a few months "normal".

Precisely in this way the idea of "return to normality" that in general these societies have tended to implement anyway, appeared somewhat artificial. The pandemic has clearly shown, in fact, that today the "normalization" of a contagion can be

---

55   *Security, Territory, Population*, p. 62.
56   *Security, Territory, Population*, p. 65.

dramatically hindered by the "novelty" and the poor preventive knowledge of certain infectious diseases: this "novelty", in particular, makes it difficult – as happened in 2020 – to promptly have vaccines to be used for the their "normalization". As a consequence, these same characteristics of the emerging diseases will perhaps end up forcing more and more often the governments of contemporary societies to face the dangers of pandemic oscillating between jumps back in the history of biopolitics to rehabilitate the model of quarantine and reckless jumps forward towards the improbable normalization of aberrant-mutant pathogens.

There remains, however, the possibility that certain governments will progressively orientate themselves to making use of surveillance technologies different from that practiced on a global scale by world organizations for preventive purposes. This is a possibility experienced during the pandemic of 2020, which implies a mixed strategy between the security and disciplinary approach, a strategy based on remote surveillance and contact tracing: on the one hand, it tends to control the movement of people through smartphones and other telematic devices, allowing it to continue to unfold; on the other, to impose the selective quarantine of infected or potentially infected individuals traced through the same devices.[57]

One may consider, on the other hand, that in the future there will also be room for governments willing to deny the seriousness of the health emergencies they will face and which will therefore tend to propose both pandemics and their mass deadly effects as normal.[58]

---

57   On this subject see Luca Ferretti and others, 'Quantifying SARS-CoV-2 transmission suggests epidemic control with digital contact tracing', *Science*, 368, 6491 (2020), https://science.sciencemag.org/content/368/6491/eabb6936/tab-article-info (accessed June 2, 2020).

58   A significant example of this is illustrated in Julie Ricard and Juliano Medeiros, 'Using misinformation as a political weapon: COVID-19 and Bolsonaro in Brazil', *The Harvard Kennedy School (HKS) Misinformation Review*, 1, 2 (2020), https://misinforeview.hks.harvard.edu/wp-content/uploads/2020/04/final_brazil.pdf (accessed June 2, 2020).

3.2 *Analytical tools to rethink*

3.2.1 *Exception*

At this point it is appropriate to dwell on some general questions. We must first consider the fact that anti-epidemic biopolitics have a privileged relationship with the emergency aspect. From this point of view, they seem to confirm Agamben's thesis, according to which there is a sort of structural link between the biopower and the sovereign power that decides on the state of exception, whose implications have been expressed in a catastrophic way in totalitarianisms: in short, anti-epidemic biopolitics would show that biopower, as intimately linked to sovereign power, would always be ready to use the exception to suspend legal freedoms and decide unconditionally on life.

Agamben's theses deserve attention since at the beginning of the pandemic of 2020 he denounced with extreme clarity the danger for democracy, which – according to him – the state of emergency declared by the Italian government to face the contagion entailed: «what is once again manifest – he said – is the tendency to use a state of exception as a normal paradigm for government».[59] It should be noted that the position taken by the Italian philosopher was based on a hasty press release from the National Research Centre (CNR), in which – just before the infection spread in the country – it was claimed: «there is no SARS-CoV2 epidemic in Italy».[60] Nonetheless, Agamben was perhaps too easily deceived by what seemed to him an

---

59 Giorgio Agamben, 'The Invention of an Epidemic' (February 26, 2020), *European Journal of Psycoanalysis*, https://www.journal-psychoanalysis. eu/ (accessed May 3, 2020).

60 Centro Nazionale delle Ricerche (CNR), 'Coronavirus. Rischio basso, capire condizioni vittime' (February 22, 2020): https://www.cnr.it/ it/nota-stampa/n-9233/coronavirus-rischio-basso-capire-condizioni-vittime (accessed May 3, 2020). In the text it was further alleged that: «The infection, according to the epidemiologic data available as of today and based on tens of thousands of cases, causes mild/moderate symptoms (a sort of influenza) in 80-90% of cases. In 10-15% of cases a pneumonia may develop, but one with a benign outcome in the large majority of cases. It has been estimated that only 4% of patients require intensive therapy».

unrepeatable opportunity to definitively demonstrate the validity of his well-known thesis according to which «the state of exception tends increasingly to appear as the dominant paradigm of government in contemporary politics».[61]

The question raised by the Italian philosopher certainly cannot be resolved by denying the danger that individual and collective freedoms run when an emergency offers a government the possibility of taking measures to limit mobility, activities and relationships. What should be noted, however, is that in order to support his position, Agamben felt the need not only to rule out that a pandemic was about to invest what turned out to be one of the countries most affected by the infection in the world ('The Invention of an Epidemic' is the title of his first article on the subject); subsequently he also believed that he could diminish the fact that – at least in some Italian regions – the pandemic was causing a very high number of deaths.[62]

Bringing the matter back on a general level, one cannot help but frame it in a different way. It can also be admitted that an unconditional sovereign power can "invent" a state of exception to broaden its ability to decide beyond any legal limit; however, it should be added that in general the purpose of a sovereign decision on a state of exception – "true" or "invented" that it is – is not to impose it in order to keep it indefinitely to one's advantage; its purpose is rather to establish or restore an order that can only be primarily legal. In short, Agamben with his stance showed the limits and consequences of his reading of the conception that Carl Schmitt proposes of the relationship between sovereign decision and exception. The Italian author, in fact, in his works maintains that the exception is the true condition of sovereignty, or that the latter finds its foundation in the exception. What he has always underestimated in this regard is that for Schmitt the ruler's decision is far more important than the exception for a very simple reason: for the German author, the decision is an

---

61   Agamben, *State of Exception*, p. 2.
62   See Giorgio Agamben, 'Sul vero e sul falso', *Una Voce*, April 28, 2020: https://www.quodlibet.it/giorgio-agamben-sul-vero-e-sul-falso. (Accessed May 3, 2020).

expression of the legal order, also if it is something other than the legal norm.

> After all – claims Schmitt –, every legal order is based on a decision, and also the concept of the legal order (...) contains within it the contrast of two distinct elements of the juristic – norm and decision. Like every other order, the legal order rests on a decision and not on a norm.[63]

This reference to the relationship, theorized by Schmitt, between the decision and the norm as a legal norm, allows us to show by contrast the meaning that the concept of norm can assume instead when a government power takes decisions on a biopolitical problem such as a pandemic or a danger of pandemic. Beyond the tools – laws or decrees – that this power uses to enforce such decisions in circumstances like these, its main purpose is neither the invention nor the use or indefinite perpetuation of a state of exception; its purpose is rather to impose or make sure that a norm is imposed by itself as a criterion for distinguishing between what is normal and what is not. In other words, if the sovereign who decides on the exception tends to establish an order, the government that decrees on a biopolitical emergency aspires to restore normality, albeit precarious and problematic. And in this regard it is particularly useful to recall what we have seen through Foucault regarding disciplinary quarantine and vaccination security practices as different strategies for dealing with an epidemic. In the first case we are very close to the proclamation of a state of exception, but in reality we are dealing with the rigid imposition of a normalizing norm by means of an ironclad regulation; in the second we are instead faced with a dynamic application of the norm as a statistically considered normal level of the spread of a

---

63 Schmitt, *Political Theology*, p. 10. That which allows Agamben to supports his theses is the fact that he declines the Schmittian concept of state of exception in the terms in which Walter Benjamin elaborates it, according to which, «[t]he tradition of the oppressed teaches us that the "state of emergency" in which we live is not the exception, but the rule». Walter Benjamin, 'On the Concept of History', in *Selected Writings, Volume 4, 1938-1940*, trans. by Edmund Jephcott (Cambridge, Mass.: The Belknap Press of Harvard University Press, 2003), p. 392.

disease, beyond which it is thought to be dangerous for society and for the government itself.

We can therefore say that, if there is a privileged relationship between an unconditional sovereign power and a paralyzing state of exception, this relationship does not necessarily reproduce in the case of a government that intervenes on an epidemic by evaluating in biopolitical terms the danger, the emergency and the normality. If we think about what happened with the 2020 pandemic, we can understand first of all that the powers that contribute to the decisions of a government in circumstances of this kind are varied and largely extraneous to the political and legal sphere of sovereignty: they are, in fact, epidemiological, virological, immunological, statistical, economical knowledge-powers. In a certain sense, it is a paradoxical suspension of the power to sovereignly decide what puts a government in conditions, not only to intervene biopolitically on an epidemic danger or emergency, but also to vary its measures if necessary; therefore it can go, for example, from the more or less rigid imposition of a quarantine to the dynamic and selective regulation of previously prohibited activities and forms of mobility; or let things run their course, taking this as a "normal" decision to be combined, possibly, with a broad and flexible use of remote monitoring technologies. All this, undoubtedly, entails problematic risks and consequences for freedom and democracy, which, in any case, are to be assessed with the morality of critical discernment, rather than with the presumption of a priori complaint.

It must be added that Agamben in an article following those mentioned, naturally did not fail to consider the influence of medical knowledge on the management of the pandemic; however, it did so by simply comparing this knowledge to a religion capable of pushing the whole society to subject its existence to a general health obligation. In reality, if the question were really so simple, it could however not be overlooked that Agamben himself let himself be influenced – before and more than others – by the "religion" of medical science, when he believed without uncertainty to a scientific institution (the Italian CNR) which expressed from a medical point of view the belief, however provisional, that there was «no SARS-COV2 epidemic in Italy».

Beyond what Agamben has advocated, in any case, if the condition in which the medical and biological sciences have come to be with the pandemic is not brought into sharp focus, we risk completely misrepresenting the direct and indirect consequences that this event had on them. These sciences, at least initially, were undoubtedly the main reference to which both the rulers and the governed clung to find a way to orient themselves in the face of contagion and its effects. But during the pandemic it became completely clear that medicine and life sciences proceeded by continuously varying their indications on the characteristics of the virus, on the therapies, on the possibilities of being able to develop a vaccine, on the trend, the severity, the duration of the epidemic, and so on. To this, on the other hand, it can be added that the pandemic has offered clear and perhaps definitive evidence that contemporary medicine has largely lost its "war" against contagious diseases.

3.2.2 *Immunity and individualization*

Another general question that should be considered is that anti-epidemic biopolitics have been taking the immune approach for some centuries as a strategy for reducing the dangers of epidemics. If we refer this question to the COVID-19 pandemic, we can ask ourselves whether, by pushing society to rediscover the importance of vaccinations (even or above all if they are not immediately possible), we are faced with a risk theorized by Roberto Esposito: that of indirectly legitimizing the immune approach to political problems, which would push modern biopolitics to regularly turn into thanatopolitics: tending to immunize society from factors of real or presumed danger, this biopolitics – according to him – sooner or later comes to promote policies of radical exclusion and death.

In reality, the new importance assumed by vaccinations allows us to ascertain once again that the thesis of the Italian philosopher is reliable insofar as the concept of immunization is understood in a general metaphorical sense, that is, if it is taken as a synonym of discrimination of individuals or groups perceived as bearers of dangers for society. If, on the other hand, the concept is traced back to its strictly medical meaning, which is expressed in vaccination practices, it confronts us with strategies for normalizing pathological situations considered dangerous and therefore abnormal for individuals and for society. From this point of view, what appears problematic is neither immunizing vaccination itself – except to the extent that it too can create risks for those who are subjected to it – nor the search for normality, generally understood as a concern to avoid dangers. Rather, problematic is the possibility that certain political, biopolitical and economic logics steer the medical immunization and the consequent normalization strategies in a certain direction: for example, if you think that a certain "normal" number of deaths should not be exceeded so that an epidemic situation remains controllable, you can even get to make selective use of immunization and consider acceptable the suffering and death of those who "exceed" this number considered normal. It is difficult, however, to establish how likely this use of medical immunization is in different situations; however, it alludes to something that can easily happen during an epidemic or pandemic: getting used to considering "normal" a number of infections or deaths that in other circumstances would be considered serious or "abnormal".

However, as we saw in the third chapter, an interesting aspect of Esposito's thesis is that according to which the (metaphorically) immune character of modern politics is revealed in the fact that it tends to reproduce the social bond in a paradoxical way, i.e. so that neither the individual nor society are involved in sharing intensely community relations. In this sense, it can be said that the social bond in modernity is reproduced by "immunizing" it from the risk of this sharing, that is, "purifying" it from an unconditional sociality and therefore substantially denying it.[64] This, in fact, is an effective way of describing the process that historically led liberal governmentality to prevail over other ways of governing: it can be said that liberalism tended to "defend society" above all by safeguarding the interests of individuals and thus taking the functioning of an immune mechanism such as that described by Esposito to the extreme consequences.

---

64   Esposito, *Bíos: Biopolitics and Philosophy*, pp. 50-2.

If we take into account the theses of Nikolas Rose, on the other hand, we can consider that this process is devoid of destructive consequences for the social bond, or that these consequences are only apparent or are a sort of false problem: after all, it is precisely by downsizing the importance of society as a totalizing community that – according to the British author – advanced liberal societies have freed themselves from the most dangerous biopolitical implications (racism, eugenics, nationalism, etc.) of the union between the state and the collective understood as population or as a nation.[65]

Beyond the assessments we have already made on Rose's vision, the COVID-19 pandemic appears to have added additional reasons for questioning it. The pandemic has made the historical biopolitical centrality of the population clearly emerge as a collective aggregate to which the health needs of the individual can be connected and, in some way, subordinate. In other words, the population can regain this centrality even in an era permeated by the individualizing policies of neoliberalism. Furthermore, the management of the pandemic has also given the state an important role and, moreover, has provoked sentiments of "national solidarity" in many countries. On the other hand, as we saw in the fifth chapter, many other phenomena (neo-racism, neo-nationalism, sovereignism, etc.) have long indicated the limits of Rose's thesis, according to which the biopolitical role of the population is destined to weaken in advanced liberal societies. In 2020, these societies – having been hit more widely than others by the pandemic – had to deal with the impossibility of ignoring the link that can be created between the individual contraction of a disease and the possibility that it spreads disastrously to an entire population. In addition, as we have already observed, many of the difficulties of these societies in coping with the pandemic stemmed from their policies of downsizing the social, communal and public character of their health systems and from the preference for personalized biomedicine which – according to Rose – is the decisive condition of the new biopolitics of the

---

65   Rose, *The Politics of Life Itself*, pp. 52-66.

21st century, based on the genetic responsibility of the biocitizen-consumer of health.[66]

The COVID-19 pandemic has evidently overturned or greatly complicated this prospect. This, however, must not simply lead us to take note of the essential importance that the population and the state regain in a time like ours. The scenario created with the pandemic must urge us, rather, to consider that the oscillation between the privileging of the population-species and that of the individual-organism will still remain an essential element for a long time and, at the same time, a crucial problem of contemporary biopolitics: depending on whether the attention paid to the population or that paid to the individual prevails, the lives and freedoms of individuals or the life and collective freedoms may be dangerously questioned.

Furthermore, the fact that the pandemic has given back to the state a role which it seemed to have largely lost, should not lead us to think that in this way the public and communal character of life-care services surely recover the lost importance. It must be assumed, in fact, that in the case of advanced liberal societies this possibility could have been largely compromised by the role that the state has played since the end of the last century as a vehicle for the privatization of medicine and health services; in the case of the "socialist", centralist and authoritarian states, however, this possibility could have been compromised by the fact that they often actively promoted collective adherence to the logic of the global market, becoming the main culprits of: the deterioration of collective health, caused by upsetting and highly polluting forms of industrialization and urbanization; the consequent alterations of ecosystems, from which many of the new epidemic diseases arise. Needless to say, China – the country where many of the most serious epidemics in recent decades have exploded – is the clearest example of this type of situation.

On the basis of these considerations, in short, the pandemic must be understood as a historical opportunity to problematize the importance of the oscillation between state and market which has characterized the history of biopolitics.

---

66   *The Politics of Life Itself*, pp. 131-54.

3.2.3 *Individual and population*

Ultimately, the issues we face are not resolved simply by trying to tip the balance again in favour of the state which has been leaning for too long in favour of the market. The historical "ambiguity" of the state can be overcome only if one can manage to make it function as "custodian" and promoter of the "public" and of the "common" as irreducible dimensions both to the sphere of the population-species and to that of the individual-organism. Be that as it may, if new perspectives are to be developed starting from the epochal experience of the pandemic, it is appropriate to take into account exactly its biopolitical specificity. Although it has brought to light the importance of the collective dimension of the population, this experience will not easily help contemporary individual to overcome the retreat upon himself and upon his biological life, to which he has been constantly encouraged by the medicalization processes on which biopolitics is historically based. The pandemic has exacerbated this inclination, to the extent that it has increased his fears, has pushed him to live in alarm and permanent attention to his own survival.

One of the attempts that perhaps should be made to seek a way out of this condition is to overcome the insurmountable importance that we spontaneously attribute not so much to life, as to its anthropocentric conception. If the experience of the pandemic and the history of biopolitics can teach us something in this sense, it is that precisely by remaining tied to the oscillation between population and individual we continue to blindly reproduce this conception; also or above all in this way we continue to remain at the centre of our self-referential attention as biological beings constantly at risk. Undoubtedly the pandemic, as a danger that has become permanent, reduces the possibility of thinking differently. However, it should also encourage us to rediscover the alternatives that the oscillation between individual and population – and between state and market – continues to make us lose sight of; it should urge us to think that the dimension that goes beyond the sphere of the individual towards a wider dimension of existence is not simply that of the family, society or population-species, but that of the worldly sphere which – according to the cases and viewpoints that we adopt – can be defined as ecosystem, environment, territory, place, city, world, cosmos. At the same time, the experience of the pandemic should lead us to consider that the human animal does not connect to life only through the somatic matter that inhabits it in cellular and genetic form; he relates to it also or above all through trans-specific and ecosystemic relationships which due to their irreducibility to a molecular microcosm can become decisive in provoking unexpected and sometimes catastrophic events such as a pandemic.

It is also for reasons such as these that it remains difficult to accept the idea that the alternative to the bio-thanato-political dimension in which the pandemic pushed us could consist in the "normality" of the economic governmentality of each and every one in the name of the global market.[67]

3.3 *Beyond the plague-stricken city*

The reasons why the pandemic represents an important reason to question both the rationality forms of biopolitics, and those that inspire the economic governmentality of society, can be grasped if it is reflected on the crucial importance that the urban dimension assumes on the occasion of the epidemics.

As we have seen, since the beginning of modernity, the city – as a place of intense aggregation, cohabitation, exchange, mobility and frequentation – easily becomes a space of biopolitical government for the danger of contagion. The experience of the COVID-19 pandemic, on the other hand, shows us that the city can even turn into the triggering cause of a pandemic when it takes on the enormous dimensions that it has reached in our time. Its current trend towards unlimited expansion makes even the definition of metropolis to indicate the prevailing examples of this expansion inadequate,

---

67   This is, in fact, the ground on which the "centralistic" regime of the country in which the pandemic originated, already during its most acute phase, declared itself ready to collaborate with the governments of advanced liberal societies to overcome the destructive effects of the pandemic itself. See: 'Working Together to Defeat the COVID-19 Outbreak. Remarks by H.E. Xi Jinping President of the People's Republic of China At the Extraordinary G20 Leaders' Summit', Beijing, 26 March 2020: *Xinhuanet*, 2020-03-26: http://www.xinhuanet.com/english/2020-03/26/c_138920685.htm (accessed June 3, 2020).

making the idea of megacity appear more appropriate. It does not take much effort to find that some of the places where the pandemic has caused the most disastrous consequences are precisely large metropolis, megacities and densely urbanized regions: Wuhan and its province, New York, London, Madrid, Sao Paulo, New Delhi and their metropolitan areas, Milan and its region, etc.

The more or less strict application of the lockdown and the subsequent transition to regulated forms of activity and mobility in these places have taken on meanings that should be compared with those of the management of epidemics through the disciplinary and security interventions examined by Foucault. In this sense, we must first highlight the inaugural meaning that the imposition of the quarantine regulation on plagued cities at the end of the 17th century may have had for the formation of the modern state. The deployment of a capillary surveillance system of the life of each inhabitant of the city gave a very powerful impulse to overcome the separation between the private and public sphere of existence, which the economic government of modern society would have pursued in other ways as well. The quarantined city announced the transformation of public space into an exemplary dimension of the economic government of society, in which the promotion of private activities tending to develop wealth for wealth would become the essential task of political institutions. What took place in the plague-stricken city was the transformation into a public problem of what was happening in the private space of the *oikos* from which everyone had to disclose himself for «answering to his name and showing himself», and participate in «the great review of the living and the dead».[68]

In a 2007 article, Agamben was able to grasp this type of implications of the imposition of quarantine, analysed by Foucault, precisely by avoiding to compare it to a simple declaration of the state of exception. He opportunely connected that event with the progressive rise of the metropolis as a model of the urban space of modernity. The metropolis would no longer be the "mother city" of other cities founded by its inhabitants, as happened at the time of the *polis*. It would become the destiny of the modern city as

---

68   *Discipline and Punish*, pp. 195-6.

a place where the public space of the citizen's political freedom would be transformed into the privileged sphere of economic governmentality, of the private productive and commercial initiative, and therefore also into a space of depoliticization.[69] From this point of view, what was announced with the quarantine of the plague city of the 17th century was the biopolitical centrality that in 2020 the anti-pandemic lockdown would have assigned to the private and family reality locked within the home walls and celebrated by the media as a reality to be safeguarded in view of the recovery of economic activities; a reality moreover capable of keeping alive, at least in part, these activities with smart working and online shopping.

Precisely if we intend the organization of quarantine in the embryonic modern city as an inaugural act not only of biopolitics, but also of economic government, we can grasp the ideal continuity that is thus established between the health discipline of individual behaviour and dynamic protection of life as an essential resource of society and the free market metropolis. In fact, the historical transition to a securitarian and probabilistic management of the risk of epidemic contagion has this meaning: as Foucault argues, this management has its main seat in «the market town» of which the government must guarantee the proper functioning taking into account that it is also «the home of disease» and «the place of revolt».[70]

The overcoming of the lockdown and the resumption of the activities of the postmodern megacities after the peak of the pandemic can only have a similar meaning. The contemporary metropolis and megalopolis, however, present themselves as extreme forms of the city's modern mutation. These tend to dissolve the public space of political citizenship not only through their immense growth, but also by transforming themselves into places dedicated to extreme forms of privatization, economization and general commercialization of activities, relationships, spaces and structures.[71] Therefore, they have become anything but

---

69   Giorgio Agamben, 'La città e la metropoli', *Posse*, 13 (2007): https://www. sinistrainrete.info/teoria/133-la-citta-e-la/amp (accessed May 25, 2020).

70   *Security, Territory, Population*, p. 63.

71   On these issues see Maria R. Marella, 'Lo spazio urbano come bene comune', *Scienze del Territorio*, 3 (2015), 78-87; 'The Law of the

accidentally ideal places of unexpected health emergencies that go beyond the problems of individual health to be addressed with the means obtained from private activities. For the same reasons, when these emergencies take the form of a pandemic, the governments of these places of unlimited urbanization end up oscillating between the temporary blockage of the danger of biopolitical catastrophe and the unstable normalization of the risk deriving from the material development of the economic traffic. Thus the communal and public space of the city itself – once its civic and political vocation has been dispersed in the megacity for the benefit of the economic one – after a pandemic that promises to return, paradoxically risks becoming the residual site of an always potentially infected reality from which to keep at a distance as much as possible by transferring most of the dealings, activities and businesses themselves into the virtual dimension of the telematic platforms.[72]

A need is felt for a new politics – more than a biopolitics – to escape what this perspective promises. In reality, while this book ends, something similar already foreshadows in various megacities capable of returning to city: in Hong Kong, one returns to the squares to counter the liberticidal threats of the Chinese regime, after having largely avoided the contagion coming from other megacities that it governs; in large cities around the world – after the killing by the US police of the African American George Floyd – people are mobilizing against racism, the most classic problem before which biopower continues to pose us from its origins.

Urban Common(s)', *South Atlantic Quarterly*, 118, 4 (2019), 877–93. See also: Ugo Rossi and Alberto Vanolo, *Geografia politica urbana* (Rome and Bari: Laterza, 2010); Sonia Paone, *Città in frantumi. Sicurezza, emergenza e produzione dello spazio* (Milan: Franco Angeli, 2008); Alberto Magnaghi, *The Urban Village* (London and New York: Zed Books, 2005).

72 On this perspective, see Naomi Klein, 'Screen New Deal', *The Intercept*, May 8, 2020: https://theintercept.com/2020/05/08/andrew-cuomo-eric-schmidt-coronavirus-tech-shock-doctrine/ (accessed June 1, 2020).

EPILOGUE
If the History Starts Again,
a Book Must End

Georg Wilhelm Friedrich Hegel, one of the most influential philosophers of modernity, in his posthumously published work: *Lectures on the philosophy of world history*, proposes his vision of universal history by affirming that it has found its fulfilment in Europe by realizing the culmination of political and spiritual civilization of humanity.[1] In that work the German philosopher maintains that one of the determining factors of the course that history has taken is constituted by the different environmental conditions in which the various peoples of the earth have found themselves living. In this sense, according to him, the different natural contexts of the countries of the world can be considered the «geographical basis of world history». Each of these contexts has placed the populace who have inhabited them in conditions more or less favourable to their participation in history itself; the influence of geographical environments has been so important, in his opinion, that in many cases it has determined the impossibility for certain peoples to contribute effectively to the achievement of historical progress. Countries that are too hot or too cold, for example, have certainly prevented them from establishing «national spirits» adequate to the task of geographically accomplishing the stages of this progress. Hegel deduces from all this that the development of history towards ever higher levels of civilization took place in the northern temperate zone of the Old World – Asia and Europe – heading from East to West and finding precisely in the European continent the conditions to

---

1   See Georg W. F. Hegel, *Lectures on the philosophy of world history. Introduction: Reason in history*, trans. by Hugh B. Nisbet (New York: Cambridge University Press, 1975).

express its most advanced results. In his opinion «World history – travels from east to west; for Europe is the absolute end of history, just as Asia is the beginning».[2]

Of course, today it is all too easy to recognize in this vision an exemplary testimony of the arrogance with which Europe and the West have sought to propose and impose the idea of their superiority on the whole world.[3] But at the end of this book – and after the considerations on the pandemic theme – there is the possibility of adding some further consideration on a vision like this.

That geographical path that universal history – according to Hegel – has taken from Asia to Europe, largely corresponds to the path that COVID-19 took in 2020, before spreading all over the world. This simple fact should prompt the West, Europe, advanced liberal societies in particular, to remember that – well before the German philosopher elaborated his narrative – a long sequence of pandemic events had denied in advance the credibility of this same narrative. This is the sequence that began with the Black Death which – like the universal history of Hegel – also came to Europe from the East. This placed, repeatedly and for centuries under the eyes and in the bodies of Europeans, the evidence of the impossibility of thinking that the progress of humanity takes place according to a progressive logic, recognizable even in an orderly succession of its geographical stages. Above all, it denied Europe and the West the possibility of considering themselves to be the custodians of a vocation and a historical right to impose their own model of civilization on others, while remaining immune from the side effects of this imposition. Nonetheless, the modern West – through Hegel and his emulators – has shown that it never wanted to thoroughly read the book of history that preceded it. Black Death, on the other hand, did not contradict in advance the Hegelian narrative by indicating a perverse vocation of the East to generate pandemics, rather than universal history; it told a story that at least we contemporaries of the successes of COVID-19 can

---

2   Hegel, *Lectures on the philosophy of world history,* p. 197.
3   See Enrique Dussel, *The Invention of Americas: Eclipse of "the Other" and the Myth of the Modernity* (New York: Continuum, 1995)

understand well: epidemics would not be such if they remained within the confines of their places of origin; sometimes they go so far that they can fully claim the right to define themselves as universal or – if one prefers – global.

Hegel, for his part, perhaps had the opportunity to suspect the historical importance of these events when he faced a cholera epidemic that – at least officially – caused his death. Certainly, however, he lacked the time and energy to draw philosophical consequences; time and energy that, however, his followers have wasted without being aware of it.

Foucault was also taken by surprise by a historic epidemic caused by an emerging infectious disease of our time: AIDS. However he had already prepared sufficient tools to allow us to approach the first real pandemic of the 21st century with some hope of understanding its meaning and implications and, at the same time, of thinking of it as the last and most surprising metamorphosis of biopolitics.

NAME INDEX

Agamben, G., 16, 91n, 143-5, 145n, 146, 146n, 147, 147n, 148-50, 150n, 151, 151n, 152, 152n, 153, 153n, 155, 157-8, 158n, 159, 159n, 160-1, 161n, 162-4, 193-4, 425, 425n, 426, 426n, 427n, 428-9, 435, 436n

Agar, N., 275n

Agrawal, A., 358-9, 359n, 360n

Ahmed, A.-K., 391n, 406n

Arendt, H, 14-5, 87-8, 88n, 89, 101, 128n, 132, 132n, 133, 139-40, 140n, 145-6, 148, 164, 165n, 194-5, 232, 389-90

Aristotle, 12, 14-5, 85, 85n, 86-7, 89-90, 90n, 91, 94-6, 100, 100n, 101-2, 107, 124, 124n, 125, 127-8, 128n, 129, 131-3, 133n, 134, 135n, 136, 136n, 137-8, 161, 380

Asclepius, 103-4, 106, 118

Ashford, R.W., 396n, 410n

Bacher, J., 318n

Barbier, G., 281n

Barrat, J., 185n

Barry, A., 66n

Barry, D., 271n

Basaglia, F., 57n

Bateson, G., 29, 364-5, 365n, 366, 366n, 367, 367n, 368-76, 382-5, 400

Bateson, M.C., 367n

Baudelaire, C., 175-76

Baudrillard, J., 343n

Bazzicalupo, L., 193n, 343n

Beck, U., 320, 320n, 345, 345n, 346n, 348

Becker, G. S., 23, 254, 254n, 255, 255n, 256, 256n, 257, 257n, 258, 258n, 259, 259n, 261, 288, 305, 362

Behrent, M.C., 254n

Béland, D., 228n

Benasayag, M., 281, 281n, 282, 282n

Benjamin, W., 147n, 427n

Bentham, J., 343n

Benveniste, E., 191n

Benyus, J., 350n, 351n

Berenbaum, M.R., 397, 397n

Berns, T., 389n, 411n

Beveridge, W., 18-9, 233, 233n, 234, 234n, 235, 239, 239n, 241, 241n, 242n, 243n, 244, 244n, 246n, 247, 247n, 252, 253n

Bismarck, O. von, 229-31, 242n

Blanchot, M., 191n

Bock, G., 251n

Boer, W.F.de, 400n

Borgna, P., 185n

Botelho, A., 392n

Botero, G., 68n

SUBJECT INDEX

Philanthropy: philanthropism/philanthropic associations/organizations, 202-4, 214-5, 219-20, 224, 259

Physicalism, 29, 364, 383; *see also* bioenergetic paradigm

Police, 44, 76-81, 83, 138, 156, 201, 437; sciences/theory, 68, 68-69n, 154, 166; state, 79-81, 83, 138, 156, 201, 217

Polis, 13, 16, 88, 90, 95, 97, 101, 105, 132-6, 140, 147-9, 182, 195, 232, 390, 435; *see also* city-state

Population, 12, 18-9, 21-2, 26-7, 32, 36, 40, 44-6, 48-9, 65, 67-8, 71-7, 82-3, 95, 124, 127, 128n, 134, 154, 156, 175, 200-1, 204-6, 206n, 208-14, 224, 230, 234, 243, 254-5, 259, 273-6, 278-9, 282-3, 287, 324-6, 329-31, 333-4, 336, 340-3, 362-3, 372, 393, 398, 400, 421-3, 431-3; as species, 32, 39, 325, 335, 432, 433; overpopulation/surplus population, 19, 59, 208-14, 224n, 243; *see also* demography *and* ecology: population

Post-ecological knowledge, 28-9, 356-7, 364, 375-6

Power-knowledge, 48, 58, 68, 89, 104, 153

Precautionary principle, 316-7, 317n; precautionary strategies, 403

Pre-emption, 317-8

Preparedness, 316, 403, 419, 419n; unpreparedness, 407, 418

Private sphere, 85, 87, 100-2, 179, 232, 249, 390

Privatization, 20, 23, 267, 285, 289, 307, 386-7, 411, 418, 432, 436

Procreation, 13, 23, 38, 96, 98, 108-11, 111n, 131-2, 208, 214, 249, 255-7, 260, 274, 288

Protector state, 235

Public space/Public realm, 87, 133, 145, 147, 389, 435-7

Quarantine, 31, 419-24, 427-8, 435-6

Race, 36-7, 96, 98-9, 110, 151, 181, 184, 187, 232, 259, 275-6, 278-80; racism, 21-2, 37, 63-4, 105, 260, 277, 280, 345, 431, 437; state racism, 36, 38, 79, 96

Raison d'État, 68, 68n, 83-4

Risk(s), 19, 25, 51-2, 59, 61-2, 118, 151, 207, 214-5, 217-9, 219n, 221-2, 228-9, 230n, 256, 266, 282, 295, 316-7, 319, 321-2, 329, 341-2, 347-8, 357, 369, 385, 433; environmental/ecological, 317, 320, 344, 346-7; epidemic/pandemic, 46, 394, 403, 405-6, 408-9, 416-7, 419-20, 422, 430, 436-7; genetic, 22, 185, 260, 269, 270-1, 284, 287, 293, 296, 321, 362; society, 320-1, 345-6

Security, 65, 69, 73, 82, 86, 95, 111, 119-20, 208, 215, 217-8, 225-6, 238, 266, 309, 312, 318, 324, 326, 329, 340, 343-4, 411-2, 419, 419n, 424; apparatuses/mechanisms/technologies, 59, 70-6, 82, 340-1, 422, 427, 435; social, 17-8, 40, 215, 217-8, 222, 228-9, 232, 238-40, 244, 245-246n, 263, 313, 320-1, 329, 344

Social defence, 59, 284n

MIMESIS GROUP
www.mimesis-group.com

MIMESIS INTERNATIONAL
www.mimesisinternational.com
info@mimesisinternational.com

MIMESIS EDIZIONI
www.mimesisedizioni.it
mimesis@mimesisedizioni.it

ÉDITIONS MIMÉSIS
www.editionsmimesis.fr
info@editionsmimesis.fr

MIMESIS COMMUNICATION
www.mim-c.net

MIMESIS EU
www.mim-eu.com

Printed by
Geca Industrie Grafiche – San Giuliano Milanese (MI)
July 2020